CENTURY
of STRUGGLE

The Woman's Rights Movement in the United States

CENTURY
of STRUGGLE

The Woman's Rights Movement

in the United States

By

ELEANOR FLEXNER

ATHENEUM

New York

1970

Published by Atheneum
Reprinted by arrangement with Harvard University Press
Copyright © 1959, 1968 by Eleanor Flexner
All rights reserved
Library of Congress catalog card number 68-18410
Manufactured in the United States of America by
The Murray Printing Company, Forge Village, Massachusetts
Published in Canada by McClelland & Stewart Ltd.
First Atheneum Printing January 1968
Second Printing February 1970

TO THE MEMORY OF

ANNE CRAWFORD FLEXNER
JUNE 27, 1874 — JANUARY 11, 1955

My mother's life was touched at many points by the movement whose history I have tried to record. Born in Georgetown, Kentucky, she graduated from Vassar (class of '95) at a time when relatively few Southern girls went away to college. She marched in the New York suffrage parades. She made her mark as a playwright at a time when such an achievement was still unusual for a woman. She was active in organizing playwrights into a professional association, and served for years as an officer of what is now the Dramatists Guild of the Authors League of America.

Her hope for me was that I would be a writer; her own success made it possible for me to write this book, which I dedicate to her with respect and gratitude.

PREFACE TO THE ATHENEUM EDITION

1970 will mark an anniversary for American women—a half-century since they acquired the right to vote for President and for every other elective office in the United States.

Few women—or men—under seventy are aware that there was a time when women could not vote—or earn their livelihood, go to college, or choose a profession. They do not know what was involved in reaching these goals which they now take for granted.

The reason they do not know is that they have not learned these things in school or college as part of their American history studies. Few general historians have shown much awareness of how different the circumstances of women's lives were from those of the men in their families as the exploration, settlement and development of this country took place. There are exceptions—one thinks in particular of the late Arthur M. Schlesinger, and of Allan Nevins. But for the most part historians—in particular social historians, whose concern is less with dates, political evolution and military matters than with how the American people lived and how their ways of living changed—continue the tradition of omission and neglect. A recent instance is the *Oxford History of the American People,* by Samuel Eliot Morison (New York, 1965), in which the winning of woman suffrage by the Nineteenth Amendment to the Constitution rates two sentences of a section entitled "Boot-Legging and Other Sports" in the chapter on post-World War I developments; the issue of prohibition and the Eighteenth Amendment, however, rate three pages.

Only an occasional paragraph in these books deals with the long struggle for the right of women to vote, the history of higher education for women, their slow but steady entrance into industrial production and the labor movement, or the contribution made by women to the growth of that social concern which is one of the distinctive characteristics of our time. The names of Susan Anthony and Jane Addams may be mentioned—barely; the names of so many other women who have left their imprint on our society—never.

Ask students who invented the steamboat or the cotton gin, explored the sources of the Mississippi River, led the Populist Movement or the Progressive Party—and if they do not remember they will look for the answers in their history books. Ask them who founded the early women's colleges, who led the seventy-five-year campaign for their right to vote, who pioneered in protective legislation for working mothers, who developed the concept of settlement houses and social work among the underprivileged—ask them to identify Mary Lyon, Elizabeth Blackwell, Leonora Barry, Elizabeth Cady Stanton, Lillian Wald, Florence Kelley —and they will have to head for the nearest library. Negro history having suffered its own special form of suppression and oblivion, the Negro women who took part in the long endurance contest are even less likely to be known, with the possible exception of Harriet Tubman and Sojourner Truth.

Yet the history of women in this country continues to be relevant because even today almost every woman who seeks to widen her sphere of activity beyond her home encounters conflict. The ambiguities and obstacles facing her will not be the same as those facing the women who lived a hundred or even fifty years ago. *They* had to prove to others, and to themselves as well, that a woman's brain was capable of the same kind of intellectual activity as a man's. They had to combat not only public prejudice but their own fears of being unladylike, of becoming unsexed creatures if they tried to be doctors or mathematicians. The girls who first went away to college worried about whether they would find husbands if they showed themselves too bright or too interested in science or politics. No one really knew whether they might not sicken and die if they were exposed to logarithms—or physical education. It had to be proved, not once but over and over again, that they would survive—until these things were finally taken for granted.

Today women face another problem—the balancing of rights against responsibilities. The prejudices they once challenged, the fears they overcame, had their origin in nature's fiat that woman is the child-bearer and, by extension, the child-rearer and home-maker. Habit and custom had combined to make her a creature believed to be capable of very little else. Today's woman who knows she can do a great deal else is faced, once she takes up the option of motherhood, with the decision of *how much else?*—and how soon? Somewhere in the wide arc between the credo of Solange Hertz (that a woman's role remains and will remain within her home, at least until all her children are grown) and that of Betty Friedan (that an educated woman is not fulfilled unless she has a career) each married woman and mother must make her own choice and commitment.

Today working women supposedly have the law on their side. The Equal Pay for Women Act (1963) guaranteed them equal pay for equal work, thereby removing (in law) any sex differential in wages or salary. By the Equal Rights Act (1964) they have (under Title VII) the right to employment without regard to race, color, creed—or sex. Critics have pointed out that such legislation threatens laws for the protection of women workers (see p. 328). Moreover, having rights guaranteed in law and enforcing them is not the same thing, as minority groups have learned to their abiding bitterness; it can only help. Employers will inevitably still be influenced by the uncertainty of whether women—any particular woman—will put work or family first, whether she will follow her husband if he is transferred elsewhere by *his* employer, how long a young unmarried woman can be counted on to stay at work before she marries and leaves to raise a family. Whatever the legislation —and agitation—this uncertainty about a woman's priorities—often uncertain to a woman herself—will continue to have a depressing effect on women's pay and women's opportunities for promotion and advancement.

The challenge to women today is therefore somewhat different from that which faced their forerunners. It involves not so much the winning of their rights as how best to reconcile rights with responsibilities. If the problem appears insoluble, it may help to look at the long road American women have traveled since 1790, when Judith Sargent Murray demanded more intellectual stimulus than was provided "by the mechanism of a pudding, or the sewing of the seams of a garment."

A more comprehensive history of American women than this will be written in the light of the wealth of research now taking place, and eventually the fruits of this work should find their way into the general and social histories offered to students and to the public. We may hope for this, not in the interests of feminism, but of better history.

Eleanor Flexner

Northampton, Massachusetts
September, 1967

PREFACE

For more than a hundred years women in this country have tried to achieve full citizenship, the right to take part in the political and social life of their time and to stand on a plane of equal human dignity with men in their personal relationships. While not many will claim that these goals have been finally achieved, women have come far enough for us to look back and see where they started, and how they reached their present status.

The story of the woman's rights movement has never been completely told. It deserves telling, not only because it is a story of gallantry and devotion, and thus a rich part of our common heritage, but because knowing and understanding something of the social forces involved in that movement may help us to cope with the problems we — men as well as women — confront today.

There is controversy at this time as to whether women have achieved loss, rather than gain, as to whether the "girl in the gray flannel suit" has not brought in her wake fresh problems worse than the old ones. Without necessarily advocating, in so many words, that women should give up working (if they could), or abandon the political rights they have held for less than half a century, or relinquish higher education, and devote themselves solely to their homes and their families, it is frequently hinted or implied, and occasionally stated point-blank that they would be better off if they did some or all of these things, and that the course of events has been, at best, unfortunate.

The most objective historian must have a point of view. This book has been written in the belief that opportunity for complete human development could not, and should not, have been witheld from one-half of the nation because such opportunity inevitably brought with it new problems. The extension of greater participation (and responsibility) to additional sections of the population is the essence of democratic growth; it has always brought fresh complications in its wake, whether it took the form of extending political suffrage to all adult males, or the spreading of popular education, or the growth of labor unions, or racial emancipation and integration.

Some women reformers thought that woman suffrage, or higher education for women, would bring the millenium; others were wiser. This writer believes that it is still too early to strike a final balance: to expect women to have accomplished anything like a satisfactory adjustment to the enormous changes of the past fifty years, especially since these have occurred in an era beset, like our own, with so many different and continuing kinds of changes — technological, scientific, social, and political — all of which throw additional stresses and strains on both men and women.

The alterations in the status of American women did not arise solely from the efforts of a relatively small but active group of feminists. They arose from, and these feminists themselves received impetus from, the same forces that transformed the United States in a comparatively brief space of time from a small, undeveloped, and unexplored agrarian country, to one in the forefront in wealth, industrialization, and international responsibilities.

Women played many roles in that transformation — not as presidents, inventors, generals, or business leaders, but as mothers and homemakers, producers, reformers, and eventually as citizens. The end is not yet; their roles will continue to evolve, along with all changing social relationships, in a society kept dynamic by the accelerating pace of scientific discovery and technological growth.

Unfortunately, historians have paid little attention to women's changing role. Some thirty years ago Professor Arthur M. Schlesinger took his colleagues to task for their neglect in *New Viewpoints in American History* (New York, 1928):

An examination of the standard histories of the United States and of the history text-books in use in our schools raises the pertinent question whether women have ever made any contributions to American national progress that are worthy of record. If the silence of the historians is to mean anything, it would appear that one-half of our population have been negligible factors in our country's history. . . [And] any consideration of woman's part in American history must include the protracted struggle of the sex for larger rights and opportunities, a story that is in itself one of the noblest chapters in the history of American democracy.

Since this criticism was voiced, little progress can be reported, whether in the fields of history, sociology or economics. One could cite volume after volume in which the share of women in the process of democratic growth has either been omitted, or only briefly referred to. This book can take only a limited step toward filling the gap. It does not presume to be a history of American women or a rounded sociological study of the changes that gradually took place in their status. Its aim is to give an account of the movement, consisting largely but by no means entirely of women, to gain for women broader rights and opportunities, beginning with a brief survey of their position during the colonial and revolutionary periods before the woman's rights movement itself can be properly said to have begun, then tracing its slow development, from scattered beginnings early in the nineteenth century on a number of different fronts, down to the enactment of a woman suffrage amendment to the constitution in 1920.

Something should perhaps be said in explanation of why so much of this narrative — almost a quarter of it — has been devoted to the final dozen years that it took to win woman suffrage. Actually, even less attention has been paid by historians to this phase, in proportion to its significance, than to other aspects of the woman's movement — such as the Seneca Falls convention in 1848, the founding of the first women's colleges, or the work of women like Jane Addams and other social reformers among her contemporaries.

Yet political citizenship was, for women as for any other group arbitrarily deprived of it, a vital step toward achieving human dignity, and the recognition that they too were endowed with the faculty of reason, the power of judgment, the capacity for social responsibility. The achievement of that recognition was extraordinarily difficult, infinitely more so than anyone today remembers or believes, except for the rapidly diminishing few who took part in the struggle. What the vote cost the more active and conscious sections of several generations of American women is perhaps best summed up by two who led them, in *Woman Suffrage and Politics* (New York: Scribner, 1923) by Carrie Chapman Catt and Nettie Rogers Shuler:

It is doubtful if any man, even among suffrage men, ever realized what the suffrage struggle came to mean to women, before the end was allowed in America. How much of time and patience, how much work, energy and aspiration, how much faith, how much hope, how much despair went into it. It leaves its mark on one, such a struggle. There were some women in every state who knew nothing about it. Not all the women in every state were in it. But most of the women in all the states were at least on the periphery of its effort, and interest, even when they were not in the heart of it. To them all its success became a monumental thing.

That success did not overcome the remaining obstacles to equality of opportunity, but it did mark a solid historical milestone. Never since then has there been the same measure of agreement among women as to the further goals they desire, or how these can be achieved, and consequently there has never since been the same heroic mustering of effort, except for a nationwide cause. The history of women's efforts on their own behalf since 1920 must be written from the perspective of a later date.

E. F.

Northampton, Massachusetts
May 1959

CONTENTS

PART I

PART II

CONTENTS

PART III

ILLUSTRATIONS

ILLUSTRATIONS

PART I

Chapter I

THE POSITION OF AMERICAN WOMEN
UP TO 1800

For more than a hundred years after the discovery of North America and its fringe islands, the vast majority of Europeans who reached it were men. Some were explorers or *voyageurs,* ranging from the Caribbean Sea to Hudson Bay, probing the innumerable coastal estuaries and inlets for the legendary passage to Cathay, or looking for gold; others were fishermen, reaping a rich annual harvest from the Banks, or trappers skirmishing with the forbidding New England and Canadian forests.

The first colonies reflected the prevailing idea that wealth might be found quickly and easily on the new continent, and that settlers need only be transients who would soon return home wealthy from gold dust or tobacco planting. Not until Mistress Anne Forest and her maid Anne Buras reached Virginia in 1608 was a new chapter opened in the history of colonization along the northern Atlantic coastline. Anne Buras herself wrote a new page when she married the laborer John Laydon. When the London merchants who were putting capital into the Virginia colony as a business venture began to realize that men alone would not build a stable community, but would remain a loose, constantly shifting aggregation of adventurers, they began to send out women. Ninety came on one ship alone in 1619: "Agreeable persons, young and incorrupt . . . sold with their own consent to settlers as wives, the price to be the cost of their own transportation." [1]

Perhaps the knowledge that each would find a husband among the several hundred bachelors eagerly awaiting them made up for subsequent hardships, but they cannot have found life easy. Virginia was only a toehold in the wilderness, fighting an unceasing war against plague, encroaching vegetation, and the Indians, who bitterly resented the white influx.

Even worse lay in store for eighteen married women (three of them pregnant) and eleven girls among the hundred and one passengers on the Mayflower, which headed for Virginia a year later, went off her course, and ended up off the Massachusetts shore.

Some of these settlers were of a different stamp from those in Virginia; in addition to the indentured servants, hired craftsmen, and adventurers, there were fugitives from religious persecution. Many came with whole families to plant their faith in a new world for the sake of their children.[2] Yet even women supported by strong religious faith might have quailed as they looked out on that rocky November coastline or went through the pains of child-birth in the crowded, stench-ridden hold. Elizabeth Hopkins had already born a child at sea, a son named Oceanus — and as the little ship nosed into Cape Cod Bay, Susanna White bore a daughter; Mary Allerton's son was stillborn before the settlers went ashore. Young Dorothy Bradford, wife of the man who was to lead the colony through the first terrible years, drowned beside the ship while it lay at anchor and Bradford and a few others were looking for a place to settle; whether she fell by accident or flinched before that bleak rampart of rocks and forest, we do not know.

"Clinging like wasps to the rim of a continent," Stephen Vincent Benét described that first winter:

> There was the fierce
> New climate, the scanty food, and the great toil,
> And the sickness came — not the fever of the marsh,
> But scurvy at last, and the sicknesses of the cold . . .
> . . . It was a grim
> Business of back-break labor in whirling snow,
> In the gusty, heart-chilling rain. They could faint and die,
> But the wood must be cut and gathered, the fire kept lit.*

While the men cut and dragged firewood, and built a "community house" and a few more cabins, the women nursed the sick. When spring came, only four of eighteen women were left. All

---

* Stephen Vincent Benét, *Western Star* (Rinehart & Company Inc., copyright 1943 by Rosemary Carr Benét) pp. 145–146, 165.

but six of the children had been saved; twenty boys and eleven girls were still alive.

The children grew up; ships brought more settlers with many motives; new colonies sprang up from Maine to Georgia and began reaching inland, up the rivers and through the forests. There was little difference at first in the rigors endured by the women, gently-born mistress, servant, artisan's wife, or indentured maid. Whether they came for conscience' sake or to escape pauperism or prison, they faced the common task of achieving survival for themselves and their families in a wilderness that yielded nothing easily. While the men hunted, chopped, built, plowed, fought the Indians, and sat in council together, the women cared for one another in childbirth and sickness with no skill to call on save their own, wrestled with strange foods in a climate savage in both its heat and cold compared with that of England and western Europe; they toiled from sunup to sundown, converting the raw skins and meat brought home by the men into the necessary food and clothing, and planted and tended the ground the men had cleared.

While many came as wives and daughters of settlers, there were not nearly enough of these to guarantee the growth of stable communities or to satisfy the insatiable demand for more working hands. The answer was, on the one hand, Negro slaves, and on the other, indentured servants.

Many of the latter came voluntarily because life in England held little promise for them; they bound themselves to service for a specified term, from five to seven years, to pay their passage. During their period of bondage they were under heavy restrictions: any offense they committed was punished more heavily than that of a free citizen, and their term of service could be increased, a threat which hung over any attempt to run away from their master. Nor could they marry or engage in any occupation without the latter's permission. To be a bondsman or bondswoman was to be, for the time specified, little better than a slave.

Perhaps some of those who came voluntarily might have stayed away, had they known the kind of existence awaiting them. But there were others, a large proportion of the indentured class, who came, not of their own volition, but as victims of a highly organized, thriving kidnapping business, which snatched them off the streets of London and other large cities — grown men and women or young boys and girls — and dragged them in bonds aboard ship. Others were sold by their jailers out of prisons packed to suffocation with the victims of the heavy sentences of that day for petty misdemeanors, destitution, or major crimes. Still others received court sentences for deportation or, given their choice, preferred indenture to long prison terms or the gallows.

If they survived their indenture period they were free to seek other service, to enter a trade they might have learned, or to marry; the Beards remark (p. 105) that many sank "into that hopeless body of poor whites, the proletariat of the countryside."

As growth and increased wealth produced social stratification, generalization about "colonial women" became more difficult. It was one thing to be the lady of a southern tobacco plantation or the wife of a New England merchant; it was quite another to be a pioneer raising a family in western Massachusetts or the Allegheny valleys, the self-supporting widow of a Marblehead fisherman, or a servant girl working out her indenture period.

Even the most prosperous of these was liable to be suddenly uprooted and thrust back into an earlier, grimmer mode of life, if the family sought new fortunes in the ever opening West. When this happened, there were only differences in degree between the hardships endured by the Pilgrim women, and those who, at first on foot and later in Conestoga wagons, filtered through the eastern mountain passes, up into the Northwest Territory, or who crossed the deserts and sierras to the Pacific Northwest, two hundred and fifty years later. Life never got any easier; the women, tied to the young children, to the drudgery of the frontier cabin and the small patch of garden beside it, endured the same racking loneliness, the same frustration and despair.

In the 1830's the traveler and observer Tocqueville, visiting such a frontier outpost whose geographical location he has not identified, has left us one picture:

By the side of the hearth sits a woman with a baby on her lap . . . in the prime of life; her appearance seems superior to her condition, and her apparel even betrays a lingering taste for dress; but her delicate limbs appear shrunken, her features are drawn in, her eye is mild and melancholy. . . . Her children cluster about her, full of health, turbulence, and energy: they are true children of the wilderness. Their mother watches them from time to time with mingled melancholy and joy: to look at their strength and her languor, one might imagine that the life she has given them has exhausted her own, and still she does not regret what they have cost her. . . .

The house inhabited by these emigrants has no internal partition or loft. In the one chamber of which it consists, the whole family is gathered for the night. The dwelling is itself a little world, an ark of civilization amid an ocean of foliage; a hundred steps beyond it the primeval forest spreads its shades, and solitude resumes its sway.[3]

When the famous orator and suffrage leader Anna Howard Shaw was eight years old, mother and children emigrated to the backwoods of Michigan, where her father (who remained behind to work in a Lawrence textile mill) had built a "home" for them:

What we found awaiting us were the four walls and the roof of a good-sized log house, standing in a small cleared strip of wilderness, its doors and windows represented by square holes, its floor also a thing of the future, its whole effect achingly forlorn and desolate. It was late in the afternoon when we drove up to the opening that was its front door, and I shall never forget the look my mother turned upon the place. Without a word she crossed the threshold and, standing very still, looked slowly around her. Then something within her seemed to give way and she sank upon the floor. She could not realize even then, I think, that this was really the place father had prepared for us, that here he expected us to live. When she finally took it in she buried her face in her hands, and in that way she sat for hours, without speaking or moving . . . While my eighteen year-old brother was picketing his horses and building his protective fires, my mother came to herself, but her face when she raised it was worse than her silence had been. . . . [it] never lost the deep lines those first hours of her pioneer life had cut upon it.[4]

Whatever their social station, under English common law, which became increasingly predominant in the colonies and among all religious denominations (until the advent of the Quakers), women had many duties, but few rights. Married women in particular suffered "civil death," having no right to property and no legal entity or existence apart from their husbands.

Man and wife are one person, but understand in what manner. When a small brooke or little river incorporateth with Rhodanus, Humber or the Thames, the poor rivulet looseth its name, it is carried and recarried with the new associate, it beareth no sway, it possesseth nothing during coverture. A woman as soon as she is married, is called

covert, in Latin, *nupta,* that is, *veiled,* as it were, clouded and over-
shadowed, she hath lost her streame. . . . To a married woman, her
new self is her superior, her companion, her master.[5]

The concept of the *femme coverte* would carry over into the
nineteenth century and be a handicap to the married women who,
whether from economic necessity or independence of spirit, tried
to override its taboos. Married women could not sign contracts;
they had no title to their own earnings, to property even when it
was their own by inheritance or dower, or to their children in case
of legal separation. Divorce, when granted at all by the courts or
by legislative action, was given only for the most flagrant abuses:
adultery, desertion and non-support, and extreme cruelty. With
respect to women's ability to gain redress on an equal basis with
their husbands, both law and practice varied widely, from the
relative liberality in New England to the stringent limitations
of the mid-Atlantic colonies. In the South divorce statutes were
for a long time non-existent, and the legal dissolution of marriage
was infrequent and difficult to achieve.[6]

Next to common law, the most potent force in maintaining
woman's subordinate position was religion. The colonists might be
dissenters of one kind or another against the Church of England,
but they were at one with it in believing that woman's place was
determined by limitations of mind and body, a punishment for
the original sin of Eve. However, in order to fit her for her proper
role of motherhood, the Almighty had taken especial pains to
endow her with such virtues as modesty, meekness, compassion,
affability, and piety.

The "Lady's Books" of colonial days spelled out in detail a
woman's responsibilities — and limitations; they also dwelt on the
desirability of her virtue, in contrast to the latitude permitted her
husband. She was advised to keep any knowledge she might have
of his extramarital activities to herself.

"Civil death" also applied to all women in political matters.
But this was hardly an anachronism in a society where only some
classes of males, usually on a propertied basis, were enfranchised,
and where all were governed as a colony with little voice in any
major issues. There were a few scattered instances during the pre-
Revolutionary period where women voted, but suffrage for women

did not become an issue until long after the country had become an independent republic.[7]

Although women would be regarded as inferior, and therefore properly subordinate human beings for hundreds of years, forces were at work undermining such attitudes from the earliest colonial days. It was not merely that Protestantism held idleness to be a sin, and therefore required of women that they weave, spin, make lace, soap, shoes, and candles, as well as care for their households and families. The economy itself demanded such a division of labor because at first there was no other source for these goods and services. Nor did all women work within the sheltering confines of the home. The toll which exploration, hunting, fishing, Indian wars and migration to the West took of manpower, left many women widowed, often with small children to provide for. Frequently they carried on a former husband's business, such as innkeeping, printing, managing a store or even a newspaper; sometimes they struck out for themselves in such endeavors; or they became seamstresses, milliners, house servants, etc. In a struggling society in which there was a continuous labor shortage, no social taboos could keep a hungry woman idle.[8]

Moreover, by the demands it made on human beings for survival, frontier economy established a certain rough egalitarianism which challenged other, long-established concepts of propriety. Women were just as indispensable as men, since a household which lacked their homemaking skills, as well as nursing, sharpshooting and hunting when needed, was not to be envied. As colonial society became more complex this tradition became obscured, but its roots remained in American life and thinking; as the frontier moved westward in a changing world, the idea that women were the equals of men traveled with it, with far-reaching results.

The question of equal status for women was first raised in the earliest days of the founding of New England, when Anne Hutchinson challenged the Puritan theocracy of Boston, not only in the field of religious dogma, but also in its assumption that no woman could have a voice in church affairs. The battle was drawn along strictly theological lines, but the issue was implicit in her unprecedented demand that she, a woman, be permitted to think for herself about God and provoke others, women included, into doing the same.

Our knowledge of Anne Hutchinson is scant and one-sided:
she left no letters, no journal; no one in her family or among her
followers set down a portrait of her or a description of her famous
"conversations" that has come down to us. Most of our knowledge
comes from the pen of the man who hated her most — John
Winthrop, governor of the Massachusetts Bay Colony. It is as if all
that we knew of Joan of Arc were from the testimony of her mortal
enemy, Pierre Cauchon. "A woman of a haughty and fierce carriage," wrote Winthrop, "of a nimble wit and active spirit, and a
very voluble tongue, more bold than a man, though in understanding and judgment, inferior to many women." [9]

The Puritans had followed the Pilgrims and come to Massachusetts Bay in 1630, fleeing from Stuart Catholic England. They were
Calvinists who believed that only a small group were the repositories of divine enlightenment and leadership, and that salvation
could be attained only through prayer, charity, and churchgoing:
the so-called "Covenant of Works."

Mistress Hutchinson and her family did not come to Boston
until 1634. By that time the Calvinist faith had hardened into
dogma. But Mistress Hutchinson in the meantime had come to
believe in the individual's direct communion with God, and in His
existence in every human being — the "Covenant of Grace." She
could not submit to an orthodoxy so rigid that it denied her right
to express her beliefs. She had already begun to do so on board
ship during the long ocean crossing. Once in Boston she won
adherents in growing numbers by her rare knowledge of healing
herbs, and by her eloquence. The horrified authorities began to
hear that groups of sixty or more, mostly women but even a few
men, were meeting at the Hutchinson home, listening to Mistress
Hutchinson's theories of the "indwelling Christ" and to her penetrating criticism of the local ministers.

Winthrop and his associates feared, with some grounds, that
the whole fabric of the community was being subverted: it was
impossible to challenge established religion in Puritan Boston
without challenging the State as well, since there was no separation between them. In maintaining that an individual could commune directly with God, Mistress Hutchinson was claiming

equality for herself and everybody else with the men who ruled, with a dominion as absolute as that of the Stuart kings, the lives and minds of the Massachusetts Bay Colony.

The new heresy made alarming inroads, and the authorities moved ruthlessly to protect their power. They attacked Anne Hutchinson on two fronts, through the civil court and by religious proceedings. At the time of her civil trial, she was pregnant and seriously ill. Yet she was not allowed to sit down until it became obvious that she could no longer stand: "her countenance discovered some bodily infirmity," says Winthrop's terse record.[10] During the course of the trial she was subjected to the harassments common to persecution from that day to this: her words were falsified; she was denied the right to introduce evidence in her own defense; her judges declared their minds made up before they examined her witnesses, who were bullied and browbeaten. The Court found her guilty as charged and ordered her banished from the colony. Its findings were far from clear, but when Anne Hutchinson asked: "I desire to know wherefore I am banished?" the great Winthrop could only answer, "Say no more, the Court knows wherefore, and is satisfied." [11]

Civil punishment alone could not break Mistress Hutchinson's strong hold on her followers; her heresy must be established beyond question. She was confined to the home of one of her opponents, and after weeks of inquisition, during which she was ill most of the time, she finally voiced certain *questions* on points of doctrine. These were immediately pounced on as *statements of belief,* blown up into twenty-nine heretical errors, and made the basis for her trial for excommunication.

During the trial, Anne Hutchinson's fearlessness, her knowledge of scripture, and her eloquence terrified and infuriated her accusers. Faced with her repentance *in writing,* they fell back on unanswerable prejudice: "Her repentance is not in her countenance." [12] What else could one do with a woman who, in the midst of abstruse haggling over the nature of the human soul, could say: "I think the soul to be nothing but Light." [13]

But she was still weak from illness, and her defense, at first lucid and brilliant, gradually faltered into confusion and silence. When she left the church under ban of excommunication, only one arm was raised to support her: that of Mary Dyer, who — first roused to questioning by Mistress Hutchinson — would pay the price twenty-two years lated when Boston's rulers, still hot for orthodoxy, hanged her as a Quaker.

Anne Hutchinson and her family (who, it is pleasant to record, remained consistently loyal to her) journeyed first to Roger Williams' colony of Rhode Island. Such was still her power that some thirty-five families followed her, away from the relative security of the tiny Boston colony, into the wilderness. Apparently finding traces of intolerance appearing even among these faithful disciples, she migrated once more, and settled near the shores of Long Island Sound on what is now Pelham Bay on the outskirts of New York City. She believed the Dutch had sold her land for which they had paid the Indians in good faith, but she was deceived. The Indians, thinking her party to the fraud, killed her and her family. The tiny meandering river and the great motor highway that pass through Pelham Bay Park bear her name today.

The ruthlessness of Anne Hutchinson's punishment is the measure of her stature and her threat to the Puritan way of life and faith. Unschooled — save for her knowledge-of the Bible — because she was a woman; inexperienced in rhetoric or debate — because she was a woman — she nevertheless won a large portion of a community highly conscious of theology to her beliefs. She challenged its best educated, best-trained minds until they had to fall back on falsehood and compulsion. Like Roger Williams, Anne Hutchinson challenged church and state on behalf of new ideas of tolerance and religious freedom; as a woman she went further, questioning, for the first time on this continent, the validity of the place assigned to her sex.

Molly Pitcher, who sprang to load her husband's cannon when he was wounded at the battle of Monmouth, was a brave woman; so was Deborah Gannett, who is reputed to have served during a large part of the Revolutionary War as an enlisted soldier before being discovered. But women were active in more widespread and effective ways in the struggle for independence, and in the years immediately preceding it.

When feeling ran high against the enforced importation of British tea, high-priced because of the excessive duty, there were a number of instances in the New England and Middle Atlantic

States of women organizing anti-tea leagues, which popularized the use of such substitutes as raspberry, sage, and birch brews. The most popular, called "Liberty Tea," was made from the four-leaved loosestrife by an elaborate process that required boiling its leaves twice and drying them in the oven.[14]

Some of these associations achieved brief cohesion and called themselves Daughters of Liberty, although they never reached anything like the degree of organization of the Sons of Liberty under Samuel Adams. Such groups tried to aid the boycott of British goods by spinning and making clothes and by publicly pledging to buy only domestic products:

Early in February [1770] the females of Boston made a public movement on the subject of non-importation, and the mistresses of three hundred families subscribed their names to a league, binding themselves not to drink any tea until after the Revenue Act was repealed. Three days afterward the *young ladies* followed the example of the matrons, and multitudes signed a document in the following terms: "We, the daughters of those patriots who have, and do now, appear for the public interest and in that principally regard their posterity — as such, do with pleasure engage with them in denying themselves the drinking of foreign tea, in hopes to frustrate a plan which tends to deprive a whole community of all that is valuable in life." [15]

During the war, some merchants hoarded sugar and coffee, and on at least one occasion such stores were forcibly "opened" by women. Abigail Adams wrote to her husband John, sitting as a delegate to the Continental Congress in Philadelphia in 1777:

One eminent, wealthy, stingy merchant (who is a bachelor) had a hogs-head of coffee in his store, which he refused to sell the committee under six shillings per pound. A number of females, some say a hundred, some say more, assembled with a cart and trunks, marched down to the warehouse, and demanded the keys, which he refused to deliver. Upon which one of them seized him by his neck and tossed him into the cart. Upon his finding no quarter, he delivered the keys when they tipped up the cart and discharged him; then opened the warehouse, hoisted out the coffee themselves, put it into the trunks and drove off. It was reported that he had personal chastisement among them but this, I do believe was not true. A large concourse of men stood amazed, silent spectators of the whole transaction.[16]

During the war, the absence of men serving with the continental armies created a vacuum which women had to fill, to enable

family and farm to survive and to keep the economy of the thirteen states functioning. The most novel contribution they made
was that of supplying clothing to the army, foreshadowing the
famous Sanitary Commission of Civil War fame and the later Red
Cross. There is no record of such activity during the winter that
Washington's sorely pressed and ragged men held out at Valley
Forge. But in 1780 Mrs. Esther De Berdt Reed, the wife of Washington's Adjutant General, headed an "association," at first made
up of Philadelphians but subsequently joined by women from
other Pennsylvania communities as well as from Maryland, New
Jersey and Delaware. Some $7,000 (in specie) was raised to pro-
vide badly needed clothing, principally shirts. The list of donors
ranges from a Negro laundress who gave seven shillings to women
of means who gave large sums. Mrs. Reed died before the work
had ended, and her place was taken by a committee of five, among
them Benjamin Franklin's daughter Sarah Bache, at whose home
much of the work of cutting and sewing was done: a visitor has
recorded seeing some 2200 freshly starched shirts piled high, waiting for shipment! [17] Sporadic and incidental as these efforts were,
they are the first instances we know of American women working
together towards a specified end — in other words, organizing.

No element in the life of the emerging young nation could
remain static. The same forces that were dissolving the bonds
between the colonies and the mother country would eventually
render many things obsolete in the position of the eighteenth
century woman. Explosive ideas had been unleashed. If man was
endowed with certain natural and inalienable rights, why not
woman as well? If civil authority derived from reason and the
consent of the governed rather than from divinity, could women
be maintained in a state of subjugation by the authority of the
Bible?

Tom Paine, who made all oppression his province, was perhaps the first to describe, and condemn, the position of women:

even in countries where they may be esteemed the most happy, con-
strained in their desires in the disposal of their goods, robbed of freedom and will by the laws, the slaves of opinion, which rules them with
absolute sway and construes the slightest appearances into guilt;

surrounded on all sides by judges, who are at once tyrants and their seducers . . . Who does not feel for the tender sex? [18]

There were women in close touch with the revolutionary ferment who no longer fitted the mold described by Paine: women like Mercy Warren — playwright, correspondent, and friend of Washington, Adams and Hancock; or Abigail Adams, who in 1777 wrote to her husband:

In the new code of laws which I suppose it will be necessary for you to make, I desire you would remember the ladies and be more generous and favorable to them than your ancestors. Do not put such unlimited power into the hands of the husbands. Remember, all men would be tyrants if they could. If particular care and attention is not paid to the ladies, we are determined to foment a rebellion, and will not hold ourselves bound by any laws in which we have no voice or representation.[19]

Mrs. Adams was undoubtedly writing with tongue in cheek, although acid touched her pen. She was as far ahead of her time as had been Mistress Margaret Brent in the early days of the colony of Maryland. Armed with the legal right of executrix for the deceased Leonard Calvert, brother and representative of my Lord Baltimore himself, that lady had appeared before an astounded House of Burgesses to demand, not one vote, but *two* (one as Calvert's executrix, and the other on behalf of Lord Baltimore); failing in this effort, she demanded that all proceedings of that session of the Council be declared invalid. (Her request was denied.)

Both Mistress Brent and Mrs. Adams were forerunners and prophets rather than initiators. The legal position of women, let alone any voice in political matters, would not become vital issues until the mid-nineteenth century. The first aspect of broader rights and opportunities for women to become an issue of importance was that of education. The struggle for knowledge, for training, for opportunity to envisage new goals and to grow by reaching for them, which runs like a bright thread through American social history, found its earliest expression on behalf of women in the writings of Judith Sargent Murray, some ten years before Mary Wollstonecraft in England in 1790 published her *Vindication of the Rights of Women,* from which the modern woman's rights movement is usually dated.[20]

Mary Wollstonecraft moved among the most advanced thinkers of her day: Condorcet, Paine, Godwin. Judith Murray lived in the Massachusetts seaport town of Gloucester, where her father was a prosperous merchant and sea captain who supported the revolutionary forces and sat as a delegate in the Massachusetts convention which ratified the Constitution in 1788. Mrs. Murray was hostess to, and later the guest of, President and Mrs. Washington; her portrait was painted by Stuart and Copley. Her mind explored new vistas, and some time during the Revolutionary War, she wrote an essay (not published until 1790) in which she reflected on the disparity of opportunities open to men and women:

Is it upon mature consideration we adopt the idea, that nature is thus partial in her distributions? Is it indeed a fact that she hath yielded to one half the human species so unquestionable a mental superiority? . . . Yet it may be questioned, from what source doth this superiority, in this determining faculty of the soul (the judgment) proceed? May we not trace its source in the difference of education and continued advantages? Will it be said that the judgment of a male two years old, is more sage than that of a female's of the same age? I believe the reverse is generally observed to be true. But from that period what partiality! How is the one exalted and the other depressed, by the contrary modes of education that are adopted! The one is taught to aspire, the other is early confined and limited. As their years increase, the sister must be wholly domesticated, while the brother is led by the hand through all the flowery paths of science.[21]

In answer to those critics who feared that educated women might neglect their domestic responsibilities, she wrote:

Should it still be vociferated, "Your domestic employments are sufficient" — I would calmly ask, is it reasonable, that a candidate for immortality, for the joys of heaven, an intelligent being, who is to spend an eternity in contemplating the works of Deity, should at present be so degraded, as to be allowed no other ideas, than those which are suggested by the mechanism of a pudding, or the sewing of the seams of a garment?[22]

However, in another essay published in 1798, Mrs. Murray was able to point to others who had come to share her views: "Female academies are everywhere establishing and right pleasant is the appellation to my ear. . . . I may be accused of enthusiasm;

but such is my confidence in THE SEX that I expect to see our young women forming a new era in female history." [23]

One of those who sought to establish a new pattern of education for women was Dr. Benjamin Rush, physician, scientist, and professor of chemistry at the University of Pennsylvania. Rush was a member of the Board of Visitors (all male) of the Ladies' Academy in Philadelphia, and speaking to a gathering of students, their families and friends in 1787, he declared that female education "should be accommodated to the state of society, manners and government of the country in which it is conducted." Therefore, in the newly established republic, "the equal share that every citizen has in the liberty, and the equal share he may have in the government of our country, make it necessary that our ladies should be qualified to a certain degree by a peculiar and suitable education, to concur in instructing their sons in the principles of liberty and government." [24]

Among the subjects which Dr. Rush felt that the state of society required of women were the English language and writing, geography, reading books of history, biography and travel (as an antidote to the alarming increase in the popularity of the novel), vocal music (as an aid to strengthening the body), dancing (which he considered by no means improper), and religious instruction.

Yet despite the fertilizing ideas of a few far-seeing individuals and the hopeful growth in female academies noted by Mrs. Murray, no significant change could take place in the kind of education available to women, or in the number and kind of women able to take advantage of it, until westward expansion and the beginnings of industrial production outside the home began to affect the whole social structure of the young nation. When Samuel Slater first harnessed water power to spin cotton at Pawtucket, Rhode Island, in 1790, he opened the way for the development of the textile industry some twenty years later, which would have a far-reaching impact on the position of women. Having previously supplied the demand for cloth by spinning and weaving at home, they would become, in increasing numbers, full-fledged wage earners. And if it became "proper" for a woman to work fourteen hours a day in a textile mill, just like a man, then a good many other social taboos would also come up for reconsideration.

"The new era in female history" foreseen by Judith Sargent Murray was coming into sight.

The women kidnapped from city streets, or sold out of crowded prisons and brought to this country to serve as indentured servants, had something to look forward to, if they survived: at the end of seven years they would be free. It might be the freedom of utter want or degradation, but the chance for something better than that glimmered before them.

No such vision sustained the men and women of dark skins who were torn from the African continent and brought to North and South America to be sold as slaves. For two hundred years the traders — British, French, Portuguese, Spanish, American — carried on a trade which provided labor for the southern cotton and tobacco plantations and whose proceeds fattened London and Liverpool, New York, Boston, Salem, and Newport.

It is impossible to compute accurately the numbers taken from Africa over several centuries; estimates run as high as 20,000,000. Nor is there agreement as to the proportion — somewhere between one-half and one-third — who lived to reach their final destination.[25] For, after the warlike raids on the villages in upland plain or jungle, after the breaking-up of tribes and separation of families, the march through equatorial heat and rain for hundreds of miles, the slave pens on the coast, the branding and the chains, came the Middle Passage.[26]

The 4,000 mile crossing was made at first in ships even smaller than the Mayflower, and the passenger lists were longer. There are records of one-hundred-ton vessels carrying five hundred, even seven hundred and fifty men and women; usually the small ships carried between two and three hundred. Only a small space was reserved for the crew and supplies; the rest was filled with "cargo," chained in pairs to platforms of benches which occupied most of the floor space, sometimes with as little as eighteen inches between the "floor" and the "ceiling." Each tier had its complement of manacled bodies chained side by side; occasionally they would have to double up their legs, with no room to move them. There, except for brief periods to relieve themselves or go on deck, they remained during a five or six weeks' voyage.

Approximately one third of the cargo was usually women. The

only concession to their sex was that they were chained in a separate room: "packed spoon-fashion, they often gave birth to children in the scalding perspiration from the human cargo." [27]

When wind and weather were adverse, food and water ran short, and the slaves suffered most. Provisions for removing human excreta were always inadequate, and bathing facilities practically nil. Not only could a slave ship be smelled for miles down wind, but sickness raged: smallpox, ophthalmia, "the flux," and insanity. Dead bodies were thrown overboard, and sometimes the sick as well, to check the spread of infection. On occasions a plague-ridden or damaged vessel was abandoned by her crew, leaving the cargo still chained below decks.[28]

Although the slave trade was formally abolished by both Great Britain and the United States in 1808, illicit trading by American ships continued. When a patrol ship came in view, the best guarantee for trader and crew was to dump the manacled cargo overboard, where it quickly sank from sight or was disposed of by the sharks.

The slaves themselves left no chronicle of the Middle Passage; coming from many tribes, they often could not communicate with each other. There remains the testimony of the slavers — detailed, and dispassionate, such as that of Alexander Falconbridge:

I saw pregnant women give birth to babies while chained to corpses which our drunken overseers had not removed. . . . The younger women fared best at first as they were allowed to come on deck as companions for our crew. . . . Toward the end of the run, which lasted nearly six weeks, the mortality thinned out the main hold, and some scores of women were driven below as company for the males.[29]

To reduce the high death rate, some of the later and larger ships carried doctors, one of whom wrote, with clinical detachment, of the high rate of insanity, especially among the women:

One day at Bonny I saw a middle-aged stout woman, who had been brought down from a fair the preceding day, chained to the post of a black trader's door, in a state of furious insanity. On board the ship was a young negro woman chained to the deck, who had lost her senses soon after she was purchased and taken on board. In a former voyage we were obliged to confine a female negro about 23 years of age, on her becoming a lunatic. She was afterward sold during one of her lucid intervals.[30]

Although profits from the slave trade ran high, sometimes as much as 100 per cent per voyage, the hazards were also high, and were increased by the volatility of the cargo. Unending warfare raged between slaves and traders, sometimes concealed, at other times breaking out in open revolt. If the slaves could not win control of the ship, they could at least die. They fought back not only by mutiny, but through hunger strikes; they jumped overboard, and on occasion, literally refused to breathe. The slaver faced the dilemma of using punishment, such as hanging, lashing, mutilation or starvation, impartially against men and women alike, or of keeping his commodity not only alive but marketable — able to work, or at least looking fit for it. The wonder is that even a third or a half survived, and that the women could still bear healthy children.

They were first unloaded in the West Indies for "seasoning" and training — in reality, for time in which to try and repair some of the more visible damages of the Middle Passage, and to weed out those permanently maimed or diseased. Here too began the process of teaching them to wear clothes, speak English, do plantation work, and worship the God of the Christians. The complex, highly evolved African tribal life was uprooted as completely as individual tribes and families had been atomized and scattered. Each new boatload was submerged in a rapidly increasing population of "assimilated" slaves, two million by 1830, almost four million by the outbreak of the Civil War.

Not all slaves found themselves in similar circumstances or suffered equal hardships; the institution of slavery permitted wide variations, depending on the economic status and individual personality of the slave owner. Before the Civil War a Negro woman slave might be one of the two million slaves in the so-called "cotton states"; there she might work on one of the larger plantations where life was controlled by an overseer, and slavery often assumed its most brutal and exploitative form. Or she might be a "house servant" on such a plantation, a group somewhat apart and better off than the field hands. Again, she could be on a smaller plantation or farm with fewer slaves where the master himself worked in the fields and life was apt to be less hard than under the overseer's lash. At best, it was a grueling and near-hopeless existence.[31]

On the other hand, she might be one of the two million slaves in the states of Virginia, North Carolina, Maryland, Delaware, Kentucky, Tennessee, or Missouri, where the major cash crop was not cotton, or tobacco — but slaves. Each year these states "exported" some 100,000 dark-skinned males and females to the cotton domain, traveling in chained coffles similar to those in which their African forebears had been herded to the coast. Advertisements would appear:

Negroes for Sale: A girl about twenty years of age (raised in Virginia) and her two female children, one four and the other two years old — remarkably strong and healthy — Never having had a day's sickness with the exception of the smallpox, in her life. The children are fine and healthy. She is very prolific in her generating qualities and affords a rare opportunity to any person who wishes to raise a family of strong and healthy servants for their own use.[32]

In the last analysis no slave, however benevolent his owner or privileged his circumstances, was safe from such a fate. A change of family fortunes might cause the sale of the slaves, and the breaking of every personal tie: the tragedies of *Uncle Tom's Cabin* were taken from the millionfold realities of slave life.

The female slave faced additional hazards peculiar to her sex. She was used for breeding purposes to increase her owner's labor force or his stock of saleable merchandise; under existing conditions of slave life and medical care, she had to give birth often to meet both requirements.[33] She had, moreover, no defense against the sexual advances of any white man, a fact attested to by the widespread presence of mulattoes, some 588,000 according to the Census of 1860. This particular aspect of slavery had a strong impact on northern white women and accounted in some measure for the number of them drawn into the anti-slavery movement. The Grimké sisters bore outspoken witness to its effect on white family life and morality: "It is *not* the slave who alone suffers from the licentiousness of the Master and his sons, but the wronged and dishonored wife and daughters who are deeply injured and weep in secret places." [34]

Although the African matriarchal pattern had been largely destroyed, slave life itself gave the Negro woman a unique status. It was not only that, in the constant flux of slave relations, her relationship to her children was clear while the father's was often not, but also that, in addition to her capacity as a worker, the owner profited from her child-bearing and rearing her young. She was therefore less apt to be sold out of hand than the male, and was the more stable element in what little there was of slave family life. "As a rule the Negro woman as wife and mother was the mistress of her cabin, and, save for the interference of master or overseer, her wishes in regard to mating and family matters were paramount. Neither economic necessity nor tradition had instilled in her the spirit of subordination to masculine authority." [35]

Thus, however incongruous it might appear, the slave woman had achieved one kind of dignity many white women could not boast. But across the path to full human stature stretched, more unassailable than the barriers of common law or religious precepts, the wall of human bondage.

Chapter II

EARLY STEPS TOWARD EQUAL EDUCATION

The movement to improve and widen education in the young democracy assumed many forms. It included the extension of free education to ever wider sections of the population, the professional training of teachers, provisions for financial endowment, and the development of institutions for advanced education and higher learning and research.

Within this broad framework of endeavor, women faced some particular handicaps. It was almost universally believed that a woman's brain was smaller in capacity and therefore inferior in quality to that of a man. Some of the earliest women to demand greater educational advantages did not desire greater opportunities for women; they merely believed that more knowledge would make them better mothers and more efficient housewives. Some of them opposed the nascent woman's rights movement when it began to emerge; it was, in the main, a younger generation of women, their imaginations nourished and their wits sharpened by the pioneers, who took the leadership in advancing the legal and economic position of their sex.

Perhaps it was just as well that the earliest women educators saw only so far and no further; there were enough obstacles ahead to daunt even the strongest. By 1812, despite the dissemination of a few fertilizing ideas, education for women had made little progress. It was still limited to the well-to-do few, and consisted largely of such pursuits as embroidery, painting, French, singing, and playing the harpsichord. Its foundation on woman's proper sphere had been clearly stated by the French philosopher Rousseau: "The whole education of women ought to be relative to men. To please them, to be useful to them, to make themselves loved and honored by them, to educate them when young, to care

n when grown, to counsel them, to console them, and to
fe sweet and agreeable to them — these are the duties of
women at all times, and what should be taught them from their
infancy." [1]

But vast changes were in the making which would effectively
challenge such a philosophy. In 1814 the first power-driven loom
was set up at Waltham, Massachusetts, operated by one Deborah
Skinner; in 1817 three looms were in operation in Fall River
operated by Sallie Winters, Hannah Borden, and Mary Healy.
They proved that the nimbleness and skill previously employed
in spinning and weaving at home could be put to profitable use
in factories in what was to be the first large-scale industry in the
United States.

Following the Louisiana Purchase and the opening of most of
the northwestern continent to exploration and settlement, the
Jacksonian era saw great strides in westward expansion and industrial development. Women were not only entering the new textile
mills, they were also in increasing demand as teachers for a rapidly
growing population. The need to equip them for the new duties
being laid upon them was becoming harder to deny.

Among the earliest voices raised against outworn shibboleths
was that of Hannah Mather Crocker, whose little tract, *Observations on the Real Rights of Women,* published in 1818, shows the
conflict between old and new. She admitted a heavy debt to the
writings of Mary Wollstonecraft, but hedged on "the total independence of the female sex. We must be allowed to say, her theory
is unfit for practice, even though some of her sentiments and distinctions would do honor to the pen, even of a man." [2] She had
further reservations about women studying subjects too abstruse
for their physical makeup, such as metaphysics, or about entering
public affairs:

Females may console themselves and feel happy, that by the moral
distinction of the sexes they are called to move in a sphere of life
remote from those masculine contentions, although they hold equal
right with them of studying every branch of science, even jurispru-
dence. But it would be morally wrong, and physically imprudent, for
any woman to attempt pleading at the bar of justice, as no law can
give her the right of deviating from the strictest rules of rectitude and
decorum.[3]

Nevertheless Hannah Crocker unequivocally rejected the creed that woman must forever occupy an inferior position because of her inherent frailties, as demonstrated for all time by the fall of Eve:

We shall consider woman restored to her original right and dignity at the commencement of the Christian dispensation; although there must be allowed some moral and physical distinction of the sexes agreeably to the order of nature, still the sentiment must predominate that the powers of the mind are equal in the sexes. . . . There can be no doubt but there is as much difference in the powers of each individual of the male sex as there is of the female; and if they received the same mode of education, their improvement would be fully equal.[4]

In 1819, one year after Mrs. Crocker's pamphlet had appeared, Governor DeWitt Clinton of New York (of Erie Canal fame) received *An Address to the Public; Particularly to the Members of the Legislature of New York, Proposing a Plan for Improving Female Education;* it was the work of Mrs. Emma Willard, who had been quietly carrying out some novel pedagogical ideas which were to prove a turning point in women's education.

Born in Berlin, Connecticut, Emma Hart had been fortunate in her father; he wanted the best possible education for a lively-minded daughter who enjoyed grappling with mathematical problems for the sheer delight of mastering them. But her pleasure was spoiled when she discovered that most women were deprived of the study of higher mathematics because their brains were not considered equal to the strain. Slowly she came to the realization that women would not be able to overcome such prejudices without the knowledge and the discipline afforded by a systematized course of study.

Mrs. Willard, by then married to the head of an academy for boys in Middlebury, Vermont, and herself teaching girls, requested the privilege of attending the men's examinations at the University of Middlebury, in order to familiarize herself not only with the subject matter but also with teaching methods and standards in the fields barred to herself and her pupils. Her request being denied, Mrs. Willard set herself to evolving her own teaching methods, and training her own teachers. As a prerequisite she had to study each new subject by herself. "I spent from ten to twelve hours a day in teaching and, on extraordinary occasions such as preparing for examination, fifteen; besides having always under investigation some one new subject which, as I studied, I simultaneously taught a class of my ablest pupils." [5]

She did not stop with algebra and geometry, but went on to solid geometry (which, lacking textbooks, she taught with the aid of pyramids and cones carved out of turnips and potatoes), trigonometry, and conic sections. She taught geography, not by having her pupils memorize the distance between Peking and London, but by drawing maps; history was presented as a living process rather than a list of names and dates.

Since her pupils not only survived such rigorous fare, but responded with gusto, she was encouraged to present her *Address* to Governor Clinton. Her goal was a seminary whose curriculum would also include natural philosophy (science) and domestic science; she sought not only a charter but financial endowment. Mrs. Willard spent much time in Albany, pressing her ideas on members of the legislature. Decorum did not permit her to appear publicly, but she did read the *Address* to several individuals and to at least one larger group. Her biographer, Miss Alma Lutz, has suggested that she was probably the first woman lobbyist.

Although Governor Clinton gave her his support, and the legislature voted her a charter for a seminary in Waterford, it balked at the idea of a subsidy. Mrs. Willard then turned to the prosperous town of Troy, just across the Hudson River from Albany, where she aroused the interest of some substantial citizens. The Town Council voted to raise $4000 for a building by a special tax, and additional funds for maintenance and staff by private subscription; in 1821, the Troy Female Seminary, the first endowed institution for the education of girls, opened its doors.

Here Emma Willard continued to introduce innovations into her course of study, the most daring being the subject of physiology, at a time when any mention of the human body by ladies was considered the height of indelicacy.

Mothers visiting a class at the Seminary in the early thirties were so shocked at the sight of a pupil drawing a heart, arteries and veins on a blackboard to explain the circulation of the blood, that they left the room in shame and dismay. To preserve the modesty of the girls, and spare them too frequent agitation, heavy paper was pasted over the pages in their textbooks which depicted the human body. [6]

In 1828–1829 women's education received a lively impetus from the teachings of Frances Wright. Born in Scotland in 1795, well-schooled and widely-traveled, the friend of Lafayette and of many freethinkers, Miss Wright edited a newspaper in Robert Owen's Utopian colony of New Harmony in the Indiana frontier country, and later her own paper, the *Free Enquirer,* in New York. She achieved further notoriety by pioneering as a woman lecturer and by her radical philosophy, of which her advocacy of equal education for women was an integral part. Like Mary Wollstonecraft, she argued that men were themselves degraded by the inferiority imposed on women; every relationship to which woman was a party — friendship, marriage or parenthood — suffered as long as she was regarded and treated as a lesser human being.[7]

Until women assume the place in society which good sense and good feeling alike assign to them, human improvement must advance but feebly. It is in vain that we would circumscribe the power of one half of our race, and that half by far the most important and influential. If they exert it not for good, they will for evil; if they advance not knowledge, they will perpetuate ignorance. Let women stand where they may in the scale of improvement, their position decides that of the race.[8]

Since Miss Wright cut a wide swath in her lectures, her ideas on education were linked, in many minds, with such other incendiary views as her support of political action by workingmen, her challenge of all forms of religious obscurantism, and her insistence on the rational basis of all knowledge and the importance of free enquiry:

I am not going to question your opinions. I am not going to meddle with your beliefs. I am not going to dictate to you mine. All I say is, examine; enquire. Look into the nature of things. Search out the ground of your opinions, the *for* and the *against.* Know *why* you believe, understand *what* you believe, and possess a reason for the faith that is in you.[9]

This was strong meat, and the easiest way to dispose of it as well as of Miss Wright's ideas on education for women was to fall back on accusations of atheism and free love; her reputation became such that later woman's rights advocates were tagged "Fanny Wrightists" as the worst kind of abuse.

Yet her influence was enduring. No woman in the first half of the nineteenth century who challenged tradition escaped the effect of Frances Wright's leavening thought; nor was its impact limited to women alone. The lectures which she delivered in New York, Philadelphia, Baltimore, Boston, Cincinnati, Louisville, St. Louis, and elsewhere were largely before audiences of workingmen, who also read accounts of her addresses in the active labor press of the day; they helped to feed the rising popular demand for free education.

As the electorate slowly broadened state by state to include all white males over twenty-one regardless of property qualifications, the demand that education likewise be made available to all, irrespective of income levels, became one of the important issues of the Jacksonian era; every voter needed to be responsible and intelligent, and therefore had a basic right to education. Yet it took the better part of the nineteenth century to achieve a nation-wide system of free education for males, from primary school through college. In the period before the Civil War, the states were largely concerned with establishing publicly-supported elementary schools. By 1860 there were still only some forty-odd high schools worthy of the name in the entire country. Many which called themselves such were in reality little better than elementary schools.[10]

Lacking the argument afforded by suffrage, education for girls who could not attend private schools advanced even more slowly. While they were permitted to go to elementary schools, however financed, from the earliest days, their admission into secondary and high schools took much longer. The opening of free high schools for girls in such cities as Boston and Philadelphia was a veritable milestone which occurred only after the Civil War.[11]

Since convincing taxpayers and civic authorities that women were entitled to the same educational opportunities as men was to be a long and laborious task, private institutions continued for some time to be the principal recourse of young women seeking broader schooling. But here too a problem existed. The fees were necessarily high, and thus limited the student body to those with parents able to meet them. When the heads of such seminaries sought to broaden their student body, they were confronted with the need for outside supplementary financing. From her earliest teaching days Emma Willard had sought to take education out of the realm of a privilege for the well-to-do. Her method was to make grants, in the form of loans, which were repaid by her pupils after they had found teaching posts; it is estimated that she loaned more than $75,000 over the years for this purpose. But she knew it was no real solution to the problem, and it was not the least of Mrs. Willard's contributions to women's education that she first raised the question of private endowment for women's educational institutions.

Mrs. Willard also played a pioneer role in demanding, and providing for, the training of teachers. Teaching was the first of the "professions" open to women, but since they had no training and only the most rudimentary schooling, their prestige was low and they could not command salaries anything like those of men who were often college or university graduates. The Willard Association for the Mutual Improvement of Female Teachers, founded by Mrs. Willard in 1837 as a sort of alumnae association, was the first organization to bring this matter to public attention. It was typical of Mrs. Willard's "modern" methods and also of her national reputation that she secured as Honorary Vice-Presidents of the Association such distinguished women as Sarah Josepha Hale, editor of the famous *Godey's Lady's Book* magazine, and the poet and novelist, Lydia Sigourney.

The subjects Mrs. Willard taught her girls might appear as higher education to contemporaries, but they could not compare with what was offered to young men at Harvard and other colleges. The first institution which offered women a curriculum even remotely comparable to that available to men on the college level was Oberlin, which began as a "seminary" and developed into a rudimentary college. As such it held a special and deserved place in the affections of the early woman's rights leaders; Lucy Stone referred to the opening of Oberlin as "the gray dawn of our morning."

Founded in 1833 in the 30-year-old state of Ohio, it was the first such institution to open its doors to all comers, regardless of race, color — or sex. The founders stated among its prominent objectives: "the elevation of the female character, bringing within the reach of the misjudged and neglected sex all the instructive privileges which hitherto have unreasonably distinguished the leading sex from theirs." [12]

The earliest women students at Oberlin took a shortened "literary" course in deference to the prevailing creed that their minds could not assimilate the same fare as men's. The first woman graduated the "full course" in 1841; close on her heels came Lucy Stone and Antoinette Brown, the former to become one of the outstanding orators of her day, the latter the first woman to be ordained as a minister. It is noteworthy that both had stormy careers at Oberlin because of their feminist views, which brought them into constant conflict with the authorities:

Oberlin's attitude was that women's high calling was to be the mothers of the race, and that they should stay within that special sphere in order that future generations should not suffer from the want of devoted and undistracted mother care. If women became lawyers, ministers, physicians, lecturers, politicians or any sort of "public character" the home would suffer from neglect. . . . Washing the men's clothes, caring for their rooms, serving them at table, listening to their orations, but themselves remaining respectfully silent in public assemblages, the Oberlin "co-eds" were being prepared for intelligent motherhood and a properly subservient wifehood.[13]

Among the women educators who accepted the status quo for women — with a difference — was Catharine Beecher, who conducted a successful seminary for girls in Hartford, Connecticut, from 1823 to 1827.[14] Forced to give it up by the inroads made on her health by the familiar dual job of teaching and money-raising, she turned her attention to other facets of the problem of female improvement. She was concerned that the "surplus" females in the East, forced to earn their own livelihood by the large-scale westward migration of eligible males, were going into factories where they worked long hours at low wages under insanitary conditions. Her remedy was twofold: either women should teach — and the enormous demand for properly trained teachers would go far to absorbing such a "surplus" — or they should address themselves to some form of domestic work:

When all the mothers, teachers, nurses and domestics are taken from our sex, which the best interests of society demand, and when all these employments are deemed respectable and are filled by well-educated women, there will be no supernumeraries found to put into shops and mills or to draw into the arena of public and political life.[15]

Miss Beecher's concept of woman's highest calling was quickened by something new: her insistence that, in order to discharge her housewifely obligations properly, a woman needed not only a rounded education, but a training as technical as that of a lawyer or a doctor. She developed her ideas in a series of books on domestic science, physical culture, and even what we would call "marriage problems." Her crowning work in this field, *The American Woman's Home,* contains a mass of information ranging from recipes and sewing instructions to suggestions on proper ventilation, planning a house suited to easy housekeeping, and maintaining the niceties of harmonious family living!

But it was in her approach to the training of teachers, a concern that she shared with Emma Willard, that Miss Beecher made her greatest contribution. She believed that teaching, like homemaking, must be dignified by adequate training. She developed a scheme for what we would call normal schools in a chain of middle-western cities, of which only two or three materialized, and only one, Milwaukee-Downer College, survives today. To rouse public interest in the question she established organizations, the National Board of Popular Education in 1847 and the American Women's Educational Association in 1852. Although she remained decorously in the background, working through interested gentlemen who even read her speeches for her at public gatherings, Catharine Beecher was one of the founders of modern teacher training.

Looking back from our present vantage point, we can see that the single most significant step away from the concept that women needed an improved education only to carry out their housewifely or teaching duties better came with the founding of Mount Holyoke in 1837. Generally regarded now as the oldest woman's college in the United States, it made no such claim at the time. It opened as a seminary, and there were other such institutions then in existence.[16] Mount Holyoke did not achieve collegiate status until 1893, after Vassar, Wellesley, Smith, and Bryn Mawr; yet it opened the way for them all.

Its founder, Mary Lyon, followed the path charted by Emma

Willard, but went much further; in the fifteen years between the first steps toward founding her school and her premature death at fifty-two, Miss Lyon established certain fundamental principles which succeeding institutions accepted as axiomatic: the schools must have adequate financial endowment; they must try in some degree to make education available to girls of all economic groups; they must offer a curriculum more advanced than that envisaged even by Mrs. Willard; and they must prepare their students for more than homemaking or teaching.

Miss Lyon succeeded in her ambitious undertaking because, in addition to an indomitable will and a mind which left its fiery imprint on all whom she encountered, her purpose was perfectly suited to both time and place. Hers was a New England in which wider horizons for women were becoming a household controversy: where women were already more than homemakers and pedagogues. They were working by the thousands in the red brick mill buildings springing up beside every creek and river.[17] The year Mount Holyoke opened its doors, anti-slavery women were holding their first national convention in New York, and the Grimké sisters were touring Massachusetts, speaking publicly against slavery; the storm unleashed by their unladylike behavior was convulsing the churches. There was a ferment abroad which stirred even women in obscure villages to ideas and efforts undreamed of a few years earlier. To a person of Mary Lyon's gifts and determination, here were the soil and climate that she needed.

She was born on a marginal hill farm in western Massachusetts in 1797, and as a child already showed astonishing mental capacities; like Emma Willard, she soon reached the outposts of knowledge then accessible to women. Like Mrs. Willard, she began to teach, and in the process, to continue her own education, to extend the existing curriculum, and to reshape teaching methods. With Miss Zilpah Grant she ran a successful academy, first at Derry, New Hampshire, and then at Ipswich, Massachusetts, but she was not satisfied. She saw the price paid in poor health by Miss Grant and by her friend, Catharine Beecher, for their staggering labors. She saw good schools arise, and then vanish, if a wealthy supporter died or lost interest. Like Miss Beecher she was obsessed with the need for good teachers. Most of all, she brooded over the young women who, like herself, wanted an education they could not afford: "During the past year my heart has so yearned over the adult female youth in the common walks of life, that it has sometimes seemed as if there was a fire shut up in my bones. I would esteem it a greater favor to labor in this field than in any other on which I have fastened my attention." [18] To her mother she wrote in the same vein: "I have for a great while been thinking about those young ladies who find it necessary to make such an effort for their education, as I made when I was obtaining mine. . . . I have looked out from my quiet scene of labor on the wide world, and my heart has longed to see many enjoying the privileges, who cannot for want of means. . . . Sometimes my heart has burned within me; and again I have bid it be quiet." [19]

In 1834 she laid her plan for a new kind of educational institution for women before a number of businessmen and ministers, who finally assumed the responsibility of raising the $27,000 estimated as necessary to build and open the school.

Here lay one of the major obstacles to success. Miss Lyon was herself the heart of the enterprise; yet the proprieties required that she keep in the background. It was not even considered seemly that she be present at the trustees' meeting which voted to locate the school in South Hadley, Massachusetts. She wrote to Zilpah Grant: "It is desirable that the plans relating to the subject should not seem to originate with *us* but with benevolent *gentlemen*. If the object should excite attention there is danger that many good men will fear the effect on society of so much female influence, and what they will call female greatness." [20]

But when it became apparent that the men hired as "agents" were unable to raise the needed funds in the face of not only public apathy but a gradually worsening economic situation which culminated in the panic and depression of 1837, Mary Lyon herself entered the field, carrying the green velvet bag which became famous all over New England. When her staunchest friends objected to her incessant traveling and appearances at public meetings to ask for money, as unladylike, she refused to compromise her dream for the sake of propriety:

"What do I do that is wrong?" she asked in a letter. "I ride in the stage-coach or cars without an escort. Other ladies do the same. I visit a family where I have been previously invited, and the minister's wife or some leading woman calls the ladies together to see me, and I lay our object before them. Is that wrong? I go with Mr. Hawks and call on a gentleman of known liberality at his own house, and converse with him about our enterprise. What harm is there in that? If there is no harm in doing these things once, what harm is there in doing them twice, thrice or a dozen times? My heart is sick, my soul is pained with this empty gentility, this genteel nothingness. I am doing a great work, I cannot come down." [21]

Miss Lyon herself raised the first $1,000 with which to launch the campaign, primarily from her former Ipswich students and teachers. Next she won support from men of means whom she visited under the escort of one or more of her trustees: there were two donations of $1,000 each, one of $640, one of $500. But in the last analysis the greater part of the money was raised because Mary Lyon, sometimes accompanied by a gentleman but very often alone, went to as large a cross-section of the population of New England as she could reach.

The greater portion of the total sum was raised from farmers and small townsfolk — men whose livelihood did not come easily, and women without any source of income except their handiwork, or what husbands or fathers might give them. In the old ledgers there are eloquent entries of five dollars, ones and threes, fifty cents, and one gift of six cents. Much of this money was raised at church meetings, small parlor gatherings, and sewing circles. There was a young girl in a sewing circle at West Brookfield, who was making a shirt to help a young man through theological seminary, and whose thoughts as she listened to Miss Lyon have come down to us: "How absurd it was for her to be working to help educate a student who could earn more money toward his own education in a week, by teaching, than she could earn in a month; and she left the shirt unfinished and hoped that no one would ever complete it." [22] Her name was Lucy Stone.

It took four long years to raise the money, put up the building, and open Mount Holyoke. Often the outcome seemed in doubt, even to the trustees. The building had been started long before all the funds were in hand, and it was still not quite finished on the day in November 1837 when students began arriving. Many of them spent their first night with the best families in South Hadley, whose womenfolk rallied to loan furnishings for the rooms still lacking necessary equipment.

To the first group of girls and the parents who brought them, Miss Lyon communicated her own sense of urgency and triumph; no freshman on the threshold of her college life would ever feel quite the exhilaration and significance which fused that group, under Miss Lyon's influence:

Girls, stiff with riding almost continuously since before dawn, on the last afternoon of grace were swung down from chaises by fathers and friends' fathers, to stumble through a side door into a five-storied brick building that rose, stark and blindless, out of a waste of sand. Deacon Porter was helping lay the front threshold, paint pots and work benches furnished the parlors, and Miss Lyon met them in the dining-room. There stood tables spread for the hungry; near by, a merry group of young women were hemming linen and finishing off quilts and counterpanes. Hammer strokes resounded through the house. Coatless, on his knees in "seminary hall," Deacon Safford tacked matting, looking up with a smiling word to newcomers: "We are in glorious confusion now, but we hope for better order soon." . . . Trustees' wives washed dishes in the kitchen . . . A girl's journal remarks: "Helped to get the first breakfast at Holyoke. Miss Lyon and I were the first to appear in the kitchen.". . . Examinations began to go forward amid the clamor of alien activities. Singly, in twos, in groups, the girls took them, teachers and students seated together on the stairs, or side by side on a pile of mattresses in a hall-way, little oases of scholarly seclusion. . . . And then at four o'clock, when the last tack had been driven in "seminary hall," a pause fell on the fleet occupations. With examinations far from finished, and many loads of furniture still on the road, a bell rang, and Mount Holyoke opened.[23]

Behind this adventurous group of students was an admission policy as startling as anything else in Miss Lyon's scheme: an age limit (no girl less than sixteen years old was accepted), an embryonic system of examinations, and the conscious *selection* of girls on the basis of their maturity and promise of intellectual growth. The requirements for entering the first year were roughly those in effect at the best seminaries of the day, but the substitution of a systematic three-year course instead of the usual two years, and its content, as stated in the sober prose of the 1837–1838 catalogue, marked a new era.

Prospective students were examined in the general principles of English grammar, modern geography, history of the United States, Watts' *On the Mind,* Colburn's *First Lessons,* and "the *whole* of Adams' New Arithmetic or what should be the equivalent in written arithmetic." Those fulfilling these requirements, faced the following prospectus of courses in the new seminary:

Junior (first year): English Grammar, Ancient Geography, Ancient and Modern History, Sullivan's Political Class Book, Botany, Newman's Rhetoric, Euclid, Human Physiology.

Second (or middle) Year: English Grammar continued, Algebra, Botany continued, Natural Philosophy, Smellie's Philosophy of Natural History, Intellectual Philosophy.

Studies of the Senior Class: Chemistry, Astronomy, Geology, Ecclesiastical History, Evidences of Christianity, Whately's Logic, Whately's Rhetoric, Moral Philosophy, Natural Theology, Butler's Analogy.[24]

Students were also required to take part in calisthenics, music, and French, as well as domestic duties, an item which aroused much controversy. (Miss Lyon claimed it cut costs and thus helped the school to survive; it probably also reassured some parents and supporters who might have been fearful that the students were moving too far out of their natural sphere!)

This curriculum had much the same impact on the educational world of the 1830's as did the "Harvard Annex" and Bryn Mawr entrance examinations some fifty years later. However dry the enumeration of texts, however rigid and now outworn the course of study, its significance can hardly be overstated. The long struggle first envisaged by Judith Sargent Murray and launched by Emma Willard, taking women beyond the pudding and the nursery, had passed a decisive stage. Mary Lyon had put into their hands the means by which they could carry on that struggle in many different directions. What a few had dreamed and dared was now being proved in life and practice: that women's minds were constituted, in bulk and cell structure and endowment, the same as those of their masculine counterparts; that, given opportunity, discipline, and direction, they could encompass the same subject matter as a man; and that such an education was worth a sizable financial investment on the part of the parent, the philanthropist, and the community. The way had been cleared for the opening of Vassar in 1865, of Smith and Wellesley in 1875, of the "Harvard Annex" in 1879, of Bryn Mawr in 1885. It was becoming clear, to the dismay and regret of some, that there was no telling where it would all end.

As long as the institution of slavery existed, an educated Negro was not only an anachronism but a threat. To educate him was to disprove the premise of racial inferiority on which slavery was founded, and also to arm him for the struggle for freedom. It was illegal in southern states to teach a slave how to read. Although there are reports of schools conducted by Negro women in Louisiana, South Carolina, and Georgia, they were for the children of the freed Negroes, and they were rare. When Sarah Grimké tried to teach her slave maid to read, she did so behind a locked bedroom door and by the light of blazing pine knots. They were soon discovered, and the lessons stopped.

"At the North," in the phrase of the day, where slavery was abolished state by state over a period of fifty years beginning in 1790, colored children were nevertheless barred from the common schools in many places down to the Civil War.[25] Laura Haviland, devoted crusader for freedom, testified that even in the Northwest Territory, where slavery had been abolished in 1787, there was not a school in the whole state of Michigan in 1837 that a colored child or adult could attend.[26] Negroes were taxed in Ohio in the 1840's to support "public schools," but their children could not enter them.[27]

Inevitably, the Negro girl suffered more deprivation than her brothers. If a white woman was supposed to be mentally incapable of receiving the same education as a man, and Negroes were inferior to whites, it followed that the Negro girl had the least possible potential for mental growth.

And yet, it had already been proved that a colored woman could be not only educated but capable of creative work. The honor and tragedy of such proof had fallen to Phillis Wheatley, who as a child of six had been captured in West African Senegal by slave traders, had survived the Middle Passage, and had been sold in the Boston slave market in 1759.[28] She was extraordinarily fortunate; her owners were both educated and kind. They gave her the best possible schooling, and when she demonstrated her abilities as a poet and Latinist, they freed her but kept her in their home. Writing verse in the classical style of the day, Phillis wrote among others an "Ode to General Washington," which he gracefully acknowledged. After the Revolutionary War she journeyed to England, where she was feted by literary society.

Then her patrons died; the man she married proved worthless, and left her destitute with three children. In 1784, when she was thirty-one years old, she died with a newborn child in her arms in an unheated Boston rooming-house, of cold and starvation.

There was no place in the world for a Phillis Wheatley yet. As the movement for the abolition of slavery began to pick up headway, it might have been expected that the education of Negro girls would become a matter of wider concern. That it did so even briefly was due to the heroism of one woman, and it is significant that none followed her example for some twenty years. The hazards encountered by Prudence Crandall in 1833–1834 in her effort to teach Negro pupils in a small Connecticut village are a measure of the obstacles that lay across the path of Negro girls looking for an education in the "free North" at that time.

Miss Crandall was a Quaker who conducted a successful school for young ladies in Canterbury, some forty miles southeast of Hartford. Her servant was a free Negro woman, engaged to marry the local "agent" of the *Liberator,* the fiery Abolitionist paper conducted by William Lloyd Garrison. She influenced Miss Crandall to accept a Negro girl, Sarah Harris, into her school of select and sheltered young misses. A storm of protest blew up; faced with the demand that she oust her new pupil, Miss Crandall closed her school instead.

Canterbury was taken aback, but found the episode was a mere prelude. Miss Crandall embarked on a series of journeys to Boston, Providence, and New York, where she took counsel with abolitionist leaders. Advertisements appeared in the *Liberator,* asking Negro parents to send their daughters to her for instruction. In April, just two months after she had closed one school, she opened another with seventeen Negro pupils.

Canterbury had never considered itself pro-slavery in sentiment. But such of its citizens as concerned themselves with the issue at all favored its solution by colonization: the return of the country's Negro population to Africa. They certainly never bargained for a school for Negro girls, backed — of all things — by abolitionist firebrands.

When the pillars of the community failed to close the school by threats, they resorted to other means of persuasion. Miss Crandall was jailed on a vagrancy charge — presumably laid against her pupils rather than herself — and when that failed to stand up in court, a special law was rushed through the Connecticut legislature making it illegal for a Connecticut citizen to teach a pupil from another state! [29]

While this measure dragged through the courts (where it was ultimately reversed), other time-honored methods were applied: the school's windows were broken; pupils and teachers (Miss Crandall was aided by her sister Almira) were stoned as they went for walks; manure was dropped in the well; local storekeepers refused to sell food, and doctors denied their services.

For one year and a half, Miss Crandall and her pupils held fast. She and her school became a symbol. Supporters from nearby communities brought food; her father carted water from his well two miles away. Abolitionists sent funds, and when they came to visit, the students gave recitations, dressed in their best. The girls themselves appeared as witnesses on Miss Crandall's behalf in court and wrote letters to abolitionist newspapers. In the end it was her concern for their lives that caused Prudence Crandall to retreat. One night, shortly after an attempt at arson had gutted the cellar, masked men brought battering rams into position and swung them against the walls of the house and the front door. Students and teachers spent a sleepless night upstairs while the rooms below were virtually demolished. The next day Miss Crandall announced that the school had closed.

Canterbury had won.[30] But Miss Crandall's defeat marks the beginning of a long struggle in which she is honored as a pioneer. Today a woman's dormitory in Howard University in Washington, the first institution for the higher education of Negroes of both sexes founded after the Civil War, bears the name of Crandall Hall.

Prudence Crandall's struggle is all the more memorable when viewed in the context of her day. In 1833, Mount Holyoke was still a dream in Mary Lyon's mind. The voices of the first women to speak against slavery in public had not yet been raised. The first diffident women's anti-slavery societies would not be organized for another year. Yet Prudence Crandall traveled widely ("unladylike," Miss Lyon's friends called *her* fund-raising travels!), disregarded not only threats but flying stones, and carried on her school in a virtual state of siege for eighteen months. Here was a struggle to give many a woman not only food for thought but heart as well. Prudence Crandall belongs not only to the anti-slavery movement, but also to that for woman's rights.

Chapter III

THE BEGINNINGS OF ORGANIZATION
AMONG WOMEN

The epic of Prudence Crandall's school was part of an upsurge against slavery. In 1831 the slave Nat Turner had led a slave revolt in Virginia, which had brought a wave of repressive measures throughout the South. That same year in Boston William Lloyd Garrison founded his abolitionist weekly, *The Liberator*, with its uncompromising opening salvo: "I will not equivocate, I will not excuse, I will not retreat a single inch — and I WILL BE HEARD!" The first anti-slavery societies (of men only) were formed, and the Underground Railway, that vast network of skilled "agents" and hidden "stations" which assisted runaway slaves to free territory, gained its name and began to pick up momentum.

Thousands of men and women were drawn into the work; among the latter were the first conscious feminists, who would go to school in the struggle to free the slaves and, in the process, launch their own fight for equality. It was in the abolition movement that women first learned to organize, to hold public meetings, to conduct petition campaigns. As abolitionists they first won the right to speak in public, and began to evolve a philosophy of their place in society and of their basic rights. For a quarter of a century the two movements, to free the slave and liberate the woman, nourished and strengthened one another.

The earliest rudimentary women's organizations had been church sewing circles, which were started to raise money for missionary or charitable work. Elizabeth Buffum Chace has recorded that the Smithfield (Rhode Island) Female Improvement Society met each week in the 1820's, to read "useful books" aloud, and hear original compositions by its members.[1] Later, the women began to range farther afield; in 1840 Lucy Stone wrote her brother: "It was decided in our Literary Society the other day that ladies ought to mingle in politics, go to Congress, etc., etc. What do you think of that?" [2]

Free Negro women in the North and West, while they came together for similar purposes, had other motives as well. There were Female Literary Societies of colored women in Philadelphia, New York, Boston, and other eastern cities in the 1830's; but the powerful incentive of getting an education for their children also brought about such organizations as the Ohio Ladies Education Society, "which probably did more toward the establishment of schools for the education of colored people at this time in Ohio than any other organized group." [3]

When the leading abolitionists met in Philadelphia in 1833 to found the American Anti-Slavery Society, they permitted a few women to attend, and even to speak from the floor, but not to join the society or to sign the "Declaration of Sentiments and Purposes." When the convention adjourned, some twenty women met to form the Philadelphia Female Anti-Slavery Society.

They were intrepid but still decorous; treading such an uncharted path, they asked a Negro freedman to preside at their first meeting. Within a few years other women were organizing for the same purpose in New York, Boston, and many other New England towns, and by 1837 the first National Female Anti-Slavery Society convention met in New York with eighty-one delegates from twelve states. Far from accepting the aid of a man as presiding officer, one of the delegates sent word to the abolitionist Theodore Weld: "Tell Mr. Weld . . . that when the women got together they found they had *minds* of their own, and could transact their business *without* his directions. The Boston and Philadelphia women were so well versed in business that they were quite mortified to have Mr. Weld quoted as an authority for doing or not doing so and so." [4]

From the beginning, the women showed great courage; because they were overstepping time-honored bounds, they aroused the particular fury of adherents of slavery, of whom there were many in the North, and mob violence was not unusual. In Boston in 1835 a mob swarmed into the building where Garrison was to address the Boston Female Anti-Slavery Society and stormed up the stairs to the door of the very room in which the women were meeting. Garrison was whisked out a back door (he was later dragged through the streets at the end of a rope), and the Mayor himself came to beg the women to leave in order to avoid physical harm. At the direction of Maria Weston Chapman, each white lady present took a colored "sister" by the hand, and two by two, they walked calmly down the stairs and out the building, "their hands folded in their cotton gloves, their eyes busily identifying the genteel leaders of the mob." [5]

Even small house gatherings were not immune. On one such occasion, when the women heard that violence was planned, Mrs. Chapman personally went to warn every member of the Society of what might occur:

Among those whom she visited was an artizan's wife, who was sweeping out one of her two rooms as Mrs. Chapman entered. On hearing that there was every probability of violence and that the warning was given in order that she might stay away if she thought proper, she leaned upon her broom and considered awhile. Her answer was: "I have often wished and asked that I might be able to do something for the slaves; and it seems to me that this is the very time and the very way. You will see me at the meeting and I will keep a prayerful mind as I am about my work until then." [6]

After another such gathering the British writer Harriet Martineau wrote: "When I was putting on my shawl upstairs, Mrs. Chapman came to me, bonnet in hand, to say, 'You know, we are threatened with a mob today again, but I do not myself much apprehend it. It must not surprise us; but my hopes are stronger than my fears.' " [7]

The women who took part in the operations of the Underground Railroad underwent the sharpest schooling of all. They were ready at all hours to welcome fugitives arriving at their homes, often in the middle of the night, feed and care for them, keep them in cellar or attic or secret chamber while the sheriff's posse hammered at the door or even searched the house; sometimes, in the absence of husband or father, when the danger was acute, they would mount the driver's seat and drive a wagon load of "freight" to a safer station up along the line toward freedom.

It is therefore not surprising that so many women abolitionists became active on behalf of greater rights for women. The pioneers were the Grimké sisters, who first fought for — and won — woman's right to speak in public before any and every kind of audience, and who paved the way for the long roster of famous women orators in the anti-slavery cause: Lucy Stone, Lucretia Mott, Abby Kelley Foster, Frances Harper, Ernestine Rose, Sojourner Truth, Susan Anthony, and many more.

Since the days of Anne Hutchinson, women had remained silent in public. Alone among the larger religious denominations, the Quakers permitted them a voice in church affairs, allowed them to speak in "meeting," and ordained them as ministers.[8] The other Protestant churches followed the same dicta of St. Paul that had been used against Mistress Hutchinson: "Let the women learn in silence with all subjection. . . . I suffer not a woman to teach, nor to usurp authority over the men, but to be in silence." And again: "Let your women keep silent in the churches, for it is not permitted unto them to speak." [9] The churches merely expressed a dominant social pattern which dictated that the speaking of women in public was unseemly.

The first woman to pass through the curtain of silence had been Frances Wright, whose meteoric lecturing career in 1828–1829, while highly successful, had also been unpleasantly tinged with notoriety. She did not immediately pave the way for other women because — if only by a few years — she came upon the scene and left it, too soon.

Another short-lived attempt was that of a Negro woman, Mrs. Maria W. Stewart, who spoke several times in Boston between 1831 and 1833. Uneducated, impelled by strong religious beliefs, she was also an outspoken abolitionist and eager to see greater educational opportunities open to girls.[10] Her attempts to lead her people to regeneration from the platform were not kindly received; in a "Farewell Address" to her friends in Boston she admitted failure: "I find it is no use for me, as an individual, to try to make myself useful among my color in this city. . . . I have made myself contemptible in the eyes of many." [11]

In her addresses Mrs. Stewart not only summoned her listeners to live in greater righteousness; she pleaded for the slave, and stoutly defended her right as a woman to do so in words that heralded the arguments the Grimkés were to use a few years later:

What if I am a woman; is not the God of ancient times the God of these modern days? Did he not raise up Deborah to be a mother and a judge in Israel? Did not Queen Esther save the lives of the Jews? And Mary Magdalen first declare the resurrection of Christ from the dead? . . . If such women as are here described once existed, be no longer astonished then, my brethren and friends, that God at this eventful period should raise up your own females to strive by their example, both in public and in private, to assist those who are endeavoring to stop the strong current of prejudice that flows so profusely, against us at present. . . . What if such women as are here described should rise among our sable race? And it is not impossible; for it is not the color of the skin that makes the man or the woman, but the principle formed in the soul.[12]

Those who really opened the way to public speaking, and therefore enabled women to reach large numbers of people directly, were the Grimké sisters, Sarah and Angelina, whose achievement was the outcome of a now rapidly growing stream of social development. Where the Grimkés led, other women soon followed in growing numbers.[13]

Sarah and Angelina Grimké were the daughters of a South Carolina slaveholding family; from earliest childhood they had loathed slavery and all its works. Nor could they close their eyes and live with it; first Sarah, the elder and plainer, and later the beautiful Angelina moved to Philadelphia, where they joined the Quakers. But they found that flight was no salve to conscience and for years they sought painfully for the way to strike a blow against the institution they abhorred.

In 1836 they made abolitionist friends, at whose suggestion Angelina began to write "An Appeal to the Christian Women of the South," urging them to speak out on behalf of the slave. About the same time, the American Anti-Slavery Society invited the sisters to speak at small parlor gatherings of women in New York. The response was overwhelming. More than three hundred women appeared for the first meeting, which had to be transferred to the parlor of a small church. The sisters' eloquent description of slavery at first hand aroused so much interest that the next meeting was called in a church itself to accommodate all who wished to attend. A man slipped in, and was promptly ushered out. But others came, singly, then in twos and threes; before anyone really knew what was happening, the Grimkés were addressing large mixed public audiences. From New York they were invited to New England, where local anti-slavery societies, often of women, sponsored meetings in innumerable small towns and where tremendous gatherings were held in Boston.

Meanwhile a storm of controversy broke out. The main opposition came from the churches. The most powerful blast unleashed against the Grimkés, without mentioning them by name, was a Pastoral Letter from the Council of Congregationalist Ministers of Massachusetts, then the largest denomination in the state, denouncing their behavior as unwomanly and unchristian:

We invite your attention to the dangers which at present seem to threaten the female character with widespread and permanent injury. The appropriate duties and influence of women are clearly stated in the New Testament. Those duties, and that influence are unobtrusive and private, but the sources of mighty power. When the mild, dependent, softening influence upon the sternness of man's opinions is fully exercised, society feels the effect of it in a thousand forms. The power of woman is her dependence, flowing from the consciousness of that weakness which God has given her for her protection.

We appreciate the unostentatious prayers of woman in advancing the cause of religion at home and abroad; in Sabbath-schools; in leading religious inquirers to the pastors for instruction; and in all such associated efforts as become the modesty of her sex. . . . But when she assumes the place and tone of man as a public reformer . . . she yields the power which God has given her for her protection, and her character becomes unnatural. If the vine, whose strength and beauty is to lean on the trellis-work, and half conceal its cluster, thinks to assume the independence and the overshadowing nature of the elm, it will not only cease to bear fruit, but fall in shame and dishonor into the dust.[14]

Such attacks took a heavy toll of both women. At every step of the path along which their consciences drove them, they found themselves at odds with the traditions of decorum in which nineteenth century women were bred. None who overstepped those bounds in the quest for freedom and self-realization suffered more from doubts and self-questioning than the Grimkés. Angelina, who was the better speaker and who bore the brunt of public utterance (she once spoke on six successive evenings in the Boston Opera House, with her voice reaching the topmost tier), actually broke down under the strain in May 1838 and did not speak again for many years.[15]

But while they suffered deeply, they also gained insight from the opposition they encountered. They began to answer their critics, linking the two issues of slavery and the position of women, Angelina in her speeches, Sarah in a series of articles in the *New England Spectator* on "The Province of Women," which were issued as a pamphlet the following year entitled *The Equality of the Sexes and the Condition of Women* and widely circulated.

In these articles, Sarah Grimké met the assault of the Pastoral Letter head-on. She categorically denied any Biblical justification for the inferior position of woman. An early exponent of the "Higher Criticism," she held that the Scriptures were not divine in origin, and necessarily reflected the agricultural, patriarchal society which produced them.

Accepting Eve's responsibility for Original Sin, she turned it neatly on its advocates:

Adam's ready acquiescence with his wife's proposal does not savor much of that superiority in *strength of mind* which is arrogated by man. Even admitting that Eve was the greater sinner, it seems to me that man might be satisfied with the dominion he has claimed and exercised for nearly 6000 years, and that more true nobility would be manifested by endeavoring to raise the fallen and invigorate the weak than by keeping woman in subjection.[16]

With some tartness, she added: "I ask no favors for my sex. I surrender not our claim to equality. All I ask of our brethren is that they will take their feet from off our necks, and permit us to stand upright on the ground which God has designed us to occupy." [17]

Primarily Sarah Grimké saw the question of equality for women, not as a matter of abstract justice, but of enabling women to join in an urgent task:

In contemplating the great moral reformations of the day, and the part which they [women] are bound to take in them, instead of puzzling themselves with the harassing, because unnecessary inquiry, how far they may go without overstepping the bounds of propriety, which separate male and female duties, they will only inquire, "Lord, what wilt thou have me do?" They will be enabled to see the simple truth, that God has made no distinction between men and women as moral beings. . . . To me it is perfectly clear *that whatsoever it is morally right for a man to do, it is morally right for a woman to do.*[18]

It is said, woman has a mighty weapon in secret prayer; she has, I acknowledge, *in common with man:* but the woman who prays in sincerity for the regeneration of this guilty world, will accompany her prayers by her labors. A friend of mine remarked: "I was sitting in my chamber, weeping over the miseries of the slave, and putting up my prayers for his deliverance from bondage, when in the midst of my meditations it occurred to me that my tears, unaided by effort, could never melt the chain of the slave. I must be up and doing." She is now an active abolitionist — her prayers and her works go hand in hand.[19]

The Grimkés' advocacy of woman's rights evoked mixed reactions in the anti-slavery camp. Some of their staunchest friends, such as John Greenleaf Whittier and Theodore Weld (soon to marry Angelina), begged them to drop the woman's rights question, lest it impair their advocacy of abolition. But Angelina stood firm:

We cannot push Abolitionism forward with all our might *until* we take up the stumbling block out of the road. . . . You may depend upon it, tho' to meet *this* question *may appear* to be turning out of our road, that *it is not.* IT IS NOT: we *must* meet it and meet it now. . . . Why, my dear brothers can you not see the deep laid scheme of the clergy against us as lecturers? . . . If we surrender the right to *speak* in public this year, we must surrender the right to petition next year, and the right to *write* the year after, and so on. What *then* can *woman* do for the slave, when she herself is under the feet of man and shamed into *silence?*[20]

Among the women however their words fell upon eager ears. The beautiful and gifted Maria Weston Chapman, whom the poet Lowell called "the coiled-up mainspring of the anti-slavery movement," wrote a rollicking satire in answer to the Pastoral Letter, entitled "The Times That Try Men's Souls," and signed it "The Lords of Creation":

> Confusion has seized us, and all things go wrong,
>   The women have leaped from "their spheres,"
> And instead of fixed stars, shoot as comets along,
>   And are setting the world by the ears!
> In courses erratic they're wheeling through space,
> In brainless confusion and meaningless chase.
>
> In vain do our knowing ones try to compute
>   Their return to the orbit designed;
> They're glanced at a moment then onward they shoot,

And are neither "to hold nor to bind":
So freely they move in their chosen elipse,
The "Lords of Creation" do fear an eclipse.

They've taken a notion to speak for themselves,
    And are wielding the tongue and the pen;
They've mounted the rostrum; the termagant elves,
    And — oh horrid! — are talking to men!
With faces unblanched in our presence they come
To harangue us, they say, in behalf of the dumb.[21]

Angelina herself wrote to a Quaker friend, Jane Smith: "We find that many of our New England sisters are prepared to receive these strange doctrines, feeling as they do that our whole sex needs emancipation from the thraldom of public opinion. What dost thou think of some of them *walking* two, four, six and eight miles to attend our meetings?" [22]

It was not mere restlessness or frustration that drove women into such wintry tramps; it was the knowledge, in Angelina's words, that "we abolitionist women are turning the world upside down." A dramatic instance was the series of hearings held on three separate days in February 1838 before a committee of the Massachusetts State Legislature, on anti-slavery petitions. Henry B. Stanton had suggested, half in jest, that Angelina Grimké speak for the abolitionists, and after the usual soul-searching, she agreed. When she rose to speak, the first woman ever to make such an appearance before a legislative body, she confessed:

I was so near fainting under the tremendous pressure of feeling, my heart almost died within me. The novelty of the scene, the weight of responsibility, the ceaseless exercise of mind thro' which I had passed for almost a week — all together sunk me to the earth. I well nigh despaired, but our Lord and Master gave me his arm to lean upon and in great weakness, my limbs trembling under me, I stood up and spoke for nearly two hours. . . . Many of our dear Abolition friends did indeed travail in spirit for me, wrestling in earnest prayer, and M. Chapman's "God strengthen you my Sister" just before I rose was a strength to my fainting spirit.[23]

Among the abolitionist friends present was Lydia Maria Child, the successful writer who had sacrificed her career to the anti-slavery cause, and who wrote:

The Boston members of the legislature tried hard to prevent her [Angelina Grimké] having a hearing on the second day. Among other things, they said that such a crowd were attracted by curiosity the galleries were in danger of being broken down; though in fact they are constructed with remarkable strength. A member from Salem, perceiving their drift, wittily proposed that "a Committee be appointed to examine the foundations of the State House of Massachusetts to see whether it will bear another lecture from Miss Grimké!" [24]

When Angelina Grimké wrote Theodore Weld that women would be jeopardizing their right to petition by retreating on other issues, she was not indulging in idle fantasies. Their right to petition was under fire at the time in Congress, for the same reason that she and her sister were being upbraided by the clergy for their public speaking; both were being energetically exercised on behalf of the slave.

In 1834 the American Anti-Slavery Society had initiated a petition campaign which had quickly snowballed to such proportions as to seriously perturb southern congressmen. In an attempt to stem the tide, the House of Representatives passed the Pinckney Gag Rule forbidding their presentation.

The first voice raised from the floor of the House against this infraction of basic rights was that of John Quincy Adams, former president of the United States and now representative from Plymouth, Massachusetts. The seventy-year-old Adams, who earned the title of "Old Man Eloquent" during this last phase of his venerable career at first defended merely the rights of his own constituents to petition Congress. But when his stand became known, anti-slavery petitions began flowing in to him from all over the North. A large proportion of these came from the Female Anti-Slavery Societies, which roused the particular ire of southern representatives, and Adams took up the right and propriety of women's signing petitions and collecting signatures. [25]

Adams' defense of the women was touched off by the criticisms made by Congressman Howard of Maryland, in the course of which the Southerner declared that

he always felt regret when petitions thus signed by women were presented to the House relating to political matters. He thought that these females could have a sufficient field for the exercise of their influence in the discharge of their duties to their fathers, their husbands or their children, cheering the domestic circle and shedding over it the mild radiance of the social virtues, instead of rushing into the fierce struggles of political life. He felt sorrow at this departure from their proper sphere, in which there was abundant room for the practice of the most extensive benevolence and philanthropy, because he considered it discreditable, not only to their own particular section of the country, but also to the national character, and thus giving him the right to express his opinion.[26]

It seemed altogether appropriate for Abigail Adams' son to take up the cudgels for women in the controversy thus launched, and he did so in a series of speeches from June 26 to 30, in which he spared the House nothing in the way of historical reflections on women's role during revolutionary struggles, or his own opinion that American women were moving into a broader sphere:

Why does it follow that women are fitted for nothing but the cares of domestic life, for bearing children and cooking the food of a family, devoting all their time to the domestic circle — to promoting the immediate personal comfort of their husbands, brothers and sons? . . . The mere departure of women from the duties of the domestic circle, far from being a reproach to her, is a virtue of the highest order, when it is done from purity of motive, by appropriate means, and the purpose good.

In answer to Howard's argument, that women had no right to petition because they lacked the vote, Adams went so far as to ask: "Is it so clear that they have no such right as this last?" [27]

Behind Adams' tenacity on this issue and the efforts of a small group of congressmen who gathered to support his battle for the right of free petition, there lay another saga — that of the campaign for signatures. The women who took part in it were taking a long stride ahead. Not only were they engaging in a *political act,* now on behalf of others, but they were also securing a right which they would use later in their own interests. They were the first detachment in the army of ordinary rank-and-file women who were to struggle for more than three quarters of a century for equality. It took the same kind of courage as that displayed by the Grimké sisters for the average housewife, mother, or daughter to overstep the limits of decorum, disregard the frowns, or jeers, or outright commands of her menfolk and go to her first public meeting, or take her first petition and walk down an unfamiliar street, knocking on doors and asking for signatures to an unpopular plea. Not only would she be going out unattended by husband or brother; but she usually encountered hostility, if not outright abuse for her unwomanly behavior.

Those who made the first venture came from diverse ways of life. Even a woman as courageous as Lydia Maria Child, supported by her husband in the work, found it difficult: "My husband and I are busy in that most odious of all tasks, that of getting signatures to petitions. We are resolved that the business shall be done in this town [Northampton, Mass.] more thoroughly than it has been heretofore. But, 'Oh Lord, sir!' " [28] Others faced much greater hazards: "A history of their progress from door to door, with the obstacles they encountered, would be at once touching, ludicrous and edifying. Young women, whose labors depended on public opinion, laid the claims of the enslaved to freedom before those whose simple words might grant or deny them their own means of subsistence." [29]

Today, countless file boxes in the National Archives in Washington bear witness to that anonymous and heart-breaking labor. The petitions are yellowed and frail, glued together, page on page, covered with ink blots, signed with scratchy pens, with an occasional erasure by one who fearfully thought better of so bold an act. Some are headed by printed texts, others are copied in careful, stilted script, or in a hasty scrawl. They petition Congress against the admission of more slave states into the Union — Florida, Arkansas, Texas; against slavery in the District of Columbia; against the interstate slave trade; for the total abolition of slavery. They bear the names of women's anti-slavery societies from New England to Ohio. A frequent Massachusetts petition reads:

The undersigned women have been deeply convinced of the sinfulness of slavery and keenly aggrieved by its extension in a part of our country over which Congress possesses exclusive jurisdiction in all cases whatsoever, do most earnestly petition your honorable body immediately to abolish slavery in the District of Columbia, and to declare every human being free who sets foot on its soil. We also respectfully announce our intention to present this same petition, yearly, before your honorable body, that it may at least be "a memorial of us" that in the holy cause of human freedom, "we have done what we could." [30]

In the first half of the nineteenth century, women worked in more than a hundred industrial occupations.[31] At first, some of these occupations, the making of cloth, garments, and hats, and the sewing of shoes, were carried on in the home where they had first engaged in them as housewives.

But with the invention of the spinning jenny and the power loom, home work shrank; there was a steady demand for women workers in the textile mills, due to the insatiable demand for men as agricultural workers and their migration to the west, but opportunities for factory work could not keep pace with the number whom mechanization had thrown out of work. With no skills which were in economic demand except some sort of sewing, many women found themselves in desperate competition with one another in the garment industry, which was still largely carried on at home.

These were not the only factors making for low earnings in this field. The concept of the inferiority of women barred them from training for more skilled work, and therefore from entering other occupations; it also prevented their receiving the same pay as a man for similar work.

Said the *Boston Courier* as early as 1829:

Custom and long habit have closed the doors of very many employments against the industry and perseverance of woman. She has been taught to deem so many occupations masculine, and made for men only that, excluded by a mistaken deference to the world's opinion from innumerable labors most happily adapted to her physical constitution, the competition for the few places left open to her has occasioned a reduction in the estimated value of her labour, until it has fallen below the minimum and is no longer adequate to present comfortable subsistence, much less to the necessary provision against age and infirmity, or the everyday contingencies of mortality.[32]

Another newspaper estimated in 1833 that women earned only one fourth of men's wages, while still another asserted that three fourths of Philadelphia's working women "did not receive as much wages for an entire week's work of 13 to 14 hours per day, as journeymen receive in the same branches for a single day of 10 hours." [33]

Sarah Grimké, writing in 1837, found that the prevailing concept of women's inferiority

bears with tremendous effect on the laboring classes, and indeed on almost all who are obliged to earn a sustenance, whether it be by mental or physical exertion — I allude to the disproportionate value set on the time and labor of men and women. This I know is the case in boarding and other schools with which I have been acquainted, and it is so in every occupation in which the sexes engage indiscriminately.

As for example, in tailoring, a man has twice or three times as much for making a waistcoat or pantaloons as a woman, although the work done by each may be equally good. In those employments which are peculiar to women, their time is estimated at half the value of that of men. A woman who goes out to wash, works as hard in proportion as a wood sawyer, or a coal heaver, but she is not generally able to make more than half as much by a day's work.[34]

The result was that women homeworkers in 1833 were averaging as little as $1.25 a week, *or less;* a childless woman might earn an average of $58.50 a year, but one encumbered by young infants needing her care would make only an average of $36.40 annually.[35] Three years later a contemporary estimate put women's daily average earnings at less that 37½ cents, with thousands earning a mere 25 cents a day.[36]

It was among these women, working in slum dwellings under conditions similar to those of the modern sweatshop, that the desire first emerged for contact with one another and joint action to better their conditions. Out of their plight came such short-lived organizations in the 1830's as the United Tailoresses Society of New York, led by Lavinia Waight and Louise Mitchell, the Lady Shoe Binders of Lynn, Massachusetts, and others in Baltimore and Philadelphia. Their rudimentary attempts to band together and withhold their labor met with little success. The women were not only inexperienced and working in isolation from one another, but they received little support from the men in their trades, whose attitude generally was one of fear that women's low earnings would compete unfavorably with their own.

If pay was higher and conditions in general somewhat better in the cotton and woolen mills, the difference was only relative. The typical factory working day lasted from sunup to sundown, and sometimes until after "lighting-up time." The hours ran from 12½ to 15 or 16 a day. In Paterson, New Jersey, women and children had to be at work at 4:30 A.M. and work as long as they could see, with time off for breakfast and dinner, until a strike in 1835 cut the working day to twelve hours.[37]

Women's wages, always lower than those of men on similar work, ranged from $1.00 to $3.00 a week, out of which they had to pay $1.50 or $1.75 for board in company-owned or leased boarding houses.[38] Many were young girls, away from home and earning cash wages for the first time, and at first such pay seemed ample. Their satisfaction did not endure, especially after the depression of the mid-thirties, when wage cuts and speed-up became frequent.

The earliest known strike of women factory workers took place at Pawtucket, Rhode Island, in 1824, where they joined the men operatives in striking against a wage cut and longer hours. (The hundred and two girls and women involved held their meeting separately from the men.) The first strike in which women participated alone was in Dover, New Hampshire, four years later. In Lowell in 1834 a nameless young woman, newly fired from her job, tossed her poke-bonnet in the air down in the yard as a signal to the girls watching her to leave their looms; one of them then climbed the town pump and made ". . . a flaming Mary Wollstonecraft speech on the rights of women and the iniquities of the 'monied aristocracy' which produced a powerful effect on her auditors and they determined to have their own way, if they died for it." [39]

Two years later, again in Lowell, the strikers marched through the town, singing a parody on an old song, "I Can't Be a Nun":

> Oh, isn't it a pity, such a pretty girl as I
> Should be sent into the factory to pine away and die?
> Oh, I cannot be a slave,
> I will not be a slave,
> For I'm so fond of liberty
> That I cannot be a slave.[40]

The pattern was repeated constantly, in Manchester and Taunton, in Paterson and Pittsburgh, and elsewhere: angered by a wage-cut or rumors of speed-up, the women would leave the mill, hold a procession or meeting, listen to speeches and perhaps pass a resolution — and then in a few days or even hours dribble back to work, sometimes with their leaders blacklisted.

One can follow the rise and ebb, the fainthearts catching fire from a few braver sparks, the display of enthusiasm, the dependence on a man's experience, the eventual faltering and collapse, in the pages of a journal kept by a citizen of Chicopee, Massachusetts, in 1843:

May 2 — Great turnout among the girls . . . after breakfast this morning a procession preceded by a painted window curtain for a banner went round the square, the number sixteen. They soon came past again with Mr. ——, they then numbered forty-four. They marched around a while and then dispersed. After dinner they sallied forth to the number of forty-two and marched around to Cabot under the direction of Mr. ——. They marched around the streets doing themselves no credit. Messrs. Mills and Dwight are up from Boston.

May 4 — Girls on the turnout. They had a meeting at Cabot last night and were ably addressed by Hosea Kenny. This morning after breakfast they came out and marched around the square numbering twenty-two . . . They marched to Cabot but it did no good.

May 5 — The girls had no turnout today.

May 6 — The girls have got over their excitement in some degree.[41]

The Chicopee story shows the women's basic problem: aside from frightening Messrs. Dwight and Mills (top company officers) into rushing up from Boston, they were too weak to accomplish any results. Even when their militancy was greater and more sustained than that of the early New England "turnouts," they could achieve nothing lasting, as shown by the succession of strikes for a shorter workday in the Alleghany mills, near Pittsburgh, from 1843 to 1848, part of the wide agitation for a ten-hour day. Two strikes in 1845 and 1848 were militant to the point of violence: on both occasions women were part of attacking columns, armed with sticks and stones, which actually broke down the massive wooden gates of one mill, "captured" it, and silenced the looms. They won the sought-for reduction in hours but only at the cost of a cut in pay.[42]

The only cure for such sporadic ineffectiveness was *organization*. The anti-slavery movement was one example; early, although short-lived, organizations among men workers were another incentive. It remained for a group working in the Lowell textile mills to prove that women could build a stable organization (even if only for a relatively brief period), develop leadership with intellectual ability and courage, and conduct a systematic campaign which would leave its mark. These were the achievements of the Lowell Female Labor Reform Association, which was led from 1845 to 1846 by Sarah Bagley, the first woman trade unionist of note in this country.

For a time a myth had existed that the mills in Lowell were different. The factories and the boarding-houses where the operatives lived had been built according to a master plan by the mill owners, who boasted that their "girls," as they were universally known at the time, were more intelligent and refined, better educated, better housed and cared for, and happier than those in other places. Belief in the girls' interest in educational and literary pursuits was fostered by Improvement Circles and by a magazine called the *Lowell Offering,* edited by two former mill operatives, which carried contributions from the girls and was known and extolled as far away as Great Britain.

The facts were otherwise, and eventually became known. Average wages were $2.00 weekly, plus board. The young women sometimes slept six to a room, two in a bed. They had, in periods of business recession, the same problems of wage cuts and speed-up as textile workers elsewhere. The *Offering* became an apology for the employers, whose aim was to perpetuate a fiction of "factory girl life" in Lowell as a means of recruiting ever new, cheap, docile labor from among the daughters of New England farmers.

The Lowell Female Labor Reform Association, an auxiliary of the New England Workingmen's Association, was organized as part of the same upsurge that had led to violence in Pennsylvania, but with different results. On a December evening in 1844, five mill girls met to plan how they could win the ten-hour day. They chose as their motto "Try Again," and by May of 1845 they had 600 members, with Sarah Bagley as their president.[43]

Miss Bagley was born in New Hampshire. She came to Lowell after the unsuccessful "turnout" of 1836, and at first took part in the Improvement Circles, even writing a piece on "The Pleasures of Factory Life." That life, however, taught her otherwise; she also learned that under existing conditions women in the mills could gain nothing by strikes, and must therefore have recourse to other methods to improve their lot.

Largely under her leadership, Female Labor Reform Associations began to appear in other mill towns: Manchester, Waltham, Dover, Nashua, Fall River. She wrote pamphlets, spoke, advocated that the groups keep in touch with one another, and for fifteen months was associated with a weekly newspaper published as the organ of the New England Workingmen's Association, the *Voice of Industry.*[44]

Here she spoke out in articles, editorials and letters, writing in a different vein from that in which women were ordinarily addressed in the press of the day. She described herself as

a common schooled New England female factory operative . . . long, long, even now, a sufferer among the unwieldy yet mighty mass. . . . What we lack in editorial ability, in rhetorick [sic], or historical research, be assured we will make up in heart. Our heart, yea, our whole soul, is wrapped up in the cause of the oppressed — of the downtrodden millions throughout the world.[45]

When the textile companies tried to blacklist employees for joining the Female Labor Reform Association, she thundered at them:

What! Deprive us, after working thirteen hours, of the poor privilege of finding fault — of saying our lot is a hard one! Intentionally turn away a girl unjustly persecuted, as men have been persecuted, to our knowledge, for free expression of honest political opinions! We will make the name of him who dares the act, stink with every wind, from all points of the compass. His name shall be a by-word among all laboring men, and he shall be hissed in the streets, and in all the cities of this widespread republic; for our name is legion though our oppression be great.[46]

A striking number of other women, all from the mills, worked with Miss Bagley: Huldah Stone, Mehitabel Eastman, Mary Emerson, Eliza Hemingway, Hannah Tarlton. By their ability and hard work they compelled the respect of the men leading the New England labor movement. They served as delegates to labor conventions, and in 1846 three of them became directors of the New England Labor Reform League, along with five men.

The Lowell Female Labor Reform Association succeeded in channeling the energies of its members away from fruitless strikes to more effective tactics. When one of the larger mills in Lowell tried to increase the work load from three to four looms, at the same time reducing wages a cent per piece, a meeting of the Association pledged that no such increased load would be accepted unless accompanied by an increase in pay. Almost every woman weaver working for the mill signed a pledge to this effect, and stuck to it; the attempted speed-up was canceled.[47]

Even more significant was the participation in the petition campaign directed at the Massachusetts state legislature, asking for a ten-hour-day law. The women were so prominent in the circulation and signing of petitions that the committee which the legislature was finally compelled to appoint to investigate conditions in the mills summoned eight mill operatives as witnesses, six of them women.[48] As a veiled threat, it stated that, "as the greater part of the petitioners are females, it will be necessary for them to make the defence, or we shall be under the necessity of laying it [the petition] aside." [49]

Any hope the legislators might have had that conventional ideas of propriety or fear of losing their jobs would deter the women from testifying was rudely dispelled. When the hearings opened on February 13, 1845, Miss Bagley and her associates were present — self-possessed and articulate.

They minced no words; the committee, the first ever to hold a state investigation into labor conditions, heard an earful. Eliza Hemingway, who earned an unusually high scale of pay as an experienced woolens weaver, made from $16 to $23 a month in addition to her board; however, she worked in a room with more than one hundred and fifty people, where two hundred and ninety-three small lamps and sixty-one large lamps burned mornings and evenings all winter, making the air foul; sometimes as many as thirty women were sick in one day from the fumes. A Miss Judith Payne had lost one whole year out of seven through illness; although a highly-skilled worker, she averaged only $2.93 a week above her board. Another received as little as $1.62½ after board. Others testified similarly. One woman exonerated the mill-owners.[50]

Between the stark lines of testimony as digested in the record lies a great deal that today is taken for granted in connection with legislative hearings: the preparation of testimony (one wonders when the lamps were so carefully counted!) and the alarming but perhaps heady novelty of their two-day appearance under such circumstances.

The committee, having heard the operatives as well as representatives of the employers, and desiring further evidence, journeyed to Lowell; they were charmed, among other things, by the flower beds outside the mills, and in due course issued a report recommending *no* ten-hour-day legislation. They buttressed their findings with such arguments as "Labor is on an equality with capital and indeed controls it," and stated that the "intelligent and virtuous men and women" who had appeared before them as petitioners could be counted on to take care of themselves! [51]

The Association whose motto was "Try Again" did not give up at once. Although its members could not vote, it had a hand in defeating for re-election to the state legislature the Lowell newspaper publisher, William Schouler, who had been chairman of the hearings committee, and it took public credit for the deed in a resolution:

Resolved, that the members of this Association tender their grateful acknowledgments to the voters of Lowell, for consigning William Schouler to the obscurity he so justly deserves, for treating so unjustly and ungentlemanly the defence made by the delegates of this Association before the committee of the Legislature, to whom was referred petitions for the reduction of the hours of labor, of which he was chairman.[52]

Schouler retaliated; having discovered that the personal life of one of the Massachusetts labor leaders, John Cluer, was not above reproach, and that Cluer had spoken from the same platforms as Miss Bagley, he employed highly modern smear tactics and succeeded in discrediting both Miss Bagley and the Association.

There were other reasons why neither the organization nor Miss Bagley's career were of long duration. Together with the rest of the New England labor movement they succumbed to prevailing Utopian theories. Miss Bagley, who had testified at the legislative hearing that mill work had undermined her health, suffered a breakdown, and disappeared from the labor scene, although she attained a different kind of renown in becoming the first woman telegrapher. The Lowell Female Labor Reform Association lingered only a little longer.

It was not in the cards for women, alone and unaided, to build their own labor organizations, although they made repeated efforts to do so until after the turn of the century. They lacked money, since their earnings were uniformly low; and they lacked time. (Even today, with vacuum cleaners, washing machines, and ready-to-eat packaged foods, the working woman has, by social usage, more housekeeping and family responsibilities than the man of the household; in a world without labor-saving devices and a ten-hour workday, she had even less time for herself.) But unless the movement for woman's rights is to exclude the issues of equal pay and shorter hours, which alone would enable working women to enjoy the benefits of education or full citizenship, the Lowell mill girls must be considered pioneers in the same cause as the Grimkés and Emma Willard.

Chapter IV

THE BEGINNINGS OF REFORM

The beginnings of higher education for women and their emergence as public speakers and anti-slavery workers affected with extreme slowness the legal conditions under which women lived. Change came at a snail's pace, state by state; although the number of women who were "gainfully employed" rose rapidly, women in most states continued for decades to be unable to control their own earnings, manage property legally their own, or sign legal papers.[1]

When Jane Swisshelm, one of the earliest women to publish her own newspaper, the *Pittsburgh Visiter* [sic], inherited a small estate from her mother, it was in the form of a trust, a legal device developed to circumvent women's inability to hold property. As such it was only partially successful:

[My husband] felt himself wronged and became angry, but had one remedy. Being the owner of my person and services, he had a right to wages for the time spent in nursing mother, and would file his claim against the executors. I do not know why I should have been so utterly overwhelmed by this proposal to execute a law which had never been questioned by any nation, or state, or church, and was in full force all over the world. . . . Why should I blush that my husband was a law-abiding citizen of the freest country in the world? Why blame him for acting in harmony with the canons of every Christian church? . . . . Was it any fault of his that all that [the wife] can acquire by her labor-service or act during coverture, belongs to her husband? Certainly not.[2]

Lydia Maria Child rebelled similarly at being unable to make her own will:

David has signed my will and I have sealed it up and put it away. It excited my towering indignation to think it was necessary for him to sign it . . . . I was not indignant on my own account, for David respects the freedom of all women upon principle, and mine in particular for reason of affection superadded. But I was indignant for womankind made chattels personal from the beginning of time, perpetually insulted by literature, law, and custom. The very phrases used with regard to us are abominable. "Dead in the law." "Femme couverte." How I detest such language! [3]

A working woman could be compelled to hand over every penny of her wages to a drunkard husband, even if she was left with nothing for her own subsistence or the maintenance of her children, and even if the husband was known to be making no provision for them. If she sought to divorce such a husband, he might, irrespective of the kind of father he was, be legally entitled to sole guardianship of the children. This state of affairs sometimes brought about episodes reminiscent of the seizure of runaway slaves, such as one recounted by Clarina Howard Nichols of Vermont:

Two men entered the [railway] car. In the younger man I recognized the sheriff of our county. Having given a searching glance around the car, the older man, with a significant nod to his companion, laid his hand upon the saloon door an instant, and every person in the car had risen to his feet, electrified by the wail, "O father! she's my child! *she's my child!*" . . . "Who is it?" "What is it?" were the anxious queries put up on all sides. I answered: "It means, my friends, that a woman has no right to her own babies; that the law-makers in this *Christian country* — have given the custody of the babies to the father, drunk or sober, and he may send the sheriff, as in this case, to arrest and rob her of her helpless little ones!" [4]

If a husband died intestate, the law could be stringent in disposing of his possessions. In New York, the widow was allotted the family Bible, pictures, school books, and all books not exceeding in value the sum of $50; spinning wheels, weaving looms, and stoves; ten sheep and their fleeces; two swine and their pork. Irrespective of the number of her children, she also received: "All necessary wearing apparel, beds, bedsteads and bedding; the clothing of the widow and ornaments proper to her station, — one table, six chairs, six knives and forks, six tea-cups and saucers, one sugar dish, one milk-pot, one tea-pot, and six spoons." [5]

Woman was little better off before God than before the law. The marriage service spelled out her lowly station, her submission, and her duties. Some of the early women reformers put up a pitched battle to omit the word "obey." Sometimes the husband joined in the protest; the early "marriage contracts" entered into by men and women who wished to found their marriage on a mutual concept of human dignity are eloquent not only of their aspiration, but of the conditions against which they rebelled. One of the first was that drawn up by Robert Dale Owen (son of the Utopian humanist Robert Owen), when he married Mary Jane Robinson in 1832:

Of the unjust rights which in virtue of this ceremony an iniquitous law tacitly gives me over the person and property of another, I cannot legally, but I can morally, divest myself. And I hereby distinctly and emphatically declare that I consider myself, and earnestly desire to be considered by others, as utterly divested, now and during the rest of my life, of any such rights, the barbarous relics of a feudal, despotic system.[6]

When Lucy Stone and Henry Blackwell were married in 1855, they joined hands at their wedding and read aloud a statement which declared:

While we acknowledge our mutual affection by publicly assuming the relationship of husband and wife . . . we deem it a duty to declare that this act on our part implies no sanction of, nor promise of voluntary obedience to such of the present laws of marriage as refuse to recognize the wife as an independent, rational being, while they confer upon the husband an injurious and unnatural superiority . . . We protest especially against the laws which give the husband:

    1. The custody of the wife's person.
    2. The exclusive control and guardianship of their children.
    3. The sole ownership of her personal and use of her real estate, unless previously settled upon her, or placed in the hands of trustees, as in the case of minors, lunatics and idiots.
    4. The absolute right to the product of her industry.
    5. Also against laws which give to the widower so much larger and more permanent an interest in the property of his deceased wife than they give to the widow in that of the deceased husband.
    6. Finally, against the whole system by which 'the legal existence' of the wife is suspended during marriage' so that, in most States, she neither has a legal part in the choice of her residence, nor can she make a will, nor sue or be sued in her own name, nor inherit property.[7]

Between 1839 and 1850 most states passed some kind of legislation recognizing the right of married women to hold property. In some cases this was due to the interest of large property-owners in protecting their bequests to female legatees; in others it was due to the efforts of liberal-minded men aided and abetted by a few energetic women.

In 1836 the first petition for a Married Woman's Property Law in New York reached the state legislature. It carried the signatures of *six* women and was the work of Mrs. Ernestine Rose, who had just arrived in this country. Although born in Poland, Mrs. Rose became one of the outstanding women orators of her day and was often called "The Queen of the Platform." [8] She was also one of the first women to try to improve the position of her sex through legislative action, and she found the task a difficult one:

After a good deal of trouble I obtained five signatures. Some of the ladies said the gentlemen would laugh at them; others, that they had rights enough; and the men said the women had too many rights already . . . I continued sending petitions with increased numbers of signatures until 1848 and '49, when the Legislature enacted the law which granted woman the right to keep what was her own. But no sooner did it become legal than all the women said: "Oh! that is right! We ought always to have had that!" [9]

Behind the slowly rising tide of legislative reform was the growth of a perceptible body of public opinion, educated by lecturers and writers of all shades of liberalism and vehemence. There were men like John Neal, the "downeast Yankee" from Portland, Maine, who began speaking on woman's rights in 1832 and kept it up for half a century. There was Judge Hurlbut of New York, who was converted to the cause by writing a paper against it, which he then found he could refute at every point; the result was a pamphlet by the eminent jurist called *Human Rights,* which was widely circulated.

An important force in educating public opinion was Mrs. Sarah Josepha Hale, the editor of *Godey's Lady's Book.*[10] This magazine, with an extremely large circulation (for that day) of 150,000, never embraced the cause of woman's rights as such. Writing always with the greatest circumspection, Mrs. Hale waged a number of tenacious and uncompromising campaigns — for the higher education of women, for their admission to such professions as medicine and nursing, together with adequate training in the same, on the merits of physical education for women, the menace of corsets, and many more.

Most influential of all was Margaret Fuller, whose book *Woman in the Nineteenth Century* became a beacon to generations of women. She has been called an intellectual and a "bluestocking" but the facts of her life suggest that her interest in women's problems was not purely intellectual in origin.[11] Born in 1810, she was educated by an embittered and exacting father to read the classics of six languages, including Latin and Greek. When she was twenty-five her father died, and as her mother showed little disposition to shoulder the practical problems of keeping a large family together, Margaret undertook the education of the four younger children, and eventually taught in a girls' school in Providence to earn a living. There she heard John Neal lecture on woman's rights. She returned to Boston and was caught up in the transcendentalist school of thought, which preached the liberation and fulfilment of the highest potential in all human beings; yet she saw her own sex denied that right.[12] She became the friend of men like Emerson, Channing, Alcott, and other Transcendentalists; yet all around her she saw evidence of intellectual starvation and frustration among women, who were conspicuously absent from the ferment of thought then going on in New England.

Because she needed to earn money, because she was already known as a brilliant talker, and because she wished to provide some stimulus and outlet for women, Miss Fuller inaugurated a series of "conversations" (today we would call them discussion groups or parlor meetings) in Elizabeth Peabody's famous West Street bookshop in Boston. She was less than thirty years old when she opened the first one on a November afternoon in 1839 on the subject of "Greek Mythology," a topic of more general interest then than now. Among the twenty-five ladies present were the Peabody sisters (one of whom was to marry Horace Mann and another Nathaniel Hawthorne, and Elizabeth herself), Lydia Maria Child, Maria White — fiancée of the poet James Russell Lowell — and the wives of the philosopher Emerson, the historian George Bancroft, and the minister Theodore Parker. Over a five-year period these "conversations" dealt with such additional topics as Art, Culture, Literature, and Women and Life.

Her association with the Transcendentalists led Miss Fuller

Harriet Tubman

Lucy Stone

Lucretia Mott

Sojourner Truth

Prudence Crandall

Frances E. W. Harper

Elizabeth Blackwell

Myrtilla Miner

Sophia Smith

to co-editorship (with Ralph Waldo Emerson) of the quarterly magazine, *The Dial;* she achieved another unique distinction when she left Boston in 1845 to become the first woman on the staff of the rising New York newspaper, the *Tribune,* published by Horace Greeley, as its literary critic.

A year earlier she had published *Woman in the Nineteenth Century,* which had gone through successive phases, first as one of her "conversations," later as a *Dial* article under the title, "The Great Lawsuit: Man Versus Woman — Woman Versus Man," and finally as a slim book. To modern readers it may seem poorly organized and verbose, lacking the forcefulness of Sarah Grimké's earlier work; sections of it are all but swamped with classical allusions and suffer from being a showcase for Miss Fuller's immense erudition. But to contemporary women its message was clear: woman must fulfill herself, not in relation to, and as subordinate to men, but as an individual, an independent human being. Failure to do so had made of woman "an overgrown child."

Miss Fuller would not admit that women were adequately represented in government by men, however close their family ties, because man's view of woman was distorted by his dominant relationship with her; yet her primary concern was not political:

What Woman needs is not as a woman to act or rule, but as a nature to grow, as an intellect to discern, as a soul to live freely, and unimpeded to unfold such powers as were given her when we left our common home.[13]

But if you ask me, what offices they may fill, I reply — any. I do not care what case you put; let them be sea-captains, if you will.[14]

She was not afraid of the sweeping changes that would be required to achieve such a goal, and she threw down a challenge that echoed through half a century:

We would have every arbitrary barrier thrown down. We would have every path laid open to Woman as freely as to Man . . . then and then only will mankind be ripe for this, when inward and outward freedom for Woman as much as for Man shall be acknowledged as a *right,* not yielded as a concession. As the friend of the Negro assumes that one man cannot by right hold another in bondage, so would the friend of Woman assume that Man cannot by right lay even well-meant restrictions on Woman.[15]

Once or twice her anger flashed out, as in her answer to those who contend that woman's physical nature unfits her for any but the sheltered domestic sphere:

If in reply we admit that Woman seems destined by nature rather for the inner circle, we must add that the arrangements of civilized life have not been as yet such as to secure it to her. Her circle, if the duller, is not the quieter. If kept from "excitement," she is not from drudgery. Not only the Indian squaw carries the burdens of the camp, but the favorites of Louis XIV accompany him on his journeys, and the washerwoman stands at the tub and carries home her work at all seasons and in all states of health. Those who think the physical circumstances of Woman would make a part in the affairs of national government unsuitable are by no means those who think it impossible for Negresses to endure field work even during pregnancy, or for seamstresses to go through their killing labors.[16]

In a society which preferred not to discuss such matters at all, certainly not with women, she dealt calmly and lucidly with the "double standard" of morality and prostitution. Although she had strong differences with the abolitionists which prevented her ever associating herself with them, she referred, always with respect, to their contributions to the cause of women and cited as examples of great courage and moral power, Angelina Grimké and Abby Kelley Foster.

Margaret Fuller kept herself apart from the political controversies of the day, including that of slavery. But *Woman in the Nineteenth Century* won her great prestige; some of her friends who read the passionately partisan letters she sent the *New York Tribune* from Rome, describing the downfall of the republican cause there in 1848, and who knew of her active work on its behalf with Mazzini, dreamed that on her return home she would take leadership in the crystallizing woman's rights movement.[17] But Margaret Fuller was drowned within sight of the Fire Island beaches. She was only forty years old; yet within her brief span, she had "possessed more influence upon the thought of American women than any woman previous to her time." [18]

Many who did not subscribe to *Godey's Lady's Book*, or read books by Margaret Fuller, could be reached from the public lecture platform. The Grimké sisters gave up speaking in 1838, but other women were coming forward. Outstanding among them was Lucy Stone, who won the title of "morning star of the woman's rights movement" by her years of lecturing up and down the country, from New England to Ohio and Wisconsin.

No one knew better than Lucy Stone what it meant to work as hard as any man and yet be regarded as man's inferior. On the marginal farm in western Massachusetts where she was born in 1818, husbandry was still primitive, and the women carried a heavy load of dairy work in addition to their household tasks; yet "there was only one will in our house, and that was my father's." [19] There were seven children cared for by a gentle toil-worn mother, who exclaimed when Lucy was born: "Oh dear! I am sorry it is a girl. A woman's life is so hard." [20] A few hours before the baby came she had milked eight cows, because a sudden thunderstorm had called all hands into the fields. It was more urgent to save the hay crop than to safeguard a mother on the verge of labor, or the life of one more child.

When she was twelve, Lucy decided that she would do what she could to lighten her mother's burden, and in addition to her school work she took over the household laundry. Work continued hard throughout her teens, and money was scarce; there was none to spare for a girl who wanted more education. At sixteen she began to teach school herself, not an unusual thing in those days, and for nine years she saved her earnings and kept up her own studies; at last even her father was convinced that nothing would deter her from her purpose. She was one of the earliest women to graduate from the "regular," as distinguished from the "literary," course at Oberlin in 1847, having deliberately prepared herself for a career as a public speaker on behalf of the oppressed: "I expect to plead not for the slave only, but for suffering humanity everywhere. ESPECIALLY DO I MEAN TO LABOR FOR THE ELEVATION OF MY SEX." [21]

Lucy Stone gave her first lecture on woman's rights from the pulpit of her brother's church in Gardner, Massachusetts, the year she graduated. The following year she became an "agent" or lecturer for the Anti-Slavery Society, which often entailed speaking to violently hostile audiences. She was unimpressive in appearance — small and slight, and lacking in beauty — until she opened her mouth. But her voice was unforgettable — clear and musical as a silver bell; coupled with indomitable courage, it enabled her to face down, and win over, the worst mobs.

She soon got into trouble in another direction. Like the Grimkés, she could not keep the subjects of slavery and woman's rights apart, and like the Grimkés, she roused the ire of the abolitionists who did not want them confused. Eventually a compromise was worked out by which she lectured on abolition on Saturdays and Sundays and for woman's rights the rest of the week. She gave a series of three lectures on women: the first on their social and industrial disabilities, the second on legal and political handicaps, and the third on moral and religious discrimination.

When she spoke against slavery she could count on the help of the local anti-slavery groups. She had no such support when it came to arranging meetings on woman's rights. She wrote:

When I undertook my solitary battle for woman's rights, outside the little circle of abolitionists I knew nobody who sympathized with my ideas. I had some hand-bills printed, 12 x 10 inches. I bought a paper of tacks, and, as I could not pay for posting, I put up my bills myself, using a stone for a hammer. I did not take a fee at the door. But there was always the expense of hall and hotel. To cover this, at the close of my speech, I asked help for the great work, by a collection for expenses. Then I took a hat and went through the audience for the collection, for all were strangers to me. I always got enough to pay what was due, and sometimes more.[22]

There were many who, while not resorting to mob violence to do so, longed to silence her, and hoped that her marriage to Henry Blackwell in 1855 would put an end to her career. The *Boston Post* published a poem whose concluding stanza ran:

> A name like Curtius' shall be his,
> On fame's loud trumpet blown,
> Who with a wedding kiss shuts up
> The mouth of Lucy Stone.[23]

But the pundit was wrong. The marriage made two advocates for woman's rights where there had been one, and eventually three. Henry Blackwell, Lucy Stone, and their daughter, Alice Stone Blackwell, covered nearly the entire span of the woman's rights movement, from 1847 to 1920, with their labors for the enfranchisement of women.

Chapter V

THE SENECA FALLS CONVENTION, 1848

The way had been opened, and there were workers here and there hewing away at prejudice and law; but they were scattered and isolated from one another. Grievances, even articulate voices raised in discontent, are not enough to give birth to a reform movement. What was needed now was a sharp impetus — leadership and, above all, a program. These were to be the achievement of the Seneca Falls convention in the summer of 1848, from which the inception of the woman's rights movement in the United States is commonly dated.

Although it grew naturally out of the unsatisfactory position of women in a changing world and the work of the pioneers during the preceding thirty years, the seed of the convention was actually planted in the summer of 1840. A World Anti-Slavery Convention in London was attended by an American delegation which included a number of women; but despite the strong objections of some of the American leaders, the convention ruled, after hot debate, that only men delegates should be seated.[1] Among the women compelled to sit passively in the galleries during the ensuing ten days were Lucretia Mott and the young wife of an abolitionist leader, Elizabeth Cady Stanton.

After the sessions the two women walked the London streets together or sat on a bench in the British Museum while the rest of their party explored its treasures, talking about the anomaly of devoted workers in the anti-slavery cause being denied any voice in its deliberations simply because they were women, and the need for action.

In these talks Mrs. Mott was the preceptor; aided by the circumstances of birth and religious faith, she had already cast off many of the bonds that trammeled other women.[2] She was born in 1793 on the island of Nantucket, off Cape Cod, a center of the New England whaling industry. There a sturdy tradition of feminine equality had grown out of the men's long absences at sea, during which time the women carried on their affairs. Lucretia Coffin's father was the master of a whaling ship, and her mother ran a store. Like many other Nantucketers, they became Quakers. In 1804 the family moved to the mainland.

The young Lucretia became a teacher while still in her teens and learned early that women received far less than men doing the same work. When she married James Mott, whom she met at Nine Partners Boarding School in New York state, they settled in Philadelphia; Mrs. Mott taught in a Quaker school for a short time. At twenty-eight she was ordained a minister by her Quaker "meeting," thus winning the priceless opportunity of perfecting herself as a public speaker. When the Quakers split on matters of doctrine, the Motts joined the liberal or Hicksite wing. They became increasingly active abolitionists; their home was a busy station on the Underground Railroad, and Mrs. Mott was a founder of the first Female Anti-Slavery Society. When she went to the London convention she was already a public figure.

In an age that abounded in stormy personalities that clashed continually even if they had common aims, Mrs. Mott was widely beloved. A gentle manner, luminous countenance, and soft voice concealed an inflexible rectitude and devotion to principle. In some respects initially conservative (she drew back at first from demands she felt too precipitate, such as the franchise and easier divorce laws), she never shrank from the conclusions which a fearless and rational mind imposed on her.[3] Her contribution in helping to free the gifted and eager mind of Elizabeth Cady Stanton was an incalculable one, for the younger woman was destined to be the leading intellectual force in the emancipation of American women.[4]

Elizabeth Cady's father was a judge, and the Cady home in Johnstown, New York (near Albany) was of the best. Elizabeth, born in 1815, received the finest available education: she attended Mrs. Willard's school in Troy. More compelling, in the long run, were the hours she spent as a child, crouched in a corner of her father's office, listening to the people who came to him with their legal problems. Many were wives and daughters of farmers;

often the husband had disposed of their small property, or taken their earnings for drink, or, in the event of a separation, had the sole right to guardianship of the children. Judge Cady was kind, and often dipped into his own pocket to help the women; but he reiterated patiently and endlessly that they had no legal redress, and his daughter was marked for life by that knowledge.

In 1840 she married Henry B. Stanton, an abolitionist leader who had faced down angry mobs. She also made friends with the Grimké sisters. After her meeting with Lucretia Mott in London the friendship was maintained by correspondence when the Stantons moved to Boston, where they made their first home. When Mrs. Stanton visited in Johnstown, she got in a little work with Albany legislators on behalf of the Married Woman's Property Bill which finally became New York state law early in 1848.

But the decisive turn in her life came when the family moved to Seneca Falls, in the Finger Lakes region of New York, and Elizabeth Cady Stanton suddenly came face to face with the realities of a housewife's drudgery and isolation in a small town. Her husband was often away on business, and she was left with a growing family of lively children, most of them boys who got into constant mischief. There was the usual servant problem, and even when she could get help, like all other housewives of her day, she did an immense amount of work: baking and cooking, washing and sewing, and caring for each new baby. With her restless and eager mind she found the situation, despite all the reading she managed to squeeze in, an intolerable one:

I now fully understood the practical difficulties most women had to contend with in the isolated household, and the impossibility of woman's best development if in contact, the chief part of her life, with servants and children. . . . Emerson says: "A healthy discontent is the first step to progress." The general discontent I felt with woman's portion as wife, mother, housekeeper, physician, and spiritual guide, the chaotic condition into which everything fell without her constant supervision, and the wearied, anxious look of the majority of women, impressed me with the strong feeling that some active measures should be taken to remedy the wrongs of society in general and of women in particular. My experiences at the World Anti-Slavery Convention, all I had read of the legal status of women, and the oppression I saw everywhere, together swept across my soul, intensified now by many personal experiences. It seemed as if all the elements had conspired to impel me

to some onward step. I could not see what to do or where to begin —
my only thought was a public meeting for protest and discussion.[5]

The possibility of such a meeting had been discussed by Mrs.
Stanton and Mrs. Mott from their first acquaintance. But no opportunity to realize it occurred until the Motts paid a visit in
Waterloo, New York, near Seneca Falls, where Mrs. Stanton spent
a day with them. There she also found the Motts' hostess Jane
Hunt, Martha Wright (Mrs. Mott's sister), and Mary Ann Mc-
Clintock, all of them Quakers. To them "I poured out, that day,
the torrent of my long accumulating discontent, with such vehemence and indignation that I stirred myself, as well as the rest
of the party, to do and dare anything." [6]

Seated around a mahogany table (now in the Smithsonian
Institution in Washington), the five women decided to call a convention (today we would simply call it a meeting since there were
to be no elected delegates), and wrote an announcement which
appeared in the next day's issue (July 14) of the *Seneca County
Courier:*

Woman's Rights Convention — A convention to discuss the social, civil
and religious rights of woman will be held in the Wesleyan Chapel,
Seneca Falls, New York, on Wednesday and Thursday, the 19th and
20th of July current; commencing at 10 a.m. During the first day the
meeting will be held exclusively for women, who are earnestly invited
to attend. The public generally are invited to be present on the second
day, when Lucretia Mott of Philadelphia and other ladies and gentlemen will address the convention.[7]

Having drafted the notice, the women were at a loss as to how
to proceed. Obviously what was required was some kind of declaration of sentiments, such as they were familiar with from their
experiences with anti-slavery gatherings. But what form it should
take, they had no idea. When Mrs. Stanton began to read aloud
from the Declaration of Independence, it seemed to lend itself
to their purpose; the resulting paraphrase of the original, sentence
by sentence and paragraph by paragraph, became a Declaration
of Principles that would serve three generations of women:

When, in the course of human events, it becomes necessary for one
portion of the family of man to assume among the people of the earth
a position different from that they have hitherto occupied. . . .

We hold these truths to be self-evident: that all men and women are created equal; that they are endowed by their Creator with certain inalienable rights: that among these are life, liberty and the pursuit of happiness. . . .

The history of mankind is a history of repeated injuries and usurpations on the part of man toward woman, having in direct object the establishment of an absolute tyranny over her. To prove this, let facts be submitted to a candid world.[8]

The facts presented ranged over every aspect of woman's status. In conclusion, departing from its model, the Declaration stated:

In entering upon the great work before us, we anticipate no small amount of misconception, misrepresentation, and ridicule; but we shall use every instrumentality within our power to effect our object. We shall employ agents, circulate tracts, petition the State and national legislatures, and endeavor to enlist the pulpit and the press on our behalf. We hope this Convention will be followed by a series of Conventions embracing every part of the country.[9]

The final drafting of resolutions to implement the Declaration was turned over to Mrs. Stanton, and the Motts went home to Philadelphia, leaving the young woman to cope with her household, and with a rising sense of panic. The latter was in no way mitigated when she read her husband the draft of a resolution she proposed demanding the vote for women; Henry B. Stanton declared that if it were presented to the convention he would have nothing to do with the affair, and that he would leave town. (He did.) To make matters worse, a letter arrived from Mrs. Mott, mixing encouragement with caution:

I requested (Mary Ann McClintock) . . . to tell thee how poorly my husband was, and that it is not likely that I should be able to go to Seneca Falls before the morning of the convention. I hope however that he will be able to be present the second day. . . . James says thy *great* speech thou must reserve for the second day, so that he and others may be able to hear it. The convention will not be as large as it otherwise might be, owing to the busy time with the farmers, harvest, etc. But it will be a beginning, and we hope it will be followed in due time by one of a more general character.[10]

None of the women, even Lucretia Mott, felt equal to the task of serving as chairman, and it had been planned that James Mott would fill the post. Fortunately he recovered promptly and both the Motts arrived in Seneca Falls in good time. Less auspicious was Mrs. Mott's reaction to the proposed resolution on the franchise: "Thou will make us ridiculous. We must go slowly." Only Frederick Douglass, the Negro abolitionist leader who published his paper, *The North Star,* in near-by Rochester, approved of Mrs. Stanton's daring proposal; reassured by his promise that he would be present and take the floor in her support, she resolved to stick to her purpose.

July 19, 1848, was a fine summer morning, and despite the demands of the haying season, and the fact that only one issue of the *Seneca Courier* had carried the brief notice, Mrs. Mott's fears were not realized. People came from a radius of fifty miles to the little Wesleyan chapel, which the convention initiators found locked when they arrived. (Perhaps a reluctant minister had regretted his rash act in making his premises available for such an occasion.) But the delay was brief; a nephew of Mrs. Stanton's was boosted through a window and the gathering crowd flocked inside.

One of the women told, some sixty years later, of the impression the proceedings made on a farmer's daughter. Nineteen-year-old Charlotte Woodward, who longed to be a typesetter and work in a print shop, and who might as well have aspired to fly to the moon, read the *Courier* notice and ran from one neighbor to another, to find that others had already read it, some with amused incredulity, others with the same excitement as herself. She and half a dozen of her friends planned to attend the convention, and set off early in the morning of the 19th in a wagon drawn by farm horses, fearful that they would be the only ladies present. But as they neared Seneca Falls they met many other vehicles like theirs, headed for the same destination. She sat for two days, late into the evening, in a back row, among an audience of some three hundred; no less than forty men had turned up the first day, originally planned for ladies only, and had compelled the women to modify this restriction.[11] She heard Elizabeth Cady Stanton rise to make her maiden speech:

I should feel exceedingly diffident to appear before you at this time, having never before spoken in public, were I not nerved by a sense of right and duty, did I not feel that the time had come for the question of woman's wrongs to be laid before the public, did I not believe

that woman herself must do this work; for woman alone can understand the height, the depth, the length and the breadth of her degradation.[12]

There followed a speech almost incredible for a novice: long,
scholarly but eloquent, of the kind that was to become familiar
to Mrs. Stanton's audiences over the next fifty years. There were
other speakers, and plenty of lively discussion, particularly over
resolution nine, read by Mrs. Stanton: "Resolved, that it is the
sacred duty of the women of this country to secure to themselves
their sacred right to the elective franchise." [13] This was the only
resolution not passed unanimously; it carried by a small margin.
At the conclusion of the proceedings, sixty-eight women and thirty-
two men· (a third of those present), signed their names to the
Declaration of Principles. Among them was Charlotte Woodward
who, alone of those present, lived to vote for President of the
United States in 1920.[14]

In regarding the Seneca Falls convention as the birth of the
movement for woman's rights, we are on solid ground only if we
remember that birth is a stage in the whole process of growth. In
this case the process had begun almost half a century earlier. Such
a view does not detract from the convention's importance, or from
the vision and courage of those who brought it about. They themselves were fully aware of the nature of the step they were taking;
today's debt to them has been inadequately acknowledged. The
Wesleyan chapel which saw their momentous gathering is marked
only by a signpost on the sidewalk, and itself does service as a gas-
filling station and garage.

Beginning in 1848 it was possible for women who rebelled
against the circumstances of their lives, to know that they were
not alone — although often the news reached them only through
a vitriolic sermon or an abusive newspaper editorial. But a movement had been launched which they could either join, or ignore,
that would leave its imprint on the lives of their daughters and
of women throughout the world.

Chapter VI

FROM SENECA FALLS TO THE CIVIL WAR

At the time of the Seneca Falls convention the United States was experiencing a tremendous acceleration of growth. The outcome of the Mexican War speeded up the exploration and settlement of the western half of the continent. Newspaper readers turned from articles ridiculing woman's rights to accounts of settlers' trains reaching Oregon and the Sacramento Valley of California. In January 1848 Marshall found gold in Sutter's Creek, and a year later the Gold Rush was under way.

Industrial development kept pace with territorial expansion. Hand-weaving at home had completely given way to power-driven factory looms. From 1840 to 1860 the textile industry's consumption of cotton quadrupled, and the number of spindles more than doubled, reaching over five million; two years before the Civil War, industrial output for the first time reached a total worth of almost $2 billion.[1]

By 1850 the growing labor force in manufacturing of close to one million included 225,512 women — almost 24 per cent of the total. They were to be found in a wide variety of manufacturing industries, but the greater part were in textiles, clothing, shoes, and millinery, and increasing numbers were going into cigar-making and printing.[2]

Industrial and social change was sharpening the issues before the nation. Chief among these were the extension of slavery into the new western territories and the question of freedom or continuing bondage for nearly four million slaves in the southern states. Slavery affected the position of the wage-earner, in the North as well as South. It also bore heavily on the position of the southern white woman, whether plantation lady or poor farmer's wife, who was effectively isolated by a slave society from the movement for greater equality and opportunity that began to emerge among northern women.

In 1850, the Fugitive Slave Law was passed: men and women of good will found that their consciences compelled them to wink at, or even break, a law counter to their deepest convictions. It was a time when "giants walked the earth," and American literature reached its finest flowering: the era of Emerson, Whitman, Thoreau, Melville, and Poe, as well as Hawthorne, Bryant, Longfellow, Lowell, and Greeley. In one year — 1851 — there appeared *Moby Dick, Uncle Tom's Cabin,* and *The House of the Seven Gables. Walden* was published in 1854, *Leaves of Grass* one year later.

Everywhere (except in the South), horizons were broadening, old ways being re-tested, new ideas fermenting. Transcendentalism, abolition, Utopianism, and woman's rights were currents in a broad stream of intellectual activity and reform. A nation-wide religious revival was underway.

Not only were women entering industry in growing numbers; some of them were taking an active and extremely profitable part in the cultural life of the period. Women authors such as Catharine Sedgwick, Fanny Fern, and dozens of others were turning out, with varying degrees of success, a type of fiction which won a name all to itself: "the domestic novel." Frequently they wrote serially, and were in huge demand among periodicals and weekly newspapers; the more successful made incomes which not many men writers could match. While few of them were interested in the reform causes of their era — Mrs. Stowe was an exception — their work did its part in undermining the prevailing concept of women as domestic figures and nothing more.[3]

So did the heroic labors of Dorothea Dix, who undertook singlehanded, beginning in 1838, to uncover and make known the appalling conditions prevailing in prisons and insane asylums. Her trips of investigation and inspection, alone and unescorted, to hundreds of such institutions, and her authoritative reports to state legislatures which set in motion the first prison and hospital reform legislation were eloquent evidence of what a woman could do; so was her "lobbying" of Senators and Congressmen on behalf of federal legislation to support mental institutions (comparable to the later Morrill Land-Grant Act on behalf of colleges), which passed Congress in 1854, but lacked sufficient votes to override a presidential veto.[4]

Viewed in this context, the Seneca Falls Declaration of Principles seems very much in the spirit of the times, and it was not surprising that the ideas it presented should begin, however slowly, to gather momentum. At first the results might have seemed disappointing. While a second convention was held only two weeks later, in Rochester, New York, it involved the same principals. Thereafter came a lull of a full year and a half, before another woman's rights convention was held, once more in a small town — Salem, Ohio. The most novel feature of this occasion was the barring of men from any vocal participation whatsoever:

Never did men so suffer. They implored just to say one word; but no; the President was inflexible — no man should be heard. If one meekly arose to make a suggestion he was at once ruled out of order. For the first time in the world's history men learned how it felt to sit in silence when questions in which they were interested were under discussion.[5]

Although this innovation apparently afforded the women of Salem great satisfaction, it was not adopted elsewhere. In general the women were only too glad to hear from men, either their defenders or their critics; it made for livelier sessions. Nothing produced more effective arguments than the fulminations of an outraged clergyman supporting the status quo.

On the other hand many leading men in other reform movements were the women's staunch supporters. The signers of the call to the first national woman's rights convention in 1850 included Wendell Phillips, William H. Channing, Bronson Alcott, William Lloyd Garrison, and Gerrit Smith. Speeches by Phillips, Thomas Wentworth Higginson, and Theodore Parker were standard woman's rights propaganda for decades.

The 1850 convention was held in Worcester, Massachusetts, and was largely organized by Paulina Wright Davis of Rhode Island, who brought wealth and social position to the new movement. Together with a second convention the following year, again held in Worcester, it brought into national prominence as leaders of the emerging woman's rights movement, not only such stalwarts as Lucy Stone, Mrs. Mott, Mrs. Davis, Ernestine Rose, Abby Kelley Foster, and Angelina Grimké, but new figures: Antoinette Brown, another Oberlin graduate who was to become the first woman ordained as a minister; Harriot Hunt, one of the women pioneers in the field of medicine;[6] Elizabeth Oakes Smith, already known as one of the early women lecturers on the lyceum circuit, but not previously committed to the woman's rights movement;[7] the Negro abolitionist Sojourner Truth; and many others.

From 1850 to 1860 national woman's rights conventions were held every year except 1857; in addition there were gatherings in small towns and large in Ohio, Indiana, New York, Pennsylvania, and Massachusetts. Their frequency led to the charge that the women did nothing but talk; at this stage, there was not much else they could do. Having stated their dissatisfaction with things as they were, they had to agree on what they wanted to achieve, and to develop an ideology which would serve to refute their critics and win them new adherents. What *was* the proper condition of married women? What should be woman's place in the church, the community, the professions, the state? On what basis should divorce be permitted (a question on which the widest divergence of opinion existed among the women themselves)? From the gatherings where these issues were thrashed out there emerged a body of thought, new and dedicated leadership, wide publicity, and new recruits.

Over the years the tone of the press, at first uniformly hostile save for Greeley's *Tribune,* changed for the most part to the point where news reports of the conventions were factual and serious, even if the editorial comment was not. A fair sample of the treatment meted out quite generally at first was the comment in the *New York Herald,* owned by James Gordon Bennett, on the first Worcester convention in 1850:

What do the leaders of the women's rights convention want? They want to vote and hustle with the rowdies at the polls. They want to be members of Congress, and in the heat of debate subject themselves to coarse jests and indecent language.

Presumably to give them a foretaste of what awaited them, the *Herald* continued:

They want to fill all other posts which men are ambitious to occupy, to be lawyers, doctors, captains of vessels and generals in the field. How funny it would sound in the newspapers that Lucy Stone, pleading a cause, took suddenly ill in the pains of parturition and perhaps gave birth to a fine bouncing boy in court! Or that Rev. Antoinette Brown was arrested in the pulpit in the middle of her sermon from the same cause and presented a "pledge" to her husband and the congregation; or that Dr. Harriot K. Hunt while attending a gentleman for a fit of gout or fistula in ano, found it necessary to send for a doctor, there and then, and to be delivered of a man or woman child, perhaps twins. A similar event might happen on the floor of Congress, in a storm at sea or in the raging tempest of battle, and then what is to become of the woman legislator? [8]

Although such diatribes became less frequent, the press in general did little to further the women's cause. For the exchange of information and opinion they so sorely needed, the women had to rely on the abolitionist papers, and a succession of journals published by, and for, themselves: *The Lily,* issued by Amelia Bloomer, whose masthead carried the heading "Devoted to the Interests of Women"; Paulina Wright Davis' *The Una;* Jane Swisshelm's *Pittsburgh Visiter* [sic]; and the *Woman's Advocate,* owned by a joint stock company of women, edited by Anna McDowell, and printed entirely by the labor of women.[9]

No permanent organization of the woman's rights movement emerged during the 1850's, beyond a loose steering committee known as the "Central Committee," consisting of one or more women from any state where there was activity. The women feared an organization would be cumbersome, and would restrict individual effort, while little would be gained by it; they would not change these views until their own experience during the Civil War taught them otherwise.[10]

The early woman's rights movement showed little interest in getting the vote; few felt its importance then as strongly as Mrs. Stanton. Of more immediate concern were the control of property, of earnings (not the same thing by any means), guardianship, divorce, opportunity for education and employment, lack of legal status (women still could not sue or bear witness), and the whole concept of female inferiority perpetuated by established religion.

One fact soon became apparent: the women had no weapon with which to win their demands, a handicap which was to hinder them down to the days of World War I. One of their greatest problems was *how* to press for reforms, other than through speeches and resolutions at their conventions. The possibility of winning public support from the platform or through the press was limited; the Church was largely hostile. How, without the vote, did one go about getting laws passed? Or how could one go about changing conditions not directly governed by legislation, such as clothing, for instance?

Woman's Emancipation

The attempt at dress reform, although badly needed, was not only unsuccessful, but boomeranged and had to be abandoned. The so-called Bloomer costume started out as a revolt against the fantastically uncomfortable and unhealthy garb worn by "ladies" and those desiring to appear as such: stays so tightly laced that women could hardly breathe, and half a dozen skirts and petticoats (which might weigh as much as twelve pounds), long enough to sweep up refuse from the streets and dust from the floor.

The "Bloomer costume" consisted of a tunic loosely belted at the waist, a skirt not much more than knee length, and — the most sensational feature — Turkish pantaloons which reached to the ankle. Amelia Bloomer neither originated it, nor was she the first to wear it. Nobody knows who did design it, but the first woman to come into public notice by wearing it was Mrs. Stanton's cousin, Elizabeth Smith Miller. Mrs. Bloomer advocated the costume in *The Lily* and wore it herself, and her name stuck to it. Mrs. Stanton, harassed as usual by her household chores and already an advocate of simple clothing and exercise, embraced it with enthusiasm. Mrs. Stone and Miss Anthony followed suit, and it was widely seen. Some women wore it for its comfort alone; others made it a symbol of revolt against all senseless restrictions on women. In the public mind, advocates of equal rights became "bloomers."

If the women were physically more comfortable, they suffered untold mental tortures. They were the butt of unceasing ridicule, from newspaper editors to corner loafers and small boys. Eventually the persecution became unbearable, and a handicap to the cause. Having been one of the first to adopt it, Mrs. Stanton with her clear intellect was also one of the first to weigh good against evil, and to discard it. She wrote Susan Anthony who wished to continue wearing the dress despite the anguish it caused her: "We put the dress on for greater freedom, but what is physical freedom compared with mental bondage? . . . It is not wise, Susan, to use up so much energy and feeling that way. You can put them to better use. I speak from experience." [11]

The women were on more solid ground when, following the example of the anti-slavery forces, they began sending petitions to state legislatures asking for specific remedial measures. Some of the outstanding accomplishments were in New York state under the leadership of Susan B. Anthony, who had the insight to realize that in order to get beyond the stage of merely sending in petitions and to win hearings before legislative bodies, thousands of signatures had to be rolled up, not only in the large cities but in every county in the state. Such political acumen was something new in a woman; so was the organizational ability required for the job. If Lucretia Mott typified the moral force of the movement, if Lucy Stone was its most gifted orator and Mrs. Stanton its outstanding philosopher, Susan Anthony was its incomparable organizer, who gave it force and direction for half a century. [12]

She was a late starter compared to the others, joining the ranks only after meeting Mrs. Stanton in 1851. The Anthonys were Quakers, and Susan was born in 1820 in the Berkshire town of Adams, Massachusetts. Her father owned a small textile mill but lost his business and had to make a fresh start as a farmer outside of Rochester. Young Susan helped with the housework and on the farm, and then turned to teaching, the only vocation open to a woman with any schooling. She rose as high as a woman could, to be "headmistress" of the Female Department at Canajoharie Academy. Dissatisfied with the inequities heaped on a woman teacher, she went back to the family farm.

Her mother and sister Lucy had attended the woman's rights convention held in Rochester in 1848, and first roused her desire to meet Mrs. Stanton and Mrs. Mott by their accounts of the occasion. Through her father, an ardent abolitionist, she met Frederick Douglass and other anti-slavery leaders. She tried working as a paid agent for the temperance movement, only to encounter hidebound prejudice against any kind of equal participation by the women. The women's temperance societies she organized all died for lack of funds, and this taught her another abiding lesson:

Thus as I passed from town to town was I made to feel the great evil of woman's utter dependence on man for the necessary means to aid reform movements. I never before took in so fully the grand idea of pecuniary independence. Woman must have a purse of her own and how can this be so as long as the law denies to the wife all right to both individual and joint earnings? [13]

Miss Anthony's first campaign on behalf of her new cause was for signatures to a petition addressed to the New York legislature, asking for three reforms: (1) control by women of their own earnings; (2) guardianship of their children in case of divorce; (3) the vote. Her method of work is a commonplace today; then it was a spectacular innovation. She chose sixty women, one from every county in the state, to serve as "captains," and in midwinter of 1854 they started out to get names.

Although more women were ready for such labors than twenty years earlier, they encountered many of the same obstacles — the prejudice, hostility and apathy — which had plagued Lydia Maria Child. Moreover, Mrs. Child was canvassing in her home town of Northampton; these women had to travel, and women who traveled alone were still unusual. Conditions for all but the affluent traveler were primitive, and for solitary females the problems of securing decent food and respectable accommodations were staggering. The women had no money except what they might themselves possess (an infrequent occurrence) or get from friends;

they had no organization behind them; under such conditions to arrange local meetings, have broadsides printed, and secure notices in the local paper was enough to daunt all but the indomitable.

As for their reception by those on whose behalf they toiled:

Like itinerant tin pedlars or book agents they tramped the streets and country roads, knocking at every door, presenting their petitions, arguing with women who half the time slammed the door in their faces with the smug remark that they had husbands, thank God, to look after their interests, and they needed no new laws to protect their rights. After each rebuff the women simply trudged on to the next street, the next row of houses, the next grudgingly opened front door.[14]

Yet in ten weeks they collected six thousand signatures. As still another demonstration of the new tactical sense which had been added to the women's armory, Miss Anthony had planned a New York state woman's rights convention to be held in Albany while the legislature was in session; the petitions would be used to try to gain a hearing for the bills the women were supporting.

The maneuver was successful; Elizabeth Cady Stanton appeared before a Joint Judiciary Committee of both legislative houses, the first woman to do so in New York. Her speech dealt with the legal disabilities of women, and its eloquence and careful documentation (not for nothing was she a judge's daughter) might have been expected to impress her audience, not only with the validity of her argument, but as a proof of woman's intellectual capacities.

The bill was not passed, of course; that would have been expecting too much too soon. More signatures were needed, and Miss Anthony went after them. The epic of her tour of New York State during the winter of 1855 is a saga in itself.

She started out on Christmas Day, 1854, with a bag full of literature, petitions, and $50 loaned to her by Wendell Phillips. In each town she had to make all arrangements for her meeting: engage the hall, see to the lights and ushers, and get throwaways printed and distributed, announcing the meeting. Sometimes audiences were friendly and openhanded, coming from miles around despite bitter weather, and she was able to pay not only her expenses but make a small surplus, which would be promptly swallowed up at the next stop, where the audience might be negligible, or where perhaps she could find no proper meeting place.

The physical hardships alone, in what was one of the worst winters in living memories, were major obstacles:

The snowdrifts are over the fences in many places and the roads are so badly blocked with snow that vehicles have to take to the ice-covered meadows. Susan's feet, frost-bitten no doubt, begin to give her serious trouble. She soaks them in cold water, then wraps them in woolens, but the pain merely transfers itself to her back. All the way to Malone she has to sit doubled over, clinging to the seat in front in order not to groan aloud. She holds her meeting in spite of suffering, gets to Ogdensburg, then to Canton. But when the time arrives to leave this point, she has to be carried to the stage. Ten miles from Watertown she changes to the train, barely able to walk, and arriving at the hotel in the late afternoon, she determines to give the "water cure," sovereign remedy of the age, a final test. She sends for the chambermaid, orders two buckets of ice-water, and sitting in a coffin-like tin tub, has both buckets poured over her aching body. Wrapped in hot blankets she sleeps through the night and, believe it or not, wakes in the morning as good as new.[15]

When she returned to Rochester on May 1, completely exhausted, she had spoken, and circulated her petitions in fifty-four of the sixty counties in New York State; her meticulous accounts showed that she had spent $2,291 and collected $2,367, leaving her with a balance of $76 for future campaigns.

One marvels at the stamina that could endure, not only such physical hardships, but the indignity of the report handed down by the Assembly's Judiciary Committee in response to the petitions collected by Miss Anthony and her co-workers, a report received by the Assembly with roars of laughter:

The Committee is composed of married and single gentlemen. The bachelors on the Committee, with becoming diffidence, have left the subject pretty much to the married gentlemen. They have considered it with the aid of the light they have before them and the experience married life has given them. Thus aided, they are enabled to state that the ladies always have the best place and choicest titbit at the table. They always have the best seat in the cars, carriage and sleighs; the warmest place in the winter and the coolest place in the summer. They have their choice on which side of the bed they will lie, front or back. A lady's dress costs three times as much as that of a gentleman; and, at the present time, with the prevailing fashion, one lady occupies three times as much space in the world as a gentleman.

It has thus appeared to the married gentlemen of your Committee, being a majority (the bachelors being silent for the reason mentioned and also probably for the further reason that they are still suitors for the favors of the gentler sex), that, if there is any inequity or oppression in the case, the gentlemen are the sufferers. They, however, have presented no petitions for redress; having, doubtless, made up their minds to yield to an inevitable destiny.

On the whole, the Committee have concluded to recommend no measure, except as they have observed several instances in which husband and wife have signed the same petition. In such case, they would recommend the parties to apply for a law authorizing them to change dresses, that the husband may wear petticoats and the wife the breeches, and thus indicate to their neighbors and the public the true relation in which they stand to each other.[16]

Nevertheless, the world did move. Four years later in 1860 Mrs. Stanton was once more in Albany, this time addressing a joint session of both Houses from the Speaker's desk. The bill which became the law of New York state at that time was a considerable improvement over that of 1848; it gave women the right, in addition to owning property, to collect their own wages, to sue in court, and to have similar property rights at their husband's death as the latter had when his wife pre-deceased him.[17]

If the women lacked many weapons for achieving their goals easily, they had some very real assets. Perhaps one of the greatest was the working partnership between Mrs. Stanton and Miss Anthony. Few associations have been more fruitful. Their talents and the circumstances of their lives complemented each other. Miss Anthony was an organizer, Mrs. Stanton a thinker, writer, and speaker. Mrs. Stanton was tied down by a large family for twenty years of their association; Miss Anthony was more mobile, and could either travel, or rush in answer to a distress call from the Stanton home, to care for children and household, while Mrs. Stanton shut herself up to prepare a needed brief or speech. When Mrs. Stanton on occasion wandered afield, Miss Anthony was usually able to bring her back into line. (Their co-workers frequently complained that Mrs. Stanton was forever bringing up new and controversial issues — divorce, the Bible, the "educated vote," which would "rock the boat.") Although Susan Anthony and Elizabeth Cady Stanton had their differences, the deep bond between them never frayed. In her reminiscences Mrs. Stanton has left a vivid sketch of their early labors together:

Whenever I saw that stately Quaker girl coming across my lawn, I knew that some happy convocation of the sons of Adam was to be set by the ears, by one of our appeals or resolutions. The little portmanteau, stuffed with facts, was opened, and there we had what the Rev. John Smith and the Hon. Richard Roe had said: false interpretations of Bible texts, the statistics of women robbed of their property, shut out of some college, half paid for their work, the reports of some disgraceful trial; injustice enough to turn any woman's thoughts from stockings and puddings. Then we would get out our pens and write articles for the papers or a petition to the legislature; indite letters to the faithful, here and there; call on *The Lily, The Una, The Liberator, The Standard* to remember our wrongs as well as those of the slave. We never met without issuing a pronunciamento on some question. . . . She supplied the facts and statistics, I the philosophy and the rhetoric, and, together, we have made arguments that stood unshaken through the storms of long years; arguments that no one has answered. Our speeches may be considered the united product of our two brains.[18]

Mrs. Stanton had a shrewd idea that they would leave their mark on the world. In 1857 when she was forty-two and Miss Anthony thirty-seven, when summoning her friend to help her, she wrote:

You must come here a week or two, and we will do wonders. Courage, Susan — this is my last baby, and she will be two years old in January. Two more years and — time will tell what! You and I have the prospect of a good long life. We shall not be in our prime before fifty, and after that we shall be good for twenty years at least.[19]

Yet without the work of countless others, even the Stanton-Anthony team would not have accomplished what they did. Behind them and the other leaders — the silvery-voiced Lucy Stone, the wise Lucretia Mott, the eloquent Ernestine Rose and Abby Kelley Foster, the worldly Paulina Wright Davis — were innumerable women who became leaders in their states: Frances Dana Gage, Ohio abolitionist, also known as "Aunt Fanny," who wrote stories for children; Clarina Howard Nichols of Vermont, newspaper editor and later organizer in the West; Matilda Joslyn Gage, who, although tied for many years to a home and small children in an upstate New York town, became one of the most scholarly of them all; Josephine S. Griffing, Amanda M. Way, and Caroline Severance of Ohio; Hannah Tracy Cutler of Illinois; Mary Upton Ferrin of Massachusetts; and the Negro women who, while their first interest inevitably lay in the anti-slavery struggle, consistently pointed out the relationship between freedom for the slave, and equality for women of any color — Sojourner Truth, Frances E. W. Harper, Sarah Remond.

None did more valiant service than the almost legendary Sojourner Truth. Born a slave near Kingston on the Hudson River, she was given the name of Isabella. She remained illiterate all her life. Her master forbade her to marry the man she loved, and flogged her in his presence; when she finally married a man "approved" by her owner, and bore thirteen children, most of them were sold into slavery.

In 1827, at long last, New York state freed its slaves by law. The free Negro woman Isabella came to New York, did domestic work, and then, after a period of religious revivalism, became an active abolitionist, taking the name of Sojourner Truth.

In 1851 at a woman's rights convention in Akron, Ohio, none of the women seemed able to answer an outbreak of heckling, and it looked as if their cause would be worsted at their own gathering. Sojourner Truth came forward and sat on the steps of the pulpit from which Frances Dana Gage was presiding. Many women, apprehensive that the abolitionist leader would harm their cause, begged Mrs. Gage not to give her the floor. Mrs. Gage, fortunately, thought otherwise: "[Sojourner] moved slowly and solemnly to the front, laid her old bonnet at her feet, and turned her great speaking eyes to me. There was a hissing sound of disapprobation above and below. I rose and announced 'Sojourner Truth' and begged the audience to keep silent for a few moments."

Sojourner turned the full force of her eloquence against the previous speaker, a clergyman who had ridiculed the weakness and helplessness of women, who should, therefore, not be entrusted with the vote:

The man over there says women need to be helped into carriages and lifted over ditches, and to have the best place everywhere. Nobody ever helps me into carriages or over puddles, or gives me the best place — and ain't I a woman?

With a gesture that electrified the audience, she raised her bare black arm:

Look at my arm! I have ploughed and planted and gathered into barns, and no man could head me — and ain't I a woman? I could work as much and eat as much as a man — when I could get it — and bear the lash as well! And ain't I a woman? I have born thirteen children, and seen most of 'em sold into slavery, and when I cried out with my mother's grief, none but Jesus heard me — and ain't I a woman?

Then she shifted to another, shrewder vein: "If my cup won't hold but a pint, and yours holds a quart, wouldn't ye be mean not to let me have my little half measure full?"

Mrs. Gage wrote of her achievement:

Amid roars of applause she returned to her corner, leaving more than one of us with streaming eyes, and hearts beating with gratitude. She had taken us up in her strong arms and carried us safely over the slough of difficulty, turning the whole tide in our favor. I have never in my life seen anything like the magical influence that subdued the snobbish spirit of the day and turned the sneers and jeers of an excited crowd into notes of respect and admiration.[20]

This stormy occasion served as Mrs. Gage's own baptism by fire. She found herself presiding at the convention although, as she told the audience, she had never before attended a business meeting and had no knowledge of parliamentary procedure. She then proceeded to make, as so many of these amazing women did, an able maiden speech which drew a parallel between those early settlers in Ohio who had left the security of New England for greater opportunity, and the women's cause:

The old land of moral, social and political privilege seems too narrow for our wants; its soil answers not to our growing, and we feel that we can see clearly a better country that we might inhabit. But there are mountains of established law and custom to overcome; a wilderness of prejudice to be subdued, a powerful foe of selfishness and self-interest to be overthrown. But for the sake of our children's children, we have entered upon the work.[21]

Mrs. Gage soon found herself the leader of a movement that grew quickly in soil well-ploughed by such speakers as Abby Kelley Foster and Lucy Stone, by the influence of Oberlin, and the work of the Underground Railroad. Not all the meetings were held in churches. One "convention" in the tiny village of Chesterfield in Morgan County found itself locked out of the church for which it had been advertised, and the schoolhouse as well. But a gathering-place was found "on the threshing-floor of a fine barn, and we found about three or four hundred of the farmers and their wives, sons and daughters, assembled." [22]

Then there was "John's convention."

It was two days' journey, by steamboat and rail. The call was signed John Andrews, and John Andrews promised to meet me at the cars. I went. It was fearfully cold, and John met me. He was a beardless boy of nineteen, looking much younger. We drove at once to the "Christian church." On the way he cheered me by saying "he was afraid nobody would come for his asking." When we got to the house there was not one human soul on hand, no fire in the rusty stove, and the rude, unpainted board benches all topsy-turvy. I called some boys, playing near, asked their names, put them on paper, five of them, and said to them: "Go to every house in this town, and tell everybody that Aunt Fanny will speak here at eleven a.m., and if you get fifty to come I will give you each ten cents." They scattered off upon the run. I ordered John to right the benches, picked up chips and kindlings, borrowed a brand of fire at the next door, had a good hot stove and the floor swept, and was ready for my audience at the appointed time. John had done his work well, and fifty at least were on hand, and a minister to make a prayer and quote St. Paul before I had said a word. I said my say and before 1 p.m. we adjourned, appointing another session at 3 and one for 7 p.m. and three for the following day. Mrs. C. M. Severance came at 6 o'clock and we had a good meeting throughout. John's convention was voted a success after all.[23]

An example of how the new ideas were carried westward with the tide of migration is the life of Clarina Howard Nichols of Vermont. From 1843 to 1853 she edited the *Windham County Democrat,* of which her husband was the publisher, and as early as 1847 wrote a series of editorials on the property disabilities suffered by married women. In 1852 she appeared before the lower house of the State Legislature on behalf of a bill giving women the vote in district school meetings, an ordeal which caused her such a violent attack of heart palpitations that she very nearly ended her plea before she had well begun. But she recovered her poise, and spoke at length, turning the charge that women wanted to steal the trousers in the family, back on her opponents: "I will not appeal to the gallantry of this House, but to its manliness, if such a taunt does not come with an ill grace from gentlemen who have legislated our skirts into their possession? And will it not be quite time enough to taunt us with being after their wardrobes, when they shall have restored to us the legal right to our own?" [24]

Until 1854 Mrs. Nichols editorialized and lectured throughout New England. She also spent two months in Wisconsin speaking for a woman's temperance society, interlarding her talks with arguments for woman's rights. When she visited Kansas with two of her sons who were settling there, she held woman's rights meetings, by request, on the boat going up the Missouri River to Kansas City. In 1857 she went back to Kansas to settle there, and extended her labors to the neighboring state of Missouri, and later to California. "Latter day laborers," she once wrote, "can have little idea of the trials of the early worker, driven by the stress of right and duty against popular prejudice, to which her own training and early habits of thought have made her painfully sensitive." [25]

The same tenacity crops up again and again. There was Mary Upton Ferrin of Salem, Massachusetts, who learned in the spring of 1848 that by Massachusetts law her husband owned, not only her real estate and all improvements on it, but her personal effects, unless she hid them or proved they had been loaned to her! No lawyer or judge whom she approached for help would draw up a petition for her to present to the Legislature, so she drew one up herself and began to circulate it for signatures, also unaided. Year after year she kept at it, traveling some 600 miles, a great many of them on foot. Other women joined in the work, and at last in 1854 Massachusetts passed a Married Women's Property Bill.

It was hardest for the self-supporting woman to go against the tide, especially if, in addition to going to meetings and listening to speakers, she tried to do something constructive. In Ellsworth, Maine, two women undertook to organize a course of lyceum lectures, inviting among others such controversial figures as Wendell Phillips, Dr. Harriot K. Hunt, and Susan Anthony. One of the initiators, Miss Charlotte Hill, was a violinist who played at parties, and also taught music to boys and girls. Threatened with retribution if she did not desist from "bringing such people to town," she answered: "Very well — I shall maintain my principles, and if you break up my classes I can go back to the seashore and dig clams for a living as I have done before." [26]

In this particular case the record indicates that she did not have to resort to such a drastic step, but it is certain that she would have been perfectly willing to do so rather than back down. Like any movement of social reform, the strength of that for equal rights for women lay not only in the leadership it developed, but in the dogged devotion it was able to instill in countless individuals throughout the nineteenth century down into our own. For most of its course, its sole wealth lay in the people who put a part of their lives, sometimes their whole lives, into it.

No Susan Anthony or Frances Dana Gage could emerge in the South — not because life there was a round of magnolias, moonlight, and waltzes, and women lacked neither security nor dignity. There were hundreds of thousands of them on farms belonging to non-slave-holding, middle class, and "poor white" farmers, or living in cities and small towns, who faced the same realities as their sisters elsewhere in the country. The prevailing attitude toward women, which has been called "southern chivalry," was merely the reverse side of an order which kept them largely within the domestic circle. The agrarian, plantation economy was far from universal, but its social code was dominant.[27]

It was for this reason that no movement comparable to that growing in the North and West could develop in the southern states. With political life increasingly centered on the defense and perpetuation of slavery, there was no chance for the growth of reform movements such as those which were drawing women into new activities elsewhere. With little industrial development, there was no demand for women as factory hands. The deadening influence of slavery made itself felt in the low level of education, despite the existence of some institutions for men which claimed collegiate rank, a few short-lived women's "colleges" which were no better than seminaries, and fashionable schools for planters' daughters.

Slavery stifled any tendency toward reform or dissent. The rebel who could not become reconciled to it had to leave, as did the Grimké sisters, or face social ostracism. There was no possibility that a woman from an upland farm who might have become a Lucy Stone could ever do so. There was no Oberlin to nourish her, no forum of controversy in which she might exercise her talents and grow, and in point of fact no such woman emerged. There were many planters' wives and daughters who showed administrative and organizing ability in managing large establishments, and who have left us, in letters and journals, a vivid record of their responsibilities, their culture, and charm. But their lives were set within a framework grounded on human bondage, which in turn gave them little opportunity to break into new fields of endeavor or ways of thinking.

It was otherwise with the Negro woman. Even if she was free, her opportunities for education and advancement were severely limited — she was free in what was, after all is said and done, enemy country — and if she was a slave, her energies were directed toward survival for herself and her family, manumission, or flight. The myth of her meek submission to her fate is belied by the annals of the Underground Railroad, which are filled with accounts of women making the dangerous journey, often taking young children with them, even infants in arms, heading north, and resisting capture and the inevitable return to slavery at all costs.[28] The retaken slave Lucy in *Uncle Tom's Cabin* who drowned herself when her baby was taken from her was no figment of Mrs. Stowe's overexcited imagination.[29] Her name could have been Margaret Garner, the twenty-two-year-old slave who reached "free soil" in Cincinnati with her four children, only to be recaptured almost at once by a posse from the South. In prison, awaiting transportation, she killed a three-year-old girl. On the Ohio River she allowed the baby to roll from her lap into the water, and when shipwreck overtook the boat, she eluded all attempts to rescue her, and drowned.[30] In 1838 John Quincy Adams told the House of Representatives of a slave woman in the District of Columbia who "was taken with her four infant children, and separated from her husband, who is a free man, to be sent away, I know not where. That woman in a dungeon in Alexandria killed with her own hand two of her children, and attempted to kill the others." [31] In cases where flight was impossible, slave women resorted to other forms of resistance: arson, poisoning, self-mutilation. Larceny and shamming sickness were frequent.

One former slave who grew to legendary stature while guiding others to freedom was the fabulous Harriet Tubman.[32] At first glance she was unimpressive in appearance — a mere five feet tall — but piercing eyes looked out from under a turban that always swathed her head; it was worn to conceal a deep scar in her skull, left by an iron weight an overseer had thrown at her when she was only fifteen years old. All her life she suffered from spells of unconsciousness as a result of the blow.

She was born a slave on the Eastern Shore of Maryland, not far from where Frederick Douglass grew up. When she married a free Negro, her own status was unchanged; when her master's death in 1849 made it seem likely that she would be sold, she begged her husband to go North with her. When he refused, she chose freedom without him, and made her hazardous way to Pennsylvania, and freedom, alone.

Harriet Tubman was then nearly thirty years old. She became a "conductor" on the Underground Railroad. During a period of ten years she made nineteen journeys into slave territory and brought back more than 300 men, women, and children. "Moses," they called her, a magic name among slaves planning to take the dangerous journey northward. Slave-owners paid her the compliment of putting a price on her head which mounted steadily with the years until it reached the huge figure, for that day, of $40,000. Yet she was never caught or harmed, and she never lost a "passenger." Some saw a mystical source for her infallibility, linked with the spells of unconsciousness which occasionally overtook her even when traveling with a group of runaways. But abolitionists who knew and worked with her recognized her extraordinary gifts of sagacity and courage, which, in a human being of another race and sex, would have brought her fame and public recognition. Instead, although she rendered service as a military scout and a nurse to the Union armies during the Civil War, Harriet Tubman spent most of her later years in straitened circumstances, often in dire need, struggling for a pension which a grudging Congress finally awarded her, in the amount of $20 a month, when she was eighty years old.

Such neglect was the usual lot of the Negro abolitionist, particularly the women: while Harriet Tubman and her great contemporary, Sojourner Truth, are dignified with an occasional mention in the history books, nothing whatever appears of the many other Negro women whose names at the time were known far beyond the confines of the abolition movement.

Outstanding among these was Frances Ellen Watkins Harper, noted as a poet as well as an anti-slavery lecturer of national repute. "She has a noble head, this bronze muse, a strong face with a shadowed gleam upon it," wrote Grace Greenwood, one of the most popular feminine writers of the day. "She stands quietly beside her desk and speaks without notes, with gestures few and fitting. Her manner is marked with dignity and composure. She is never assuming, never theatrical." [33]

Behind the presence that so impressed Miss Greenwood lay the familiar pattern of struggle for education and a livelihood. Her parents were free Negroes living in Baltimore, but they left her an orphan while still a child. She was fortunate enough to have an uncle who conducted a school she could attend, and later to be able to work in a bookstore, where she made the most of the merchandise whenever she had a moment to spare. When the Fugitive Slave Act was passed in 1850, Maryland was no longer safe even for a free slave, for many such were kidnapped and sold South as "runaways." Mrs. Harper was hard pressed for a time to earn a living — she taught school and did domestic work, meanwhile working with the Underground Railroad in Pennsylvania and Ohio. Out of her experience she wrote poetry which appeared in anti-slavery papers and in her first published volume in 1854. When she began to lecture as agent for the Maine Anti-Slavery Society, traveling all over the country, people came to hear her not only for her passionate eloquence and musical voice, but as the author of such verses as "The Slave Mother" and "Ethiopia":

> Yes! Ethiopia yet shall stretch
> Her bleeding hands abroad;
> Her cry of agony shall reach
> The burning throne of God.[34]

There is no mention in the accounts of the early women editors and journalists of Mary Ann Shadd Cary. A free native of Delaware, she taught school in Wilmington until the Fugitive Slave Act made it desirable that she, too, remove to safer ground than a "border state." She went to Canada to investigate the possibility of Negro freedmen and runaways settling there, and until the

Civil War she lived in Windsor, Ontario, just across the border from Detroit. There for three years she published her own newspaper, *The Provincial Freeman,* and made periodic trips into the states to give anti-slavery lectures.[35] An intrepid woman of commanding mien, she took in her stride the mobs which were a constant threat to abolitionists, particularly those of Negro descent. Once when a runaway slave boy was in imminent danger of being seized by slave catchers, she roused an entire community to his aid, and succeeded in stirring up so much feeling that "the pursuers fled from the infuriated people, happy to get away without bodily harm."[36]

There were others who lectured, wrote, or worked in selfless anonymity with the Underground Railroad: Charlotte Forten, Anna Mae Douglass (the wife of Frederick Douglass), Sarah Remond (whose brother, Charles Lenox Remond, joined Garrison in protesting the exclusion of the women delegates from the World Anti-Slavery Convention in 1848), and many more. They deserve better than the oblivion to which they have been consigned.

The education of Negro girls had made little progress since the days of Prudence Crandall. Even in the North they were for the most part barred from any schools save those taught by Negroes, who usually lacked adequate training for the task. The opening of the first school to train Negro girls as teachers, in Washington, D. C., in 1851, launched a battle hardly less vigorous or less significant than Miss Crandall's, although much less well-known today.

The school's founder, Myrtilla Miner, was one of the young women whom Mary Lyon's heart yearned over: she was poor, she came from a tiny village in central New York, and she wanted an education so desperately that she wrote to the Governor of the state, then William H. Seward, asking for advice.[37] His Honor, apparently not knowing of the opening of Mount Holyoke Seminary a year earlier, gave her only vague encouragement, saying he hoped matters would improve soon! Eventually the eager girl was admitted to a Quaker seminary in Rochester.

Here she made friends with two Negro students who told her something of slavery. She learned more when, after leaving school,

Women shoemakers of Lynn, Mass., striking for higher pay, 1860

Women Delegates to the General Assembly of the Knights of Labor, 1886

Frances Willard

Josephine St. Pierre Ruffin

Ida B. Wells-Barnett

Florence Kelley

she took a post as a teacher in a school for planters' daughters in Mississippi. When she asked to be allowed to teach the slave children on the plantations, her request was of course refused. Deeply stirred, Myrtilla Miner came back North. After consulting friends and anti-slavery leaders, she resolved to open a school for colored girls "endowed with all the powers and professorships belonging to a first class school of the other sex." The place she chose was Washington, because "it was the common property of the nation, and because the laws of the District gave her the right to educate free colored children, and she attempted to teach no other." [38]

Nevertheless the political climate in Washington in the decade before the Civil War was hardly favorable to attempts to better the position of the Negro; not all the abolitionists whom Miss Miner consulted thought her plan wise or feasible. Yet her tenacity and driving determination overcame or ignored all objections, even those of Frederick Douglass, who remembered her as "a slender, wiry, pale (not over healthy) but singularly animated figure . . . a delicate and fragile person who stood or rather moved to and fro before me, for she would not accept a chair. She seemed too full of her own enterprises to think of her own ease, and hence kept me in motion all the time she was in my office." Douglass did his best to dissuade her from her purpose: "In my fancy I saw this little woman harassed by the law, insulted in the street, the victim of slave-holding malice, and, possibly, beaten down by the mob. . . . My arguments made no impression upon the heroic spirit before me." [39]

Miss Miner opened her school in the autumn of 1851 with six pupils; within a few months she had forty, despite a host of tribulations similar to those endured by Prudence Crandall: repeated evictions, arson, and other forms of mob violence. The school survived because, as in the case of Miss Crandall, the heroism of the pupils and their parents matched that of their teacher; furthermore, the anti-slavery movement was stronger, and Miss Miner in the nation's capital could call on allies that Miss Crandall lacked in a small village. While she started out with only the slender sum of $100, contributions came to her from Wendell Phillips, Charles Sumner, Ellis Loring, Arthur Tappan, and from the Quakers in Philadelphia, New York, and New England. Harriet Beecher Stowe gave $1,000 from her royalties on *Uncle Tom's*

Cabin towards a new building; Horace Mann's sister Lydia came
to help, and there were Beechers, Manns, and Stowes active on the
board of trustees, as donors and teachers. Yet in the last analysis
Myrtilla Miner had to rely on her own fortitude. "Mob my school?
You dare not," she challenged some of her enemies. "If you tear
it down over my head I shall get another house. There is no law
to prevent my teaching these people, and I *shall* teach them, even
unto death." [40]

There were outbreaks of stone-throwing, and several times
the school had to be moved, but the worst did not happen until
1860:

At one o'clock I was awoke [sic] by the smoke of cracking fire. I
listened, felt sure that it could not be in either stove, there having
been no fire in the house during the day. I opened the door from my
chamber directly into the next, and smellt the smoke — then hurriedly
threw on a dress, rushed to the front chamber window and cried fire! —
fire! with awful fury — then with a pail I ran for water — the fire having but that moment broken out. It seemed to me that I alone could
stop it — but I ran with water and screamed *fire!* till I got the third
pailful — then the neighbors came, and one going onto the roof soon
allayed the fire, but when I got back into our room the fire had entered
there and burnt the curtain to my closet and was slowly burning a
quantity of waste paper. . . . The fire was introduced by an incendiary
between the clapboard and lathing and had burnt much between them
before bursting out. . . . For years I had been expecting this so it did
not take me unawares but for the last year the ruffians had been so
quiet I tho't they had given me up.[41]

Such courage could come only from deep conviction. "I love this
school of mine profoundly," she wrote a friend, "and have really
no idea, when I am with them, that they are not white, recognizing
their spiritual more than their physical. Some, indeed many, *spirits*
with whom I come in contact here seem far darker than they." [42]

Unfortunately Frederick Douglass had been right when he
noted that Miss Miner did not look "over healthy," and she con
sumed herself in the superhuman efforts needed to keep the school
going. It was she who bedeviled congressmen, senators, journalists,
and newspaper publishers for aid, and who carried on a mountain-
ous correspondence, much of it begging for funds, in addition to
the day-to-day load of teaching and administration. She took into
her own home orphan girls who otherwise would have been unable

to attend the school; vacations were unthought of, and often she was too ill and overburdened to write to her family and closest friends for months on end.

By 1857, although she had built up an institution that included three departments — primary teaching, domestic economy and teacher training — Myrtilla Miner had nearly burned herself out; in 1859 she was obliged to close the school, not only to try and regain her health, but to seek the kind of endowment which Emma Willard and Mary Lyon had found necessary to establish their institutions on a lasting basis. Then came the Civil War. During its course, Myrtilla Miner had a horseback riding accident from which she never recovered. She died in 1864, at the age of forty-nine.

Yet she had built a solid foundation on which those whom she had drawn into the work with her could resume the task of educating the emancipated slaves at the close of the war. Until 1955 Miner Teachers College, standing on a hill overlooking the capital close to Howard University, sent out its graduates to teach throughout the country; today it is a part of the integrated District school system under the name of the District of Columbia Teachers College.

PART II

Chapter VII

THE CIVIL WAR

During the closing months of 1862 the scattered entries in Louisa May Alcott's *Journal* record her decision to volunteer as a nurse in an army hospital:

November — Thirty years old. Decided to go to Washington as nurse if I could find a place. Help needed, and I love nursing, and *must* let out my pent-up energy in some new way . . . I want new experiences, and am sure to get 'em, if I go. So I've sent in my name.

December — I started on my long journey, full of hope and sorrow, courage and plans. A most interesting journey, into a new world full of stirring sights and sounds, new adventures, and an ever-growing sense of the great task I had undertaken. I said my prayers as I went rushing through the country white with tents, all alive with patriotism, and already red with blood. A solemn time, but I'm glad to live in it; and am sure it will do me good whether I come out alive or dead.[1]

The somber note came unpleasantly near to being prophetic: Louisa May Alcott nearly died of typhoid fever, and she was back home again within three months, still desperately ill, and with her health permanently impaired. Yet she always maintained that the brief experience had been of lasting value: how much more this must have been true of women who spent all or most of four years in such new activities?

Often their motives were just as varied as those so candidly admitted by the author of *Little Women;* they were compounded of patriotism, anti-slavery sentiment, and the restlessness produced by twenty years' agitation which now demanded release. Their origins lay in the ferment of two decades, in the teachings of Frances Wright and Margaret Fuller, or perhaps in a petition presented at the door by an unknown woman, asking for the vote.

For many, the dominant compulsion was the need to keep families whose menfolk had gone into the armies, housed, clothed, and fed. The influx of women into teaching and their entrance into government offices date from the Civil War. Thousands more broke away from stove and laundry tub to look for work in the cities, or to do the heavy manual labor required to keep the family homestead going as recorded by Anna Howard Shaw:

The problem of living grew harder with every day. We eked out our little income in every way we could, taking as boarders the workers in the logging-camps, making quilts, which we sold, and losing no chance to earn a penny in any legitimate manner. Again my mother did such outside sewing as she could secure, yet with every month of our effort the gulf between our income and our expenses grew wider, and the price of the bare necessities of existence climbed up and up. The largest amount I could earn at teaching was six dollars a week, and our school year included only two terms of thirteen weeks each. It was an incessant struggle to keep our land, to pay our taxes, and to live. Calico was selling at fifty cents a yard. Coffee was one dollar a pound. There were no men left to grind our corn, to get in our crops, or to care for our livestock; and all around us we saw our struggle reflected in the lives of our neighbors.[2]

Those more favorably situated were able to create new spheres of usefulness for their sex. Dorothea Dix, already widely known for her work in reforming prisons and insane asylums, became — at the age of sixty — head of the nursing service in the Union army hospitals. "A kind old soul, but queer and arbitrary," commented Miss Alcott's *Journal*.[3] Certainly her experience as a lone lobbyist, however persistent and devoted, was hardly the best preparation for the huge task of administration, especially when the Army Medical Corps was largely hostile in its attitude — as Miss Nightingale had found in the Crimea. Yet if Miss Dix was criticized for lack of tact and flexibility, few could question her devotion or the fact that she had some share in bringing a degree of order out of chaos.

There were other women, like "Mother" Bickerdyke and Clara Barton, who saw the possibility of saving many lives by following closely after the battle-lines.[4] Indeed Miss Barton, who had been searching all the decades of her adult life for a satisfying purpose to her existence, caught her first glimpses of it as she tended the wounded and held the heads of dying men on the battlefields of Antietam, Chancellorsville, and Fredericksburg.

Gradually an entirely new institution, the Sanitary Commission, became the right arm of the Union hospital and medical services. Behind the famous greeting, "Hello, Sanitary," which echoed down the rows of cots to the women bringing jelly, fruit, clean clothing, soap, and other essentials to the ragged men, lay the work of a complex organization which, by the end of the war, numbered some 7,000 local societies throughout the North and West, and which raised — and spent — the huge sum of $50,000,-000.[5]

Decorum — and the ability born of previous experience — both required that its leaders be men. But working closely with Dr. Henry Bellows, the Unitarian minister who served as its president, and its gifted general secretary, Frederick Law Olmsted, were women like Mary A. Livermore of Chicago and Louisa Lee Schuyler of New York. The Commission's farflung activities, and the money needed to carry them out, owed their existence to a multitude of anonymous women who ran the countless bazaars, and carried on a kind of modern Red Cross-USO program unparalleled up to that time.

There were few aspects of the war, aside from military strategy and actual combat, which the Sanitary Commission did not have its finger in. It recruited the nurses for army hospital services (whom Miss Dix required to be over thirty, *plain, not* wasp-waisted, strong enough to turn a grown man over in bed, and willing to do the most menial work — a combination of virtues which the Sanitary Commission was often hard put to find!).[6] It provided bandages, medicines, and dietary supplements to the highly inadequate hospital rations, and campaigned against scurvy and for better sanitation in the army camps. It established and maintained hospital ships, relief camps, and convalescent homes. It helped the wounded making their painful way back home, and aided frantic relatives to locate those missing in action. Many a small-town woman or farmer's wife whose tasks had been limited and whose horizon had been narrow, as well as the city matron previously caught up in a round of fashion and pleasure who became engrossed in some facet of the Commission's work, could never be quite the same person afterwards.

But the Civil War made even more novel demands on women than those of nursing or relief work; it brought them into national politics on other issues than their own enfranchisement. It gave young Anna Dickinson the opportunity to become one of the most celebrated of northern orators, although she was only seventeen when she began her meteoric career.[7] Republican Party leaders, banking heavily on her youth, beauty, and eloquence, were willing to let her speak for them, despite her extreme views against the Copperheads and in favor of emancipation. She was, observed Wendell Phillips, "the young elephant sent forward to try the bridges to see if they were safe for older ones to cross." [8] After helping to win hotly contested Congressional elections in New Hampshire and Connecticut in 1862 for Republican candidates, she went on to greater heights, culminating on the evening of January 16, 1864, when she addressed a great gathering in the chamber of the House of Representatives. Among the audience which paid admission (proceeds to go to the National Freedmen's Relief Bureau) were members of Congress and the Supreme Court, and President Lincoln himself.

The last woman's rights convention before the Civil War was held in Albany in February 1861; thereafter all activity for woman's rights ground to a standstill. Unlike the majority of their co-workers, neither Susan Anthony nor Elizabeth Cady Stanton accepted this fact gracefully. They might have been more willing to shelve the issue of woman's rights had they had any sympathy for the early temporizing of the Lincoln administration; but like many other abolitionists they mistrusted Lincoln, and were opposed to any compromise with the slave states.

They went to considerable lengths to uphold their principles. In the first months after Lincoln's election, when secession still hung in the balance, Mrs. Stanton, Miss Anthony, and Lucretia Mott were among a group of speakers which toured New York State under such slogans as "No Compromise With Slave Holders," and "Immediate and Unconditional Emancipation," and they received the roughest treatment of their lives at the hands of aroused mobs in every city where they stopped between Buffalo and Albany. In Syracuse the hall was invaded by a crowd of men brandishing knives and pistols. All ladies were escorted out of the hall except Miss Anthony who stood her ground until the mob surged onto the platform around her, while the chief of police refused to lift a finger in her defense. In Albany Mayor Thacher was of a different stripe. He personally escorted the party of speakers to the hall and sat on the platform with a loaded pistol in his lap throughout the proceedings. Nevertheless he doubted his ability to hold matters in hand during a proposed evening meeting, and asked as a personal favor that it be called off, a request which was gratefully honored.

With the outbreak of war, both Mrs. Stanton and Miss Anthony were at loose ends; they were too accustomed to intellectual and political activity — and leadership — to fit into war relief work. Moreover they continued to be highly critical of the Administration's policy towards slavery, and even the Emancipation Proclamation itself failed to dispel their pessimism. It remained for Henry B. Stanton to point out a way in which they could serve a worthy cause. Charles Sumner had introduced into Congress a constitutional amendment forever banning slavery (the Proclamation had only freed slaves in areas still in rebellion), and in the gloom of early 1863 after a succession of Confederate victories, it seemed uncertain whether the measure could command the needed two-thirds majority in both Houses. In January Stanton wrote to Miss Anthony: "The country was never so badly off as at this moment . . . You have no idea how dark the cloud is which hangs over us. . . . We must not lay the flattering unction to our souls that the proclamation will be of any use if we are beaten, and have a dissolution of the Union. Here then is work for you. Susan, put on your armor and go forth." [9]

As usual, Miss Anthony and Mrs. Stanton buckled on their armor together. After consulting abolitionist leaders, they sent out a call to women all over the country who were known to them through their work on behalf of abolition or for women, calling a meeting of "The Loyal Women of the Nation" in New York on May 14, 1863. The summons bore the unmistakable imprint of its authors:

At this hour the best word and work of every man and woman are imperatively demanded. To man, by common consent, is assigned the forum, the camp and field. What is woman's legitimate work, and how she may best accomplish it, is worthy our earnest counsel with one another. . . . Woman is equally interested and responsible with man in the settlement of this final problem of self-government; therefore let none stand idle spectators now.[10]

Hundreds of women crowded into Dr. Cheever's Church of the Puritans on Union Square, just ten days after the northern armies had suffered another defeat at Chancellorsville. Many of them had next of kin in uniform, and consecration and controversy mingled in the proceedings. Some found fault with any injection of the woman's rights issue into the resolutions under debate, while others held that even abolitionist sentiments were out of place, and that support of President Lincoln's policies was the sole issue.

It took the combined eloquence not only of Miss Anthony and Mrs. Stanton, but of Lucy Stone, Ernestine Rose, and Angelina Grimké Weld, who came out of retirement to raise her voice with all of its old fire, to achieve some measure of agreement.[11] The resolutions adopted pledged the women's support to the government, as long as it continued to wage a war for freedom; they also pledged to collect a million signatures to a petition asking Congress to pass the Thirteenth Amendment. Since many of the women present knew in their own bones what collecting signatures to a petition entailed, the pledge was no idle one. Before the gathering adjourned, it organized the National Woman's Loyal League, with Mrs. Stanton as president and Miss Anthony as secretary. By the end of May a tiny office had been opened in Cooper Union, and the gigantic project was underway.

For fifteen months Mrs. Stanton and Miss Anthony labored. A stream of letters went out from the tiny office, strengthening their ties with women as far away as California, Wisconsin, and Michigan. Some two thousand men, women, and children actually circulated the petitions and the League grew to number five thousand members.[12] When hands were lacking for the work of sorting, counting, and wrapping the petitions, Mrs. Stanton enlisted children, her own sons among them, offering a badge of honor to any boy or girl who brought in one hundred names. Miss Anthony got her first taste of office experience, which was to stand her in good stead in later years. She lived on the sum of $12 a week (made available to her by Wendell Phillips from a fund left by Charles F. Hovey for anti-slavery and woman's rights work), boarding at Mrs. Stanton's, spending ten cents a day for lunch, and traversing on foot the long distances she had to cover around the city.

One million signatures would have meant the names of one-twentieth of the population of the northern states, an impossible goal; yet by the time it disbanded in August 1864 the League had gathered nearly 400,000, no mean figure then, or now.[13] On February 9, 1864, two tall Negroes, symbolic figures, carried enormous bundles made up of petition rolls into the Senate Chamber and placed them on the desk of the Senator from Massachusetts, who rose to speak:

"Mr. President," said Sumner, "I offer a petition which is now lying on the desk before me. It is too bulky for me to take up. I need not add that it is too bulky for any of the pages of this body to carry. . . . It will be perceived that the petition is in rolls. Each roll represents a State. For instance here is New York, with a list of seventeen thousand, seven hundred and six names; Illinois with fifteen thousand, three hundred and twenty, and Massachusetts with eleven thousand, six hundred and fifty-one. . . . This petition is signed by 100,000 men and women, who unite in this unparalleled manner to support its prayer. They are from all parts of the country and every condition of life. They are from the seaboard, fanned by the free airs of the ocean, and from the Mississippi and the prairies of the West, fanned by the free airs that fertilize that extensive region. They are from the families of the educated and the uneducated, rich and poor, of every profession, business and calling in life, representing every sentiment, thought, hope, promise, activity, intelligence which inspires, strengthens and adorns our social system. Here they are, a mighty army, 100,000 strong, without arms or banners, the advanced guard of a yet larger army." [14]

Perhaps one of the most far-reaching effects of the League's work was to accustom the women themselves to the value of organization as a means to accomplish their ends. Their experience in the League, fortified by the many other activities they carried on during the war, acted as a powerful solvent in changing their earlier views that organization could only be constricting and harmful.

Today few Civil War histories refer to Anna Dickinson. Even more infrequent is any mention of the achievements of the National Woman's Loyal League. One is led to suspect that the reason for the oversight is the same in both cases: they throw the accepted historical timetable out. At a time when even the most advanced women were supposedly concerned only with their own betterment or with good works, some of them were active in national politics and playing a not insignificant role.

No organization similar to the Loyal League, or for that matter to the Sanitary Commission, developed among the women of the

Confederacy; neither existing notions of propriety, nor the women's own past experience, nor existing conditions permitted it. A few strong-minded individuals founded their own hospitals, or penetrated into those of the Army, where they sometimes served as superintendents. Many women worked in their local hospital relief societies or sewing circles, rolling the inevitable bandages and collecting delicacies for the wounded. But those in the hospitals were hampered by prejudice, which kept many young and unmarried women out completely, and sharply curtailed the number available as sorely needed nurses.[15]

Many published journals and collections of letters record the privations women underwent for the Confederate cause. It was they who kept the family fed and clothed, and the farm or plantation going, no small tasks under the steadily worsening conditions of four years of blockade. In a few cities, such as Richmond and Mobile, women took part in bread riots in 1863 and '64, caused by high prices, and actual food shortages.[16]

The tremendous economic and social dislocation resulting from the loss of manpower, and the painful changeover from an economy based fundamentally on slavery, would eventually dislodge large numbers of southern white women of all classes from their homes and make them breadwinners, seekers for education, and potential voters.

Chapter VIII

THE INTELLECTUAL PROGRESS OF WOMEN, 1860–1875

Before taking up the struggle which women had to wage in order to win admission to the professions, we should take into account what a profession *is*. According to one modern definition, "professions involve essentially intellectual operations with large individual responsibility; they derive their raw material from science and learning; this material they work up to a practical and definite end; they possess an educationally communicable technique; they tend to self-organization." [1]

Even in their relatively primitive state a hundred years ago, the professions required of a woman wishing to enter one of them that she be creative in more than the biological sense with capacities greater than those involved in "attending to the mechanism of a pudding," as Mrs. Murray put it. The idea that women might possess creative intellectual powers was an explosive one, and accounted for the reaction rescribed by Jane Swisshelm with her usual verve:

It is well known that thousands, nay, millions of women in this country are condemned to the most menial drudgery, such as men would scorn to engage in, and that for one fourth the wages; that thousands of them toil at avocations which public opinion pretends to assign to men. They plough, harrow, reap, dig, make hay, rake, bind grain, thrash, chop wood, milk, churn, do anything that is hard work, physical labor, and who says anything against it? But let one presume to use her mental powers — let her aspire to turn editor, public speaker, doctor, lawyer — take up any profession or avocation which is deemed honorable and requires talent, and O! bring cologne, get a cambric kerchief and feather fan, unloose his corsets and take off his cravat! What a fainting fit Mr. Propriety has taken! Just to think that "one of the deah creathures" — the heavenly angels, should forsake the sphere — woman's sphere — to mix with the wicked strife of this wicked world! [2]

The Declaration of Principles adopted at Seneca Falls in 1848 pointed out the absence of women from such fields as medicine, law, and theology. The fact that women in limited numbers had made a place for themselves in literature and journalism did little to help those who aspired to the learned professions (except insofar as the women writers and editors gave them support); writing and editing involved a training and discipline that was largely individual and self-acquired. Far more difficult was the achieving of professional training and licensing by the state, which involved a social sanction of non-domestic pursuits far-reaching in its significance.

The same year as the Seneca Falls convention, the American Academy of Arts and Sciences elected to membership the astronomer Maria Mitchell, who during the preceding year had discovered the comet which bears her name. Two years later the great naturalist Louis Agassiz sponsored Miss Mitchell's election (by unanimous vote) to the newly formed Association for the Advancement of Science. The earliest woman to be elected to either body, Miss Mitchell appeared at first glance the complete antithesis of the militant reformer. A quiet spoken Quaker, she presided by day over the Athenaeum Library which was one of the riches of Nantucket; at night she was the companion and co-worker of her astronomer father, William Mitchell. Through summer heat and winter storms she swept the skies from the roof of their home, and at the age of twenty-eight discovered her comet, a feat which brought her international friendships and acclaim.[3]

But Maria Mitchell was also unremitting in trying to advance the position of women — in the field of science, as a Vassar College professor, as an advocate of woman suffrage, and as president of the Association for the Advancement of Women, which she helped to found in 1873. She longed to infuse the process of social development, the search for solutions to perplexing social problems, with the adventurous spirit of the true scientist: "I wish something of the physicist's readiness to try experiments would come into our moral reform work. We are all afraid of new experiments, as if the law of growth through failure were not similar in moral, mental and material work." [4]

She was a passionate believer in woman's potential contribution to forward development: "I wish we could give to every woman who has a novel theory dear to her soul for the improvement of the world, a chance to work out her theory in real life" — [5] words that forecast the appearance, among others, of Clara Barton and Jane Addams.

Maria Mitchell was unusually fortunate among women pioneers. The occasional difficulties she met as a woman ahead of her time were in no way characteristic of the harassments visited on other women attempting to achieve professional status. Outstanding among them all, for hardships and for the courage with which she countered them, was Elizabeth Blackwell in medicine.

Like Columbus, she trod in the footsteps of others who had tried before: Mary Gove Nichols, who gave lectures on anatomy to women as early as 1838;[6] Paulina Wright Davis, who tried to use a manikin to illustrate elementary lectures on physiology, only to find some of her auditors dropping their veils, hastening from the room, or even fainting in their seats before they could do so;[7] and Harriot K. Hunt, denied admission to the Harvard Medical School, who practiced without a license for years, although she confined herself largely to what today would be called physiotherapy.[8]

There was nothing simple or single-minded about Miss Blackwell's motives in seeking to become a doctor; she had in fact a repugnance to illness and the practice of medicine. Among her motives were rebellion at a life of social ease and passive study, deep emotional frustration and the influence of a family in which woman's rights were a basic principle (one brother married Lucy Stone and another Antoinette Brown). Lastly she believed that women, because of their role as mothers, could play a special part in improving human health and welfare. Once fairly launched on her endeavor, the challenge of overcoming the tremendous obstacles in her path outweighed all other considerations: "The idea of winning a doctor's degree gradually assumed the aspect of a great moral struggle, and the moral fight possessed immense attraction for me." [9]

Once Elizabeth Blackwell had made up her mind, she spent two years in correspondence with and visits to leading doctors, some of whom helped her while others derided or ignored her.

While she was saving up money for her tuition, she applied to twenty-nine medical schools, before she was able to matriculate. The circumstances of her admission to Geneva College (later absorbed into the University of Syracuse) were hardly such as to cover that institution with glory: the faculty unanimously opposed her admission, but did not want to bear the onus of saying so; they put the decision up to the students (with the proviso that a single negative vote could blackball the applicant) in the happy belief that there could be only one outcome. The students turned the tables on their teachers, also for any but idealistic reasons: they voted unanimously to admit the woman applicant because they saw in her presence endless opportunities for diverting themselves.

There were painful episodes ahead. Miss Blackwell had to insist on her right to attend *all* classes, including those in anatomical dissection. She had to sit through demonstrations she knew no woman had ever witnessed before, her quivering nerves masked in apparent imperturbability, while some students sniggered, or made tentative advances. The townspeople, even the other boarders at the house where she lived, made no effort to conceal their hostility to such a monstrosity as a would-be woman doctor. She was lonely and racked with self-doubt. In the end what carried her through, and won her the unqualified admiration and respect of her fellow-students, was her unassailable dignity and her ardor as a student; she graduated on January 23, 1849, at the head of her class. We catch a glimpse of the contradictions out of which such women were made, in her decision, although she had battled to be allowed to witness the dissection of the reproductive organs, against walking in the Commencement procession because it would be unladylike!

After graduation Elizabeth Blackwell went to Europe for further training, but found the way no easier than it had been at home. When she finally gained admission to La Maternité, the great Paris hospital for training midwives, she contracted ophthalmia and lost one eye, thus putting an end to all her hopes of becoming a surgeon.

Undaunted, she continued her studies in Germany and in England, where she formed a lifelong friendship with Florence Nightingale, who was still struggling unsuccessfully to break the bonds of idleness and futility, but was already bursting with ideas. Dr. Blackwell always gave Miss Nightingale credit for awakening her interest in sanitation and hygiene, in which field she made her most important contributions to medical science.

When she returned to New York in 1851, she encountered a stone wall. She had great difficulty in finding a place to live or an office to rent. No private patients came to her; she could not gain access to the wards of city hospitals or even the chance to work in a dispensary; and she was shunned by her fellow physicians. A mind eager for further growth and for the exchange of ideas was completely cut off from professional companionship or stimulus.

At times the burden seemed too heavy. In 1853 she wrote to a sister, regarding some gossip that had been willfully circulated about her:

These malicious stories are painful to me, for I am woman as well as physician, and both natures are wounded by these falsehoods. Ah, I am glad that it is I, and not another, who have to bear this pioneer work. I understand now why this life has never been lived before. It *is* hard, with no support but a high purpose, to live against every species of social opposition. . . . I *should* like a little fun now and then. Life is altogether too sober.[10]

But Elizabeth Blackwell would not admit defeat. Faced with intellectual as well as economic starvation, she proceeded to create her own opportunities. She gave a course of lectures on bodily hygiene and the physical education of girls; among those who came were a number of Quakers. Impressed with the grave, slender, deep-voiced young woman, her learning and her commonsense, they brought her patients and supporters. For a while she was able to maintain a tiny dispensary of her own in one of the city's worst slums, on East 7th Street near Tompkins Square, where the combined medical and embryonic social service she offered that teeming, insanitary community, was a harbinger of Lillian Wald's nursing service, still fifty years away.

When this project foundered for lack of funds, Dr. Blackwell, far from trimming her sails, shook out fresh canvas. She launched an appeal for $5000 to finance, for one year, a 40-bed hospital; a house was bought at 64 Bleecker Street, and on May 12, 1857, the New York Infirmary, staffed entirely by women, opened its doors.[11] Among those who aided Dr. Blackwell were Emily Howland, who had been a strong supporter of Myrtilla Miner's school, and the novelist Catharine Sedgwick. The medical staff consisted of herself, her sister Emily, who had just completed her own herculean struggles for a medical degree, and Dr. Marie Zakrzewska, a Polish-born midwife who had come to this country in the hope of becoming a doctor. Dr. Blackwell found her earning a precarious livelihood by doing fine embroidery, and helped her to achieve her goal.[12]

The opening of the hospital — and its survival — were also made possible by a small group of men doctors whose support Elizabeth Blackwell had finally won; but there were more doubters than friends.

A host of objections were raised by those whom the early friends of the institution attempted to interest in their effort. They were told that no one would let a house for the purpose; that female doctors would be looked upon with so much suspicion that the police would interfere; that if deaths occurred their death certificates would not be recognized; that they would be resorted to by classes and persons with whom it would be an insult to be called upon to deal with; that without men as resident physicians they would not be able to control the patients; that if any accident occurred, not only the medical profession but the public would blame the trustees for supporting such an undertaking; and, finally, that they would never be able to collect enough money for so unpopular an effort.[13]

Some of these calamities occurred, as well as a few others not anticipated; mobs assaulted the hospital, believing that a patient who had failed to recover had been killed by the "lady doctors." In between their surgical and medical work the women carried the brunt of raising funds to keep the enterprise afloat. Nor was Dr. Blackwell satisfied with just a hospital. Eight months after its opening, she introduced a nurses' training school. The enormity of this step may be gauged by the fact that Florence Nightingale had only just returned to England from the Crimea, where the profession of nursing had actually been born, and did not open a nursing school herself until 1860.[14]

There was more to come. With the outbreak of the Civil War, Dr. Blackwell took part in launching the drive for army nurses, and in selecting and sending them to Miss Dix in Washington. But in 1865 the hospital's trustees, goaded by the Blackwell sisters, applied to the State for a college charter to open a medical school; the step was necessary because the existing reputable schools in New York still barred women students, and there were rumors that an inferior school for women might be opened. The Woman's Infirmary Medical School, which opened in 1868 contained a number of innovations, which had an impact on the field of medicine: "It is in some measure due to the example and success of the school of the Doctors Blackwell that the system of teaching medicine changed from the lecture to the recitation — from theoretical to practical work in laboratories, in hospitals and clinics." [15]

Elizabeth Blackwell was English-born, and always felt a strong pull back to her native land, where the entrance of women into medicine took longer than in the United States.[16] In 1869, secure in the knowledge that others were carrying on the struggle she had initiated, she returned to England.

Fortunately for the women who followed in her footsteps, Dr. Blackwell, although she was not a great physician, made her own distinct contribution to that science, particularly in the area of hygiene. Later women attempting to enter medicine and other professions gained from the fact that she had shown herself, not merely a human being of tough fiber and high courage, but capable of excellence.

In no other profession did women encounter the same degree of resistance as in medicine; it almost seemed as if, once they had worked on the same level with men against death itself, opposition elsewhere became relatively inconsequential. They did, of course, encounter endless deprivations and harassment in their attempts to become lawyers, ministers, scientists, architects, etc.; advancement was more difficult for a woman, the economic problem more acute.

Dr. Anna Howard Shaw, the robust and eloquent minister who became the great orator of the generation which achieved woman suffrage, went through some dark hours as a theological student. Already a licensed preacher and a graduate of Albion College in Michigan, she entered Boston University in 1875 to study for a higher ministerial degree, and found that her main enemy was hunger:

My class at the theological school was composed of forty-two young men and my unworthy self, and before I had been a member of it an hour I realized that women theologians paid heavily for the privilege of being women. The young men of my class who were licensed preachers were given free accommodations in the dormitory, and their board, at a club formed for their assistance, cost each of them only $1.25 a week. For me no such kindly provision was made. I was not allowed a place in the dormitory, but instead was given $2 a week to pay the rent of a room outside. Neither was I admitted to the economical comforts of the club, but fed myself according to my income, a plan which worked admirably when there was an income but left an obvious void when there was not. . . . I lived, therefore, on milk and crackers, and for weeks at a time my hunger was never wholly satisfied.[17]

On one occasion she did a week's revival preaching (which required plenty of physical energy), sustained by nothing more than her faith, and a box of crackers. She had of course expected some small remuneration, and when, after all her efforts and a gratifying crop of converts, she was told the church could afford to pay her nothing, she was saved from actual starvation — and abandoning her vocation — only by a gift of five dollars from a woman whose apparently irredeemable grandson she had converted. Shortly thereafter, through the good offices of the superintendent of the Woman's Foreign Missionary Society, who had found her sitting on a flight of stairs because she was too weak to climb them, she began to receive a weekly stipend which at least enabled her to eat, and to forgo preaching engagements for concentrated study.

Women wishing to become lawyers encountered another type of obstacle. They were obliged to apply to the Supreme Court of their state for a license, and the date when each state finally admitted women to the bar differed widely from one state to another. One of the first to make the attempt was Mrs. Myra Bradwell of Illinois, in 1870. In its denial of her application, the Illinois Supreme Court clearly indicated that the position of women was in a state of flux, and the progress already achieved had induced near panic in some higher judicial bodies:

That God designed the sexes to occupy different spheres of action, and that it belonged to men to make, apply and execute the laws, was regarded as an almost axiomatic truth. . . . We are certainly warranted in saying that when the Legislature gave to this court the power of granting licenses to practice law, it was not with the slightest expectation that this privilege would be extended equally to men and women.

. . . It is not merely an immense innovation in our own usages as a court that we are asked to make. This step, if taken by us, would mean that in the opinion of this tribunal, every civil office in this State may be filled by women — that it is in harmony with the spirit of our Constitution and laws that women should be made governors, judges and sheriffs. This we are not yet prepared to hold.[18]

While bowing in the direction of wider spheres of activity for women, the Court also raised a doubting eyebrow as to whether "to engage in the hot strifes of the Bar, in the presence of the public, and with momentous verdicts the prizes of the struggle, would not tend to destroy the deference and delicacy with which it is the pride of our ruder sex to treat her." [19]

Thereupon the Court tossed back the responsibility of introducing "so important a change in the legal position of one-half of the people" to the legislative bodies of the state and the nation. Mrs. Bradwell carried her appeal to the United States Supreme Court, basing her plea on the Fourteenth Amendment to the Constitution, which forbade the several states to make or enforce any law abridging the privileges or immunities of any citizen, and on Section 2, Article IV, of the Constitution: "The citizens of each state shall be entitled to all privileges and immunities of citizens in the several states."

The Court ruled against Mrs. Bradwell in 1872, on the grounds that citizenship, whether state or federal, did not in itself confer the right to practice law, which a state might deny. The Illinois legislature settled the matter a year later by passing legislation which provided that "no person shall be precluded or debarred from any occupation, profession or employment (except military) on account of sex. (Provided that this act shall not be construed to affect the eligibility of any person to an elective office.)" [20] Other states were already permitting women to practice, and in 1879 the United States Supreme Court admitted Belva Lockwood as the first woman lawyer entitled to practice at its bar.

Opportunities for women to teach advanced students while carrying on research themselves were largely limited, then as now, to women's and co-educational institutions. Having won the battle, albeit with difficulty, to go to college, they still encountered the same obstacles to more advanced training. (When M. Carey Thomas went abroad in 1879, to work for and win her doctorate in

Germany, her mother wrote to her that family friends never mentioned her name, as she was felt to be a disgrace to her kin.)[21] The entire community considered plans for research and teaching as tantamount to relinquishing any hope of, or interest in, marriage; nor was there much possibility of advancing to the higher academic posts or being taken seriously as scholars and investigators.

Because it took so long for women to be admitted on a basis of equality to existing professional organizations, they were compelled to establish their own, in medicine, law, and other fields. These organizations continue to exist today as evidence that professional women still encounter prejudice and special difficulties in carrying on the work of their choice.[22]

By 1865 the higher education of women had made little progress except in the Middle West. In 1852 Antioch joined Oberlin as a coeducational college; the latter had granted 79 women the degree of Bachelor of Arts, while 290 had passed its "literary course," which was hardly more than seminary level.[23] Iowa in 1858 was the first state university to accept women, and Wisconsin opened a special normal school training course to them in 1863. A step with far-reaching consequences had been taken one year earlier with the passage by Congress of the Morrill Land-Grant Act, which gave each "loyal" state 30,000 acres of public domain for every senator and representative in Congress, for the endowment of so-called agricultural and mechanical colleges. In actual practice such funds were also available to state institutions which, in addition to such specialized training, offered a liberal arts degree. More and more of these were opened to women, mainly in the Middle West, but also in the East, where Cornell was founded in 1868 (with a special branch for women, Sage College, in 1874). New educational opportunities were thus available to a whole generation of women; time would show the significance of Carrie Chapman Catt's admission to Iowa State College in 1877 and of M. Cary Thomas to Sage College in the same year, followed a year later by Florence Kelley.

Nevertheless such victories, even in the West where many of the traditional barriers did not exist, were not automatic. The story of the admission of women to the University of Michigan is an instance. Here the women's efforts were sparked by Miss Sarah Burger, who as a girl of sixteen had been present at a woman's rights convention held in Cleveland in 1853, where she had heard such speakers as Ernestine Rose, Lucretia Mott, Lucy Stone, and Frances Dana Gage — renewed evidence, if such were needed, of the seminal role played by these gatherings. Three years later Sarah Burger began to prepare herself for application to the University of Michigan; moreover, by corresponding with a number of schools, she enlisted eleven other young women in the attempt with her.

They applied to the Board of Regents in July 1858; although they had given that body due notice of their intention, the Regents turned down the application on the grounds that more time was needed for so momentous a decision! In September the girls renewed their application, again without success, although they did begin to attend a few lectures on an informal basis. Another group made application in June 1859 without success. By fall, public resentment had been sufficiently aroused to replace some of the more conservative Regents by men with a more liberal viewpoint. Yet the first woman student did not enter Michigan until February 1870. In the autumn of that year eleven women enrolled in the Literary Department, three in the Department of Pharmacy, eighteen in the Department of Medicine, and two in the Department of Law! [24] In the same year the Universities of Illinois and Ohio State also withdrew restrictions against women students.

In the East progress took a somewhat different course. A few institutions did adopt coeducation: little St. Lawrence University graduated its first woman student in 1866; Boston University became coeducational in 1869; Cornell in 1874; a few coeducational institutions were founded, such as Swarthmore in 1869. But the main impetus came from carrying Mary Lyon's idea of an endowed institution for girls beyond the seminary level at which Mount Holyoke had remained, to that of the best existing institution for men.

It should be borne in mind that even the best men's colleges at that time were a far cry from what they are today. Very few of the 350 institutions claiming the title of college in 1870 would be able to do so now, including the "Big Three":

Harvard was a poverty-stricken and struggling college . . . Many of its courses were on the level of a present-day high school. . . . Yale's facilities were even more wretchedly insufficient. . . . Its curriculum was antiquated. . . . Princeton followed a course of study almost identical with that pursued by undergraduates when Madison was in the White House. . . . The colleges were used to the spectacle of professors filling several or even half a dozen chairs at once. Thus Yale had one heroic savant expounding physics, astronomy, meteorology and mechanics, while at Columbia an intellectual Hercules dealt with moral and mental philosophy, English literature, history, political economy, and logic.[25]

However inadequate the training offered under such conditions, it was still better than any available to women in the East, even though Elmira "College," opened in 1855, attempted to bridge the gap. The first real step toward closing it came in 1865 with the opening of Vassar College, which also re-emphasized the fact that the differential existed not only at the collegiate level, but went back into the realm of preparatory education.[26]

The college was chartered by the state of New York at Poughkeepsie in the Hudson River valley in 1861. Its founder, Matthew Vassar, was a leading citizen of the town who had made his fortune as a brewer, banker, and real-estate owner. He owed his interest in the education of girls to his niece, Lydia Booth (whose seminary for young ladies he supported), and even more to Dr. Milo P. Jewett, who had conducted a seminary in Alabama for many years, and who deserves a major share of the credit in guiding Mr. Vassar toward the concept of Vassar College.

Its original name was "Vassar Female College," and Mrs. Sarah Josepha Hale, the energetic editor of *Godey's Lady's Book,* is credited with finally convincing the founder that such an appellation was derogatory — who ever thought of qualifying a "male" college in such a manner? The offending adjective was dropped. Vassar had to await the end of the Civil War to open. When it did so, it was with a building which far outdistanced any yet constructed for women students; it also boasted a "museum" and "art gallery," neither of the same caliber as the astronomical observatory available to Maria Mitchell, who was easily the most distinguished member of the teaching staff. How Mary Lyon, who had been grateful for pennies and quarters from New England farmers, would have rejoiced at the opening day, when a faculty of thirty (eight of them men) greeted a student body of 300 girls.

Yet financially Vassar was in a more precarious position than even Mount Holyoke had been at the start. The erection of so expensive a building had seriously depleted Mr. Vassar's endowment of $400,000; in order to remain solvent, the building must be kept filled. Nevertheless it was clear almost at once that few among the early students were prepared for anything like a collegiate standard of instruction. The only solution therefore was "to be patient and create a constituency, and themselves do the preparatory work which had not been done in the schools of the country." [27] For years — until 1888 — the Preparatory Department at Vassar was responsible for a large proportion of its registration and absorbed part of the energies of its faculty to the detriment, an increasing body of alumnae felt, of its academic standing.

Whatever its shortcomings, Vassar was an important pioneer and made possible the next step, which took place with the opening of two more women's colleges in Massachusetts in 1875. In some respects the beginnings of Wellesley duplicated those of Vassar.[28] It was the product of the generosity and vision of one man — a wealthy Boston lawyer, Henry Fowle Durant, who turned first to evangelism and then to education, after the death of a dearly loved son. The building and grounds surpassed even those at Vassar — they cost $1,000,000 — and again there was the problem that, since most of the endowment had gone into building, the college must be kept filled from the beginning with 300 students in order to maintain itself. This was the more difficult, even though preparatory school work was improving, because Wellesley set entrance standards very nearly the equivalent of those of Harvard (with the exception, for the first few years, of Greek). Once again the answer was a Preparatory Department, which the college was able to discontinue in 1881.

The Vassar faculty had always included both men and women, but Maria Mitchell felt that the male president and the all-male Board of Trustees preferred men for the higher academic posts, resisted equalizing the salaries of men and women on the same academic level, and were reluctant to appoint women to faculty committees.[29] Wellesley had women presidents from the beginning, following the early policy of Mount Holyoke (although to all intents and purposes Mr. Durant *was* the president in his life-time), and during its first year the Wellesley faculty was composed entirely of women. Durant held that there was no other way open to them to achieve high academic rank, and that when the women he wished to appoint lacked the needed experience and training, he would give them the opportunity to get both. He kept his word; however, within a year of its opening, Wellesley also began to appoint men to its faculty.

Smith was the first college for women to be endowed by a woman. No greater contrast could be imagined than that between Mary Lyon's single-minded, life-long intensity of purpose, and the shy, deaf, doubt-ridden Sophia Smith of Hatfield, Massachu-setts, who at sixty-eight inherited a fortune in whose accumula-tion she had played no part, and who sought long and anxiously for guidance as to its disposition. Both women shared a deep religious feeling, but what was the bread and breath of life to Miss Lyon — "concern for the adult female youth in the common walks of life" — had to be nurtured in Miss Smith over long years by her friend and pastor, John M. Greene.

Himself so strongly impressed with the importance of higher education for women that he persuaded his own fiancée to com-plete her course at Mount Holyoke before their marriage, he succeeded in instilling his wealthy parishioner with his beliefs. She set aside the larger portion of her fortune to found a girls' college, which she hoped would be "a perennial blessing to the country and the world."

One day later than Wellesley, Smith College opened its doors in Northampton, Massachusetts, but at the opening exercises the spacious auditorium, capable of seating four hundred, held only fourteen girls and a handful of teachers; in the words of President Seelye, "it seemed a long time off before there would be enough students and teachers to fill it." [30] For Smith was the first of the women's colleges to insist, from the beginning, on the same en-trance requirements as the best men's colleges, including Greek and mathematics. That it was able to do so and to forgo the preparatory departments resorted to by Wellesley and Vassar was due not only to the founder's high standards, but also to the stipulation in her will that half the endowment (originally some $350,000) be maintained in a general fund, "the interest of which alone shall be used forever for furnishing teachers, library and apparatus." Such farsightedness enabled the college to grow steadily, and to add, in conformity with Miss Smith's expressed wish,

such other studies as coming times may develop or demand for the education of women and the progress of the race. I would have the education suited to the mental and physical wants of women. It is not my design to render my sex any the less Feminine, but to develop as fully as may be the powers of womanhood, and furnish women with the means of usefulness, happiness and honor, now witheld from them.[31]

The founders of these earliest women's colleges had this in common with some suffragists: they believed higher education would be the panacea to remedy all evils, just as some suffragists thought that giving woman the vote would open the way to a new golden age (an illusion cherished by reformers in all ages). Sophia Smith in her will put her dream into words: "It is my belief that by the higher and more thorough Christian education of women, what are called their 'wrongs' will be redressed, their wages adjusted, their weight of influence in reforming the evils of society will be greatly increased, as teachers, as writers, as mothers, as members of society, their power for good will be incalculably enlarged." [32]

That the reality fell short, in Sophia Smith's century as in our own, of her hopes, does not detract in the least from her stature; despite her physical isolation and her intellectual limitations, of whom no one was more conscious than she was herself, Miss Smith was in the mainstream of progress.

Tremendous obstacles faced the Negroes emerging from bondage. They were free — in a predominantly white society which regarded them as enemies, except as they were essential to it as low-paid, unskilled labor. They were for the most part illiterate, and still considered incapable of rising above the status of slaves. They needed work, but lacked training for any but the same agricultural and domestic tasks they had pursued before emancipation. The men had political freedom, to the extent that it could be explicitly stated in a constitutional amendment, but they were not allowed to exercise it except during the turbulent Reconstruction era.

The handicaps confronting Negro women were even greater; no group ever pulled itself up further by its own bootstraps. The dominant pattern set by white society decreed that opportunity should go first of all to the man or boy. Many a male Negro received education or a start in a small business through the laborious efforts of the woman in the household over the washtub or ironing board:

The mothers are the levers which move in education. The men talk about it, especially about election time, if they want an office for self or their candidate, but the women work most for it. They labor in many ways to support the family while the children attend school. They make great sacrifices to spare their own children during school hours. . . . In some cases the colored woman is the mainstay of the family, and when work fails the men in large cities, the money which the wife can obtain by washing, ironing and other services, often keeps pauperism at bay.[33]

Fortunately the schools established for Negro children were open to girls as well as boys. More boys attended, and they stayed longer, but some girls persevered despite enormous difficulties. A few struggled through secondary or normal school; a mere handful got through college.

Of these, the greater number attended predominantly Negro institutions: Howard, Wilberforce, and Atlanta. Mrs. Anna J. Cooper, who taught Latin in the colored schools of the District of Columbia, looking for reasons why only thirty Negro women had received college degrees by 1890, laid the blame principally on the men of her race:

While our men seem thoroughly abreast of the times on every other subject, when they strike the woman question they drop back into 16th century logic . . . I fear the majority of colored men do not yet think it worthwhile that women aspire to higher education. . . . A self-supporting young girl has to struggle on by teaching in the summer and working after school hours to keep up with her board bill, and actually to fight her way against positive discouragement to higher education. . . . Let money be raised and scholarships be founded in our colleges and universities for self-supporting, worthy young women.[34]

Yet the small number of Negro women college graduates cannot be explained only by factors within the Negro community, North or South, or even by the differential in secondary schooling

available to white and colored students. There was a growing
Negro population, in the North and West, with access to better
schools than in the South; yet the number of Negro graduates
from the major women's colleges was still infinitesimal at the time
of a study made under the direction of Atlanta University in 1900,
and not much better when a second one was made ten years later.[35]
Before 1899 Mount Holyoke had graduated one Negro student,
Radcliffe and Wellesley two each, and Vassar one (the latter not
being known as colored while she was in college); Oberlin (which
was a much older institution) had graduated fifty-five. In 1910,
Smith and Radcliffe reported four Negro graduates each, Mount
Holyoke two, Wellesley three, Vassar still only one, and Bryn
Mawr, Mills (in California) and Barnard (in New York City)
none. Clearly no special efforts were being made to attract or assist
the gifted Negro student who might lack preparation in some
requisite subject, or who could not afford the relatively high cost
of such institutions, or who perhaps feared social isolation.[36]

A very few Negro women were able to enter the professions at
an early date. Miss Charlotte E. Ray, daughter of the New York
abolitionist Charles B. Ray, graduated from Howard University
Law School in 1872, and appears to have been the first Negro
woman qualified to practice law in the United States.[37] Another
early lawyer was Mary Ann Shadd, later Mrs. Cary, who, after
serving as teacher and principal in the District of Columbia
colored schools after the war, entered Howard University Law
School at the age of sixty, graduated in 1883, and practiced law
until her death ten years later.[38]

Among the earliest Negro women to enter the field of medicine
was Caroline V. Still, daughter of two famous "agents" on the
Underground Railroad, William and Letitia Still of Philadelphia.[39] Dr. Still interned at the New England Hospital for
Women and Children which had been founded by Elizabeth
Blackwell's distinguished co-worker, Dr. Marie Zakrzewska; it
was also from the nursing school of this institution that the first
Negro trained nurse, Mary Elizabeth Mahoney, graduated in
1879.[40]

The Negro women who achieved such training, especially
those who spent their lives in the South teaching others of their
race, carried on seminal work of heroic proportions. As teachers

and school principals, nurses and doctors, founders and directors of normal schools, of rural education institutes and health centers, and of teachers' associations and women's clubs, they served as life-giving elements to a group of human beings hitherto denied knowledge or the opportunity to put it to use.

Chapter IX

WOMEN IN THE TRADE UNIONS,
1860–1875

Industrial development in the northern states, already under way before the Civil War, was tremendously accelerated by the four-year conflict. Equipping and maintaining large armies, in addition to steadily increasing westward expansion, brought about large-scale capital growth, which was further stimulated by the outcome of the war — the victory of free over slave labor. The maturing of the American business and industrial giant had begun.

The struggling young labor movement, which had all but succumbed to the recession and panic of 1857, stirred to renewed life, its rebirth the outcome of high wartime prices, bitter struggles over wages, and the introduction of labor-saving machinery. In one industry after another, nationally organized unions came into existence for the first time: by 1870 there were thirty-two: iron molders, railway workers, miners, mechanics, ship caulkers, construction workers of all kinds, cigarmakers, printers, etc.

Women factory workers were increasing steadily in numbers. The 225,922 shown in the 1850 census rose to 270,987 by 1860 and to 323,370 by 1870.[1] Thousands of women were forced into the labor market when their menfolk joined the Federal armies, came back crippled, or died in action. Most of them, with no other skills to fall back on, glutted the sewing trades, where their situation was desperate. Early in 1865 a group of sewing women in Cincinnati petitioned President Lincoln to end the system of subcontracting for army uniforms since it reduced their earnings below the level of subsistence. Protesting their patriotism and their wish to do the work needed by the army, they pointed out that we are unable to sustain life for the price offered by contractors, who fatten on their contracts by grinding immense profits out of the labor of their operatives. As an example, these contractors are paid one dollar and seventy-five cents per dozen for making gray woolen shirts, and they require us to make them for one dollar per dozen. . . . The manufacture of pants, blouses, coats, drawers, tents, tarpaulins, etc., exhibits the same irregularity and injustice to the operative.[2]

Women in such dire straits were available to employers looking for cheap labor and constituted a threat, in any trade they entered, to the men's attempts to better their standards by organizing. The first two national unions to admit women to membership because so many of them were entering their industries were the cigarmakers in 1867, and the printers in 1869. Similarly, the increase of women in various trades lay behind the concern for them shown by the National Labor Union, a short-lived, loosely knit federation of national unions led by William Sylvis. Sylvis was president of the Ironmolders Union, a man of radical sympathies who gave support to the woman's rights movement and who saw that in the last analysis the interests of men and women workers were indivisible. At its first convention in 1866, the National Labor Union resolved that

we pledge our individual and undivided support to the sewing women and daughters of toil in this land, and would solicit their hearty cooperation, knowing, as we do, that no class of industry is so much in need of having their condition ameliorated as the factory operatives, sewing women, etc., of this country.[3]

The organization of working women at this time took several forms. One was that of the bona fide trade union, either an independent group limited to the women in a particular industry, or part of an existing union to which women were admitted. Another form was the Working Woman's Association which took in any and all women who worked for their livelihood. A third was the Protective Association, which also took in women regardless of trade or occupation, but which confined itself to such welfare problems as legal aid or finding reputable employment.

Protective Associations of women workers arose in many cities, such as Chicago, St. Louis, Indianapolis, Boston, Philadelphia, and New York, out of the suffering of the underpaid women during the war, many of them on the verge of starvation. In New York during the winter of 1863–1864, a nameless mechanic suggested to Moses S. Beach, editor of the *New York Sun,* the idea of hiring a hall and advertising a meeting for such women in the pages of his newspaper. They came by the hundreds, but with little idea of how to proceed:

The hall was filled — *full* — with eager, trembling women, but they knew not what to do or how to act, and soon the scene was one of supreme confusion. At this juncture a motherly woman approached the gentlemen, and begged their interference. In response to her earnest pleading a dry goods merchant — afterward a member of Congress — consented to preside, and under his direction, the business of the evening was discussed. Then a committee was appointed, who were to consult with a sub-committee of gentlemen, and devise suitable measures of relief, to be reported at a subsequent meeting. For very many hours, at a hotel in the Bowery, this joint committee debated the subject; examining and cross-examining many working women, who appeared for the purpose. But no conclusion appeared possible until one present remarked that the only remediable difficulty suggested was that of securing payment for work when complete. At this point the women present exclaimed, as with a single voice, *"Oh, if we could always get paid for our work, we could get along."* [4]

We can only surmise whether the purpose of the "gentlemen" present at this gathering was to see to it that the ladies did not get out of hand, and that they confined themselves to "remediable difficulties," that is, grievances an employer considered legitimate. In any case the outcome was a form of Legal Aid Society which in its near half-century of existence, aided by some of the leading lights of the New York Bar, did help the women collect some of the meager sums due them. It is also entirely possible that even without the intervention of merchants and businessmen anxious to deflect organization among needy women into non-militant channels, the women would not have accomplished any more lasting results. Certainly they were no more successful (with one exception) under the leadership of Susan B. Anthony, who, during the two years she was publishing her own weekly newspaper, *The Revolution,* devoted considerable time and effort to helping such women organize, especially during the latter part of 1868.

Typical of the items it often carried was the following: "A meeting of ladies was held on September 17 at noon, in the offices of *The Revolution* newspaper, 37 Park Row, for the purpose of organizing an association of working-women, which might act for the interests of its members, in the same manner as the associations of workingmen now regulate the wages, etc., of those belonging to them." [5]

The gathering, which formed a Working Women's Association, represented a cross-section of the currents of thought then emerging among women. There was Mrs. Stanton, convinced that women could never engage in the pursuits of their choice unless they won the ballot, urging the young organization to take a position endorsing woman suffrage. Also present were several women engaged in the novel occupation of setting type, among them Miss Augusta Lewis ("a brunette lady with pleasing dark eyes") who knew her fellow typographers well enough to declare that identifying the organization with woman suffrage would also label it in their minds with "short hair, bloomers and other vagaries"; it would be better to call the women typesetters together for "business purposes" first, and educate them on the suffrage question later. Miss Lewis had her way on this point. However she herself had illusions which she had to unlearn in the course of the next two years. One of them was the belief that the chief obstacle to women's being paid as much as men for the same amount of work was their failure to learn their craft or trade as thoroughly as the men did, because they expected to get married. Miss Lewis was also certain, at the start, that men would be open to conviction on the matter of equal pay, "if it were put to them properly." [6] She was to learn otherwise.

Miss Lewis was an educated woman who had written newspaper articles and who lived up to her own principles by mastering the art of typesetting so well that she was known for her ability to set the entire text of *Rip Van Winkle* (consisting of 24,993 ems of solid agate type) in six and a half hours.[7] When Women's Typographical Union No. 1 sprouted from the Working Women's Association, Miss Lewis became its president. The new union received encouraging support from the established men's printing union in New York, Local No. 6. At its very first meeting the corresponding secretary of Local No. 6 read a letter in which the latter pledged itself to

aid you all we can in your movement, knowing that your interests are identical with our own. We have agreed to hire a hall for your meetings, furnish you with books, stationery, etc. and assume all other expenses which it may be necessary for you to incur in getting your Association into working order, and to continue to do so until your Union shall be in a condition to support itself.[8]

Never before had working women received such assurances and encouragement. No wonder Miss Anthony, who was present to see her fledglings get underway, took fire and urged them on to greater efforts:

Girls, you must take this matter to heart seriously now, for you have established a union, and for the first time in woman's history in the United States, you are placed, and by your own efforts, on a level with men, as far as possible, to obtain wages for your labor. I need not say you have taken a great, a momentous step forward in the path to success. Keep at it now, girls, and you will achieve full and plenteous success.[9]

For a time matters looked promising. In June 1869 at the national union's convention in Albany, the delegation of Local No. 6 presented a petition from Women's Local No. 1 applying for a charter. Miss Lewis and the local's treasurer, Eva B. Howard, attended all sessions of the convention, working hard for the recognition of their organization, and Miss Lewis addressed the convention. The charter was granted after the national president pointed out that the women had certainly earned it:

Though most liberal inducements were offered to women compositors to take the places of men on strike, not a single member of the women's union could be induced to do so. Offers have been made to the president of their organization to furnish women compositors to other cities for the purpose of reducing the wages of men, and in every instance have been declined.[10]

When Augusta Lewis appeared at the convention of 1870 as a delegate from Women's Local No. 1, she received the distinction of being elected corresponding secretary of the national union for the ensuing year. This post was no sinecure: of greater importance than the honor paid to her was the fact that she filled it with singular ability. [11] Her report to the union's 1871 convention, presenting a comprehensive picture of the printing industry, including employment conditions and wage scales in a dozen cities, is the first such document to emanate from a woman in American labor history. Her information was amassed through correspondence with men who were unaccustomed, in that day and age, to dealing with a woman in such a capacity; that Miss Lewis was able to elicit their cooperation is in itself a tribute. Said the President in his annual report to the convention:

The distrust of her abilities expressed by Miss Lewis upon accepting the position of corresponding secretary has not been sustained by the facts. She has displayed industry, zeal and intelligence in the position rarely met with. . . . The details of the state of the trade in the various localities in our jurisdiction are so fully and clearly set forth by her, that I have only to refer you for information on that head to her very comprehensive report.[12]

Nor did the corresponding secretary overlook in her work the principal reason which had led her to overcome her hesitations and accept the post: "to add a link to the chain that would span the chasm that has heretofore divided the interests of the male and female printers." [13] Through personal interviews and by correspondence, Miss Lewis tried to widen the opportunities for women printers already in the union, and to help others to organize. Unfortunately the hopes with which she herself had joined the union, that the men in the trade might see the reasonableness of women's demands for equal pay, and their common interest in such a goal, were not realized. The objectivity of her report to the convention of 1871 does not obscure its bitterness:

We refuse to take the men's situations when they are on strike, and when there is no strike if we ask for work in union offices we are told by union foremen "that there are no conveniences for us." We are ostracized in many offices because we are members of the union, and although the principle is right, disadvantages are so many that we cannot much longer hold together. . . . It is the general opinion of female compositors that they are more justly treated by what is termed "rat" foremen, printers and employers than they are by union men.[14]

In 1871 Augusta Lewis married Alexander Troup, who had been the union's secretary-treasurer and of great assistance to the women printers. The couple moved to Hartford, where Troup launched a newspaper, and his wife disappeared from the labor scene. Without her, the tiny Woman's Local No. 1, which numbered forty members at its peak, encountered heavy going for the reasons so cogently stated by Miss Lewis. By 1874 it had shrunk to some twenty-eight hardy souls, and in 1878 it went out of existence;

the national union thereafter adopted the policy of chartering no further women's locals but of admitting women to membership on the same basis as men, which corresponded to the practice of the Cigarmakers Union.

Such a policy had pronounced disadvantages. Women remained a minority, and an unwelcome one, in whatever trades and organizations they were admitted to. They had no opportunity to develop their own leaders, or to focus attention on their particular problems, as Miss Lewis had been able to do by virtue of her position as a convention delegate and union official.

There was no solution possible yet for the problem. Attempts by the women to organize among themselves always resulted in failure, even though they sometimes received sporadic assistance from men's unions. The repeated efforts to form unions made by women capmakers, collar and laundry workers, tailoresses, textile operatives, shoebinders and stitchers, umbrella sewers and salesladies, through the Civil War and down to 1873, are evidence not so much of optimism as of the desperation of their plight.[15]

The women's union which became best known throughout the labor movement during its brief history was that of the collar makers and laundry workers of Troy, New York, just across the Hudson River from Albany, and the home of Emma Willard's famous seminary. It is unlikely that any of the collar workers enjoyed the benefits of this institution, although the making of separate collars for men's shirts was first carried on in the homes of respectably comfortable ladies who wished to earn some pin money.[16] But the making and laundering of collars became a major industry in Troy. Mrs. Hannah Lord Montagu grew weary of washing and ironing a whole shirt every day because the neck band had become soiled, and made the first detachable collars, and her husband Orlando, a retired Methodist minister, built a profitable business out of his wife's idea.[17]

We first learn of the women in the laundries, where they worked long hours in temperatures near one hundred degrees "while the implements with which they work are throwing out an equal amount of heat with increasing intensity." [18] In 1863 they banded together, went on strike, and won a wage increase. Three years later their organization was sufficiently substantial to donate the phenomenal sum of $1,000 to aid the locked-out and striking Iron Molders Union, a gesture which neither the union nor its leader, William Sylvis, forgot. In 1868 they won further increases in pay, and their leader, Kate Mullaney, was chosen by Sylvis as assistant secretary of the National Labor Union.

Beyond this fact, and that she was known to Susan Anthony and other outstanding women of the day, we know nothing of what must have been a dynamic and indomitable woman beside the bare facts of the rise of the Laundryworkers Union and its eventual defeat. In the spring of 1869 the collar ironers demanded a raise of one-half, one, one-and-a-half, and two cents per dozen pieces "according to the size of the article"; when their demand was refused they went out on strike again, and the starchers, although making no wage demands themselves, went out with their sister unionists, to the number of 430 in all. The *Troy Whig,* usually liberal in tone and in its support of unions, termed it an "unfortunate and ill-timed strike," but support flowed in from a long list of unions in printing, the building trades, iron work, shoemaking, etc., the individual sums ranging from $25 to $250; in one week alone $558 was received.[19]

A mass meeting on the steps of the town court house was addressed by prominent union men; plans were announced for a cooperative laundry which hoped to take the patronage of working people away from the established firms. A picnic held on July 19 was highly successful — the conservative *Troy Times* called it "a monstrous affair" and the *Whig* reported that the streets of neighboring villages were deserted because everyone had gone to the picnic;[20] it netted the strikers $1,200.

Yet on June 23 another large meeting which was to have been addressed by Richard Trevellick, a national labor leader, was canceled without explanation. Just one week later on July 31 a meeting of the union voted not merely for its members to return to work, but to dissolve the organization.

The most logical explanation for the debacle lies in the sudden death of William Sylvis after a brief illness, which threw the entire labor movement into near panic, and diverted further aid from the collar workers. The employers were not slow to press their unexpected advantage. On July 30, the day before the union meeting, the *Troy Times* ran four prominently displayed advertisements of a new *paper* collar, developed "for the accommodation of the growing demand among our citizens for this celebrated goods," a threat to the jobs of the laundry workers. The employers also met to confer on a common policy of re-employing the "old hands," many of whom were offered positions in a large new plant.[21] These onslaughts, coupled with the demoralization resulting from Sylvis' death, had the desired results. The union vanished overnight, and the cooperative laundry it had launched lasted only a few weeks longer.

Another brief chapter in the organization of women workers was written in Lynn, Massachusetts, long the center of the shoe industry. Like Troy, Lynn had not yet been reached by recent waves of immigrant labor; the women who stitched shoe tops, which they had previously done in their own homes but did now in factories, were largely of Irish-Scotch and English extraction but Americans for several generations. Out of their discontent over low pay and long hours developed a short-lived but unique trade union which spread to other growing centers of shoe manufacturing, and became a national organization — the Daughters of St. Crispin, patterned on the union of men shoe workers, the Knights of St. Crispin, and occasionally aided by it.

Like all these earlier women's organizations (with the exception of the Lowell textile operatives) they left no records, and what is known of their history is scattered in the labor press of the period. The founding convention was held on July 28, 1869 (just at the time the Troy collar workers union collapsed), and two Lynn women — Miss Carrie Wilson and Miss Abbie Jacques — were elected president and secretary, respectively. Within a few months the organization had grown to twenty-four lodges, fourteen in Massachusetts, the others scattered in Maine, New York, New Hampshire, Pennsylvania, Ohio, Illinois, Wisconsin, and California.[22]

Annual conventions were held until 1872, and two officers were present as delegates at the 1870 convention of the National Labor Union. That year the Daughters of St. Crispin passed a resolution demanding "the same rate of compensation for equal skill displayed, or the same hours of toil, as is paid other laborers in the same branches of business; and we regard a denial of this right by anyone as a usurpation and a fraud." Then, perhaps feeling that such strong language might cost them the support of opponents of equal rights for women, they added a conciliatory note: "Resolved, that we assure our fellow-citizens that we only desire to so elevate and improve our condition as to better fit us for the discharge of those high social and moral duties which devolve upon every true woman." [23]

In 1872 the shoe manufacturers of Lynn attempted to cut wages and compel every worker to sign a pledge that she would give two weeks' notice before leaving her position, or else forfeit five dollars of her pay. A meeting of nine hundred women voted unanimously not to comply with such a demand and adopted a set of resolutions which deserve quotation in full:

We, the Workingwomen, in convention assembled, do accept the following resolutions, as an earnest expression of our sentiments;

Whereas, we have long been sensible of the need of protecting our rights and privileges as free-born women, and are determined to defend them and our interests as workingwomen, to the fullest extent of our ability; therefore, be it

Resolved, That we, the workingwomen of Lynn, known as Upper Fitters and Finishers of Boots and Shoes, do enter a most solemn protest against any reduction of wages, on any pretext whatever; and that we will not submit to any rules that do not equally affect our employers.

Resolved, that we feel grateful to the shoemakers of Lynn for their interest and determination to stand by us in our time of need.

Resolved, that we, the free women of Lynn, will submit to no rule or set of rules that tend to degrade and enslave us.

Resolved, That we will accept no terms whatever, either with regard to a reduction of prices, notices to quit, or forfeiture of wages. That while we utterly ignore the spirit of selfishness and illiberality which prompted the late action of our would-be oppressors, we will not hesitate to resist, in a proper manner, the unjust encroachments upon our rights.

Resolved, that a copy of these resolutions be given to every one of the committee, to be by them presented to each girl in every shop, and her signature thereon obtained; and should anyone of the employees of the shop be reduced in her wages, or ill-treated, we will desist from our work until she has obtained her rights.

Resolved, that a copy of the above be inserted in the Lynn papers, and a large surplus number be provided for distribution among the girls.[24]

Obviously, these women knew how to handle themselves: what to expect in the way of reprisals, how to protect themselves through united action, the mechanics of using the press, and of distributing their resolution in order to gain support in the community. They were determined as well as experienced, and as a result the employers backed down — neither the wage cut nor the dismissal notice went through at that time.

Although there is no mention of the Daughters of St. Crispin as the organization through which the women functioned on this occasion, at least some of them must have been members, for although the order declined rapidly after its brief heyday, traces of it remained longest in Lynn, up to 1876. But like many other unions, it could not weather the prolonged panic and depression, touched off by the bankruptcy of the banking firm of Jay Cooke & Company in September of 1873, which lasted until 1878.

The next surge of organization among women workers did not come until the emergence of the Knights of Labor in the 1880's. Many of the women who entered its ranks had taken part in the short-lived organizations of the '60's and '70's, but organization of women workers lacks the continuity to be found among the men. Individual women appear briefly, then vanish; a promising start in one industry or one town sputters out. Unskilled and poorly paid, the women leave one trade for another that seems more promising — or they leave work to marry and bear children. There is no money even for dues, let alone strike-funds, or the mechanics of maintaining an organization (such as Local No. 6 offered the young local of women typesetters). Women of means, with contacts and influence, such as those who kept the nascent suffrage movement alive for decades, had not yet become interested in the problems of working women, or seen the relationship between their goals; they did not do so, on any appreciable scale, until the turn of the century.

But the grievances remained — low, unequal wages, the long hours, the indignities inflicted by foremen and employers — and the unremitting, sporadic, unsuccessful attempts to organize against them also continued. However fugitive they might appear, they showed the way to those who came after, and who succeeded in building more enduringly.

Chapter X

THE EMERGENCE OF A SUFFRAGE
MOVEMENT

The emancipation of the slaves had brought to the fore the question of enlarging the electorate. If the Negro was free and a citizen, he was entitled to the suffrage rights of a citizen (though it quickly became apparent that he would not be able to exercise them in the South without special guarantees). The woman leaders saw this moment as one which might bring women the vote as well.

No longer was Mrs. Stanton alone in believing that they had the same inherent right to vote as men. Seventeen years, from 1848 to 1865, had brought vast changes, due to the many woman's rights conventions, the speechmaking and the articles and pamphlets, as well as to their contributions to the war effort in the North, and to the growing numbers of wage earners among them. Mrs. Stanton had had trouble in rallying support for her epochal resolution at the Seneca Falls Convention favoring women's efforts to win the franchise; now there were many others who shared her and Miss Anthony's convictions (although as it turned out there were not as many as both women had supposed).

The woman's rights leaders who had put away their cause for the duration of the Civil War believed that, when peace came, a grateful country would reward them, spurred on by the Republican party. They were still so inexperienced in politics that they failed to estimate the extent and complexity of the forces arrayed against them. While they were used to the lamentations of conservatives who foresaw the downfall of home, church, and state if women should get the vote, they were totally unprepared for the opposition of the Republican politicians. The latter had their eyes fixed on a windfall of 2,000,000 potential male Negro voters in the South, which they had no intention of jeopardizing by stirring up an unnecessary tempest over woman suffrage. Nor did the women reckon on desertion of their cause by the abolitionists, long their staunch allies, but now convinced that this was "the Negro's hour" and that nothing must be allowed to interfere with it.

The first inkling of what was in store came in the wording of a proposed Fourteenth Amendment to the Constitution, which was introduced into Congress in the early summer of 1866. The difficulty lay in the second section, which was designed to insure the new freedmen the vote and other rights:

Representatives shall be apportioned among the several states according to their respective numbers, counting the whole number of persons in each state, excluding Indians not taxed. But when the right to vote at any election for the choice of electors of President and Vice-President of the United States, Representatives in Congress, the Executive and Judicial Officers of a State or the members of the Legislature thereof, is denied to any of the male inhabitants of such state, being twenty-one years of age and citizens of the United States, or in any way abridged except for participation in rebellion or any other crime, the basis of proportion therein shall be reduced, in the proportion which the number of such male citizens shall bear to the whole number of male citizens twenty-one years of age in such State.

Women with the acumen of Mrs. Stanton, Miss Anthony, and Mrs. Stone were naturally appalled at the appearance, for the first time, of the word "male" in the Constitution. Its three-fold use in the proposed Fourteenth Amendment, always in connection with the term "citizen," raised the issue of whether women were actually citizens of the United States.

Previously the question of whether or not they might vote had been regarded as a state matter, along with their property rights, marriage and divorce status, and legal position. In the early years after the American Revolution they had voted in some parts of Virginia and New Jersey, and their *right* to vote had been specifically denied only with the adoption of constitutions in the several states which limited suffrage to white male voters in certain property categories. The franchise had been gradually broadened state by state to include, first, white males over the age of twenty-one, then (in the North and West) all males. Adoption of the Fourteenth Amendment would require another constitutional amendment to give women the vote in federal elections. An appalling vista of herculean labor opened up before the women leaders; Mrs. Stanton was of the opinion that woman suffrage would be set back a full century if the proposed amendment were adopted.

Her indignation and that of Miss Anthony knew no bounds. The latter made the pledge that "I will cut off this right arm of mine before I will ever work for or demand the ballot for the Negro and not the woman." Mrs. Stanton made derogatory references to "Sambo," and the enfranchisement of "Africans, Chinese, and all the ignorant foreigners the moment they touch our shores." She warned that the Republicans' advocacy of manhood suffrage "creates an antagonism between black men and all women that will culminate in fearful outrages on womanhood, especially in the southern states." [1]

She might have listened to Frederick Douglass (who had so staunchly supported her unprecedented plea for woman suffrage at the Seneca Falls convention) when — speaking in the spring of 1869 — he drew a distinction between the predicament of the freedmen in the South and that of the women:

When women, because they are women, are dragged from their homes and hung upon lamp-posts; when their children are torn from their arms and their brains dashed to the pavement; when they are objects of insult and outrage at every turn; when they are in danger of having their homes burnt down over their heads; when their children are not allowed to enter schools; then they will have an urgency to obtain the ballot.

When a voice from the audience asked, "Is that not all true about black women?" Douglass answered vehemently: "Yes, yes, yes; it is true of the black woman, but not because she is a woman, but because she is black." [2]

Frances Harper, who traveled throughout the South during the period after the war, bore similar witness: "When it was a question of race, she let the lesser question of sex go. But the white women all go for sex, letting race occupy a minor position. . . . If the nation could handle only one question, she would not have the black women put a single straw in the way, if only the men of the race could obtain what they wanted." [3]

There were white women who agreed with Mrs. Harper. Lucy

Stone urged that the wording of the amendment be changed, but in the event that this was impossible to achieve, she favored its passage: "I will be thankful in my soul if *any* body can get out of the terrible pit." [4] Still others, such as Julia Ward Howe whose great hymn had carried thousands of soldiers into battle, opposed any attempt at modifying the amendment and thereby endangering its passage.

In all fairness to such irreconcilables as Mrs. Stanton, Miss Anthony, and those who sided with them, it must be said that they believed that the moment in history called by some "the Negro's hour" could be the woman's hour as well, and that such a moment might not recur in a lifetime. Many factors had been at work in bringing about an unprecedented interest in the issue of popular suffrage: the women's admitted contributions to the Union cause during the war, the emancipation of the Negro, the issues of Reconstruction in the South, state referenda on woman and Negro suffrage in Kansas in 1867, and a New York state constitutional convention the same year which rewrote that state's outworn constitution. Those who held out for linking the two issues of Negro and woman suffrage believed in all sincerity that they would help, not harm, each other.

From a historical vantage point, their optimism seems unfounded. Slavery and the condition of the Negro had been a boiling national issue for thirty-five years; a war had been fought over it. No such intensity of feeling existed yet regarding the status of women, even among the women themselves, excepting in a still relatively small group. Opinion in Congress and throughout the North was concerned with assuring the vote for the Negro; it was relatively uninterested in how such a controversial measure would affect women.

Mrs. Stanton and Miss Anthony and their followers held doggedly to their views and worked hard to secure petitions against the Fourteenth Amendment. The first signs of a split in the forces backing greater rights for women became apparent in the gatherings of the American Equal Rights Association, which was organized at the close of the war to further the interests of both Negroes and women, but whose emphasis, under the leadership of Wendell Phillips, Horace Greeley, Gerrit Smith, and others, shifted to passage of the Fourteenth Amendment at all costs.[5]

The deepening rift was thrown into sharp focus by the referendum campaign which took place in Kansas in 1867. One proposition offered to the voters of that state would take the word "male" out of the voting requirements; the other would remove the word "Negro." It was the first time that woman suffrage had come up for a political test, and the women leaders not only put their best efforts into it, but looked to their former supporters for help — largely in vain. This was particularly true of the eastern liberal newspapers — Greeley's *Tribune,* Phillips' *Anti-Slavery Standard,* and Theodore Tilton's *Independent,* all of which were widely read in the state, and all of which were silent on the question of woman suffrage until the very last moment, when support was meaningless.

During the spring of 1867 Lucy Stone and her husband Henry Blackwell broke the ground. They were followed successively by Olympia Brown, one of the earliest women ministers, who came all the way from her Massachusetts parish, Mrs. Stanton, and Miss Anthony. The first comers were highly optimistic, although they found themselves facing frontier conditions. Henry Blackwell wrote to friends back East:

Lucy and I are going over the length and breadth of this state speaking every day and sometimes twice, journeying from twenty-five to forty-five miles daily, sometimes in a carriage and sometimes in an open wagon with or without springs. We climb hills and dash down ravines, ford creeks and ferry over rivers, rattle across limestone ledges, struggle through muddy bottoms, fight the high winds on the high rolling upland prairies and address the most astonishing (and astonished) audiences in the most extraordinary places. Tonight it may be a log school house, tomorrow a stone church; next day a store with planks for seats, and in one place, if it had not rained, we should have held forth in an unfinished court house, with only four stone walls but no roof whatsoever.[6]

In September Susan Anthony reported from Salina: "We are getting along splendidly. Just the frame of a Methodist church with sidings and a roof, and rough cottonwood boards for seats, was our meeting place last night here." [7]

Transport, food, and accommodations were all primitive, even when the former governor of the state traveled with Mrs. Stanton. Sometimes, driving in utter darkness, they forded streams so deep that ex-Governor Robinson would go ahead to find the ford, walking in his white shirt so that Mrs. Stanton, holding the reins, could follow him.

To delicate eastern stomachs, the food was inedible — bacon swimming in grease, coffee without milk and with sorghum for sugar, and few fruits or vegetables. The speakers sustained themselves with purchases at an occasional settlement: dried herring, crackers, gum arabic, and slippery elm.

The nights were an unending, unsuccessful struggle against overwhelming odds, as best described in Mrs. Stanton's pithy memoirs, "owing to the general opinion among pioneers that a certain species of insect must necessarily perambulate the beds in a young civilization." One night she tried to avoid the bedbugs by sleeping in the springless carriage:

I had just fallen into a gentle slumber, when a chorus of pronounced grunts and a spasmodic shaking of the carriage revealed to me the fact that I was surrounded by those long-nosed black pigs so celebrated for their courage and pertinacity. They had discovered that the iron steps of the carriage made most satisfactory scratching posts, and each one was struggling for his turn. This scratching suggested fleas. Alas! thought I, before morning I shall be devoured. I was mortally tired and sleepy, but I reached for the whip and plied it lazily from side to side; but I soon found nothing but a constant and most vigorous application of the whip could hold them at bay one moment. . . . I had a sad night of it, and never tried the carriage again, though I had many equally miserable experiences within four walls.[8]

A dispassionate onlooker would have anticipated only one outcome to the campaign, since Kansas was a Republican state. The women lost, receiving only 9,000 votes out of a total of 30,000. What was more surprising was that the Negro franchise, although backed by the Republicans and the reform press, also lost, with only 2,000 more votes. The campaigners were not as cast down as they might have been had they realized that the struggle they had just undergone was to be only the first in *fifty-six* such state referendum campaigns which would take place between 1867 and 1918.[9]

The Fourteenth Amendment to the Constitution was ratified in July 1868. Six months later the Radical Republicans, still seeking to guarantee the Negro freedman's right to vote, introduced a Fifteenth Amendment into Congress, which read: "The right of citizens of the United States to vote shall not be denied or abridged by the United States or any State, on account of race, color, or previous condition of servitude."

It would have been so easy, argued Mrs. Stanton and Miss Anthony, to have included the word "sex"; they failed to see that such a step was still far ahead of practical political possibilities. The state of opinion in Congress on woman suffrage had been demonstrated in a debate in 1866 on a bill to extend the vote to Negroes in the District of Columbia; Senator Cowan of Pennsylvania had offered an amendment to strike out the word "male," which brought about the first debate on woman suffrage in the Senate.[10]

Suffrage advocates took their sober and reasoned arguments from the ammunition provided by Mrs. Stanton, Lucretia Mott, and the other women leaders. Their opponents used the same emotional arguments which characterized all such debates down to 1919. Said Senator Williams from the young state of Oregon (where there was still little stir among women, and indeed very few women at all):

Sir, it has been said that "the hand that rocked the cradle ruled the world," and there is truth as well as beauty in that expression. Women in this country by their elevated social position, can exercise more influence upon public affairs than they could coerce by the use of the ballot. When God married our first parents in the garden according to that ordinance they were made "bone of one bone and flesh of one flesh"; and the whole theory of government and society proceeds upon the assumption that their interests are one, that their relations are so intimate and tender that whatever is for the benefit of the one is for the benefit of the other. . . . The woman who undertakes to put her sex in an adversary position to man, who undertakes by the use of some independent political power to contend and fight against man, displays a spirit which would, if able, convert all the now harmonious elements of society into a state of war, and make every home a hell on earth.[11]

Senator Frelinghuysen of New Jersey shared his fears:

It seems to me as if the God of our race has stamped upon [the women of America] a milder, gentler nature, which not only makes them shrink from, but disqualifies them for the turmoil and battle of public life. They have a higher and a holier mission. It is in retiracy [sic] to make the character of coming men. Their mission is at home, by their blandishments and their love to assuage the passions of men as they come in from the battle of life, and not themselves by joining in the contest to add fuel to the very flames. . . . It will be a sorry day for this country when those vestal fires of love and piety are put out.[12]

It is worth noting at this point that for fifty years to come, no rational appeal to fact was able to make a dent in either of these two arguments in the anti-suffrage arsenal. Even when woman suffrage became a reality, spreading slowly from one state to another, and one would have thought it patent even to the blind that women did not vote against men, but divided along party lines in much the same proportion as male voters, the anti-suffrage cohorts went on conjuring up hideous visions of an Amazonian sex pitted against "man." Similarly, they never admitted for one moment that there were single women, in considerable numbers, either widowed, possibly divorced, or just plain unmarried, who lacked the protectors and defenders vouchsafed their married sisters, and who might possibly need to look out for their own interests. They could not make such an admission, since the basic argument on which their whole philosophy was grounded was that women *should* not vote or hold office because they *could* not. Here, too, the living record to the contrary in the growing total of suffrage states was either ignored, or willfully distorted.

The vote in the Senate on the District of Columbia amendment mustered only nine votes in favor of extending the franchise to women, with thirty-seven Senators opposed.[13] Clearly, there was an enormous amount of work to be done before sentiment on behalf of the vote for women could equal that favoring the Negro voter.

Friends of the women's cause in Congress were realistic. Since there was little hope of either amending or opposing the Fifteenth Amendment, they acted instead to keep the woman suffrage issue alive by taking steps towards a federal woman suffrage amendment. The distinction of being the first to sponsor such legislation belongs to Senator S. C. Pomeroy of Kansas, who presented his bill in December 1868, followed by Representative George W. Julian of Indiana, who offered a Joint Resolution to both Houses in March 1869.[14]

Even before the Fifteenth Amendment had begun deepening the rift between the two camps in the women's movement, Mrs. Stanton and Miss Anthony had found a new friend. Like the abolitionists of an earlier day, they asked only one question of would-be supporters: where did they stand on woman's rights? As a result they made some strange allies and brought down on their heads fresh wrath from former adherents. None roused a greater outcry than their brief but lively association with George Francis Train — financier, speculator, opponent of "sound money," a Democrat, and, allegedly, a former Copperhead.

Train was certainly one of the eccentrics of his day — a man who dressed like a dandy, but never smoked, drank, or chewed, possessed of apparently limitless wealth, part of which he had made in organizing the Crédit Mobilier (although he got out before the scandal broke, and was never linked with it), a supporter of Irish freedom, the eight-hour day, and — woman's rights! An accomplished speaker, he joined Mrs. Stanton and Miss Anthony during the Kansas campaign, an act of faith which they deeply appreciated in contrast to the silence of onetime friends.

Apparently quite casually, Train asked Miss Anthony one day why she and her friends had no paper through which they might propagandize their cause. When she made the obvious answer, he remarked, "I will give it to you." At Junction City, Kansas, in the course of a meeting the same evening, he announced to a startled audience (not to mention Miss Anthony herself) that on her return to New York the latter would launch a weekly newspaper jointly with Mrs. Stanton, to be called *The Revolution* — subscription price $2.00, with the motto: "Men, their rights and nothing more; women, their rights and nothing less!"

To be handed a newspaper literally on a silver tray was a miracle that would have canceled out any idiosyncrasies Train might possess, in the eyes of Susan B. Anthony and Elizabeth Cady Stanton; moreover, he compounded his benefactions, immediately after the Kansas defeat, by subsidizing a return trip to the East, which became a succession of public meetings in the large cities, at which the two women argued their cause, while Train took charge of all the routine arrangements — and paid the bills.

One month after their arrival in New York, the first issue of *The Revolution,* dated January 8, 1868, was on the newsstands. Another backer had joined Train — David Melliss, financial editor of the *New York World* — and it was just as well. For it was again completely characteristic of Train that almost immediately after having launched the two women on brand-new careers he departed for abroad, where he spent the better part of the ensuing year in a British jail. He wrote highly colorful articles on Fenianism and the currency question, which *The Revolution* loyally printed; meanwhile Mr. Melliss, whose funds eventually ran out, and Miss Anthony, whose duties were those of publisher and business manager, were left holding a debt-ridden newspaper.

The weekly sixteen-page paper, smaller than today's tabloids, made a contribution to the women's cause out of all proportion to either its size, brief lifespan, or modest circulation. Especially during the first year, when Mrs. Stanton was its sprightly editor (a task she shared with the veteran reformer Parker Pillsbury), it was a lively mirror of the status and struggles of women on many fronts. Here was news not to be found elsewhere — of the organization of women typesetters, tailoresses, and laundry workers, of the first women's clubs, of pioneers in the professions, of women abroad.

But *The Revolution* did more than just carry news, or set a new standard of professionalism for papers edited by and for women. It gave their movement a forum, focus, and direction. It pointed, it led, and it fought, with vigor and vehemence. Its editorials and leading articles inveighed against discrimination in employment and pay, the inequities of divorce procedure, the derogatory concept of women fostered by established religion, as well as the injustice of the Fourteenth and Fifteenth Amendments. It exhorted women to equip themselves to earn their own livelihood, to practice bodily hygiene in the matter of fresh air, dress, and exercise, and it campaigned for the vote as basic to any kind of equality. It even took up the cudgels on behalf of the unfortunate women involved in some of the more lurid criminal cases of the day and dealt, with a forthrightness that would have been applauded by Margaret Fuller, with such incendiary topics as the double standard and prostitution.

The actual split in the woman's movement took place in May 1869. A "convention" called in January to discuss the issue of woman suffrage, and woman suffrage alone, had given Mrs. Stanton the opportunity to call for a woman suffrage amendment to the Constitution. The Equal Rights Association broke wide open on the issue, and immediately following its annual meeting in New York, Mrs. Stanton and Miss Anthony, moving with the speed and secrecy necessary for a coup d'état, organized the National Woman Suffrage Association, for women only.

They did so in the belief that it was largely due to the preponderance of men in the Equal Rights Association leadership that women's interests had been betrayed, and that the women who followed the men's lead — Mrs. Stone, Mrs. Howe, and others — had been misled or duped by them. They opened membership in the new association to any woman who believed in suffrage, but in point of fact only those joined who were willing to follow the uncompromising policies of its leaders.

In November 1869 in Cleveland, a second organization was set up, calling itself the American Woman Suffrage Association. (For purposes of brevity the two groups will hereafter be referred to as the "National" and the "American.") Anxious to keep out all those it considered undesirable, the American was organized on a delegate basis. Only representatives from "recognized" suffrage organizations were seated at the convention, a new development, since up to that time the women's "conventions" had admitted and given the floor to anyone who walked in and asked to speak.[15]

At first Susan Anthony tried to work with the new Association, but more schismatic developments followed. It soon appeared that the American would have its own paper as well. On January 8, 1870 — the anniversary of the founding of *The Revolution* — the *Woman's Journal* made its appearance, published in Boston. Handsomely produced, adequately financed by a joint-stock company, and by several giant bazaars, and conservatively edited by Mrs. Stone, Mr. Blackwell, and Mrs. Mary Livermore (who had given up her own paper in Chicago, *The Agitator,* to join the new venture), it drew around it as contributors and readers the rapidly growing numbers of women emerging into the greater social freedom and multiple activity of the '70's — club women, professionals, and writers. The *Woman's Journal* spoke for this group, many of whom were not yet ready to espouse the cause of woman suffrage, just as *The Revolution* spoke for and to the exploited woman worker or social outcast.

Of the two, there could be no question which would survive. For almost two and a half years Miss Anthony had kept her paper going, despite rising monumental debts, fighting every inch of the way for advertisers, subscribers, and backers. But the field was too small for more than one such paper, and *The Revolution* succumbed in May 1870.

Except for one or two abortive attempts at reconciliation, the two suffrage associations continued to operate independently of one another for twenty years. While some authorities have pleaded mystification as to the reason for the split between women once so closely united and with the same basic aims, the reason seems simple enough. It lay in deeply opposing social viewpoints — the conservative and the radical — which clashed, not on whether women should vote, but on *how* that goal could be won.

The American believed that it could be won only by avoiding issues that were irrelevant and calculated to alienate the support of influential sections of the community. Its leaders had no interest in organizing working women, in criticizing the churches, or in the divorce question, certainly as matters of public discussion. While paying lip service to the principle of a Federal woman suffrage amendment, they concentrated their practical work for the franchise within the several states.

Mrs. Stanton, Miss Anthony, and their followers, on the other hand, continued to regard woman's rights as a broad cause in which the vote might be of primary importance but other matters were also important. Their catholic attitude toward issues and allies led them into more than one quagmire, similar to the Train episode. The most unfortunate of all was their brief alignment with the notorious Victoria Woodhull and her sister Tennessee Claflin.

Mrs. Woodhull, a woman of beauty and wit, championed woman's rights, as well as free love, spiritualism, and quack healing, in her paper, *Woodhull & Claflin's Weekly*. The sisters furnished an additional outrage to convention by making a tidy fortune on the stock market under the wing of Cornelius Vanderbilt, the Great Commodore himself. Not content with invading Wall Street, hitherto a male sanctum, Mrs. Woodhull next claimed her right to vote, in an able speech before a Congressional committee in January 1871.[16]

However, she made a serious error the following year in trying to take over the National Woman Suffrage Association to further her own political aspirations. Miss Anthony foiled the attempt, and Mrs. Woodhull and her supporters withdrew and set up their own "party," which nominated her as a candidate for the presidency of the United States and the unfortunate Frederick Douglass (without his knowledge), as vice-president.

That was the extent of Mrs. Woodhull's political career; more notable was her connection with the Beecher-Tilton scandal. News of a prolonged love affair between Henry Ward Beecher, tower of piety and liberalism, and Elizabeth Tilton, wife of the reform editor Theodore Tilton, both of them Beecher's parishioners, appeared in Mrs. Woodhull's paper in November 1871. Tilton later sued Beecher for misconduct; the sensational trial dragged its miry course for weeks, and eventually resulted in a hung jury, accurately reflecting the division in public opinion.

The case, and by inference Mrs. Woodhull's action, did the women's cause no good. Those who had always tried to link it with free love and lax morals made the most of the Beecher-Tilton scandal. They were aided by two circumstances: one, that Beecher was a former president of the American Woman Suffrage Association, the other that Mrs. Stanton and Miss Anthony both took up the cudgels on behalf of Mrs. Tilton. Neither lost a chance, in print or from the public platform, to point out that under existing social customs, the woman in the case inevitably was its principal victim, and that under the existing laws of New York State Mrs. Tilton could not even testify in court on her own behalf.

Despite its connection with Beecher, the American suffered less in loss of prestige from the Beecher-Tilton case than the National; while it stood up for Mrs. Tilton, it gave the case little coverage in the *Woman's Journal*. Nor did the scandal set the cause of woman suffrage back for many years, as has been maintained; it was no help, but there were far too many other forces pushing it forward for the case to have any lasting impact.

The division in suffrage ranks was unfortunate; but it was inevitable during the 1870's and '80's, a period of intense economic development and change during which social forces polarized in the midst of widespread unrest. The break would continue until one trend or the other — respectability or radicalism — became dominant. In the meantime victories would also continue to be won, and the last major area in which, until now, no gains had been registered — that of politics — would be breached.

Chapter XI

FIRST VICTORIES IN THE WEST

It was no accident that the first round of the political struggle to win women the vote should have taken place in the state of Kansas. During the violence and upheaval of its territorial period in the 1850's, many New England women had come with their menfolk to try and make Kansas "free soil," bringing with them the ideas sown by Margaret Fuller and Lucy Stone. In the decade following the Civil War, its pioneering days were only twenty years away; it was still close to the westward-moving frontier.

In the wake of the trappers and explorers who first pierced the Continental Divide, crossed the alkali deserts, and penetrated the Snake and Truckee defiles to reach the coast, came the settlers: gold-seekers, homesteaders — the land-hungry, the dreamers, the law-breakers. Almost from the beginning there were women among them, cut off as irrevocably by the 2,000 mile journey from their home, family, and friends as if they had made the Atlantic crossing two centuries earlier.[1]

At best it was a hazardous journey, not only for the men who broke trail, searched for water, rounded up straying cattle, and fought the Indians resisting invasion of their lands, but for the women with them: "We had some frightful places to pass," runs an 1838 diary. "We passed along the steep sides of mountains where every step the loose earth slid from beneath our horses feet. . . . My horse fell and tumbled me over his head. Did not hurt me. . . . Left the camp ground half past four in the morning after a sleepless night with toothache." [2]

There was nothing unusual in such an experience, or in the experiences of women who drove the great wagons, gave birth to children despite hunger and exhaustion, tended one another, and sometimes succumbed to the manifold dangers of the Oregon and

California trails. There were many women in that most notorious of all wagon train disasters, the Donner party which headed for California and was marooned in the high Sierra snows during the winter of 1846–1847, who survived its horrors of cold, hunger, and even cannibalism.[3] There were women in the first missions sent to proselytize the unwilling Indian tribes of the Pacific Northwest, women who lived in primitive huts amid scenery that struck terror to the hearts of some reared in the open mid-western plains or the friendly New England farm country.

Like the early eastern settlers, those who were building for a future in the West saw the need of encouraging men to marry and settle down as homesteaders, and of persuading women to make the journey from the East. One method employed was the Oregon Land Donation Act of 1850, which gave a man and wife 640 acres (the wife could hold her share as her own separate realty), while a single woman was entitled to 320 acres.

The settlers brought with them a legacy of values still in a state of conflict and transition. Among these was the dominant attitude that women were destined, because of their own bodily and mental limitations, for a subordinate existence, chiefly in the home. This view was leavened by the agitation and education already under way in the East, and by the realities of frontier life where the demands for survival made on both sexes did not encourage the idea that women should be sheltered and dominated. Moreover, women gained in prestige by their very scarcity: in 1865 California had three men for each woman, the territory of Washington (which included the later states of Oregon and Idaho) four men to every woman, Nevada eight, and in Colorado the ratio was as high as twenty to one.[4] While later writers have made a good deal of the comic aspects of such a state of affairs, it had very real sociological and political repercussions.

A good deal of western history has dealt with its heroic aspects: the romance of discovery and exploration which, no matter what the hardships, brought a reward peculiarly its own to the men who endured and survived. An account of women's role in the same historical process would have to emphasize a different kind of effort, and of satisfaction, if that is the word for it.[5]

The wife of the missionary Elkanah Walker collected rock specimens, dried plants, and stuffed animals in efforts to appease her restless and eager mind; in other circumstances she might have been an eminent naturalist. Instead her energies were largely diverted into other channels, as recorded in her diary:

Churned and made a cheese, used a deer rennet. . . . Find bed bugs have come to reside with us; have commence [sic] a war of extermination. . . . Painted Mr. E.'s front door. Washed and cleaned furniture ready for painting. Painted chairs, settees, stools. They look better than I expected they would.

Dipped 24 dozen candles. Milked. Made cheese. Washed. Cooking, scolding, etc., as usual. . . . Painting the window casings. Have been 4 days occupied in finishing the windows. Our house is wholly glassed tho to complete it I had to set 47 squares of glass that were more or less injured.

Have made a pair of pants for Cyrus out of a pair of his father's old ones and glad I am that they are done for it makes me sick to think of doing tailor's work. . . . Washed children and floors, cut hair, and sewed.[6]

In one of the wagon trains reaching Oregon in 1852 was a seventeen-year-old girl who, as Abigail Scott Duniway, was to lead the fight for woman suffrage in the Northwest, and in her seventies, write the woman suffrage proclamation for the state of Oregon, just sixty years after her arrival in the Oregon Territory. Her mother, weakened by childbirth and already an invalid when the family left their home in Illinois, died of cholera in the Black Hills of Dakota, a circumstance her daughter never forgot. Grown up and married, Mrs. Duniway lived, not in isolation like Mrs. Walker, but in a pioneering community, which brought its own problems with it:

It was a hospitable neighborhood composed chiefly of bachelors, who found comfort in mobilizing at meal times at the homes of the few married men in the township . . . I, if not washing, scrubbing, churning or nursing the baby, was preparing their meals in our lean-to kitchen. To bear two children in two and a half years from my marriage day, to make thousands of pounds of butter every year for market, not including what was used in our free hotel at home; to sew and cook, and wash and iron; to bake and clean and stew and fry; to be, in short, a general pioneer drudge, with never a penny of my own, was not pleasant business for an erstwhile school teacher.[7]

Mrs. Duniway also learned the hard way that, although they had no legal rights of their own, married women were jointly liable for commitments made by the husband; the farm into which she had put as much work as he, was lost because he signed three notes for a friend, and then had to meet them. During the years she was raising a family of five and also supporting them (for Mr. Duniway became incapacitated by illness), she absorbed a multitude of bitter lessons; at the age of thirty-six she was ready to make woman suffrage her life work.

Following the example of Emily Pitt Stevens, who was publishing her own paper, *The Pioneer,* in San Francisco, and of the women reformer-editors in the East, Mrs. Duniway launched *The New Northwest* in 1871 in the mushrooming town of Portland. She was alone as the women back East, after Seneca Falls, were never alone; she had no such co-worker as Miss Anthony or Mrs. Stanton to strengthen her. Geography made the problems of organizing conventions or a cohesive organization nearly insuperable, and the readers of her paper were spread in straggling communities over a vast area. Yet she continued to publish her paper until 1887; her articles while touring the Northwest are a vivid source of regional social history, as well as day-by-day history of an embryo social movement, that for woman's rights.[8] She traveled literally thousands of miles in all seasons, by stage coach, river boat, and sleigh, to speak wherever a few would gather to hear her.

Despite later peccadilloes — she never worked harmoniously with the national suffrage leaders (except Miss Anthony), disagreeing violently with them on the advantages to be gained from cooperating with temperance groups, and once threatened to have Anna Howard Shaw arrested if she crossed the Oregon state line! [9] — Abigail Scott Duniway remained the hardiest and most tireless suffrage worker the western states produced.

The first victory for woman suffrage on the American continent came very quietly in contrast to later gains, so quietly that very little was known back East about the events leading up to it until the battle was over. It took place, neither in California, then in the throes of heady expansion, nor in the Northwest, but in the Territory of Wyoming — a sparsely settled area where the main occupation was cattle-raising, with a population whose chronicler could have been Bret Harte or Mark Twain, hard-working, hard-drinking and hard-shooting.

The largest settlement was South Pass City, today a "ghost town," then a mining camp of 2,000 where rich placer gold deposits had been found in 1867. Near by was the main route for wagon trains headed for California and Oregon. Some of the women realized that, in a new area just taking administrative form and unhampered by existing legal impediments, they had a chance not even remotely available in the world they had come from.

At least one of them was of outstanding leadership caliber — Mrs. Esther Morris, six feet tall, with a craggy, granite-like face, whose life reflected the westward movement of a nation. Born in western New York State in 1813, she had conducted a successful millinery establishment in the town of Oswego. When her first husband died, he left her property in Illinois, where she settled, and remarried. When her husband and three sons went to Wyoming in 1869, she promptly followed them.

Finding the outlook for woman suffrage a promising one, Mrs. Morris invited a group of community leaders and legislators to her home (some versions have it for dinner, others for tea) and made an appeal for the vote, drawing heavily on a lecture by Susan Anthony she had heard just before leaving Illinois.[10] Those present pledged their support. At the first territorial election — distinguished for rowdyism even in a part of the world where lawless voting was the rule rather than the exception — the presidency of the territorial council, or Senate, went to William H. Bright, who had not only been among Mrs. Morris' guests, but was married to a "strong" suffrage woman. Interparty jockeying also favored the women — some accounts state that the legislature passed the bill as a joke on the governor — but whatever the motives, the measure passed the tiny Senate by a vote of 6 to 2 (one abstention) and the lower house by 6 to 4 (one abstention).[11]

At this point anti-suffrage forces woke up and put tremendous pressure on the governor to veto the bill. He was unfortunately a bachelor, so there was no one in his family to plead with him But the women were lucky in another respect: some twenty years earlier, he had sat in the back rows of one of the earliest woman's rights conventions — in Salem, Ohio, where no man had been allowed to take part — and watched the amazing spectacle of women conducting such a gathering for and by themselves, and the memory had sunk deep. Governor Campbell signed the woman suffrage bill.

The Wyoming elections of 1870 and '71 confounded all predictions of disaster. Women did not, as prophesied, descend upon the polling places in hordes and upset the established order. Uncertainty and fearfulness held many back, and others simply did not care to exercise their newly acquired right. Those who did so came through the ordeal unscathed. A New England minister newly arrived in the state reported:

I saw the rough mountaineers maintaining the most respectful decorum whenever the women approached the polls, and heard the timely warning of one of the leading canvassers as he silenced an incipient quarrel with uplifted finger, saying "Hist! Be quiet! A woman is coming!" And I was compelled to allow that in this new country, supposed at that time to be infested by hordes of cut-throats, gamblers and abandoned characters, I had witnessed a more quiet election than it had been my fortune to see in the quiet towns of Vermont. I saw ladies attended by their husbands, brothers or sweethearts, ride to the place of voting, and alight in the midst of a silent crowd, and pass through an open space to the polls, depositing their votes with no more exposure to insult or injury than they would expect on visiting a grocery store or meat market. Indeed, they were much safer here, every man of their party was pledged to shield them, while every member of the other party feared the influence of any signs of disrespect.[12]

In addition to giving the women of the state control of their own property, and protecting them against discrimination as teachers, Wyoming witnessed another novel development: once enrolled as voters, their names appeared on the lists of prospective jurors. This was one of the most basic demands voiced by women. How, asked Mrs. Stanton and others, could a woman ever consider herself tried by a jury of her peers as long as juries were entirely made up of men?

The jury issue in Wyoming blew up a far greater storm than even the women's appearance at the ballot box, both in and out of the territory; such pressure was put on husbands to forbid this new departure that "some were so inflamed that they declared they would never live with their wives again if they served on the jury." [13] When the issue came up before Chief Justice J. H. Howe, sitting in the Laramie City Court in the spring of 1870, he de-

clared that the matter was one for each woman to decide for herself: if they wished to be discharged on grounds of inconvenience,
he would do so. Only one woman withdrew; the rest served the
full term, and if we are to believe contemporary testimony, that
particular jury "became such a terror to evil-doers that a stampede
began among them, and very many left the state forever." [14]

Mrs. Morris was appointed to serve as Justice of the Peace in
South Pass City, the first woman justice on record; despite the
inevitable hooligan attempts to prevent her from carrying out her
duties, and the usual newspaper hue-and-cry across the country,
not one of the forty-odd cases she handled was reversed by a higher
court.

The neighboring territory of Utah enacted woman suffrage in
February 1870, and a few women voted in city and municipal
elections even before their sisters in Wyoming exercised their
newly acquired prerogative. Curiously, historians have not asked,
let alone cast any light on, why a Mormon society should have
given women the vote without any discernible demand for it
among the women themselves. Mormon writers have interpreted
the action as the logical extension of an egalitarian attitude toward
women basic to the Mormon creed, which had permitted women
a voice in church affairs ever since the founding of Mormonism
in 1830.[15] They saw nothing derogatory to woman's dignity in
plural marriage (Mormons never used the term "polygamy"), holding it far superior to the "double standard" tacitly accepted in
the Christian community. While women were debarred, by the
tenets of the Mormon faith, from the all-important ecclesiastical
hierarchy which controlled all aspects of Mormon life, they were
not, for the most part, the embittered and rebellious victims of
polygamy that critics of Mormonism considered them; the truth
lay somewhere in-between. Moreover plural marriage was not a
standard practice; it was necessarily limited to a small upper
stratum — between 2 and 3 per cent — of men who could assume
the economic support of several, or many, wives.[16]

The causes for Utah women receiving the vote so early seem
less related to Mormon ethics than to an interplay of social forces.
Brigham Young's vision of a flourishing paradise in the wilderness
was threatened from Washington, a threat expressed largely in

Women voting for the first time in Wyoming, September 6, 1870

Abigail Scott Duniway

Esther Morris

Mary Church Terrell

Jeannette Rankin

opposition to polygamy, which became an excuse for denying Utah much desired statehood and self-government (free of interference from a territorial governor appointed by the federal government). When the Cullom Bill was introduced into Congress in the winter of 1869–1870, to illegalize polygamy, the Mormons saw a chance to enlist the help of their women against such interference by giving them a voice in territorial affairs.

The meetings held by Mormon women that winter protesting the proposed Cullom Bill are vivid evidence of the extent to which some of them, at least, were already active and articulate.[17] While this arose in part from the conditions of frontier life, it was also due in good measure to the fact that Mormon women had been organized in "relief societies" as far back as 1842, when the center of the Mormon community was still in Nauvoo, Illinois. These societies were re-established in Utah, beginning in 1867; they undertook not only the care of the sick and the indigent in the scattered Mormon settlements, but later such planned activities of the Mormon state as the preservation of grain, and the fostering of new industries.[18] They were eventually joined in the National Women's Relief Society; their organ, beginning in 1872, was the *Woman's Exponent,* edited for many years by Emmeline B. Wells, who was well known to the national suffrage leaders.[19]

In 1887 Congress passed the Edmunds-Tucker Act, illegalizing plural marriage; in addition, one clause in the bill revoked woman suffrage in Utah territory. Utah women and suffragists elsewhere argued that the measure compounded injustice, since on the one hand it disfranchised women, but not men, for the alleged crime of plural marriage, while on the other hand it bore with equal weight on all women, regardless of whether they had been married to a man who practiced plural marriage or not. The bill was therefore in its effect anti-woman suffrage as well as anti-Mormon. Nevertheless the Utah women did not regain the vote until 1896, following the Mormon Church's renouncement of plural marriage, when Utah was admitted to statehood under a constitution providing for woman suffrage.

Chapter XII

BREAKING GROUND FOR SUFFRAGE

Although small and divided, the woman's movement showed considerable vitality on the suffrage issue during the 1870's and '80's. Activity fell into three categories: demonstrative, legal, and political. At the end of a decade, the first two had been abandoned in favor of the third, which came to include a variety of techniques: organizing state suffrage associations, educating public opinion, conducting campaigns in the several states for suffrage referenda, and maintaining pressure on Congress for an amendment to the federal constitution.

What was perhaps the earliest demonstration for woman suffrage took place in New Jersey, a state with unusual historical antecedents for such action. Unlike most states, New Jersey's constitution, which was adopted as early as 1776, did not specifically disfranchise women, and they voted sporadically until the legislature limited the franchise to free, white, male citizens, in 1807.[1]

On November 19, 1868, a presidential Election Day, the small grape-growing community of Vineland in southern New Jersey witnessed an unusual sight. Tables stood at either side of the platform at one end of Union Hall, at which sat election judges — men at one table, at the other women. During the day large numbers of women "voted" in the box designated for them (having first attempted to deposit their ballots with the men electors, and been "courteously refused"). On the women's side sat stalwarts like Margaret Pryor, who had faced anti-slavery mobs when Abby Kelley Foster first spoke from the lecture platform in the '40's. Now 84 years old, serene in her Quaker bonnet, Mrs. Pryor was pictured as having "the spirit, elasticity and strength of one thirty-five." A reporter described the scene in *The Revolution:*

There was no lack of friends and supporters. Men as well as women, gave us the light of their countenances and the benediction of their souls. The platform was crowded with earnest, refined, intellectual women, who felt it was good for them to be there. One beautiful girl said in my hearing, "I feel so much stronger for having voted.". . . It was pleasant to see husbands and wives enter the Hall together, only they had to separate, one turning to the right hand and the other to the left, when no separation should have taken place. Some women spent the day in going after their friends and bringing them to the Hall. Young ladies, after voting, went to the homes of their acquaintances and took care of the babies, while they came out to vote. Will this fact lessen the alarm of some men for the safety of the babies of enfranchised women on election day? [2]

Although it had been gloomily predicted that not five women would appear to show their desire for the vote, both critics and supporters as well were confounded by the turnout: 172 women cast their "ballots," four of them Negroes. *The Revolution* carried the story far and wide, and further demonstrations took place for several years. In the worst storm of the winter of 1870, forty women of Hyde Park, Massachusetts, led by Angelina Grimké Weld and Sarah Grimké (the latter nearly eighty years old) walked through the driving snow to deposit their ballots in a separate box. [3]

In 1871 and 1872 some 150 women tried to vote in ten states and the District of Columbia. Nearly seventy of them did so in the District of Columbia; being unsuccessful, they tried to win the right to vote through court action, also without success. Here and there individual women actually succeeded in having their votes counted: Marilla M. Ricker in Dover, New Hampshire; Mary Wilson in Battle Creek, Michigan; Nanette Gardner in Detroit. [4] The most famous of the court cases arising from such attempts to register and vote was that of Susan Anthony, who led a group of sixteen women in Rochester, New York, first in registering, and then in voting, in the presidential election of 1872. [5]

There was nothing light-minded about the step these women took. Warned by a Rochester newspaper, Miss Anthony knew that "illegal voters" were subject to a fine as high as $500 and a possible prison sentence running up to three years. Her biographer, Katharine Anthony, has pointed out that the group could hardly be dismissed as mere sensation seekers: some were Quakers, all were sober housewives; one of them, Rhoda DeGarmo, had been recording secretary at the woman's rights convention held in Rochester immediately after that in Seneca Falls, back in 1848.[6]

It was entirely characteristic of Miss Anthony that, knowing the possibilities, she left nothing to chance. Before the group went to the polls she assured herself of first-rate legal advice, and promised the election inspectors (whom she had convinced by the force of her arguments that they should register her group) that she would cover all costs if legal steps were taken against them!

President Grant's Republican Adminstration, confronting the widely-publicized fact that sixteen Rochester women had committed a federal offense by casting their ballots illegally, left no stone unturned to assure a conviction, and thereafter to prevent the case from going to the Supreme Court. Miss Anthony was of course made the test case, the criminal indictment against her charging that she "knowingly, wrongfully and unlawfully voted for a representative to the Congress of the United States." In the weeks preceding the trial she took her case directly to the citizens (and prospective jurors!) of Monroe County, speaking in every one of the county's twenty-nine postoffice districts. The tour attracted so much attention that the prosecuting attorney became alarmed and obtained a change of venue to Canandaigua in neighboring Ontario County, where trial was set for June 17, 1873. Nothing daunted, Miss Anthony sallied forth again, and in the little more than three weeks available to her, spoke in another twenty-one postal districts of Ontario County, while her friend and co-worker Mathilda Joslyn Gage spoke in the other sixteen.[7] The main line of her defense was that by voting in good faith, since she considered herself legally entitled to do so, she could not be held guilty of criminal action or intent.

Perhaps her amazing efforts had some bearing on the unorthodox court procedures followed during the trial by the presiding judge, Justice Ward Hunt, a political adherent of Republican senator and machine leader Roscoe Conkling, trying his first case and anxious to produce the results desired by the Administration. In any case, the high-handedness of the ensuing trial has rarely been surpassed.

When former Appeals Court Judge Henry R. Selden, acting as counsel for Miss Anthony, attempted to call her as a witness on her own behalf, the prosecution held she was incompetent to testify, and was sustained by the judge. On the other hand the court admitted (over Selden's objections) testimony she had given at a pre-indictment hearing before the Commissioner of Elections, as recorded by a court attendant.

Moreover, although a jury trial in criminal cases is mandatory, the defendant was in effect denied such right: when prosecution and defense both rested, Justice Hunt informed the jury that in his opinion, "there is no question for the jury, and the jury should be directed to find a verdict of guilty." Overruling the protests of counsel, he then read a statement (prepared before the trial) which declared:

The question . . . is wholly a question or questions of law, and I have decided as a question of law, in the first place, that under the 14th amendment, which Miss Anthony claims protects her, she was not protected in a right to vote. And I have decided also that her belief and the advice which she took does not protect her in the act which she committed. If I am right in this, the result on your part must be a verdict of guilty, and I therefore direct that you find a verdict of guilty.[8]

The Court denied Selden's plea that the jury be polled, and also his plea for a new trial.

At this point Justice Hunt seems to have faltered and made a tactical mistake: he asked the defendant whether she had anything to say as to why sentence should not be served. She had; over his repeated admonitions, once he realized what he had unleashed, Susan Anthony gave Justice Hunt, the jury, and the packed court-room a blistering denunciation not only of the trial itself, but of the whole issue of women's disfranchisement. When Justice Hunt finally succeeded in silencing her, and sentenced her to $100 fine and costs (a mild sentence), Miss Anthony promptly stated that she would never pay one dollar of it.

Once again Hunt ignored accepted procedure; he deliberately did not order her to be committed until the fine was paid. Had he done so, he would have enabled her to take her case directly to the United States Supreme Court on a writ of habeas corpus, which, because of the crass illegalities committed during the trial, might have set it aside and ordered a genuine jury trial. He thus robbed Miss Anthony of her only remaining legal weapon. She never paid the fine; but no further move was made against her, and the Rochester election inspectors who had permitted the women to register and vote were quietly pardoned by President Grant.

The explanation for the Administration's failure to press charges further against Miss Anthony lies in the fact that the issue involved was in process of settlement in its favor (on less vulnerable legal grounds than in the Anthony case as conducted by Justice Hunt) in the Minor case, which did reach the Supreme Court. This suit had been based on a new theory of women's existing voting rights, developed by a St. Louis lawyer, Francis Minor, whose wife was president of the Missouri Woman Suffrage Association.

Late in 1869 *The Revolution* had published a set of resolutions adopted by a convention of this body, drawn up by Mr. Minor, contending that the Constitution and its amendments already gave women the right to vote and that no enabling legislation by the states to permit them to do so was necessary. Declaring that "all persons born or naturalized in the United States and subject to the jurisdiction thereof, are citizens of the United States and the state wherein they reside," the resolutions pointed out the distinction between the "immunities and privileges" conferred by the Constitution, and the right of the several states to contravene them:

> Resolved, 1: That the immunities and privileges of American citizenship, however defined, are National in character and paramount to all State authority.
>
> 2: That while the Constitution of the United States leaves the qualifications of electors to the several States, it nowhere gives them the right to deprive any citizen of the elective franchise which is possessed by any other citizen — to regulate, not including the right to prohibit the franchise.
>
> 3: That, as the Constitution of the United States expressly declares that no State shall make or enforce any laws that shall abridge the privileges or immunities of citizens of the United States, those provisions of the several State Constitutions that exclude women from the franchise on account of sex, are violative alike of the spirit and letter of the Federal Constitution.
>
> 4: That, as the subject of naturalization is expressly withheld from the States, and as the States clearly have no right to deprive of the franchise naturalized citizens, among whom women are expressly in-

cluded, still more clearly have they no right to deprive native-born women of this right.[9]

This new approach to women's right to the vote was wholeheartedly adopted by the National Association, and first publicly expounded by Mrs. Stanton in January 1870 at a hearing before the Congressional Committee on the District of Columbia on behalf of a bill to extend the vote to women in the District. Had the new gambit been successful, it would have saved more than half a century of work and sacrifice. It was blocked by the Supreme Court's decision against Francis and Virginia Minor, who filed suit in 1872 against a St. Louis registrar, one Reese Happersett, who refused to permit Mrs. Minor to register in order to vote; Happersett had acted under a clause of the Missouri state constitution which specifically barred women from voting. The Minor case ran more or less concurrently with that of Miss Anthony.

When they lost the case in the lower courts, the Minors appealed to the Supreme Court and in October 1874 that body handed down a unanimous opinion written by Chief Justice Morrison R. Waite, upholding the lower court.[10] The decision held, in substance, that the Constitution did not confer the right of suffrage on those who were citizens at the time it was adopted, and that suffrage was not co-extensive with citizenship; that the States, having withheld voting rights from certain classes of males (under property qualifications, because of color, the mentally unfit, and the criminal), were equally within their rights in withholding suffrage from all women. The Court did not consider such questions, raised by the Minors in their appeal, as the hardship to women, or the merits of woman suffrage; as in the Bradwell case, it sidestepped the basic issues at stake.[11]

Subsequent rulings of the Court on cases having a bearing on the right to confer suffrage showed some inconsistencies, apparent to the lay if not the judicial mind. The decision in the Minor case did not appear to jibe with that in the so-called Slaughter-House Cases in 1873, which flatly stated that "The negro having by the Fourteenth Amendment been declared a citizen of the United States, is thus made a voter in every state in the Union." [12] Subsequently in the Yarbrough decision in 1884, the Court again ruled: "It is not true, therefore, that electors for members of Congress owe their right to vote to the state law in any sense which makes the exercise of the right to depend exclusively on the law of the State." The Court further stated that the guarantees of the Fifteenth Amendment were confined to male citizens of African descent, even though it added: "the principle . . . that the protection of the exercise of this right is within the power of Congress is as necessary to the right of other citizens to vote as to the colored citizen, and to the right to vote in general as to the right to be protected against discrimination." [13] Small wonder that the authors of volume IV of the *History of Woman Suffrage* commented: "This legal hair-splitting is beyond the comprehension of the average lay mind." [14]

Like earlier efforts to make provisions for woman suffrage part of the Fourteenth and Fifteenth amendments, the Anthony and Minor cases demonstrated that the time was not yet ripe for woman suffrage. To try to bring it about by judicial fiat was a long step ahead of social realities; to win it through act of Congress was politically an impossibility.

For while women were playing an ever larger role in the life of the country as wage-earners and professionals, they were still not able to make their influence felt because they were not organized. Without adequate organization in sufficient numbers, they could not hope to challenge deeply rooted prejudice and encrusted tradition in the citadels of economic and political power. Not only would more extensive social progress on all fronts be required, but also the conscious, directed efforts of far greater numbers of women, and of men as well, to win women the vote.

During the summer of 1876, amid great public interest, the nation celebrated its Centennial with a huge exposition in Philadelphia, the first of its kind in America. The National Woman Suffrage Association hoped to use the occasion to draw attention to the still inequitable position of women, and also to bring women from all over the country together to exchange their experiences and knowledge. They opened headquarters in Philadelphia, after great difficulty in finding premises. On one occasion when a lease had actually been signed, it turned out that the property belonged to a woman, who, under Pennsylvania law, could not make any disposition of it without her husband's consent, which he refused to give. When other rooms were finally found, it was Susan Anthony — single, and therefore legally entitled to enter into a business contract — who signed the lease.

A huge Fourth of July celebration in Independence Hall was to be the principal occasion of the whole celebration, with the Emperor of Brazil as guest of honor (a personage some of the women felt hardly suited to keynote the democratic tradition which the Centennial was intended to commemorate); no woman was scheduled to speak at the gathering. When the National asked General Hawley, chairman of the Centennial Commission, for permission to present a Declaration of Rights for Women, similar to that drawn up at the Seneca Falls Convention, the request was refused for fear it would attract too much attention; another request for a large number of admission tickets was also refused. However, General Hawley subsequently relented and sent the ladies five tickets, an act which proved to be a mistake.

On the great day, and at the very moment when the entire audience rose to greet the Brazilian monarch, five women, headed by the indomitable Miss Anthony, went up on the platform and bore down on the chairman, president *pro tempore* of the United States Senate, Thomas W. Ferry. The startled Ferry, a supporter of woman suffrage, incidentally, grasped the parchment Miss Anthony handed to him and bowed; the women, expecting every moment to be taken into custody, turned and walked off the platform and out of the hall, first drawing from their capacious reticules large handfuls of printed broadsides carrying their Declaration, which they scattered left and right. There was great confusion as men stood on their seats reaching for the handbills and hundreds of arms were stretched out for them, while General Hawley shouted for order to be restored.

Emerging from the building, the five women saw another golden opportunity and snatched it. Although the day was unusually hot, in a generally broiling summer, a large crowd was milling about Independence Square; there in the blazing sun stood a bandstand, erected for the evening's program, and now empty. The ladies surged toward it, and while one of them held an umbrella over Miss Anthony's head, she read the Declaration in a clear voice that carried far out across the listening throng. Then, after distributing still more copies, the well-satisfied suffragists adjourned to the First Unitarian Church, where a crowded five-hour meeting took place. In addition to a long list of speakers, the capacity audience heard the famous Hutchinson Family singers, familiar from many an abolition and woman's rights meeting; one of their most popular numbers was Frances Dana Gage's "A Hundred Years Hence," of which one verse ran:

> Then woman, man's partner, man's equal shall stand,
>   While beauty and harmony govern the land;
> To think for oneself will be no offense,
>   The world will be thinking, a hundred years hence.[15]

The absence of any furor over the Woman's Declaration of 1876, comparable with that aroused by the Seneca Falls Declaration, was indicative of the progress that had taken place. There was more evidence to the same effect in the document itself.[16] Not only were some of the earlier demands notably absent, such as those for equal education, public speech, the right to preach, teach, write, and earn a livelihood, but the strident note of complaint against *man* — all men — had given way to charges leveled against the state — an all-male government. The new Declaration demanded jury trial by one's peers — meaning the inclusion of women in juries — no taxation without representation, and repeal of the qualifying word "male" in state constitutions and judicial codes. It also reiterated the earlier protest against a double standard of morality, and stressed the unequal position of the woman under existing divorce statutes. While admitting considerable legislative gains, the Declaration pointed out that these were uneven, subject to amendment or outright repeal, and that many forms of flagrant discrimination were still prevalent.

The American Woman Suffrage Association did not associate itself with the Declaration (much less with its unorthodox "presentation") or attempt to maintain any headquarters at the Centennial. It did ask for a place on the July Fourth program, and when that was refused, for exhibition space. Eventually the women got wall space to display some printed matter, but "so high that few could see it." [17]

While probably not many women felt with Mrs. Stanton that the Supreme Court decision in the Minor case had as far-reaching implications for their cause as the Dred Scott decision did for that of the slave, it did close one path of action to win the vote, and direct them to others. The American Association continued the method of state-by-state action to which it was already committed; the National, while cooperating in state campaigns, centered its efforts on a woman suffrage amendment to the Federal constitution. Either path presented a staggering perspective to political realists, which, perhaps fortunately, the women were not. After woman suffrage had been won, Carrie Chapman Catt attempted some computation of the amount of human effort involved:

To get the word "male" in effect out of the Constitution cost the women of the country fifty-two years of pauseless campaign. . . . During that time they were forced to conduct fifty-six campaigns of referenda to male voters; 480 campaigns to get Legislatures to submit suffrage amendments to voters; 47 campaigns to get State constitutional conventions to write woman suffrage into state constitutions; 277 campaigns to get State party conventions to include woman suffrage planks; 30 campaigns to get presidential party conventions to adopt woman suffrage planks in party platforms, and 19 campaigns with 19 successive Congresses.[18]

The first measure providing for a woman suffrage amendment had been introduced into Congress in 1868. Early in 1878 Sen. A. A. Sargent of California, a close friend of Susan Anthony's, introduced a woman suffrage measure, usually referred to as the "Anthony Amendment," which, without any change in wording, was to be used until it was finally passed by Congress more than forty years later. "The right of citizens of the United States to vote shall not be denied or abridged by the United States or by any state on account of sex." [19]

This bill was referred to the Senate Committee on Privileges and Elections, and Mrs. Stanton headed a galaxy of the women's best speakers when hearings were held. The adverse report on the bill came as no surprise to those who had witnessed the Committee's behavior; Mrs. Stanton wrote:

In the whole course of our struggle for equal rights, I never felt more exasperated than on this occasion, standing before a committee of men many years my junior, all comfortably seated in armchairs. . . . The peculiarly aggravating feature of the present occasion was the studied inattention and contempt of the chairman, Senator Wadleigh of New Hampshire. . . . He alternately looked over some manuscripts and newspapers before him, and jumped up to open or close a door or a window. He stretched, yawned, gazed at the ceiling, cut his nails, sharpened his pencil, changing his occupation and position every two minutes, effectively preventing the establishing of the faintest magnetic current between the speakers and the committee. It was with difficulty that I restrained the impulse more than once to hurl my manuscript at his head.[20]

Supporters of the bill continued to reintroduce it at each session of Congress, and hearings were held, usually at the time of the National's annual Washington convention. Although there were always some congressmen who behaved like Senator Wadleigh, these hearings nevertheless furnished excellent opportunities for making new friends, and the proceedings were always reported in the press. They also served to keep the attention of women suffragists fixed on Congress, and a stream of petitions continued to pour in on senators and representatives.

Gradually changes took place. In 1882 both houses appointed Select Committees on Woman Suffrage, and both reported the measure favorably. This action was repeated by the Senate Select Committee in 1884 and 1886, and the bill was called up on the Senate floor on December 8, 1886, by Senator Henry W. Blair of New Hampshire, who made an able speech in its favor.[21] Declaring that "the right to vote is the great primitive right in which all freedom originates and culminates. It is the right from which all others spring," he dealt exhaustively with all the serious objections raised by anti-suffragists: that voting must be based on military service (but this restriction does not apply to men who do not perform military service); that women's intellectual capacity is inferior (men's intellect is not questioned); lack of time due to maternal and housewifely duties (why not leave this problem to the individual female as to the individual male voter?), and so on, down the line.

The main debate was held over until January 25, 1887.[22] Blair received able and reasoned support from such men as Dolph of Oregon and Hoar of Massachusetts; the opposition showed itself, as in subsequent debates, of a very different caliber: Senator Brown of Georgia was fearful of the enfranchisement of Negro women; so was Vest of Missouri, who in addition foretold the long-expected dissolution of the American home and the ruin of women's femininity:

For my part I want when I go to my home — when I turn from the arena where man contends with man for what we call the prizes of this paltry world — I want to go back, not to the embrace of some female ward politician, but to the earnest loving look and touch of a true woman. I want to go back to the jurisdiction of the wife, the mother; and instead of a lecture upon finance or the tariff, or upon the construction of the Constitution, I want those blessed loving details of domestic life and domestic love.[23]

He closed with a blood-curdling peroration portraying the role of women in the French Revolution: "Who led those blood-thirsty mobs? Who shrieked loudest in that hurricane of passions? Women. . . . In the city of Paris in those ferocious mobs . . . the controlling and principal power came from those whom God has intended to be the soft and gentle angels of mercy throughout the world." [24]

The vote, sixteen in favor to thirty-four opposed, with twenty-six absent, put seven more senators on record favoring suffrage than had voted for it in the District of Columbia in 1866. A geographical breakdown of the tally showed that the South was solidly in opposition, yielding 22 "no" votes, with 10 absentees, and not a single "yes."

The Anthony amendment continued to be introduced (with a few exceptions) and to be reported out of committee until 1896. Then, for reasons to be discussed later, it virtually disappeared from the Congressional agenda and from public notice until 1913.

While Miss Anthony and Mrs. Stanton kept their main fire concentrated on Congress, the American Association (although paying lip service to the idea of a federal amendment) turned its energies to amending the constitutions of the individual states.

For decades the method of state referenda on woman suffrage produced meager results in return for exhausting labors. The 1867 campaign in Kansas was only the first in a long series, most of which ended in defeat: from 1870 to 1910 there were exactly seventeen state referenda held, bunched in eleven states (all but three west of the Mississippi) of which just two were victorious. Among the earliest, after the first Kansas vote, were Michigan in 1874, Colorado in 1877, Nebraska in 1882, Oregon in 1884, Rhode Island in 1887, Washington in 1889, and South Dakota in 1890.[25]

In the main, these campaigns all followed the same outline. They were conducted with very little money, and the main burden was carried by a very small group of workers, among whom there were always a few devoted men supporters. Whatever the favorable conditions which originally led to undertaking the campaign, such as promises of support from one or another major party or favorable commitments from large newspapers, they usually evaporated long before Election Day. Flagrant graft was usually in evidence, and the liquor interests stood out increasingly as a major source of opposition.

Against such opponents the women could muster few resources. The financial affairs of both suffrage associations were conducted on a perpetually frayed shoestring, and state suffrage associations, as they later came to be, were almost non-existent. The work of collecting signatures to petitions requesting a referendum was still arduous, particularly in the rural areas where great distances had to be covered. The women were developing a corps of able speakers, and support could be found among the growing number of women's clubs and the network of community activities in which women were coming to the fore: temperance, missionary, charity, educational, trade union, and church. But while woman suffrage, as has always been the case with "causes," could usually produce some devoted workers when a crisis arose, sustained work was still exceptional, whether because of timidity, inertia, or the press of most women's domestic or economic responsibilities. If the need and the hour produced ability, it dribbled away when both had passed, because no adequate organization existed to enlist and develop it.

In the face of an unbroken series of defeats for universal woman suffrage, certain gains were made in the direction of partial or limited suffrage, on such matters as schools, taxes, and bond issues. As far back as 1838, Kentucky had given "school suffrage" to widows in country districts who had children of school age, the first instance of such limited suffrage on record; no other state did likewise until Kansas gave its women the school vote in 1861. Michigan and Minnesota followed suit in 1875, and thereafter the number increased steadily to nineteen states by 1890, while three had granted tax and bond suffrage.[26]

While this seemed a favorable step forward, limited suffrage brought real problems in its wake, as was conclusively demonstrated after Kansas gave women municipal suffrage in 1887.[27] As soon as women received any vote, even if only on the local level, they became objects of interest to political parties; once enlisted in any party, they were subject to party loyalty, on suffrage strategy as well as other issues. Their allegiance was divided, since woman suffrage became as much of a political football as any other issue. This fact emerged with great clarity in the second Kansas referendum campaign in 1894. The Republicans reneged on their promises to put woman suffrage into their party platform; the Populists adopted a suffrage plank, but with a rider saying that support of the issue was not to be considered a test of party loyalty. Suffrage leaders active in both parties were caught in the middle.

Another drawback to partial suffrage was that it never brought enough women to the polls to constitute a convincing demonstration that women wanted the ballot; on the contrary, it furnished the opposition with the argument that women were simply not interested in voting. The numbers who went to the polls varied greatly, depending on the degree to which women had been involved in one aspect or another of the struggle for broader opportunities, and on the obstacles they encountered if they did wish to vote. The latter were at times not inconsiderable, and reflected the disinterest of the major parties in the protection of such limited voters, in sharp contrast to what had happened in Wyoming when women received the full vote, and all parties therefore had a political stake in seeing that they received fair treatment. In the New York state school board elections of 1880, such deterrents ran the full gamut: outright denial of the right to vote (in defiance of the law); threats of reprisal — clerical, anonymous, even husbandly; crowded or unsuitable polling premises, uncouth behavior by loiterers and even election officials (some of whom puffed smoke in the women's faces), and actual cases of stone-throwing. Small wonder that the turnout of women varied from one locality to another and did little to strengthen their case for the full vote.

In 1889 a new state was seeking admission to the Union. Having been the first territory to grant women political equality, Wyoming now asked for the privilege of being the first state to do so; its newly adopted state constitution naturally contained provision for full woman suffrage.

Since the Civil War had settled the issue of free versus slave states, the granting of statehood had ceased to be a controversial question and had become partisan only insofar as it involved the likelihood of one party rather than another increasing its Congressional strength. Wyoming was expected to be a Republican state; consequently its admission was opposed by the Democrats, who relied heavily on the argument that admitting a full suffrage state would open the door to further extension of the practice — as indeed it did.

The Congressional battle over admission was therefore a sharp one. In the House, southern Democrats led by Oates of Alabama took the entirely inconsistent position of opposing the right of a state to decide a matter such as the franchise for itself.[28] Anxious women, Susan Anthony among them, listened in the gallery while these men argued that the Wyoming suffrage provision was unconstitutional (in the light of the Supreme Court decision in the Minor case), or dwelt on that ultimate horror, the appearance of a woman in their midst as a duly elected representative of the people, and the insoluble problem of how to address her.

When chances for Wyoming's achieving statehood appeared at a low ebb, territorial delegate Joseph M. Carey telegraphed his legislature that woman suffrage might have to be abandoned as the price of admission to the federal union. The legislature, mindful of a twenty-year history in the territory of successful woman suffrage, answered in the only terms open to it under its mandate from the voters: "We will remain out of the Union a hundred years rather than come in without the women." [29]

The vote in the House on March 28, 1890, in favor of admitting Wyoming with its constitution providing for woman suffrage intact was 139 to 127 (hardly a large margin). It took three months more before the Senate voted for admission on June 27, 29 to 19.[30]

The bill was duly signed by President Benjamin Harrison. When Wyoming celebrated its newly won statehood in Cheyenne on July 23, 1890, the flag honoring the occasion was presented to the Governor by Mrs. Esther Morris, "the mother of woman suffrage in Wyoming."

Chapter *XIII*

THE GROWTH OF WOMEN'S ORGANIZATIONS

Many factors contributed to the growth of organizations, especially among middle-class women. From 1865 on, a veritable domestic revolution was under way, which freed those able to take advantage of it for pursuits other than housework. The development of gas lighting, municipal water systems, domestic plumbing, canning, the commercial production of ice, the improvement of furnaces, stoves, and washtubs, and the popularization of the sewing-machine aided growing numbers of women to escape from the domestic treadmill.[1] Increasing immigration threw large numbers of unskilled women on the labor market as cooks and nursemaids, thereby giving women with means, education, and imagination more leisure than had been the lot of young Mrs. Stanton, rebelliously tied to home and children in the 1840's.

College and professional women were also increasing in numbers. In the year 1889–90, a little more than 2,500 women had taken a bachelor of arts degree (in institutions of varying standards). The 90,000 or more women teachers of all kinds in 1870 had risen to almost 250,000 in twenty years; 544 women loosely categorized in the 1870 census as "physicians, surgeons, osteopaths, chiropractors, healers, and medical service workers" had risen to almost 4,500 by 1890.[3] Even in the decades immediately following the Civil War, a Julia Ward Howe who read Greek, Latin, and the philosophical works of Kant was no longer the anomaly that Margaret Fuller had been a scant thirty years earlier.

Yet in a very real sense such women were still "all dressed up and no place to go." In 1868 Charles Dickens visited the United

States and was given a dinner by the New York Press Club. By this time there were a number of recognized women journalists, but none of them belonged to the Press Club, and when some applied for tickets to the affair, they were refused. One of those rebuffed was Mrs. Jennie C. Croly, whose indignation led her to become the founder of one of the earliest women's clubs, Sorosis. During the same year Julia Ward Howe, Caroline M. Severance, and other Boston women founded the New England Women's Club.

What set these clubs, and others which followed them, apart from earlier literary and debating societies was the multiplicity and breadth of their interests added to their concern for "self-improvement." Aimed primarily at intellectuals, and avowing in its constitution that it wished to "furnish a quiet central resting-place and place of meeting in Boston, for the comfort and convenience of its members," the Boston club also stated its intention of becoming "an organized social center for united thought and action." It lived up to this aim in such a fashion that Edward Everett Hale later remarked: "When I want anything in Boston remedied, I go down to the New England Women's Club." Similarly, the concern of Sorosis ranged from high infant asylum mortality to the admission of women students to New York's Columbia University. Other groups developed programs reflecting the interests of their members and the nature of their community, but breadth of interest was their hallmark. Soon Chicago had its Fortnightly and San Francisco its Century Club, and countless others sprang up, indicating that the new form met a deep need. While some clubs were short-lived, others proved hardy, and by 1890 there were enough stable and influential ones to form the General Federation of Women's Clubs. In 1894 State Federations were inaugurated, whose programs were educational in the broadest sense of the word.[4]

Although farm women did not have their own organizations yet, they were from the very beginning equal members (although never leaders) in the Patrons of Husbandry, or Grange. Starting from small and unpromising beginnings to bring the farmer knowledge of scientific advances in agriculture, the Grange had become a nation-wide organization by 1873, and developed wider social and educational functions. The diversification of its program arising from the membership of women strengthened the organization, while its influence on otherwise isolated farm women was well-nigh incalculable.[5]

Following local clubs with varied programs came national organizations with more specific aims. The origins in the 1860's of the Young Women's Christian Association go back to the concern of a few women with the religious life and moral problems of young girls, working away from home. The forerunner of the American Association of University Women appeared in 1882, only a few years after the earliest graduates were receiving their degrees at Vassar, Wellesley, and Smith. While the work of such organizations lies outside the scope of this narrative, mention of their appearance does serve to indicate the extent to which women were participating in the life of their day and assuming leadership in social welfare. By the 1890's these activities would broaden to include the settlement-house movement and the organization of women as consumers with social responsibilities; in the long run they would be a potent force in making the political enfranchisement of women inevitable.

Women reformers had been concerned with the temperance question since the 1840's, not merely out of sympathy with an abstract ideal, but because the law placed married women so much at the mercy of their husbands. What might be a moral injustice if the latter was a sober citizen became sheer tragedy if he were a heavy drinker who consumed not only his own earnings but his wife's, and reduced her and her children to destitution. Alcoholism was wide-spread in a society lacking in social hygiene, medical therapy, and any kind of welfare work, and whose recreational facilities were non-existent except for the well-to-do. A combination of idleness, boredom, and misfortune could make a man the bane instead of the mainstay of his family, while his wife would have no legal redress.

Small wonder that Lucretia Mott, Lucy Stone, and the rest were temperance crusaders almost as soon as they became abolitionists, and before they espoused the cause of woman's rights as such. Forced by male prejudice to organize their own temperance societies, they were unable to keep these going, because women had no money of their own for such purposes; moreover they soon saw the impossibility of achieving reform without a broader social program and political influence. It was the peculiar gift of Frances Willard, one of the ablest women of the nineteenth century, that she saw the possibility of harnessing women's newly released energies in a multi-purpose organization which might work, not for temperance alone, but for a broad welfare program appealing to women, including woman suffrage both as means and end. She was not the founder of the Women's Christian Temperance Union, but it was she who made it the largest women's organization in the country.

In 1874 a temperance movement with strong evangelical overtones originated in the Middle West, beginning in Hillsboro, Ohio, and spreading throughout the country. Bands of singing, praying women held meetings, not only in churches but on street corners, penetrating into the saloons themselves and closing them by the thousands.

But although the "Crusade" was enormously dramatic, its effects were short-lived; most of the saloons reopened, and the more knowledgeable women saw that a permanent organization was needed to accomplish lasting results. In November 1874 the Women's Christian Temperance Union was organized in Cleveland. It elected as president Mrs. Annie Wittenmeyer, who had been active in the Civil War Sanitary Commission; as corresponding (we would say organizing) secretary, it chose Frances Willard, a young woman recently converted to the temperance cause.[6]

Like many of the new rising group of women leaders, Miss Willard was a product of the westward-moving frontier, a daughter of the Middle Border. Her parents had left New England to study at the newly founded college in Oberlin, and settled in Wisconsin when Frances was fifteen years old. After graduating from one of the seminaries which then hopefully described themselves as colleges, Miss Willard taught school, becoming president of the Evanston (Illinois) College for Ladies. When the latter was transformed into the Women's College of Northwestern University, she became Dean, but found the experience of working with an all-male and singularly inflexible board of trustees an unhappy one, and resigned after three years. Within a matter of months she had become a leader, first in the Illinois state, and then the national temperance organization.

Her choice of the temperance field has been interpreted by her biographer, Mary Earhart, as arising less from an overriding interest in that cause itself than from a belief that it could be the means of drawing large numbers of women hitherto not receptive to the issue of greater rights for women, into activity which could lead them in that direction. Like the earlier temperance leaders, she saw that political influence would be a determining factor in achieving their goal, and she decided to combine the two.

She began by herself espousing woman suffrage openly at a W.C.T.U. convention in 1876. Encountering strong opposition from Mrs. Wittenmeyer, leading the so-called "conservative" bloc, she unseated her as national president within three years, and swung the organization over, not only to support of suffrage, but to intensive work for it.

Her approach was shrewd. She achieved success by a series of tangential moves, in the course of which women as yet unready for the brand of forthright argument employed by a Susan B. Anthony were gradually led to understand that they could not protect their homes and families from liquor or other vices, without a voice in public affairs. The first actual step toward a position on woman suffrage was a demand for the vote, but only on the issue of local option with respect to the manufacture and sale of intoxicating beverages:

We want [the temperance ballot] because the liquor traffic is entrenched in law, and law grows out of the will of majorities, and majorities of women are against the liquor traffic. . . . Some of our sisters have feared lest attention to this branch of work might interfere with our holding Gospel meetings, circulating temperance literature and training the children to right habits. But we invite comparison between states active in the petition battle for the temperance vote and those who have excluded this method of work.[7]

The earliest "Home Protection" drive, organized by Miss Willard in Illinois, centered around a petition to the Legislature asking for local option. It was headed by the slogan "For God, for home, and native land." Although by 1878 petitions from women were no longer a novelty, the results of this campaign were something new. A combination of the broad appeal carried by the slogan and Frances Willard's formidable talent for organization produced such results that when the petition reached the lower house of the Illinois legislature it carried 110,000 names (about half of them women), and by the time it got to the state senate it had picked up 70,000 more. Women involved in such a project gained a new consciousness of their potential strength, and press and politicians alike were profoundly impressed.

A persuasive speaker who was not afraid of what sophisticates might consider clichés, with a flair for turning the Union's conventions into dramatic and festive occasions, Miss Willard did not rely solely on either talent for attracting a broad cross-section of women to the W.C.T.U. She coined a motto for the Union: "Do Everything"; to carry it out, she organized a long series of "departments," each with its own program of activity, with a special appeal for women at different levels of awareness. There were departments for work in kindergartens, prisons, and with the "shut-in" sick; departments concerned with physical culture and hygiene, prostitution, and mothers; and a department for work for the franchise. At one time there were thirty-eight of them. Not surprisingly, they were not all equally effective; during Miss Willard's regime, the franchise department was among the most active.

Within a remarkably short space of time the Women's Christian Temperance Union had reached into every state in the union, and claimed to speak for more than two hundred thousand women. While individual local groups varied in effectiveness, no other woman's organization approached it in scope and influence for many years. Its wide appeal is attested by the variety of able women whom it drew into activity and leadership at some period during their lives: the labor organizer Leonora Barry, the Negro lecturer and author Frances Harper, Anna Howard Shaw, Mary Livermore, Zerelda Wallace, Mary McDowell, and many others.

Yet within the W.C.T.U.'s multiple activities and its large and active membership lay the basis for a sharp conflict between the two causes of woman suffrage and temperance, which Frances Willard believed could strengthen one another. Because — for reasons previously stated — women reformers had so often been workers for temperance, the liquor interests were to be found in the opposition camp from the very first steps towards political enfranchisement for women, as far back as the Kansas referendum in 1867. As the W.C.T.U. grew, and its franchise department developed and began to furnish increasing numbers of workers in state campaigns, the liquor interests' opposition became stronger and more vitriolic. Sentiment grew among some suffrage leaders that the two issues should not be permitted to become identified in the public mind, and that the work of W.C.T.U. members for woman suffrage raised obstacles out of all proportion to the help they contributed. Abigail Scott Duniway of Oregon was never more irascible than on this question, and always maintained that it was the meddling of national suffrage leaders linked with the W.C.T.U. which was responsible for the long succession of referenda, six in all, required before Oregon finally gave its women the vote.

Miss Anthony's feelings were mixed. Despite a strong personal friendship with Miss Willard, and willingness to accept the Union's aid when the situation required it (as in the desperate and unsuccessful South Dakota referendum campaign of 1890), she was aware of dangers. In 1896 she asked Miss Willard not to hold a national W.C.T.U. convention in California as planned, because of the effect it would have on a state referendum for woman suffrage. Miss Willard was understanding and cooperative, and the convention was held in St. Louis instead (a fact which did not prevent the defeat of the suffrage proposal in California anyway). But the conflict was never resolved until the liquor companies, threatened by the Prohibition amendment, shifted their main energies to more pressing concerns. Even so, Mrs. Catt attributed a referendum lost as late as 1916 in West Virginia to the fact that the campaign was led and largely staffed by active W.C.T.U. members.[8]

With Miss Willard's gradual withdrawal from active leadership, and her death in 1898, the Union's attention became restricted to its original aim of temperance. Whatever problems it may have raised for the suffrage cause, the fact remains that no other nineteenth century organization reached and influenced so many women. Those which developed later — the General Federation of Women's Clubs, the National Federation of Business and Professional Women's Clubs, the Young Women's Christian Association, the suffrage associations, and countless church, farm, professional, and other specialized groups — all benefited in varying degrees from the fact that Frances Willard had succeeded in building up as large and many-sided an organization as the Women's Christian Temperance Union in its hey-day of multiple activities.

Organization among Negro women owed its particular character not so much to the fact that by and large they were excluded from white women's groups, as to the totally dissimilar circumstances of their lives.

Because they were barred from all but the most menial jobs, they were not concerned with trade unions, nor was suffrage an issue except to a small educated number among them. Even in those sections of the country where Negroes had greater opportunity than in the South, they remained for a long time second-class citizens, dependent largely on themselves for those social benefits which were increasingly a matter of civic responsibility in the white community: care of the sick, homeless and aged, and concern with health and education. In addition, the southern Negro woman faced wanton assault and the danger of prostitution on a scale unknown to her white sister. The frequent separation of families, often caused by the husband's search for work or for sheer physical safety, brought with it another whole complex of problems, including actual destitution.

Under such circumstances clubs assumed an importance and a content quite different from that found among the white women's groups, less often related to the earlier literary and educational societies than to such matters as care of the indigent, the sick and the aged, support of a church, or aid for a needy student. As the women gained in experience, as their horizons broadened and leadership developed, club programs became diversified to the point where, as one woman expressed it, they embodied "the organized anxiety of women who have become intelligent enough to realize their own low condition, and strong enough to initiate the forces of reform." [9]

By the 1890's there was widespread feeling among the colored women that a national organization for their group was needed. When plans were launched for the Columbian Exposition in Chicago in 1893, Miss Hallie Q. Brown of Wilberforce University strongly urged the chairman of the Board of Lady Managers, Mrs.

Potter Palmer, to appoint a Negro representative to the Board. When she was told that membership on the board could only be given to a representative of a national organization, Miss Brown began urging the federation of the existing colored women's clubs into an association. A number of such clubs in Washington, D. C., had already joined forces in the Colored Women's League, with a program which included classes in English literature, German, sewing, cooking, and gardening, a model kindergarten, and a day nursery for the children of working mothers.[10]

To understand the catalytic force which brought about nation-wide organization of Negro women requires taking into consideration factors which faced only the Negro woman: the belief among whites that she was incapable of monogamous morality, and the violence under whose threat she lived in the South.

Even some of the northern white women who worked with rare devotion as teachers and missionaries among the former slaves after the Civil War were inclined to put the blame for a high illegitimate birthrate of Negro children on her:

The negro women of the South are subject to temptations, of which their white sisters of the North have no appreciation, and which come to them from the days of their race enslavement. They are still the victims of the white man under a survival of a system tacitly recognized, which deprives them of the sympathy and help of the Southern white women, and to meet such temptations the negro woman can only offer the resistance of a low moral standard, an inheritance from the system of slavery, made still lower from a life-long residence in a one-roomed cabin.[11]

The Negro women leaders did not talk about "temptations." Mrs. Fannie Barrier Williams, northern-born and educated, a founder of the first training school for Negro nurses at Provident Hospital in Chicago, minced no words when she addressed a nationwide and world-wide gathering of women at the World Columbian Exposition:

I regret the necessity of speaking to the question of the moral progress of our women because the morality of our home life has been commented on so disparagingly and meanly that we are placed in the unfortunate position of being defenders of our name. . . . While I duly appreciate the offensiveness of all references to American slavery, it is unavoidable to charge to that system every moral imperfection that mars the character of the colored American. The whole life and power of slavery depended upon an enforced degradation of everything human in the slaves. The slave code recognized only animal distinctions between the sexes and ruthlessly ignored those ordinary separations of the sexes that belong to the social state. It is a great wonder that two centuries of such demoralization did not work a complete extinction of all the moral instincts.[12]

Threats to her own person were only one aspect of the violence in whose shadow the southern Negro woman often lived, worked, and raised a family; another was lynching. Violent and often fatal attacks by the Klan and its allies were without any legal redress, while resistance brought further retribution. It is significant that one of the earliest and most challenging voices against a wave of southern lynchings in the 1890's was that of Ida B. Wells, who was also closely identified with the efforts of colored women to overcome the moral stigma attached to their reputations.

Ida Wells was born in the little town of Holly Springs, Mississippi, just six months before the Emancipation Proclamation, of slave parents.[13] Father, mother, and three children died during an epidemic of yellow fever, leaving her, at the age of fourteen, to raise four younger children. She applied for a teaching position, saying that she was eighteen, and taught school for seven years. In 1884 she removed to Memphis, Tennessee, and in addition to her teaching, began writing articles for the small newspapers then springing up under Negro ownership. In 1889–1890 she bought a third share in the *Memphis Free Speech,* and became its editor.[14]

Because Miss Wells used her paper to criticize the inferior schools which Negro children had to attend, the Memphis School Board failed to renew her teacher's contract. She became a traveling correspondent throughout the South, writing of what she saw and heard of the circumstances of her people. The real turning-point in her life came in 1892, when three men, all personal friends of hers, were lynched near Memphis. The *Free Speech* denounced the crime, pointing out that the familiar pretext of punishment for the rape of a white woman was a cover-up for the lynchers' economic motive: the victims had been prospering as owners of a small store and were becoming threats to the white storekeepers who wanted to take over their trade. For this crime of plain speaking, a mob attacked the offices of the *Free Speech;* the business manager fled for his life, and Miss Wells, then in

Philadelphia, was warned not to return. She launched a veritable one-woman crusade against lynchings through the columns of other papers, on the lecture platform, and by helping to found colored women's clubs in Boston, New York, Chicago, and the Middle West. A record of individual lynchings which she compiled for 1892–1894, published with an introduction by Frederick Douglass under the title of *The Red Record,* roused fresh public anger against her. So did a tour, by invitation, of Great Britain, where she lectured and organized anti-lynching societies.

In June 1895 *The Woman's Era,* a Negro paper published in Boston, announced that Miss Florence Balgarnie, a pioneer British suffragist who was also deeply interested in the cause of Negro emancipation and betterment, had received a letter from John W. Jack, the editor of a small Missouri newspaper, denouncing the morality of American Negro women.[15] The letter, which was apparently never published, was widely circulated among influential Negro women, and proved to be the spark which brought a national organization of colored women into being. The New Era Club (which Miss Wells had helped to found) sent out invitations to other clubs inviting them to confer on the question, over the signature of Mrs. Josephine St. Pierre Ruffin.

Nothing could have been more dissimilar from the early life of Ida Wells than that of Mrs. Ruffin, and they would have had little in common had it not been for their Negro heritage. A New Englander by birth, Mrs. Ruffin had a mixed ancestry typical of the American "melting-pot": Indian, French, English — and Negro. Her childhood illustrated the problems of the free colored child. When she first entered school, Boston still maintained segregated schools, and her parents sent her to Salem, where no such bar existed. The day after the ban was dropped in Boston, she returned to her home to complete her education. After her marriage to George L. Ruffin, the young couple tried at first to escape discrimination by living in England. They came home after the outbreak of the Civil War, and Mr. Ruffin became one of the first colored graduates of the Harvard Law School, and one of the earliest Negroes to serve on the Boston Common Council and to sit on the Massachusetts bench.[16]

Mrs. Ruffin was active in public affairs — she was a suffragist, one of the first of her race to become a member of the New Eng-

land Women's Club, and editor of *The Woman's Era*. It was natural for her to take the lead in calling on Negro women to organize. Her address to the representatives of some twenty clubs who
met in Boston July 29–31, 1895, deserves a place in the annals of
American women:

> All over America there is to be found a large and growing class
> of earnest, intelligent, progressive colored women who, if not leading
> full, useful lives, are only waiting for the opportunity to do so, many
> of them still warped and cramped for lack of opportunity, not only
> to do more but to *be* more; and yet, if an estimate of the colored
> women of America is called for, the inevitable reply, glibly given, is:
> "For the most part, ignorant and immoral, some exceptions of course,
> but these don't count."
>
> Now for the sake of the thousands of self-sacrificing young women
> teaching and preaching in lonely southern backwoods, for the noble
> army of mothers who gave birth to these girls, mothers whose intelli-
> gence is only limited by their opportunity to get at books, for the sake
> of the fine cultured women who have carried off the honors at school
> here and often abroad, for the sake of our own dignity, the dignity
> of our race and the future good name of our children, it is "meet,
> right and our bounden duty" to stand forth and declare ourselves and
> our principles, to teach an ignorant and suspicious world that our
> aims and interests are identical with those of all good, aspiring women.
> Too long have we been silent under unjust and unholy charges. . . .
> Year after year southern women have protested against the admission
> of colored women into any national organization on the ground of
> the immorality of these women, and because all refutation has only
> been tried by individual work, the charge has never been crushed, as
> it could and should have been at first. . . . It is to break this silence,
> not by noisy protestations of what we are not, but by a dignified show-
> ing of what we are and hope to become, that we are impelled to take
> this step, to make of this gathering an object lesson to the world.

Mrs. Ruffin addressed a direct challenge to those white women
who had excluded the colored women from their organizations:

> Our woman's movement is woman's movement in that it is led and
> directed by women for the good of women and men, for the benefit of
> *all* humanity, which is more than any one branch or section of it. We
> want, we ask the active interest of our men, and, too, we are not draw-
> ing the color line; we are women, American women, as intensely inter-
> ested in all that pertains to us as such as all other American women;
> we are not alienating or withdrawing, we are only coming to the front,
> willing to join any others in the same work and cordially inviting and
> welcoming any others to join us.[17]

The Boston convention organized the National Federation of Afro-American Women and chose Mrs. Booker T. Washington, wife of the founder of Tuskegee Institute in Alabama, as president. In a few months *The Woman's Era* listed active affiliates in sixteen states — Alabama, California, Georgia, Illinois, Kansas, Louisiana, Massachusetts, Missouri, New York, Nebraska, North Carolina, Pennsylvania, Rhode Island, South Carolina, Tennessee, and Virginia — showing that the yeast was working in every section of the country.[18] Within one year a merger had been effected with the Colored Women's League of Washington and a new organization formed, the National Association of Colored Women, whose first president, Mrs. Mary Church Terrell, was a representative of the newly emerging college-bred Negro woman.

Like Mrs. Ruffin, Mrs. Terrell was of mixed descent, but she came from Tennessee, and her mother had been a slave.[19] After graduating from Oberlin she taught school and became the first Negro woman to serve on the District of Columbia Board of Education. She worked actively for woman's rights, speaking at several national suffrage conventions. She was also an accomplished linguist, who electrified the International Council of Women, meeting in Berlin in 1904, by addressing it successively in English, German, and French.

The National Association of Colored Women continued to provide leadership for Negro women for many years.[20] Mrs. Ruffin's appeal for cooperation was not reciprocated by the organizations of white women, although efforts were made by individual clubs to break down the color line. Mrs. Ruffin herself was the storm center of one such episode, which took place at the Milwaukee convention of the General Federation of Women's Clubs in 1900. She presented two sets of credentials, one from the New England Federation of Women's Clubs, the other from the New Era Club, and at first both were accepted. When it was discovered that the New Era Club was composed of colored women, the uproar was not confined to verbal exchanges: efforts were made on the convention floor to snatch Mrs. Ruffin's badge; she resisted stoutly, and the fracas was widely headlined.[21] The "solution" of the credentials committee in admitting her as the representative of the federation of white clubs while rejecting the credentials of the Negro group, was in line with the practices of other groups, such as the Women's Christian Temperance Union, which admitted Negro women within their own separate units, and the Young Women's Christian Association. There would be no real solution until the issue was tackled at its root decades later; it continued to arise each time Negro women attempted to take their place beside white women for the achievement of their common aims. [22]

Chapter XIV

WOMEN IN THE KNIGHTS OF LABOR
AND THE EARLY A.F. OF L.

The 1880's and '90's were a period of huge and rapid industrial growth. The founding of the Standard Oil Company was followed by more "trusts," at first in the distilling, sugar-refining, and lead industries, later in steel, tobacco, and elsewhere. Railroads spread north and south, in a network all the way to the Pacific Coast, spurred by such financiers as Henry Villard, James J. Hill, and others.

Cheap tractable labor was needed for these giant enterprises: in the decade after 1880, immigration from impoverished European countries topped five million. Women workers were in rising demand, always for the lowest-paying jobs; the 2,647,000 gainfully employed in 1880 grew to 4,005,500 ten years later, from 15.2 per cent to 17.2 per cent of the total working labor force.[1]

Outside of the large number classified as housekeepers, stewards, hostesses, and family servants of all kinds, totaling almost a million, the greatest number were to be found in the same occupations they had carried on at home before the era of industrialization: making cloth and clothing, keeping these clean, and other so-called service occupations. The largest groups of women factory workers were distributed as follows:[2]

Clothing manufacture	389,231	Tobacco	10,868
Laundries and cleaning	109,280	Printing	9,322
Cotton textiles	92,394	Silk and rayon	9,211
Other textiles	42,420	Carpets and rugs	7,674
Shoes	21,007	Hats	6,357
Containers and boxes	14,126		

Although the demand for labor appeared insatiable, soaring immigration enabled employers to keep wages down. The 1880's consequently saw the first really serious attempt to build a national labor organization. The Knights of Labor, founded in 1869 as a secret fraternal order, discarded the bulk of its ritualistic features in 1881 and began organizing working men and women on an equal basis.[3] Sometimes they were in the same "assemblies," sometimes in separate ones; these were set up on either craft or geographic lines — the Knights never achieved any standardized and stable form of organization. The first "woman's assembly" was chartered in 1881, and others were added with increasing rapidity until 1886, the year which marked the organization's high-water mark, and which also saw one hundred and thirteen women's assemblies chartered.

Since membership turnover was constant and many assemblies kept inadequate records, it is impossible to arrive at an accurate number of the women in the Order, at any one time or in the aggregate. In Massachusetts, however, where industrial employment was high in both groups, the proportion of women members was approximately one in seven; elsewhere it was probably lower.[4]

Whatever the exact figures, women joined the Knights all over the country in an upsurge the like of which had not been seen before. They included clerks, shoe workers, waitresses, printers, glass packers, domestics, textile workers, tailoresses, tobacco workers, dressmakers, farmers, teachers, laundresses, watchmakers, students, writers (the Knights never drew any hard and fast lines, and admitted many members who were not wage earners, as a trade union today would define the term), rubber workers, agents, music teachers, milliners, factory operatives of many kinds, type dressers, eyelet makers, hatters, tack makers and squib makers.[5]

Most of these women had never belonged to a labor organization before, but some of them were undoubtedly carrying on the tradition of earlier organizations, such as the Daughters of St. Crispin. There were assemblies of women shoe workers in Lynn and other Massachusetts towns, and an assembly of collar workers in Troy, the scene of the embattled women's union in the '60's. There were assemblies of women stocking knitters in St. Louis, whiteware makers in San Francisco, lead-pencil makers, feather curlers and gold cutters in New York, cabinet makers in Detroit, tailoresses

Elizabeth Cady Stanton and Susan B. Anthony

Carrie Chapman Catt

Alice Stone Blackwell and Anna Howard Shaw

in Newark and Milwaukee, and cloak makers in Chicago and Boston. There were assemblies of "housekeepers" in the South, of laundresses in Pensacola, Florida, of laundresses, cooks, washers and housekeepers in Virginia, and one of farmers in Arkansas.[6]

Although the women were admitted, and their dues payments welcomed, what little effort was made to help and organize them was sparked largely by the small group of leaders from their own ranks. Miss Mary Stirling, a Philadelphia shoe worker who was the lone female delegate at the 1883 "General Assembly," as the annual conventions of the Knights were called, took an active part in the proceedings, apparently undaunted at being outnumbered by several hundred men. The next year two women were seated as delegates, one of whom, Miss Mary Hanafin, was a charter member of the first woman's assembly to be established. She proved to be sufficiently intrepid and forceful to win the convention's support against attempts by some officials to set up another assembly to rival the one she represented as a delegate. In 1885, when she was once again present at a General Assembly as a delegate, she and the two other women delegates were appointed, on her motion, to serve as a committee "to collect statistics on women's work."

(We shall see how this cry for facts and statistics is raised repeatedly from this time on, for the simple reason that so little reliable information was available. What information the unions possessed had little bearing on women, since so few of them were organized; the earliest state labor bureaus were just coming into being, following the pioneering example of Massachusetts under the leadership of Carroll D. Wright, later the first U. S. Commissioner of Labor, and always keenly aware of the special hardships suffered by women workers.)

None of the three women appointed to the fact-finding committee had any previous experience to fit them for the task: Miss Hanafin was a sales clerk, and the other two were shoe workers. Nevertheless they went to work; they sent out a questionnaire to the women's assemblies in the Knights — the only source of information open to them — and duly reported at the convention of 1886 that the replies showed that average hours for women workers were ten a day, with wages at $5.00 a week, except in the shoe industry where they were slightly higher.[7]

This General Assembly of 1886 in Richmond, Virginia, not only marked the high point of the Knights of Labor as an organization; it made history for working women. Of the 660 delegates, sixteen were women: the tireless Miss Hanafin, six shoe workers, five textile operatives, one machine hand, one dressmaker, one ironer, and one housewife. The housewife was Mrs. George Rodgers, who had won the position of Master Workman (or head) of the entire Knights' organization in the Chicago area, except the stockyards. The mother of twelve children, she brought the youngest, a three-weeks-old baby, to the convention, and was "interviewed" by Frances Willard (herself a member of the Order):

Mrs. Rodgers is about forty years of age; height medium; figure neither stout nor fragile; complexion fair, clear and healthful; eye an honest gray; mouth sweet and smiling; nose, masterful Roman; head square and full; profile strong and benignant. . . . "My husband always believed that women should do anything they liked that was good and which they could do well," said Mrs. Rodgers proudly; "but for him I would never have got on so well as a Master Workman. I was the first woman in Chicago to join the Knights. They offered us the chance, and I said to myself, "There must be a first one, and so I'll go forward." "How do you speak to them?" I asked. "Oh, just as I do here to my children at home," she answered simply. "I have no time to get anything ready to say, for I do, and always have done, all my own work, but I just talk as well as I can at the time." [8]

One of the textile operatives was Miss Mary O'Reilly from Providence, Rhode Island. Miss O'Reilly subsequently served three active years with the Order. Following passage of the first factory inspection bill in the state of Pennsylvania, she was deputy factory inspector for six years, one of the first women to hold such a position.

The outstanding member of the group was the "machine hand" from a hosiery mill in Amsterdam, New York, named Leonora M. Barry. When the group of women, serving as a committee to consider Miss Hanafin's report to the General Assembly and make suggestions for further action, recommended that a Department of Woman's Work be established with a General Investigator to inquire into "the abuses to which our sex is subjected by unscrupulous employers, [and] to agitate the principles which our Order teaches, of equal pay for equal work and the abolition of child labor," they recommended Mrs. Barry for the post.

The convention thereupon elected Mrs. Barry; for the next three and a half years she traveled around the country, investigating, speaking, and organizing, on a scale that only two other women had equaled until then: Susan Anthony and Frances Willard. The wonder grows when one realizes that both the latter were well educated by the standards of their day and had served long apprenticehoods in such activity; Mrs. Barry was catapulted from a stocking machine to national leadership, and the only schooling she had to draw on was that of experience.

She had been born in Cork, Ireland, and brought to this country when still a young child. Her parents settled in Pierrepont, in upstate St. Lawrence county, New York, and necessity converted her from a homemaker into a factory hand:

I was left, without knowledge of business, without knowledge of work, without knowledge of what the world was, with three fatherless children looking to me for bread. To support these children it became my duty to go out in the army of the unemployed, and in one of the largest factories of central New York, I went, and for four years and seven months remained a factory woman for the support of my little ones.[9]

Her earnings the first day she went to work were eleven cents; for the first week they amounted to sixty-five cents.[10]

Little wonder that Mrs. Barry joined the Knights when the opportunity arose. She quickly made her mark, becoming the Master Workman of an assembly of nearly a thousand women, and delegate to the 1886 General Assembly. By 1888, speaking as head of the Woman's Department, she could report to the delegates once more assembled:

There have come to the Woman's Department, from November 1, 1887 to October 1, 1888, 537 applications for my presence, 213 of which have been filled by actual service, and all others answered from the office. Communications requesting advice and information, 789, all of which have been answered by the faithful and efficient secretary, Mary A. O'Reilly.[11]

Despite the enormous volume of her work, Leonora Barry left no enduring organization to show for it, which may be one reason why she has been so easily forgotten by historians and students. Her failure was not primarily due to her own shortcomings. She could not accomplish her assignment of investigating at first hand the conditions under which women were working because employers would not admit her to their premises; the women themselves were afraid to talk freely for fear of reprisals. On the other hand, when she tried to bring more women into the Order, or to assist their assemblies to achieve greater stability and gains, she suffered from the fact that she was working in an organization rent with factional discord.

Her task could not have been easy for one who was not as consistent a feminist as either Miss Anthony or Miss Willard. Leonora Barry believed that women should leave their homes to work only when absolutely necessary, as it had been in her case. She did not relish having enemies in her own organization call her "a lady tramp," and she flatly refused to carry on any activities she considered unladylike, even when legislation in which she had the deepest interest, such as the Pennsylvania Factory Inspection Bill, was at stake: "I have to [sic] much regard for my reputation to go lobbying around a state Capitol or buttonholing legislators." [12]

Nevertheless, for the period when she worked for the Knights, she was the conscience of the labor movement, and of a growing section of public opinion, where working women were concerned. Wherever she could find a platform — addressing members of the Knights or its conventions, or women wishing to organize, or such bodies as the International Council of Women — Leonora Barry raised her uncompromising and eloquent voice against the abysmal conditions under which too many women had to earn their livelihood. Nor did she talk in generalities: the former hosiery mill machine hand knew how to translate her protests into dollars and cents and aching backs.

Were wages low? It was not enough to state the fact: it must be documented: "A seal-plush cloak, selling for from $40 to $75, is made by the cloak-makers for eighty cents and $1 apiece, one being a day's work for an expert operative." [13] Her reports are peppered with such figures. Worst of all in her opinion was the menace of the sweatshop, where piece-work — on garments, artificial flowers, etc. — was farmed out and completed at appallingly low pay and under the worst possible health conditions:

I speak of the contract sweating middleman or slop-shop plan, which works ruin, misery, sin and shame to toilers, and death or failure to the legitimate or regularly established industry with which it competes. Instance the following: Men's pants that retail at prices from $1 to $7 per pair, are taken by the contractor at 15 cents per pair. Operatives are then employed and huddled together in a close stifling backroom, where the machine operatives furnish their own machines, and, in most cases, thread, and do all the machine work on pants, without basting, for 5 cents a pair. They are then passed over to the finisher, who puts on the buttons, makes buttonholes and puts on buckles for 5 cents per pair; 6 pairs is an average day's work.

Supposing 5 operatives to be employed, and there are often more than less, the contractor makes 30 cents a head, which nets him or her $1.50 per day while his or her victim gets 30 cents per day. Men's vests are contracted out at 10 cents each, the machine operative receiving 2½ cents and finisher 2½ cents each, making 5 cents a vest for completion. Twenty vests is a day's work. Here again, with the 5 operatives, he or she nets $1 per day for doing nothing, while his unfortunate victim has 50 cents for 11 and 12 hours of her life's energies.[14]

Mrs. Barry was here reporting to a General Assembly of the Knights; in addition to herself, there were just two other women present. As she spoke to that crowd of men, her wrath and compassion as a woman blazed out:

These women are required by society to meet all the requirements of nature in an honest woman. Think of their ability to do so under such opportunities! Oh, brothers of the Knights of Labor, I implore you, by your love for mothers, sisters, wives and daughters, those sweet little innocent girls who today gladden your heart and brighten your hearthstone, unite as one man in some course that will have a tendency to remove this curse of our fair land — this blot upon American liberty and independence — ere the tender feet of your loved ones are compelled to press this life's pathway of thorns.[15]

Unfortunately she was addressing an organization which was increasingly demonstrating its inability to unite on any course at all, and rapidly disintegrating in consequence. Moreover, Mrs. Barry herself admitted that in the face of such conditions as she described, the response of women to attempts at organization was disappointing, due to ignorance, apathy, hopelessness, and

the habit of submission and acceptance without question of any terms offered them, with the pessimistic view of life in which they see no ray of hope. Such people cannot be said to live, as living means the enjoyment of nature's gifts, but they simply vegetate like partially petrified creatures. Every effort has been made to perfect and extend the organization of women, but our efforts have not met with the response that the cause deserves — partly because those who have steady employment, fairly good wages, and comfortable homes seem to see nothing in organization outside of self-interest, and, because they are what they are pleased to term "all right," do not feel it incumbent upon themselves to do anything to assist their less fortunate co-workers. Again, many women are deterred from joining labor organizations by foolish pride, prudish modesty and religious scruples; and a prevailing cause, which applies to all who are in the flush of womanhood, is the hope and expectancy that in the near future marriage will lift them out of the industrial life to the quiet and comfort of a home, foolishly imagining that with marriage their connection with and interest in labor matters end; often finding, however, that their struggle has only begun when they have to go back to the shop for two instead of one. All this is the results or effects of the environments and conditions surrounding women in the past and present, and can be removed only by constant agitation and education.[16]

While this outburst reflects the bitterness of a woman who knew from her own experience that marriage was no guarantee against the problems of a wage earner, it also shows that Leonora Barry understood the source of such illusions. By and large the reluctance of women to join trade unions, and the difficulties encountered in trying to organize them, are still very much with us. In any case, attempts to organize them into the Knights of Labor came to an end when Mrs. Barry resigned her post in 1890 to marry Oliver R. Lake, a St. Louis printer and member of the Knights; the organization, already in the process of dissolution, never replaced her.[17]

Throughout the 1890's and early 1900's, women continued their sporadic and usually unsuccessful attempts to form unions. Despite the long depression of 1893–1896 which brought widespread unemployment and destitution, they succeeded in setting up unions for varying lengths of time in meat packing, glove making, retail, domestic and janitor work, textiles, men's and women's garments, knit goods, shirtwaists, millinery and men's hats, cleaning and dyeing, paper boxes, twine, rubber, boots and shoes, laundries, cigar and cigarette making, tobacco, printing, teaching, and many other fields.[18]

Some were completely independent unions, and these, lacking resources and experience, usually fared the worst; others were so-called "federal locals," chartered by the American Federation of Labor and limited to women in one trade; still others affiliated with, or grew out of organizing done by established unions belonging to the A.F. of L. The latter, founded in 1881, and taking its better-known name in 1886, remained for decades an association of highly autonomous unions, mainly organized along craft lines among skilled and therefore relatively highly paid workers, such as carpenters, plumbers, printers, etc.

Attempts by the Federation to organize women on any large scale foundered on the disinclination of the majority of its unions to spend money organizing low-paid, unskilled trades far removed from their own immediate interests. Despite an occasional convention resolution or statement by President Samuel Gompers endorsing the principles of organizing women or of equal pay, only sporadic attempts were made to implement such pronouncements, and these were usually sparked by the women themselves.

In 1892 the A.F. of L. finally appointed a woman organizer — for a term of five months. Mary E. Kenney was a bindery worker, who had organized the women of her trade in Boston into a "Ladies Federal Union." During her brief tenure as organizer she worked with women in a number of industries in New York and the New England states. It must have been a thankless job, for in addition to encountering all the obstacles enumerated by Leonora Barry, the Federation officials were not enthusiastic supporters of her work, and it was discontinued long before she had received a chance to prove its value. Fortunately Miss Kenney's interest in organizing women was less ephemeral; she served as assistant factory inspector in Illinois under Florence Kelley, participated in shoe and textile strikes in Haverhill and Lawrence, and became one of the moving forces in the organization, ten years later, of the Women's Trade Union League.

Miss Kenney belonged to a generation of women unionists who bridged the gap between two eras: that of apparently fruitless sacrifice and devotion, and that of achievement. Most widely known of this group, among her own contemporaries, was Leonora O'Reilly, today largely forgotten.[19]

Like so many of the women who pioneered in organizing, she was Irish; her parents came to this country on the wave of immigration created by the famines of the mid-nineteenth century. Winifred O'Reilly was married to a printer who died leaving his wife and year-old daughter in bitter want, and during the panic and depression of 1873 mother and daughter were often cold and hungry. Leonora remembered her mother coming home night after night with bundles of work from the shirt factory which employed her, sewing on them until midnight, then taking up her own household tasks. Winifred O'Reilly took her daughter to labor and political rallies, even as a baby in arms.

Leonora never finished school. In 1881 when she was eleven, she went to work in a New York collar factory, earning $1.00 per dozen finished collars; in three years, the rate declined to fifty cents per dozen. In 1886 she joined the Knights of Labor and took part in her first strike.

That same year she also joined with other women in organizing a Working Women's Society which had more enduring results, since it led to the formation of the Consumers League. She came to know such influential women as Josephine Shaw Lowell and Louisa Perkins, who eventually made it possible for her to leave her factory job and get some education.

At this moment of writing there are people still living who recall the incandescence and impact of Leonora O'Reilly's personality. She became a friend and potent influence in the lives of some of the most socially creative minds of her time: Lillian Wald, Felix Adler, William Dean Howells, Mary Dreier, Margaret Dreier Robins, and a host of others. She never went back to factory work, but she remained an active force in the labor movement, always primarily concerned with women. After teaching for a number of years at the Manhattan Trade School for Girls, she became an organizer for the Women's Trade Union League (of which she was a founder) and helped bring into existence the unions that still endure today in the garment trades.

An ardent suffragist, a Socialist, an eloquent speaker, Miss O'Reilly was sought after as organizer, spokesman at legislative hearings, a voice wherever fiery protest was needed. By 1915, when she was only forty-four, she had burned herself out. Except for brief periods of activity in the Woman's Peace Party and for the Irish Fenians, she remained in virtual retirement until her death in 1927.

Chapter XV

THE REFORM ERA AND WOMAN'S RIGHTS

The rapid development of a predominantly industrial society brought about, not only an immense increase in productivity and wealth, but heightened poverty and social tension. Pyramiding incomes at one end of the scale (the *New York Tribune* estimated in 1892 that there were 4,047 millionaires in the United States),[1] were in acute contrast with sweatshops and congested slums. Violent industrial struggles took place, on a scale hitherto unknown, between a growing labor movement and employers fighting for the open shop and cheap labor as a vital source of their huge profits.

The farmers, too, were pinched between a waning "frontier" where available land was increasingly marginal and expensive to farm, the collapse of the long and fabulous land boom, and a world-wide recession in agricultural prices. There was ample basis for a revulsion against what Mark Twain had called the Gilded Age, and Vernon L. Parrington more recently christened the Great Barbecue.

Like all social protest movements, that revulsion was rooted in more than a sense of ethical injustice. Unlike the earlier anti-slavery impulse, which drew largely for its philosophy on the concept of the rights of man, it was influenced by the more recent theories of evolution. Going beyond a rigid, mechanical application of Darwinian principles of biological development to the processes of social change, the American sociologist Lester Ward was the first to evolve a body of thought which held that social evolution is not merely a continuation of natural selection and the survival of the fittest, but that the human will can consciously enter the process as a directing force.

To minds that shrank from the toll in human suffering which

so-called progress appeared to bring in its wake, and rejected the impossibility of ameliorating social injustice, such thinking was enormously liberating and stimulating. Ward's *Dynamic Sociology,* which appeared in 1883, was only the first of a series of books expounding his views, but his early influence was limited by comparison with the hundreds of thousands who read Edward Bellamy's *Looking Backward,* a description of an ideal society founded on utopian socialist principles, published in 1888, and Henry Demarest Lloyd's *Wealth Against Commonwealth* in 1894, one of the early "muckraking" exposures of big business, directed principally against the Standard Oil Company.

A number of church leaders, troubled at the gap between Christian ethics and the glaring inequities of life around them, also began to demand reform, notably those in the Church Association for the Advancement of the Interests of Labor (C.A.I.L.) led by Walter Rauschenbusch, W. D. P. Bliss, and others. On the political side, the upsurge against the vested interests took shape in the Populist Party around the farmers' demands for monetary reform, cheaper currency, and free silver, and the curbing of the trusts, the railroads (whose freight charges were ruinous to them), and land speculators.[2]

Such ferment produced new forms of organization through which women could achieve greater participation in social action. These enabled an heiress like Grace Dodge, or middle-class women of sensitivity and conscience like Josephine Shaw Lowell, Margaret Dreier Robins, and Jane Addams to bridge the gap between their own immunity and the women working in stores and factories who needed their help. Out of their joint efforts came, not only the settlement houses, but such organizations as the Working Girls Clubs, the National Consumers League, and the Women's Trade Union League, which brought women workers new allies possessed of money, influence, and dedication.

The heightened tempo of protest and fresh intellectual activity sent increasing numbers of girls to college (particularly those with a bent toward community service) and into the professions, and it eventually heightened the agitation for woman suffrage as well.[3] At every turn such women were faced with the handicap of their utter political impotence, and, with the exception of Miss

Dodge, every woman who was to any degree active in the social reform movement was also an active and articulate suffragist.

In 1884, at the same time that increasing numbers of women were joining the Knights of Labor, another form of organization began among working women. The first "Working Girls Club" was formed in New York by twelve factory workers and a young woman named Grace Dodge[4] in the upstairs room of a Tenth Avenue tenement belonging to a silk worker.

Miss Dodge came from a family which was making a fortune in copper mining. At the age when she would normally have made her society debut, she told her parents she was more interested in doing something useful. Although Dorothea Dix in the 1840's had first made prison reform and care of the indigent sick and insane the province of public-spirited women, and the Sanitary Commission had legitimized such interest, the problem was still sufficiently unfamiliar to cause Mr. Dodge to take his daughter to Miss Louisa Schuyler for counseling. Miss Schuyler, late of the Sanitary Commission, had continued her philanthropic work in peace times, becoming a founder of the New York State Charities Aid Association, and a mentor to young women like Grace Dodge.

In the end Miss Dodge, although she took part in philanthropic work for a time, found her own path, determined largely by her strongly religious bent and her growing interest in education. Through a Sunday school class which she conducted, she met some factory girls, and initiated a series of "practical talks" dealing with religious and moral questions. She was perceptive enough to grasp that the girls needed more than preachments — that they longed for education, for beauty, for an opportunity for self-expression and creation, and that, given some help, they were capable of achieving these things for themselves. By 1885, just a year after the first club was launched, there were enough clubs in New York to form the Association of Working Girls Societies. The idea spread to New England, Philadelphia, and as far away as Chicago and St. Louis. National conventions were held in 1890 and 1894, and for several years the organization had its own monthly magazine, *Far and Near,* edited by Maria Bowen Chapin.[5]

Although Miss Dodge furnished financial aid and was a guiding spirit, the individual clubs were conducted along democratic lines. They were named for a street or a neighborhood, or as an indication of the varied impulses which brought them into existence: Endeavor Club, Working Girls Progressive Society, Enterprise, Steadfast, Far and Near, Good Will, etc. The strongest clubs maintained their own houses — residences with housekeepers, a nurse, permanent lodgers, libraries, and a flourishing program of activities: classes in millinery and dressmaking, stenography, literature, physical exercise, and medical care. Their "practical talks" were in reality group discussions, often on religious subjects, on "Purity" or "Womanhood," as well as on such matters uppermost in girls' minds then as now: "How To Get a Husband," and "Money — How To Get It and Keep It." [6]

The clubs did not endure as a form of organization because they could not solve the most basic problem that beset the young girl trying to earn a livelihood and also maintain her own personal dignity and individuality. They could not help her to earn a living wage under conditions which would make it possible for her to escape illness and prostitution. Into this battle Miss Dodge could not lead them.[7] But she could, and did make other valuable contributions — to education, as one of the first women to serve on the New York City Board of Education and in aiding the development of Teachers College; and again to young working women, as the president of the unified and strengthened Young Women's Christian Association, whose work among industrial girls owed a good deal to Miss Dodge's early experience with their problems.

More characteristic than Grace Dodge of the new trend toward reform developing among women of means was Josephine Shaw Lowell, who clove nearer to the heart of the problem. She wrote to a friend:

The interests of the working people are of paramount importance, simply because they are the majority of the whole people, and the indifference and ignorance and harshness felt and expressed against them by so many good people is simply awful to me and I must try and help them if I can, and leave the broken-down paupers to others.[8]

Mrs. Lowell, the widow of a young officer who had been killed in the Civil War, had also turned to Miss Schuyler for guidance in rebuilding her life after the war. An apt pupil, she was the first woman appointed a member of the New York State Board of Charities in 1876; she made a name for herself by ability and hard work in prison reform, and in improving the administration of poor relief and institutions caring for indigent women and children.

But she grew profoundly dissatisfied with such palliatives for human suffering. It seemed more important to tackle the problem nearer its roots, *before* the individual man or woman became a public charge through destitution. In 1889 when she resigned her position on the State Board of Charities, she wrote to her sister:

Nellie says you think I ought to continue on the Board, but I think there is far more important work to be done for working people. Five hundred thousand wage-earners in this city, two hundred thousand of them women and children, and seventy-five thousand of those working under dreadful conditions or for starvation wages. That is more vital than the twenty-five thousand dependents, counting the children. If the working people had all they ought to have, we should not have the paupers and the criminals. It is better to save them before they go under, than to spend your life fishing them out when they're half-drowned and taking care of them afterwards! Exactly what I can do, I do not know, but I want the time to try.[9]

Within a year Mrs. Lowell had discovered the instrumentality through which she might accomplish some of her aims. In 1886 a group of working women founded a society because, as they stated: "For united effort there is need of a Central Society which shall gather together those already devoted to the cause of organization among women, shall collect statistics and publish facts, shall be ready to furnish information and advice, and, above all, shall continue and increase agitation on this subject."[10]

The moving spirit was a woman somewhat older than the rest, named Alice Woodbridge, who had worked for many years as a clerk and saleslady in retail stores. It was largely at her instigation that the Working Women's Society undertook to make a survey of working conditions in New York stores. Without funds or trained staff, by word-of-mouth questioning, they found — what some of them, like Miss Woodbridge, already knew at first hand — conditions so deplorable that they took their findings to a group of influential citizens, among them Mrs. Lowell, Miss Louisa Perkins,

Mrs. Frederick Nathan, Dr. Mary Putnam-Jacobi, and several interested clergymen.

The problem was not one which could be most easily solved by trying to organize a trade union of the retail workers, for reasons set out in a Consumers League report in 1895:

They are all women; and consequently usually timid and unaccustomed to associated action.

They are young, many being between the ages of fourteen and twenty; and therefore without the wisdom, strength of character, or experience which would enable them to act in their own behalf.

Their trade, although it has highly skilled departments, is mostly unskilled, and therefore there is an almost unlimited supply of applicants for their situations in case they do not accept the conditions offered them.[11]

What was needed was to bring into action a group not mobilized heretofore: the buying public. This public, where clothing, food, house furnishings, and white goods were concerned, was, then as now, largely one of women, with this difference: because wages were low, and many necessities for low-income families were still made at home by the housewife, the largest consumer was the woman of means, middle or upper class, often one still far removed from any kind of public activity or cause.

The New York Consumers League, founded in 1890, turned its attention to arousing this group. Similar Leagues followed shortly in Philadelphia, in Massachusetts, and elsewhere. In 1899 the National Consumers League was established. It made itself the militant and highly articulate conscience of the buying public on such conditions as wages of $2.00 a week for women not living at home; hours from 7:45 A.M. till midnight, with only a few minutes off for lunch; a six-day-work week, with sometimes stocktaking on Sundays at no additional pay; no seats behind the sales counters; no lockers; no vacations; and no place to eat lunch except in the toilets and stockrooms.[12]

One of the League's earliest weapons was the "White List," on which appeared the names which met its "Standards of a Fair House," such as a weekly minimum (for experienced workers) of $6.00; hours no longer than 8 to 6 with three quarters of an hour for lunch; a six-day week, with a half holiday each week during July and August; one week's paid vacation; no child labor; and such amenities as seats behind the counters, lockers for outdoor clothing, and adequate eating space. The first New York "White List" carried the names of just eight establishments which met these requirements.[13]

Under the leadership of Mrs. Lowell (its president until 1896) and later of Maud Nathan and Florence Kelley, the League grew until at its peak there were affiliates in twenty states. Its efforts soon went beyond the field of retail stores, to the conditions under which apparel was manufactured (which brought it into collision with the sweatshops), and the preparation of certain food products, such as milk.[14] Recognizing that moral public suasion was not enough, it worked for legislation which would compel employers to conform to standards set, not by organizations of private individuals, but by the state. When such legislation was challenged in the Courts as unconstitutional, it was the National Consumers League which led in the long struggle to establish governmental responsibility for limiting working hours, as well as other aspects of the individual worker's safety and welfare.

The settlement houses, a unique and highly individual form which social service developed in the reform era, arose from more complex motives than altruism alone. Along with a desire to help the needy and underprivileged, men and women of education and means felt the need, not just of seeing "how the other half lives," but of sharing, day by day, the problems and aspirations of a large section of the urban population with whom they would ordinarily have no communication whatever. As such, the settlements seemingly have no place in the movement for woman's rights. That they did is owing to a number of factors. A group of their founders and leaders were women, and exceptionally gifted women, comparable in prestige and achievements to those who emerged from abolitionist struggles to bring the women's cause to the forefront, and far more widely regarded than these as important citizens. The settlement houses also played a role in the woman's movement because, in seeking out those who most needed their services, they inevitably found working women at the bottom of the heap.[15]

The early settlement leaders, mostly women, had in common a high degree of imagination and sensitivity, together with a conviction that nothing in the way of emergencies or crises was alien to the settlement house, whether it grew out of mass epidemics, unemployment, labor disputes, poor housing, or political hysteria. They also came, not surprisingly, to strikingly similar conclusions: that beneath the surface conditions such as overcrowding, dirt, disease, and ignorance was a basic factor: people were too poor. To overcome poverty they needed, not merely counseling, or nursing, or classes in English (the overwhelming majority of slum dwellers were recent immigrants from non-English speaking countries), or vocational training: they needed trade-union organization. Among the inhabitants of New York's East Side or Chicago's South Side and the other city slums, none were paid less or needed unions more desperately than the women who were unskilled and more backward because they still carried with them the inhibitions of European traditions where women were concerned. Despite their needs, the American Federation of Labor showed little interest in them.

Inevitably, although quite unexpectedly, the settlement leaders found themselves involved in the attempts of such women to better their working conditions; sometimes indeed they were in positions verging on the ludicrous. Even before the Henry Street Settlement was born, while Lillian Wald was still working as a visiting nurse on New York's lower East Side (with a growing reputation of interest and helpfulness in that teeming area's problems which foreshadowed the part the settlement house would later play there), she received a visit from a young woman who lived in the apartment on the floor below:

Our pleasure was mingled with consternation to learn that she wished aid in organizing a trades union. Even the term was unknown to me. She spoke without bitterness of the troubles of her shop-mates, and tried to make me see why they thought a union would bring them relief. It was evident that she came to me because of her faith that one who spoke English so easily would know how to organize in the "American way," and perhaps with a hope that the union might gain respectability from the alliance. We soon learned that one great obstacle to the organization of young women in the trades was a fear on their part that it would be considered "unladylike," and might even militate against their marriage. The next day I managed to find time to visit the library for academic information on the subject of trades unions. That evening, in a basement in a nearby street, I listened to the broken English of the cigarmaker who was trying to help the girls.[16]

It was not surprising that Miss Wald had to resort to a library to find out what a union was. She came from a comfortable middle-class home, and her sole preparation for the world of slum life she would make her own was the brief and limited training then offered by a nursing school. Sympathy and perception carried her across the gap, just as they did Jane Addams, who had grown up in a small Illinois town, and whose slowly maturing social convictions led her to establish a settlement in the wilderness of slums along Chicago's Polk and Halsted streets, many without even water or sewage connections.[17] Hull House was open to working girls (as to all other comers) whatever their interests: recreation, education, or organization. Mary Anderson, a shoe worker who became Director of the U. S. Women's Bureau, has recorded what such hospitality could mean:

After I joined the union I began to know Jane Addams and Hull House. We had meetings at Hull House, where Miss Addams would speak to us, and sometimes I would meet her at trade union meetings and in other places. It was always interesting to go to Hull House. Sometimes Miss Addams would ask us to come for tea on Sunday afternoons and we would meet prominent people from other parts of the country and from abroad. . . . For me, and I think for many others too, Hull House and Jane Addams opened a door to a larger life.[18]

Mary McDowell, the first director of Chicago's University Settlement, had the advantage over Miss Wald and Miss Addams of a previous broader range of experience: she had been active in relief work during the Chicago fire of 1871, a friend of Frances Willard's, and for a time Illinois state organizer for the W.C.T.U. before she became, very briefly, one of the earliest Hull House "residents." When in 1894 the University of Chicago established a settlement in the jungle "back of the yards" to serve as the new Sociology Department's "window" on real social problems, Miss McDowell was appointed, on Miss Addams' recommendation, to be its head. Before long she was in touch with the movement to organize the men working in the yards for the huge packinghouse concerns into unions, and in 1902 in a speech to Chicago club men, she criticized the failure of the unions to organize the women who were coming in growing numbers into the industry, and also the women themselves for not following the example of the men and organizing.

Two young women named Mollie Daly and Hannah O'Day, who worked in the yards, read a newspaper account of this speech. They were already members of a girls' club named for the Irish patriot Maud Gonne; they came to the University Settlement to ask Miss McDowell's help in converting their club into a union. Miss McDowell sent for Michael Donnelly, leader of the stockyard unions, who gave the women encouragement. At their request she herself attended their meetings. They organized a union which was chartered as Local No. 183 of the Amalgamated Meat Cutters and Butchers Workmen of North America, and which lasted until an unsuccessful strike in 1904 wiped out all the stockyard unions for a time. The extent of Miss McDowell's contribution in aiding the women's local, which set a new mark by its success in uniting diverse nationalities — Irish, Polish, Negro, German, etc. — is attested by a letter Miss McDowell received from Mollie Daly, while the settlement house leader was on vacation:

We carried on such a business meeting last night I could not wait to let you know about it. . . . Hannah O'Day and I went to the Packing Trades Council Sunday, it was a special meeting the men had for to decide on a scale of wages and there was no new business taken up only our letter of appeal. It was read to the delegates and the council donated $25 and a delegate from each local was given one of the copies, with instructions to act on it at their first meeting and last night one of the new locals sent $5 which I think was very good from one just started. And at our meeting we elected a committee to make a constitution and by-laws for our local also an auditing committee and sick committee to visit our sick members and last but not least a committee to go with Mr. Donnelly to Mr. Armour to have us reinstated. We also past [sic] a resolution to have a written invitation sent to Mr. Donnelly and to the president and officers of the Packing Trades Council to our social.[19]

Although the full story of the National Women's Trade Union League belongs in a later chapter, its founding in 1903 was one more expression of the fusion of two streams — the educated, middle-class women, sometimes, but not always, professionals, and working women — for common effort on the latter's behalf. In the continuing absence of any consistent effort by the American Federation of Labor or its affiliates to organize women, the League came into existence at a series of meetings held during the Federation's convention in Boston.[20] To these sessions, held, appropriately enough, in Faneuil Hall, came a few male delegates, mostly from garment unions; but the initiative came from the indomitable Mary Kenney (now Mrs. O'Sullivan), Leonora O'Reilly, Mrs. Mary Morton Kehew, a wealthy Bostonian who had been trying to organize working girls in trade unions since 1892, the philanthropist and socialist William English Walling, and that indefatigable trio: Miss Addams, Miss Wald, and Miss McDowell.[21] Nor was the latters' interest a passing or perfunctory one; they continued active in League affairs until a new generation of leaders had emerged, many of them from the shops of the garment and allied trades, who were to carry the League through its most influential years.

It was also from the same group of settlement leaders — conscious, from their experience in trying to stir up public opinion, of the crying need for authoritative, indisputable *facts* — that there emerged the idea of a comprehensive investigation into the condition of women workers, financed by Congress, but conducted by *experts*. The plan seems to have had its inception in the minds of Sophonisba Breckinridge, Edith Abbott, and Mary McDowell. It took two years to get the bill authorizing the inquiry and appropriating the needed funds through Congress, at the urging of the General Federation of Women's Clubs, the Women's Trade Union League, assorted church, labor, and civic groups, and, at long last, of President Theodore Roosevelt himself. No individual contributed more to the final outcome than Miss McDowell.

The investigation and preparation of the nineteen-volume report took four years, from 1908 through 1911, and covered the condition of child as well as women wage earners. The report ranged over a wide area, covering not only conditions in a variety of industries employing women, but the history of women in trade unions, family budgets, the mortality of children in relation to the employment of mothers, and related topics. The report, a landmark when it was issued, is still required material for the student today.

With the publication of the report and with the pioneering work being done during the same period by such investigators as Edith Abbott, Mary Van Kleeck, Josephine Goldmark, and others, the basis was being laid for legislation to protect women and child workers for decades to come. Moreover, experience would show that, once such laws were on the statute books, comprehensive legislation covering male workers as well would follow more easily. Beyond the employer, the union, and the helpless unorganized individual worker, man, woman or child, now stood the state, increasingly responsible for safeguarding the welfare of the citizen with respect to working conditions, hours, health, and fire hazards.

Such an enlargement of its powers (which effective enforcement of such statutes amounted to) did not take place without considerable resistance; the role which so-called "protective legislation" for *women* workers played in extending the state's responsibilities for *all* wage earners is sometimes lost sight of today. One of the earliest problems, going back, as we have seen, to the 1830's, was limitation of hours. Recognizing that overworked young women are handicapped for motherhood, the state of Wisconsin had passed the first "hour law" for women in 1867. By 1907 there were already laws in twenty states, limiting, in some industries and in varying degrees, the working hours of women. Yet advocates of such legislation recognized that it had been gravely threatened by an adverse ruling of the United States Supreme Court in the case of *Lochner vs. New York* in 1905, and that further progress would be jeopardized until a law affecting women workers could win an appeal to the highest court.

The next real test came in *Muller vs. Oregon* in 1907, dealing with the hours of women working in Oregon laundries. The case is memorable today, not because it settled the issue once and for all (there were advances and losses for years thereafter), but because of the nature of the brief presented on behalf of the state of Oregon by Louis D. Brandeis, later Justice of the United States Supreme Court. Brandeis entered the case at the request of Florence Kelley of the Consumers League, a passionate crusader for protective legislation for women. What was so novel in what is now called the "Oregon Brief," was the extensive marshaling of facts in support of the thesis that overlong hours are harmful, rather than relying simply on legal points. Today the approach taken in the Oregon Brief is standard in such cases; then it was completely new (and incidentally served to bolster the demand for further research, because in providing Brandeis with material, Josephine Goldmark and Miss Kelley had to draw far more heavily on existing European sources, principally British, than they could on almost non-existent American ones).

In the light of more advanced medical knowledge, Brandeis' contention that "women are fundamentally weaker than men in all that makes for endurance; in muscular strength, in nervous energy, in the power of persistent application and attention" is today open to question. But his arguments against the injurious effects of too long hours on their feet for young women, of over-work, during pregnancy and after, for mother, child, and succeeding generations, as well as for the need of assuring both married and unmarried women the opportunity of enjoying "the decencies of life outside working hours," is hardly open to serious challenge. The scope and documentation of the Oregon Brief, its emphasis on the human implications of the legislation at stake rather than legal and constitutional considerations, profoundly affected the course of later legislation directed towards social needs. It is well to recall a fact too often forgotten — that without the vision and fighting spirit of Mrs. Kelley and the organization she built up, the Oregon Brief might not have been written. [22]

Chapter XVI

THE UNIFICATION OF THE SUFFRAGE
MOVEMENT

During the decade of 1880–1890 it was becoming increasingly evident that the factors which had brought about the existence of two separate suffrage associations were steadily diminishing in importance.

The National Woman Suffrage Association had been launched by the intellectually irrepressible Elizabeth Cady Stanton and the ever catholic Susan B. Anthony. Both were ready to work with anyone, whatever their views on other matters, as long as they wholeheartedly espoused woman suffrage. Consequently in its earlier years the National was both aggressive and unorthodox. It damned both Republicans and Democrats who brushed the suffrage question aside. It was willing to take up the cudgels for distressed women whatever their circumstances, be they "fallen women," divorce cases, or underpaid seamstresses.

The American Woman Suffrage Association, by contrast, took its tone and outlook from a New England which had turned its back on those fiery days when abolitionists, men and women alike, had stood up to angry mobs. Its advocacy of worthy causes was highly selective. Lucy Stone was not interested in trade unionism and wished to keep the suffrage cause untarnished by concern with divorce or "the social evil." The very epitome of the American's attitude was its most distinguished convert and leader, Julia Ward Howe — erudite, honored lay preacher, the revered author of "The Battle Hymn of the Republic," who cast a highly desirable aura of prestige and propriety over the women's cause.

It was not that Mrs. Howe in herself made suffrage respectable; she was a symbol of the forces that were drawing the suffrage movement into the camp of decorum. American society was becoming rapidly polarized. The middle class was learning to identify organized labor with social turmoil. A succession of strikes during the depression of 1873–1878, in textiles, mining, and railroads, culminated in the Great Railroad Strike of 1877 involving nearly 100,000 workers from the Atlantic coast to the Mississippi valley; they did not help to reassure women taught by press and pulpit to identify any kind of militancy with radicalism. Nor was this trend allayed by the hysteria whipped up over the Molly Maguire trials for secret conspiracy among Pennsylvania coal miners, or the alleged communistic influences at work in such growing organizations as the Knights of Labor and the A.F. of L. The existence of a small number of socialists was used to smear all organized labor with the taint of "anarchism." The crowning touch took place during the widespread agitation for an eight-hour day in 1886 when a bomb, thrown by a hand unknown to this day into a radical meeting in Chicago's Haymarket Square, touched off a nation-wide wave of panic.

The steady trend of the suffrage movement toward the conservative and the conventional during the last twenty years of the nineteenth century must be viewed in this setting, in order to avoid the misconception that a few conservative women took it over, through their own superior ability and the passivity of the former militants. Even the latter were changing their views, judging by their actions. It was one thing to challenge the proprieties at the Centennial of 1876; ten years later it would have been inconceivable even to the women who took part in that demonstration. Susan Anthony herself would have thought twice about flouting Federal election laws and going to jail in an era which witnessed the Haymarket hysteria.

Moreover the social makeup of the suffrage leadership was changing perceptibly. There were fewer housewives or women who did the greater part of their own work, and more professionals, writers, and women of substantial means. Those who had begun the struggle in want and penury — living, like Lucy Stone and Abby Kelley, on whatever pittance they could wring out of their lecturing — had by now achieved some measure of comfort and ease. The courage of the Grimké sisters and Lucretia Mott in pioneer days was no longer called for, as shown by Theodore Weld's excuse for not attending suffrage meetings in these quieter times: "There hasn't been anyone mobbed in twenty years — why should I go?" [1] Even the spartan Susan Anthony, who dipped continually into her meager finances for the sake of the cause, had comfortably situated friends in most cities, who cared for her on her endless lecture and campaign trips; whenever she was in Washington she stayed at the Riggs Hotel, whose owners put a suite at her disposal, sometimes for months at a time.

Along with increased means (always more evident in the lives of the individual women than in the suffrage organization's finances, which continued on a deplorable hand-to-mouth basis) came greater influence and prestige. Twenty years had seen a profound change of public attitude. Woman suffrage was not yet generally accepted, but it was no longer considered the province of eccentrics and crackpots. It boasted influential friends in Congress, and the annual conventions of the National Association in Washington were the occasion, not only of hearings before Congressional committees and lobbying "on the hill," but of White House teas and receptions. Although resolutions continued to be passed for equal pay, and a Leonora Barry might speak at a suffrage convention and be respectfully heard, most working women would conceivably wonder about their dress, and feel out of place in the round of social functions which were now an accepted part of such gatherings. The kind of day-to-day contact which had enabled Miss Anthony to organize Working Women's Associations, and sent her and Mrs. Stanton to conventions of the National Labor Union had vanished.

The growth of an organization such as the International Council of Women and the Women's Congress of the Chicago Columbian Exposition were other factors which tended to strengthen the leadership of women with independent incomes or professional prestige. The Council was conceived in 1888 as a federation of existing women's organizations around a broad program of activity, and its first chairman was Frances Willard. It never fulfilled its aim, but it held several meetings which led to the establishment of an International Council of Women, gave excellent opportunities for registering the gains made by women in legal status, in the professions, and in community standing, and was respectfully reported by the press. So was the Women's Congress of the Columbian Exposition of 1893, whose Lady Board of Managers was headed by none other than Mrs. Potter Palmer, leader of Chicago's social elite.

Another generation of women leaders was developing in this new atmosphere, even while veterans like Miss Anthony, Mrs. Stone, and Mrs. Stanton were still on the scene.[2] The younger women were not, for the most part, distinguished by the breadth of their social views. While Miss Anthony to the end of her days retained her gift of sympathy and rapport for women of whatever class — the humblest suffrage worker could still, to the end of her life, draw an answering letter from her tireless pen or typewriter, or greet her at public functions as a friend — the same could hardly be said for Rachel Foster Avery, May Wright Sewall, Carrie Chapman Catt, or Harriet Taylor Upton. (The exception was Anna Howard Shaw, who always retained the ability to meet and work with working women as her equals because of the bitter battles she had endured to achieve education and professional training, and her work as a doctor in the Boston slums.)

Another reason for the widening gap between working and more privileged women in the suffrage movement was the antagonism many of the latter felt for the huge and increasing numbers of immigrants. Large numbers of these newcomers came from social and religious backgrounds which had imbued them with highly conservative beliefs as to what the role and position of women should be. Relegated to the slums and therefore often dominated by political machines, their votes were the means by which, in one state suffrage referendum after another, native-born, educated, and often professionally skilled and wealthy women continued to be denied the franchise. Understandably these women resented the fact that such men, speaking little or no English, stood between them and the vote. Yet in the long run such rancor could only do them injury, since the immigrant, like any other voter, must be won to their cause. Not until Jane Addams and Lillian Wald began to hammer home the fact that *no* woman, whether she worked in a sweatshop or drove down Fifth Avenue in her own carriage, could win the vote until the support of the immigrant had been won — in good part through the influence of his own wife and daughters — did the suffrage movement set itself to heal this particular breach.

But such enlightenment was still in the future in the late

'80's, when, lacking any continuing basic disagreement on principle or tactics, the merger of the two suffrage associations became only a matter of time, the time needed to heal old scars.

Alice Stone Blackwell, the gifted daughter of Lucy Stone and Henry Blackwell, is generally given major credit for the final result. In reality, the fact that the policies it had been advocating for twenty years had now become dominant was the main reason why the American Association, which was smaller and had done less organizing than its one-time rival, could initiate the proposal and actually take the National into camp. The merger negotiations began in 1887, dragged on for three years, and were finally consummated at a joint convention of the two associations in February 1890.

Although Mrs. Stanton was elected the first president of the National American Woman Suffrage Association, and continued to hold the position until 1892, her active leadership of the cause of woman suffrage had come to a close. She became increasingly interested in the divorce question and in an educated (as opposed to universal) franchise. But her primary concern became the responsibility of established religion for woman's inferior position. In 1895 and 1898 she published successive volumes of an astringent critique of the Old Testament, called *The Woman's Bible,* consisting of detailed analyses of Biblical passages derogatory to woman. There was strong opposition to the work among suffragists on the grounds that it harmed the cause by alienating religious believers. Despite impassioned pleas by Miss Anthony and other liberal thinkers for the tolerance of conflicting views shown in earlier years, the suffrage convention of 1896 passed a resolution explicitly disavowing any responsibility for *The Woman's Bible,* which was in effect a sharp rebuff to the old leader. Mrs. Stanton, however, took the slap with seeming imperturbability and continued writing up to the time of her death in 1902.

She was not the only pioneer to withdraw after the merger. The 1892 convention was the last one which Lucy Stone attended; she died the following year. Susan Anthony remained at the helm, having replaced Mrs. Stanton as president of the suffrage association, although she was not without misgivings. She welcomed unification but regretted some of the changes which followed in its wake; none more so than the decision of the 1893 convention, on a motion made by Miss Blackwell, to hold the annual convention in Washington only in alternate years.

The arguments in favor of such a change stressed the cost to delegates from western suffrage associations of an annual trip to Washington and the advantage of holding conventions, with their great educational and publicity impact, in different parts of the country. But Miss Anthony saw the danger of interrupting the steady pressure which the old National Association had kept up on Congress, and she left the chair during the debate to speak on the floor against the proposal:

The sole object, it seems to me, of this organization, is to bring the combined influence of all the States upon Congress to secure national legislation. The very moment you change the purpose of this great body from National to State work you have defeated its object. It is the business of the States to do the district work; to create public sentiment; to make a national organization possible; and then to bring their united power to the capital and focus it on Congress. . . . I shall feel it a grave mistake if you vote for a movable convention. It will lessen our influence and our power.[3]

The issue was the old one of state versus federal action as the best path to winning woman suffrage. Miss Anthony continued to argue the point, without success. In 1899 she wrote to one of her most trusted younger helpers:

The one vital point of holding our Convention in Washington . . . is the securing of hearings before the Congressional Committees, and having before them in person women representing the different states of the Union. If we did not desire to secure Congressional action in the adoption of a constitutional amendment resolution, we might consider . . . nothing but the difference in the expenses of the delegates, of the halls, hotels, and the numbers attending our meetings. But I suppose it will be impossible to make any considerable number of our young women comprehend the far reaching importance of our Hearings before the committees, of the publication of the speeches by the government, and the sending out of the speeches under the frank of the Members to the friends in the several States of the Union. I have always believed, and never more strongly than now, that the educational work done by these hearings was farther reaching and did quite as much good work in the rural districts as the holding of meetings in each.[4]

Events confirmed Miss Anthony's worst forebodings. Although formal hearings were held during the years when the suffrage association convened away from Washington, neither House gave the bill a favorable committee report after 1893. To all intents and purposes, the federal woman suffrage amendment vanished as a political issue until 1913.[5]

The alternative "route" to woman suffrage, through amendment of state constitutions, did not appear on the record to be a promising one, and it became less so as the years passed. From 1870 to 1910, there were 480 campaigns in thirty-three states, just to get the issue submitted to the voters, of which only seventeen resulted in actual referendum votes. All but three of them were in states west of the Mississippi; of the exceptions, one had been Michigan, back in 1874, and the other two were in the politically minor states of Rhode Island (1887) and New Hampshire (1902).[6]

Only two referenda were successful, those in Colorado and Idaho, both sparsely populated states where victory had little significance as far as winning the rest of the country was concerned; the other two additions to what came to be known as "the suffrage column" were through the admission of new states, Wyoming in 1890 and Utah in 1896.

The victory in Colorado in 1893 was important because it was the first state where men voters actually went to the polls and gave women the vote; both the liquor and political machines were caught napping because they did not believe suffrage could win. In Idaho in 1896 there was little organized opposition; however, the campaign here was of interest chiefly as the first instance where suffrage work was done on an election precinct or district basis, a form of organization that was to reach its highest development, and prove the determining factor for victory, in the most bitterly contested battleground of all — New York State — just twenty-one years later.[7] In both cases the job was done under the direction of Carrie Chapman Catt, whose name in 1896 was still relatively new.

In contrast to these small victories was the endless succession of campaigns to get state legislatures to place the suffrage issue before the voters, each one involving untold work and expense, and the interminable series of defeats at the polls. Each campaign or vote could serve as an example of the obstacles inherent in the referendum as a weapon to win woman suffrage. A very few instances will suffice.

The South Dakota campaign in 1890 was one of the most rigorous that suffrage workers ever endured — blazing hot all summer, while the seventy-year-old Susan Anthony and the veteran Henry Blackwell (a mere sixty-five) toured the state, and freezing cold during Mrs. Catt's tour in the fall. In addition, living conditions were primitive, and all the speakers had to cover immense distances. The decision for the newly united suffrage association to enter the campaign had hinged on pledges of support from farm and labor organizations. Instead, when the campaign was already under way, the Knights of Labor and the Farmers Alliance launched a third party, which refused to encumber itself with the controversial issue of votes for women. The outcome was a defeat of almost two to one, after a murderous campaign: Mrs. Catt came down with typhoid fever immediately afterward and very nearly died, and when Miss Anthony returned to her home in Rochester, her sister Mary commented that for the first time she realized that Susan was growing old.[8]

The experience of the Kansas referendum in 1894 confirmed Miss Anthony's deep-seated distrust of "partial" suffrage such as the school or the municipal ballot. Kansas women had won the latter in 1887, and the measure had been hailed as a landmark of progress. The difficulty was that the women promptly aligned themselves with a political party, and forthwith became responsible to it on decisions regarding suffrage tactics as well as other matters of political expediency. Mrs. Laura M. Johns, the able head of the Kansas State Suffrage Association, became president of the Republican Woman's Association in the state, and yielded to the insistence of Republican leaders that endorsement of the suffrage measure be omitted from the party's platform, thus reversing previous assurances of Republican support. Despite the wrath of the national suffrage leadership, the Kansas women stuck to their party rather than to the measure aimed at enfranchising them, and thereby sealed its doom.[9]

The California campaign of 1896 was far and away the most highly organized effort the women had yet achieved. Miss Mary Hay of Indiana set up a precinct organization in the larger cities along lines initiated by Mrs. Catt earlier that same year in Idaho; there was a formidable turnout of nationally known speakers, wide newspaper support, and formal endorsement by the Populist and the Republican parties, although the latter proved non-existent in practice.

For the first time women of wealth such as Mrs. Leland Stanford and Mrs. William Randolph Hearst gave substantial sums to the cause of woman suffrage. But the bulk of the funds still came from more modest sources, and Ida Husted Harper, state chairman of the suffrage publicity committee, wrote:

A large photograph of Miss Anthony and Miss Shaw was given for every $2 pledge, and many poor seamstresses and washerwomen fulfilled their pledges in twenty-five cent installments, coming eight times with their mite. Often when there was not enough money at headquarters to buy a postage stamp, there would come a timid knock at the door and a poorly-dressed woman would enter with a quarter or a half dollar, saying "I have done without tea this week to bring you this money;" or a poor little clerk would say "I made a piece of fancy work evenings and sold it for this dollar." Many a woman who worked hard ten hours a day to earn her bread, would come to headquarters and carry home a great armload of circulars to fold and address after night. And there were teachers and stenographers and other working women who went without a winter coat to give money to this movement for freedom.[10]

Defeat came at the hands of the liquor interests, who rallied against the formidable threat posed by the suffrage campaign. To quote the same source:

Ten days before election, the fatal blow came. The representatives of the Liquor Dealers' League met in San Francisco and resolved "to take such steps as were necessary to protect their interests." . . . From that moment the fate of the amendment was sealed. . . . The following letter, signed by the wholesale liquor firms of San Francisco, was sent to the saloon-keepers, hotel proprietors, druggists and grocers throughout the State:

"At the election to be held on November 3, Constitutional Amendment No. Six, which gives the right to vote to women, will be voted on.

"It is to your interest and ours to vote against this amendment. We request and urge you to vote and work against it and do all you can to defeat it.

"See your neighbor in the same line of business as yourself, and have him be with you in this matter." [11]

The determining importance of such tactics appears when the final results are broken down by counties. The woman suffrage amendment was carried — outside of San Francisco and Alameda counties. It lost in these two counties by 27,399 votes, while the statewide margin against the amendment was 26,734!

A change of 13,400 votes would have put California in the suffrage column in 1896, instead of fifteen years later, and, because of the size and rapid growth of the state, would have had a stimulating effect on the progress of the suffrage cause. No wonder Mrs. Catt and others referred to the liquor and brewing interests as "The Hidden Enemy." Not until Prohibition became imminent did its opposition to woman suffrage wane in potency. The year 1896, to use another phrase of Mrs. Catt's, was not yet "the woman's hour."

PART III

Chapter XVII

ENTERING THE TWENTIETH CENTURY

At the beginning of the twentieth century American women were living under very different circumstances from those under which their grandmothers and even their mothers had grown up. In addition to the changes which were taking place throughout the country in its rapid pace toward industrialization and urbanization, the position of women had altered far more drastically than that of men. While changes in the legal position of women had been uneven from one state to another and had not always taken place without setbacks, nevertheless many of the worst disabilities had been eliminated, while others had been greatly reduced.

It was easier to trace the course of progress in some eastern states: by and large, the states west of the Alleghanies had never known legal discrimination against women at its worst. Virtual equality before the law (although not in political status) had been part of western state constitutions when some of them were admitted to the Federal union. In others, progress had been more rapid, under the spur of pioneer conditions, than on the Atlantic seaboard, where society had stratified while the influence of Blackstone's Commentaries was still dominant in law, and where the heritage of religious concepts concerning women's inferiority was difficult to cast off. Here it took half a century to assure a married woman in most states the right not only to her own *property*, but (a vital distinction to the working woman) her *earnings*. Although such rights were in effect by 1900 in most eastern states, a married woman in Pennsylvania could still not enter a business contract without her husband's approval.

In general the area of greatest backwardness continued to be in the South, where economic recovery from the Civil War had been slow and proportionately fewer women were working for their own living. Education among women was still largely confined to the school level, and little pressure against existing restrictions had been exerted. But even here there were wide variations. In Louisiana the discriminatory provisions of the "Code Napoléon" inherited from the days of French dominion were still in full force: a married woman did not even have legal title to the clothes she wore. In Georgia a woman's earnings still belonged to her husband. Yet next door, in Mississippi, she was fairly well safe-guarded as to property rights, while in Florida she could control her own earnings.

The greatest inequities everywhere were in the realm of divorce. The law bore heavily on a woman who had committed adultery, while the man suffered no penalties. Minnesota, for instance, required that a woman divorced for adultery forfeit even such real estate as had been her own property; Pennsylvania forbade her disposal of it if she continued to live with the man with whom she had committed adultery, after divorce. In neither state was a man so penalized. South Carolina stood alone in forbidding divorce on any grounds whatever.[1]

While many of the changes which had taken place had been the outcome of sharply fought legislative battles, in general they reflected the continuing expansion of women's interests and activities in industry, in business, and the professions. The number of women workers continued to increase. The 1890 census listed 4,005,532 as gainfully employed; in 1900 the figure had risen to 5,319,397, and in 1910 to 7,444,787.[2]

In 1900 the largest group within this army of wage earners was that of 1,800,000 women in domestic occupations (working for families other than their own) or in so-called service industries. Some 700,000 were loosely categorized as "farm laborers and managers." Three hundred and twenty-five thousand were teachers, and 217,000 worked as sales clerks. Among factory workers, the greatest number were some 671,000 in the clothing and garment trades, while another 261,000 were to be found in cotton, silk, knit-goods, and other textile manufacturing plants.[3]

A rapidly growing field for women was that of office work. Expanding corporate business required more than the old-fashioned bookkeeper who kept the accounts without mechanical assistance, or a Bob Cratchit who handled the firm's correspondence in a beautifully flowing script. The introduction of women into government offices during the Civil War had helped to pave the way for their entry into business. So did the invention of the typewriter in 1867; by 1888 there were 60,000 of these in use.[4] Other office machines followed; and the 1900 census figures show almost 74,000 women employed as bookkeepers, accountants, and cashiers, while over 100,000 were grouped together as stenographers, typists, secretaries or were active in other occupations that today would be called "white collar" jobs.[5]

The growing numbers of women workers were providing fresh arguments for woman suffrage. In 1894 when the constitution of New York State came up for revision, Dr. Mary Putnam-Jacobi made women's participation in modern industrial life one of the main themes of a pamphlet which became a classic in suffrage literature: *"Common Sense" Applied to Woman Suffrage.* An early follower of Dr. Blackwell — she received her medical degree in 1864 — and the first woman physician to be elected to the distinguished roster of the New York Academy of Medicine, Dr. Putnam-Jacobi pointed out some of the profound changes taking place. Not only were large numbers of women no longer dependent on men for support; so-called " 'women's work' was now so frequently and evidently non-domestic . . . [that it] could no longer be considered something exclusively done in the personal service of father or husband," thus removing any basis for a man's control of his wife's property and earnings, or claim that he could "represent her" politically. Another traditional concept, that the man in the family should furnish his womenfolk with "protection," bore little relation to the realities of women's employment in sweatshops and textile factories, where they needed quite a different kind of protection: that furnished by laws, and their proper enforcement, difficult to achieve for a completely disfranchised, and therefore politically impotent section of the population.[6]

Sixteen years later President M. Carey Thomas of Bryn Mawr held that "the old-fashioned arguments for woman suffrage are being pushed into the background by the urgent practical need of the ballot felt by women today." (She was referring to the earlier philosophical arguments which had been the basis for first demands for suffrage and all forms of equal rights, used by Mary

Wollstonecraft, John Stuart Mill, and Elizabeth Cady Stanton.)
Miss Thomas reproached both women and men for their fear of
"the stupendous social revolution" underway: "Whether we wish
it or not, the economic independence of women is taking place
before our eyes." She dwelt on newspaper accounts of police
brutality against women garment strikers, and quoted U. S. Labor
Commissioner Carroll Wright: "The lack of direct political influence constitutes a powerful reason why women's wages have
been kept at a minimum." [7]

There was still another element at work in the continually
changing alchemy of social relationships. The battle launched by
Emma Willard and Mary Lyon to establish the equal potential of
women's brains was not yet won; in 1894 Dr. Putnam-Jacobi could
still write that "men, accustomed to think of men as possessing sex
attributes and other things besides, are accustomed to think of
women as having sex, and nothing else." But thanks to the advances made in the medical sciences, psychology and sociology, she
could also offer new arguments in rebuttal:

The influence of environment is only beginning today to be philo-
sophically appreciated. It is just beginning to be suspected that the
widely diffused ignorance of women is not a necessary organic peculi-
arity, but explicable by the fact that until recently they were forbidden
to learn anything. Similarly we may inquire whether much of the
observed practical feebleness of women, even in carrying out the
thoughts they may have justly conceived, is not due to the social customs which, in such multiple directions, forbid their will to have any
effect.[8]

Compared with the legions of women workers, women college
graduates were few in number, but theirs was a growing group,
full of new life and promise. Not only were the women's colleges
turning out greater numbers each year — Smith, already in the
lead, graduated 219 in 1900 — but more were coming from the
state universities and colleges in the Far and Middle West; even
in the lagging South, young women were seeking elsewhere the
opportunities for growth denied them at home. In 1900 a total of
5,237 women graduated from accredited institutions (as compared
with 22,173 men), rising to 8,437 women in 1910 (as compared to
28,762 men).[9]

More was involved here than numerical growth; with the first classes for women given by Harvard professors in 1879, followed by the formal establishment of the Society for the Collegiate Instruction of Women in 1882, and the opening of Bryn Mawr in 1885, the sights were once again being raised to correct a situation which had appeared, to those sufficiently perceptive and exacting,

discouraging, except for the delight women were beginning to show in going to college. No one knew at all how things were going to turn out. The present achievement was small; the students were immature and badly trained; the scientific attainments of the professors teaching in colleges for women, with a few shining exceptions, were practically nil. Women were teaching in Wellesley, Mount Holyoke and Smith without even the elementary training of a college course behind them.[10]

The first significant step toward closing the gap was taken in December 1878 by Arthur Gilman, a Cambridge citizen concerned with the lack of educational opportunities open to his daughter in a community whose educational standards were set by Harvard University. Individual Harvard professors had already been tutoring occasional women students, and Mr. Gilman asked President Eliot's approval of a plan to make their teaching available in a systematic way to girls passing the same entrance examinations as those required of candidates for admission to Harvard.[11]

In the autumn of 1879 twenty Harvard professors, some of them leading authorities in their specialties, offered twenty-four courses to women who had passed the Harvard Entrance Examinations in chosen subjects. Of twenty-seven candidates, twenty-five qualified, although only three took the full course that first year. The first housing, laboratory, and library facilities for them were achieved without any kind of formal organization, so anxious were Gilman and his co-workers not to antagonize either the Harvard authorities or conservative Cambridge and Boston opinion.

However, in 1882 the Society for the Collegiate Instruction of Women was organized (soon informally known as the "Harvard Annex"), an amorphous form permitting the partial reconciliation of those who wished to have women admitted to Harvard classes along with men and those unalterably opposed to any suggestion of co-education. This ambivalence continued even after Radcliffe was chartered in 1893 as a full-fledged institution of collegiate rank; its students were required to fulfill the Harvard entrance requirements, and could only graduate with the approval of the President and Fellows of Harvard "on satisfactory evidence of such qualification as is accepted for the same degree when conferred by Harvard University." [12]

However ambiguous the form, the aim and conception were clear enough, and had a profound effect on another new women's college. Bryn Mawr was founded in 1885 by a group of Pennsylvania and Baltimore Quakers, but almost from its beginnings it bore the imprint of the creative imagination and inflexibly high standards of M. Carey Thomas. An early graduate of Cornell, one of the first women to return from abroad with a doctorate degree, Miss Thomas became, at the astonishingly early age of twenty-six, dean of a college which had not yet opened its doors, but whose requirements she insisted be drastically raised even before it did so.[13] She wished not only to meet Harvard standards, but to stir up the schools to further effort by compelling them to meet the challenge of special Bryn Mawr examinations as well, and also compel other colleges to raise their sights in emulation. She succeeded so well that for decades, entrance to, let alone graduation from, Bryn Mawr was a mark of intellectual distinction.

President Thomas (as she became in 1894) was also the first successfully to fight through the issue of graduate work in a woman's college; the resident fellowships offered by Bryn Mawr were the earliest available to women who wished to pursue graduate studies. In initiating such a program, Miss Thomas achieved two ends: she imposed on her own faculty greater demands than did the teaching of undergraduate studies only; and she justified women's ability to carry on higher research work by making it possible for them to do so.

Miss Thomas' insistence on the equal potentialities of women and their consequent right to equal opportunity took her beyond the academic campus into suffrage work; she had unlimited faith in the contribution college women could and should make to that cause.[14] In 1900 a college suffrage group had been founded at Radcliffe by a student named Maud Wood, who as Maud Wood Park later became one of the leaders of the suffrage movement. At the annual suffrage association convention in 1908, suffrage groups from the college campuses of fifteen states came together at the call of President Thomas, President Mary E. Woolley of Mount Holyoke, and others to form the National College Women's Equal Suffrage League. Among its first group of officers and board members were graduates or faculty members from Bryn Mawr, Barnard, Radcliffe, Smith, and the Universities of Wisconsin, California, and Chicago. The League brought political awareness to a generation of college women who helped make votes for women a reality, meeting the challenge which Miss Thomas threw down at its very first gathering:

Women are one-half of the world, but until a century ago . . . women lived a twilight life, a half life apart, and looked out and saw men as shadows walking. It was a man's world. The laws were men's laws, the government a man's government, the country a man's country. Now women have won the right to higher education and economic independence. The right to become citizens of the state is the next and inevitable consequence of education and work outside the home. We have gone so far; we must go farther. We cannot go back.[15]

The aging Susan Anthony was not one to hold power to herself; she watched for lieutenants with ability to whom she could hand over her post, especially after the merger of the two suffrage associations in 1890. The suffrage cause was fortunate that she found two, who between them divided the leadership of the movement until the goal had been won.

Both came from the growing numbers of college-trained women. Both were from the Middle West; one was of first-generation pioneer stock, the other only a little less removed from the physical actualities of the frontier. At this point resemblance between the lives of Carrie Chapman Catt and Anna Howard Shaw ceases, save for the fact that woman suffrage became the main focus of their lives.

Carrie Lane was born on a Wisconsin farm in 1859; her family moved to northeastern Iowa when some of the land was still unploughed prairie.[16] She graduated from Iowa State College and served in rapid succession as teacher, school administrator, and journalist, first on a small Iowa town paper and then in San Francisco. When her first husband, Leo Chapman, died of typhoid fever only a few months after their marriage, she turned to lecturing and suffrage work in her home state of Iowa, where her work soon attracted the notice of state leaders. The year 1890 which produced a united suffrage movement marked her entrance into national work, and her marriage to George Catt, a successful engineer and staunch adherent of suffrage who made it possible for his wife to give more and more of her time to it.[17]

It soon became apparent to Miss Anthony that here was not only an able speaker, but a woman with tremendous potentialities as an organizer, something the suffrage movement notably lacked in Miss Anthony's later years. After trying her wings in some grueling campaigns, notably the South Dakota fiasco of 1890 and the victorious Colorado campaign of 1893, and making a report at the 1895 annual convention which flayed the suffrage association for its omissions and shortcomings, Mrs. Catt was made chairman of a newly instituted Organization Committee. Here, for the next five years, she had abundant and heartbreaking opportunity to develop the flair for planning, for check-up and detail, and for seeking out and training fresh leadership, which were to be the hallmarks of her suffrage work for a quarter of a century.

The young organizer displayed considerable brashness in some of the methods she attempted to introduce in an organization which had always operated in a highly personal and haphazard manner: definite plans of work for local groups; state headquarters; study courses in, of all things, political science and economics; a manual of organization; a consistent membership system (something no one had ever bothered about); and soundly based national association finances (a goal not to be achieved for twenty years). Yet Mrs. Catt, far in advance of anyone else, saw these things as essential to any kind of sustained, consistent work, and to final success. She labored for nine years to lay some kind of sound organizational basis for a sprawling movement of women with conflicting demands on their time and energies, and with many inhibitions, even when they believed strongly in their cause. It was unrewarding, killing work, ahead of its time. But suffragists got a whiff of organization and discipline which some of them remembered later in their hour of need.

Mrs. Catt herself was learning her job; she needed judgment and tact, and to begin with she did not have enough of either. Her letters as chairman of the Organization Committee are markedly lacking in the diplomacy and human kindness present in her communications of later years.[18] She even believed that there were promising possibilities for organizing suffrage associations in the southern states. In 1897 she sent a young Missouri woman, Miss Ella Harrison, into Mississippi, with every expectation of fruitful results: "While the South is not yet favorable to woman suffrage, it gives a very cordial hearing to it, and I may also say that when interested at all they are invariably the very best people. A year or two of work there will change the sentiment and quite revolutionize it." [19]

Experience during the two months' tour, as well as subsequent history, showed otherwise: the trip proved expensive and devastating to the suffrage association's precarious budget, but it also contributed to the eventual education of the most able organizer woman suffrage was to develop.

When the time came for Miss Anthony to step down in 1900, Mrs. Catt was the older leader's choice to succeed her as president of the National American Woman Suffrage Association, by sheer weight of merit over any personal preference; the decision was a painful one since the woman who was Mrs. Catt's only possible opponent was Susan Anthony's closest friend and co-worker for the last twenty years of her life.

Anna Howard Shaw had known a pioneer childhood of great hardship, and difficult years as a divinity student. At the age of thirty-five, feeling that her hardwon Cape Cod parish was becoming too comfortable a rut, she entered a Boston medical school and received an M.D. degree in 1885. Her experience with the impoverished women of the Boston slums, in the dual role of preacher and physician, convinced her that their basic problem was one neither religion nor medicine alone could solve:

In my association with the women of the streets, I realized the limitations of my work in the ministry and in medicine. As minister to soul and body one could do little for these women. For such as them, one's efforts must begin at the very foundation of the social structure. Laws for them must be made and enforced, and some of those laws could only be made and enforced by women.[20]

She began to lecture for the W.C.T.U., becoming a close friend of Frances Willard's, and also for the Massachusetts Woman Suffrage Association. For several years after leaving ministerial work she headed the W.C.T.U.'s suffrage department. Miss Anthony marked her originally for her gifts as a speaker; the great age of woman orators had come and gone, and for a quarter of a century Dr. Shaw was unmatched in eloquence and effectiveness. She soon gave up other causes, and made the winning of suffrage her life work, although for years she was obliged to go on lecturing for her livelihood.

But when Miss Anthony retired, suffrage needed an orator less than it did an organizer and a leader who was free to give the cause her undivided efforts. To say that Anna Howard Shaw was disappointed is an understatement. But she recognized the inevitability of the decision and continued to give her not inconsiderable best. Without close domestic ties and responsibilities, she became as peripatetic as ever Susan Anthony had been, and for years traveled up and down the land, the most sought-after speaker in every state campaign and every gathering whose aim was the women's vote.[21]

After four years, Mrs. Catt resigned the presidency of the suffrage association: she was worn out from ten years' grueling effort, and ill health in her family had become a grave concern (Mr. Catt died the following year). There was also another reason for her withdrawal: her role in the growing international suffrage movement.

The latter owed its original impetus to Susan Anthony, who had visited Great Britain in 1884 with Mrs. Stanton, and broached the idea of an international suffrage association to British leaders. The organization of the International Council of Women and its several Congresses in 1888, 1893 and 1902 served to forward the idea; beginning in 1902, Mrs. Catt undertook to bring about its realization. The International Woman Suffrage Alliance was launched at a congress held in Berlin in June 1904 with eight affiliates: Australia, Denmark, Germany, Great Britain, the Netherlands, Norway, Sweden, and the United States. The last continued to furnish leadership for the Alliance, in the person of Mrs. Catt, until 1923.

In 1904 Dr. Shaw stepped into the presidency of the National-American Woman Suffrage Association, a post she was to hold for eleven years. Susan B. Anthony was still alive and active: she had attended the Berlin Congress which founded the International

Alliance, and while she was no longer the functioning head of the movement in the United States, she remained its vital center.

She was in harness until her last illness during the annual suffrage convention in 1906 held in Baltimore; even then, ill as she was, she held out long enough to win a promise from M. Carey Thomas and her close friend Miss Mary Garrett that they would raise a fund of $60,000 which would support Dr. Shaw for a five-year period, so that suffrage work would not suffer from her lecturing for a livelihood.[22] One month after this last service to the cause which had been her life, Miss Anthony was dead. Her passing marked the end of an era. She was the last of the giants who had launched the struggle to improve the condition of women to leave the scene. She had lived and worked, without respite and without discouragement, through the years of ridicule, vilification, and apparent hopelessness, which today are all but forgotten. When she died, few thinking people denied either the logic or the inevitability of woman suffrage. The only question that remained was, "When?"

Chapter XVIII

INTO THE MAINSTREAM OF ORGANIZED LABOR

The years between 1903 and the entry of the United States into the first World War in 1917 saw the growth of the first unions composed largely of women. These unions remain a stable part of the American labor movement down to the present time.

The natural place for such unions to originate was in the garment trades, where a large proportion of the labor force was female, working under conditions which were a strong incentive to organization. Despite some progress toward factory inspection, legislation, and faint stirrings of public opinion, the establishments where clothing was made in such centers as New York, Philadelphia, and Chicago boasted of nearly every evil known to modern factory production at its worst.

For the most part the shops were small, housed in filthy old buildings which were never cleaned and where sanitary conditions and fire hazards were unbelievably bad.[1] Windows were nailed shut and little light came in the grimy panes. The hissing of power belts and grinding of machinery were deafening. The workers were largely foreign-born, newly arrived in this country. Their limited knowledge of English, their youth, inexperience, and desperate need for work put them at the mercy of boss and foreman. There were endless fines: for talking, laughing, or singing, for stains from machine oil on the goods, for stitches either too crooked or too large which had to be ripped out at the risk of tearing the fabric, resulting in more fines. Hours not infrequently ran until ten at night, with no overtime pay and only a sandwich for supper. Not only were wages (for highly skilled work) as low as $6.00 a week; they were often withheld, and poor immigrant girls had no means of collecting the money owed them.[2]

The earliest locals of what is now the International Ladies Garment Workers Union date back to 1900. There were some bitterly fought strikes in New York: the reefer makers in 1907, the pants makers the following year. But the first significant strike, not only in the history of the union but in the organization of working women, took place in 1909–1910 among the shirtwaist makers in New York and Philadelphia. Organization among these workers was proceeding very slowly when resentment against the intolerable conditions erupted in two of the larger shops: Leiserson & Company and the Triangle Waist Company, which was to achieve a more gruesome notoriety two years later. Both shops went on strike in September 1909, and matters dragged on until a mass meeting of the shirtwaist workers was called on November 22 at Cooper Union to decide on further action.[3]

The hall was jammed, and thousands who could not gain admission filled overflow halls. There were endless speeches by notables: Samuel Gompers himself, leading members of the Socialist Party (to which many garment workers belonged), Mary Dreier of the New York Women's Trade Union League, and leaders of the union. The meeting seemed in danger of petering out in speech-making, when a girl in her teens named Clara Lemlich, who worked in the Leiserson shop, stood up and asked for the floor. Despite her youth, she was known as a veteran of earlier strikes who had had several ribs broken in a police attack on a picket line. She made her way to the platform and called on the audience with electrifying effect to have done with talk and to act: "I am a working girl, and one of those who are on strike against intolerable conditions. I am tired of listening to speakers who talk in general terms. What we are here for is to decide whether or not we shall strike. I offer a resolution that a general strike be declared — now!"[4]

She carried the crowd with her in a tremendous outburst of enthusiasm, which even caught up the chairman. He cried out, asking whether they would take the old Jewish oath: "If I turn traitor to the cause I now pledge, may this hand wither from the arm I now raise!" — and the entire hall stood up to take the pledge.

The strike which followed is variously described as the Revolt or Uprising of the Ten, Twenty or Thirty Thousand.[5] Whatever the total figures, there is no disagreement as to its importance: not only was it the first "general strike" of its kind, but it was the first large strike of women workers, and it became a potent answer to the threadbare arguments that women could not be organized, and that they could not be counted on to hold out in a long, hard fight.

For the first time, also, the shirtwaist strike brought into existence something approximating the complex machinery of the modern strike. It was built painfully, day after day, by a small weak union and its still inexperienced allies. (The New York Women's Trade Union League went into the struggle with little preparation or experience, and came out of it a grown-up organization.) It had been thought that some 3,000 workers would go out on strike; instead, there were many thousands, 75 per cent of them women, of different nationalities. When 1,000 to 1,500 new members join an organization day after day, the clerical work alone is staggering, let alone such tasks as organizing this mass of human beings into picket lines, with responsible leadership to meet police violence and provide bail, strike relief, and welfare aid. In New York twenty-four halls were required for strikers' meetings alone, with speakers at each in Yiddish, Italian, and English.

The Women's Trade Union League made its greatest contribution in taking the strikers' case to the public and in enlisting the aid of women who could provide bail for hundreds of arrested pickets. Among those who gave such aid were Mrs. Henry Morgenthau, Mrs. Oliver H. P. Belmont, Carola Woerishoffer, and Mrs. Lawrence Lewis of Philadelphia. A meeting was called at the Colony Club in New York by Mrs. Belmont, Miss Anne Morgan, and Mrs. J. Borden Harriman at which the strikers presented their case. The $1,300 collected on this occasion represented an infinitesimal contribution from the group of wealthy socialites present, but the meeting gave the strikers priceless publicity. Mrs. Belmont and Dr. Anna Howard Shaw spoke at a huge rally in New York's Hippodrome, for which Mrs. Belmont paid the bill. In Philadelphia, where the strike spread late in December, the League's national president, Margaret Dreier Robins, enlisted the aid of influential club women and suffragists.

But the main burden of the strike, its sufferings and sacrifices, fell on the workers themselves. In the depths of winter the shirtwaist makers, many of them between sixteen and twenty-five years of age, held out for thirteen bitter cold and hungry weeks. Not even their new-found friends, or a labor movement finally aroused to their support, could provide the needed rent, food, medical care, and other necessities for so many thousands, although it was estimated that $60,000 was expended for strike benefits, a huge sum at the time. Despite repeated police onslaughts, with dozens dragged off in "Black Maria" police vans after indiscriminate clubbings, the women picketed day after day, carrying placards with such slogans as "We Are Striking for Human Treatments" and "We Strike For Justice."

The courts thought otherwise, and did not disguise their bias. Their treatment of the strikers was so patently prejudiced that Lillian Wald, Ida M. Tarbell, Mary Simkovitch, and other citizens protested publicly in a letter published in the press. One magistrate charged a striker: "You are on strike against God and Nature, whose prime law it is that man shall earn his bread in the sweat of his brow. You are on strike against God."

This episode provided another excellent source of publicity for the strikers. Apprised of the charge, George Bernard Shaw cabled back: "Delightful. Medieval America always in intimate personal confidence of the Almighty." [6]

In one sense the struggle, despite its heroic proportions, was unsuccessful. Settlements were made individually, shop by shop, and in some cases with few gains; on February 15 the strike was called off. But its impact on the labor movement was incalculable. Never again would it be quite so easy to argue that it was no use trying to organize women. And it led directly into the next great struggle in the industry, which took place in the men's garment trade in Chicago.[7]

The pattern was much the same as in the shirtwaist strike. Starting with a walkout of a small group of unorganized workers in a Hart, Schaffner, and Marx shop against intolerable conditions, the strike spread throughout the trade until forty-five thousand men and women of nine nationalities and all age groups were out for fourteen weeks. In the end it too was inconclusive, except in the Hart, Schaffner, and Marx shops, where an historic agreement signed with the United Garment Workers recognized the principle of arbitration, collective bargaining, and an employees' grievance committee.

Once again the Women's Trade Union League, whose Chicago branch was headed by Mary McDowell, rendered indispensable aid, and Mrs. Robins served on the committee which directed the strike and which tried, vainly, to bring about an industry-wide settlement. Through its committees, such women as Ellen Gates Starr of Hull House, Katharine Coman, professor of economics at Wellesley, and Sophonisba Breckinridge of the University of Chicago brought their influence to bear on behalf of the strikers.

The women from the shops showed their stamina again. Mrs. Robins pointed out that not only were thousands of them mothers, but that twelve hundred and fifty babies were born to strikers or to their wives during that grim winter; she told of the young woman who lay beside a new-born infant, surrounded by three other small children, in an unheated room, and told the visitor from the League: "It is not only bread we give our children. . . . We live by freedom, and I will fight till I die to give it to my children." [8]

When the Women's Trade Union League was organized in 1903, with the stated purpose of helping women workers in trade-union organization, membership was open to anyone "who will declare himself or herself willing to assist those trade unions already existing, which have some women workers, and to aid in the formation of new unions of women wage earners." To insure this aim, membership on the Executive Board was to be divided as follows: "The majority . . . shall be women who are, or have been, trade unionists in good standing, the minority of those well known to be earnest sympathizers and workers for the cause of trade unionism." [9]

This balance was not achieved in fact until after 1907, the year when new leaders began to emerge in greater numbers from the ranks of the women working in the trades: Mary Anderson and Emma Steghagen of the shoe workers, Rose Schneiderman of the cap makers, Agnes Nestor and Elisabeth Christman of the glove workers (both among the handful of women who have ever held posts as national union officers in this country), Melinda Scott of the hat trimmers, Josephine Casey of the railway ticket takers, Stella Franklin of the department store clerks, Elizabeth Maloney of the waitresses, Maud Swartz of the typographers. The opportunity afforded by the League to such women for growth, through action and the exercise of responsibility, both largely denied them within the American Federation of Labor, can hardly be overestimated.

No working woman served as president of the League until Mrs. Swartz assumed the post in 1921. Until then, it was held by a succession of three women of independent means, all of them able and wholly devoted to their task: Mrs. Kehew, Mrs. Charles Henrotin (formerly president of the General Federation of Women's Clubs), and Margaret Dreier Robins, who was president from 1907 to 1921. It is testimony to the fidelity with which the organization, under their leadership, adhered to the aims of its founders that during all this period its history is indistinguishable from that of women workers in the United States.

There was hardly a strike of women workers from 1905 on in which the Women's Trade Union League was not to be found taking an active part in organizing the strikers, or picketing, raising bail or strike funds, mobilizing public opinion, or running relief kitchens and welfare committees. The original three leagues in Boston, New York, and Chicago, had by 1911 grown to eleven, the newer branches being in Springfield, Illinois, St. Louis (founded by the waitress Hannah Hennessey, who died in 1910 from tuberculosis), Cleveland, Kansas City, Baltimore, and Denver. Through these groups, or a national officer or organizer, the League worked not only in the great garment strikes of 1910 and 1911, but with the collar starchers in Troy, New York, textile strikers in Lawrence and Fall River, Massachusetts, brewery workers in Milwaukee, corset makers in Bridgeport, Connecticut, telephone operators in Boston, and laundry workers in New York.

All this was done despite the most meager resources. For years there was so little money in the treasury that no convention or annual conference could be held; the convention in Norfolk, Virginia, in 1907, which overhauled the League's constitution and program and put Mrs. Robins into top leadership, consisted of seven women. The national office for years was a desk in the office of a Chicago labor paper, the *Union Labor Advocate*, which also gave the organization space in its columns for a Woman's Department.

Gradually the League achieved greater stability and broadened its program. The 1909 convention produced a legislative code (to guide local leagues in their work for the eight-hour day, a minimum wage in the "sweated" trades, and the elimination of night work), as well as a handbook on conditions in the trades represented in the League's membership. The 1910 convention worked out a plan for local leagues to follow in their strike work, which was the fruit of the grueling battles in Philadelphia and New York during the preceding year. In 1911 the League launched its own monthly publication, *Life and Labor,* whose lively pages, edited for years by the Australian-born Alice Henry, recorded the progress of working women.

The relations of the League to the American Federation of Labor were, on the surface, cordial and cooperative. As often as possible the League's conventions were held at the same time and place as the Federation's. But the relationship was inevitably a difficult one. The Federation gladly benefited from the new members which work by the League brought into its ranks; but to the extent that the League acted as a goad to the further organization of women by Federation affiliates, it was also an irritant. Federation leaders might praise the League for its services, particularly in such hard-fought battles as the garment strikes, but they stopped a long way short of the kind of action which would have made the League's continued existence unnecessary.

Estimates of just how many women joined unions in the first decade of the twentieth century must leave a wide margin of error. (Many unions kept no records of their membership by sex.) The estimate by Professor Wolman gives a total of 76,748 for the year 1910, of which the largest numbers were in unions in the garment trades, textile and cloth weaving, book binding, shoe making, tobacco, retail, and in the musical and theater arts.[10]

That this figure represented a mere 1.5 per cent of all women wage earners at that time, and only 5.2 per cent of the women in manufacturing establishments, underlines the dimensions of the task to be achieved, if women workers were to win reduction of working hours, higher wages, and an improvement in working conditions and job security. Only such gains could assure them some measure of equality in a country where living standards were rising and where democracy was growing.

It cannot be repeated too often that for women working a ten- or twelve-hour day, whose earnings were almost half those of men, whose lives were often bounded by the sweatshop, and whose relation to their employer lacked any safeguards to personal dignity or job tenure, "equal rights" was a question of more than education or getting the vote.[11] For them equality also meant better pay for their labor, security from fire and machine hazards or the unwanted attentions of a foreman, and a chance to get home to their domestic tasks before complete exhaustion had overtaken them. Until more of them could work for these goals through a trade union, other issues were remote and unreal, a fact partially attested to by the relatively small degree of participation by such women in the suffrage movement.

Chapter XIX

THE SUFFRAGE MOVEMENT COMES OF AGE,
1906–1913

Whatever gains women were making on other fronts, the years from 1896 to 1910 came to be known among suffragists as "the doldrums." No new woman suffrage states were won. Only six state referenda were held — three of them in Oregon, the others in Washington, South Dakota, and New Hampshire; all were lost. The Susan B. Anthony federal woman suffrage amendment appeared moribund.

The situation within the suffrage association gave little cause for encouragement. For a year or two after Miss Anthony's death in 1906, it seemed as if the withdrawal of that dominant figure had created a vacuum that would endure indefinitely. The woman who might have galvanized the association into activity was no longer at the helm. Dr. Shaw's devotion was complete and her gifts were many, but administrative ability was not among them.

Except for a brief span when Mrs. Catt had hopefully opened headquarters in New York, the National American Woman Suffrage Association had never had a functioning national center. "National headquarters" during this period was in the small city of Warren, Ohio, for no other reason than that the treasurer, Harriet Taylor Upton, lived there. Kate Gordon, now corresponding secretary, lived in New Orleans. Dr. Shaw, when not lecturing or campaigning, made her home outside Philadelphia. The rest of the National Board were scattered in New York, Chicago, Boston, and Louisville, Kentucky. They met only rarely between conventions; most business was transacted by the cumbersome method of briefing members by mail, and requesting them to vote or give their opinion in like manner, whenever a matter arose which Dr.

Shaw judged needed their attention. Since Dr. Shaw was easily prejudiced or aroused to hostility, the correspondence was voluminous, inconclusive, and irritating to all parties.[1]

Inevitably under such circumstances, differences of opinion became personal and highly charged. Friction at the top became known below. Not only was there growing dissatisfaction with such cumbersome machinery, but also with Dr. Shaw's tendency to greet any and all signs of awakening initiative in the ranks as potential insurgency.

Such a situation was not conducive to much activity. Aside from the handful of state campaigns and fruitless efforts in many other states to get referenda held, the only visible action was a petition asking President Theodore Roosevelt to recommend woman suffrage in his annual message to Congress. The petition had been suggested by Mrs. Catt in the hopes of breaking the near-paralysis that had gripped the movement, and at the 1908 suffrage convention Miss Gordon reported that she had written the President, stating that ". . . we wished to know — before going to the labor and expense involved in securing such a petition — whether its influence would have any weight in leading him to recommend woman suffrage in his message. Courteously but emphatically came the reply that it would not." [2]

Fortunately the convention retained more of the spirit of Susan Anthony than Miss Gordon, and voted to embark on the task of collecting a million signatures to a petition, directed, not at the President, but at Congress, asking for a woman suffrage amendment to the Constitution. Two years were spent in amassing, not a million, but 404,000 names, before it was formally presented in the spring of 1910.

Fortunately also, this was not the sum total of suffrage activity on all fronts. If the old National was slowing to a halt, there was new life stirring in the states. The first signs of it came in New York, then the home of the two most dynamic women in the movement. One was Mrs. Catt who, while busy with the International Woman Suffrage Alliance, was maintaining an interest in home affairs. The other was the daughter of Mrs. Stanton, Harriot Stanton Blatch.[3]

Harriot Stanton had married an Englishman, and after making her home in Great Britain for twenty years had been widowed, whereupon she returned to the United States. She expected to take an active part in the movement in which, quite literally, Elizabeth Cady Stanton had reared her, and she was appalled at the condition in which she found it:

The suffrage movement was completely in a rut in New York State at the opening of the twentieth century. It bored its adherents and repelled its opponents. Most of the ammunition was being wasted on its supporters in private drawing rooms and in public halls where friends, drummed up and harried by the ardent, listlessly heard the same old arguments. Unanswering adherence to the cause was held in high esteem, but alas, it was loyalty to a rut worn deep and ever deeper. Nothing better described the situation than the title of an address given by one of its leaders, "Enmeshed." The only method suggested for furthering the cause was the slow process of education. We were told to organize, organize, organize, to the end of educating, educating, educating public opinion.[4]

There was another aspect to the situation which disturbed Mrs. Blatch.

There did not seem to be a grain of political knowledge in the movement. . . . there was nothing which needed to be changed in the machinery of government, state or national, to advance our cause. But a great change was called for in the method of attack by the reformers themselves. A vital idea had been smothered by uninspired methods of work.[5]

Some of Mrs. Blatch's impatience arose from the fact that in England she had witnessed the beginnings of new tactics, which had also originated as a protest against sterility. Woman suffrage had been an issue there since the 1860's; however, little real progress had been made. Both the major parties refused to have anything to do with the issue, or to allow it to reach the floor of the House of Commons for debate, and dissatisfaction grew among the suffragists with such outworn methods of work as parlor meetings, presenting petitions to members of parliament who simply ignored them, or querying candidates for election on their views. Some women who had been trying to win adherents among the factory workers in Manchester and other textile centers began to hold small *outdoor* meetings and to interrupt government speakers at public gatherings to ask where they stood on woman suffrage. In 1903 a new organization was formed by Mrs. Emmeline Pankhurst, the Women's Social and Political Union.

It pursued an unostentatious course until two of its members were forcibly ejected from a meeting where they had queried — or more accurately, heckled — a leader of the Liberal Party, Sir Edward Grey. Once out of the meeting, bystanders and police joined forces to maltreat the women physically, who were then arrested: one of them, a factory worker named Annie Kenney, and the other, Mrs. Pankhurst's daughter and lieutenant, Christabel. The uproar and notoriety which followed this incident convinced the Women's Social and Political Union that it had discovered a new weapon: they set about deliberately provoking violent police reprisals in order to embarrass party leaders to the point where they would feel compelled to do something about woman suffrage.

Strengthened by new converts the women continued this kind of agitation, despite the distaste of the older suffrage societies. Later the women themselves began to use violence — throwing stones, breaking windows, pouring acid into mail-boxes, and attacking members of the government with whips or their bare hands. In prison the authorities' refusal to treat them as "political prisoners" rather than ordinary criminals led to prolonged and widely-publicized hunger strikes; brutal attempts at forcible feeding fanned the flames of militancy further.[6]

Only the earliest phase of the British militant suffrage movement had come into existence at the time Mrs. Blatch and others were casting about for means to stir up the American scene. Mrs. Blatch soon abandoned any hope of working through established suffrage groups — in New York, the State Woman Suffrage Association, affiliated with the national body — and organized her own:

We who saw the light held our first meeting in January, 1907, in New York, on Fourth Street just off the Bowery. In a dingy little room which was to become our headquarters, forty of us gathered to discuss the best means of putting new life into the suffrage campaign. We all believed that suffrage propaganda must be made dramatic, that suffrage workers must be politically minded. We saw the need of drawing industrial women into the suffrage campaign and recognized that these women needed to be brought in contact, not with women of leisure, but with business and professional women who were also out in the world earning their living. The result was the formation of the Equality League of Self-Supporting Women, later called the Women's Political Union.[7]

Just one month later the League was on the scene in Albany, bent on injecting a vigorous new note into the annual hearings on a bill for woman suffrage, which had become a formal and lifeless procedure. They did so by presenting as witnesses for the bill two working women, Mary Duffy of the Overall Makers Union and Clara Silver of the Buttonhole Workers, whose straight-from-the-shoulder testimony gave the jaded legislators a jolt. Said Mrs. Duffy:

We working women are often told that we should stay at home and then everything would be all right. But we can't stay at home. We have to get out and work. I lost my husband. He was a diamond setter, a fine workman, and he earned good money, but he fell ill and was ailing for a long time. I had to go back to my trade to keep the family together. Gentlemen, we need every help to fight the battle of life, and to be left out by the State just sets up a prejudice against us. Bosses think, and women come to think themselves, that they don't count for so much as men.[8]

When only three months old, the League organized its first big public meeting jointly with the New York Collegiate Equal Suffrage League. By December the two groups felt strong enough to stage an even more ambitious meeting at Cooper Union in honor of the visiting British suffrage leader, Mrs. Cobden-Sanderson. They made another novel departure by trying to interest labor unions in the affair; on the evening when Mrs. Blatch and a friend had planned to canvass union offices, all transportation was stalled by a blizzard, and the two women walked the five miles up Fourth Avenue from 4th to 134th streets, climbing the stairs of every trade-union headquarters on their route.

Such efforts brought results. Not only was the Cobden-Sanderson meeting a success; by October 1908 the League had a membership of some 19,000. Many of the women who found an outlet for their energies in its dynamic program already were or would become well-known public figures: Charlotte Perkins Gilman, one of the most widely-read women of her day, Florence Kelley, Leonora O'Reilly, Lavinia Dock from the Henry Street Settlement, Gertrude Barnum from the Women's Trade Union League, Jessie Ashley, Helen Hoy Greeley, Inez Milholland, and Rose Schneiderman. The League continued to break new ground: holding the first open-air meetings on behalf of woman suffrage in thirty years, setting up card files of its members by political districts (something that became so axiomatic in suffrage as well as all political organization that its origins are forgotten), and holding outdoor meetings at the gates of the General Electric and American Locomotive plants in Schenectady to build up sentiment against recalcitrant members of the legislature. It campaigned actively against assemblymen opposed to suffrage in New York City, and fought in Albany for the right of women to serve as poll-watchers on election day.

It was also Mrs. Blatch's organization which deserves credit for initiating the parades which became so successful a form of suffrage agitation that the alarm with which they were viewed at first soon seemed incomprehensible. The gusto with which the Equality League launched the first one of these in New York in 1910 was such that the other suffrage groups could not afford to stay out, but the reluctance of their participation was thinly concealed: "The Woman Suffrage League of New York to the last 'marcher' . . . climbed into automobiles, and rushing down the avenue, gave the onlookers one flash of yellow and were gone. Not at all what the Parade Committee of the Equality League were seeking to accomplish." [9] Yet within a year or two parades had become so respectable that even a Mrs. O. H. P. Belmont was in line, and other cities were trying out the idea.

Fired by news of the mounting activity in England and by the League (become the Women's Political Union), as reported by the *Woman's Journal* and at state and national suffrage conventions, women in a number of other states were venturing along new paths by 1909. In Massachusetts, four of them undertook a "trolley tour" of the state, from Springfield to Boston, speaking at outdoor meetings in every small town along the way without being previously heralded, with no equipment except what they could carry with them. They aroused immense curiosity and interest. Illinois held similar suffrage tours downstate by automobile. In Maryland six hundred women, mostly from Baltimore, journeyed to the state capitol at Annapolis to demand the vote. There was a proliferation of new suffrage groups, a sure sign that the older ones were too static and restricting for the new blood, and ranging from organizations founded by socialites such as Mrs. Clarence Mackay, to a Baltimore group which included among its members a veritable galaxy of top-flight scientists from Johns Hopkins University; a Wage-Earners' League in San Francisco; and a Pennsylvania Political Equality League, which attempted to organize, along industrial lines, shirtwaist makers, bookbinders, stenographers, doctors, and dentists.[10]

Among established national suffrage leaders, Mrs. Catt was the only one who felt the new leaven working; it was no accident that she had visited Great Britain in connection with her international suffrage work and, while unconvinced that militant tactics should be used in the United States, had been deeply stirred by the upsurge they reflected. But she elected to work through the existing suffrage associations. During 1907–1908 she welded together a number of those in New York City into an Interurban Council, which became the basis a year later of the Woman Suffrage Party, its membership organized by wards and assembly districts, led by workers trained in schools she had devised. Its official launching on October 30 at Carnegie Hall, with one thousand women present as delegates and alternates from districts in the city's five boroughs, was a mere formality; the actual work had been going on for months, as the turnout attested. Mrs. Catt's plan was for a corps of 2,000 election district captains, a list of members and sympathizers in each district, and unremitting pressure on the Democratic organization, Tammany Hall, which controlled both city and state.[11]

Testimony to the appeal of such a method of work were the attempts made in other states to adopt it, especially in Massachusetts, Maryland, California, and Illinois. The results were always stimulating, but nowhere was the work successful to the degree that it eventually became in New York.

Despite the new life emerging in the eastern suffrage movement, the first victories were to come on the West Coast. All three Pacific coast states had unsuccessful suffrage histories. The tremendous yet unrewarding campaign in 1896 had set California back for years; Washington women, who had won the vote under territorial status, had subsequently lost it by court action and had been unable to regain it by referendum in 1889 and 1898; Oregon had lost *four* referenda. Yet both Washington and Oregon had another referendum vote coming up, on November 8, 1910.

Incredibly, Oregon lost once more, largely because of Abigail Scott Duniway's insistence that the quieter the campaign, the less likely the liquor interests would be to take alarm. But in neighboring Washington, Mrs. Emma DeVoe had received her suffrage training on the old National Organization Committee under Mrs. Catt: the campaign was quiet enough, but it was meticulously thorough. There were few avowed suffrage meetings, and no parades, but plenty of suffrage speakers at Grange, labor union, and church gatherings. In the small hours of November 9 the telephone rang beside Mrs. Catt's bed in New York, and she heard the news that the state of Washington had broken the fourteen-year-long deadlock by a majority of almost 2 to 1.

The news galvanized suffrage workers across the country, but more and better was to come. In California the biggest campaign yet mounted by a suffrage organization swung into full gear in the spring of 1911, and in six months' sustained activity gave women elsewhere something to shoot for in brilliance, flexibility, and scope. Nothing that had been attempted before was overlooked, and much was tried that was entirely new, such as huge billboard ads and electric signs, high-school prize-essay contests, pageants, plays, and other kinds of special entertainment.

Later campaigns were to see whole flotillas of automobiles at the service of organizers and speakers. The Northern California College Equal Suffrage League had its "Blue Liner," a seven-passenger touring car of a type long departed, which had already seen some service in the Washington campaign:

Although the car was spoken of in the daily papers, and considered by us as the "campaigning car," she carried on a sideline of business. She was the general messengerboy and magic-carpet for the College League. The troupe which acted in "How the Vote Was Won" was carried to its destination by her. She met speakers from the East at the [Bay] Ferry, conveyed relays of speakers from hall to hall for public meetings, brought materials to decorate theaters, gathered up loads of flowers and balloons for fiestas and pageants, took speakers to remote factories to speak to the men at the noon hour; carted lumber and bunting for the Labor Day float, got workers out for Election Day at the polls, took food to the watchers at the polls, crossed back and forth from Berkeley to San Francisco several times a week . . . and then off on one of the all-day, all-night campaigning trips into the country.[12]

And in the dusk the day before Election Day, the Blue Liner, trimmed with garlands of autumn flowers and "Votes for Women" pennants, carried the great singer Nordica to Union Square in San Francisco to speak and to sing the Star Spangled Banner to an audience lapping all four sides of the great square. Other speakers stood at the four corners to reach those who could not possibly hear her, so huge was the multitude, and they were kept at work until one o'clock in the morning, long after Nordica had gone home.

Although aid to a state campaign from the National Suffrage Association was nothing new, there was no precedent for the support that flowed to the women of California from all over the country: the hand of sisterhood had never reached so strongly or so far. One thousand dollars came from the newly organized Woman Suffrage Party in New York. Illinois sent two of its best speakers, Catharine Waugh McCulloch and Helen Todd, and paid their way. Gail Laughlin came from Colorado, Jeannette Rankin from Montana, Helen Hoy Greeley from New York.

Until the last week of the campaign, these, and many others, were kept out of the big cities. When the chips were down, it was the endless run of small town and village meetings and parlor talks, and the small groups organized where previously there had been no visible signs of interest in woman suffrage, that were decisive.

Never were cause and effect more clear. The strategy had been dictated by the knowledge that, as in 1896, the liquor interests would stop at nothing to buy the San Francisco and Oakland vote. The whole political machine of ward heelers and barkeepers there was in high gear, and they very nearly won out:

Wherever we left a booth unprotected, I am sure we lost votes — we may perhaps have lost thousands that way in all the large cities of the state. In my own booth I had to exercise the utmost vigilance to see that the announcer called off "yes" against our amendment, and not "no," which he could easily do . . . and to check the entries of the two tally clerks, and that they put a vote for us in the "yes" column and not in the "no" column . . . the entire election board in the booth was hostile to a marked degree. We were on duty from 5.30 A.M. to 11.30 P.M., when we saw our votes entered on the tally sheet.[13]

The morning after Election Day, when only the urban vote had been counted, exhausted suffrage workers woke to news of defeat carried in newspapers all over the country. But the rural vote was still coming in and showed a ray of hope. News also came that the returns were being tampered with in many counties, and reinforcements were sent to such areas to watch the tally, while for days volunteers and hired detectives watched the vaults in San Francisco and Oakland where the ballots had been placed, to prevent any attempt to "increase" the vote to the level needed to defeat the suffrage measure.

The woman suffrage referendum won in California by 3,587 votes, an average majority of *one vote* in every voting precinct in the state. Suffragists rejoiced — and shuddered at how close the margin had been. The politically sapient awoke to the fact that woman suffrage had, suddenly, it seemed to them, passed from the realm of speculation to that of practical politics. With the victory in California, women could now vote in six western states, with a total of 37 electoral votes for the presidency. In the following year a spate of referendum campaigns was unleashed in six states. What had been only one more social reform current was becoming a political force to reckon with.

It took time for the sap to rise and re-vivify the National Association at the top — ten years from the date of Miss Anthony's death, to be exact — until 1916. National leadership was largely absent from the successful Washington and California campaigns. The 1910 suffrage convention saw an open rift, with strong charges against Dr. Shaw, and the resignation of such stalwarts as Harriet Taylor Upton, Rachel Foster Avery, and Florence Kelley from the National Board. The withdrawal of these women showed not merely personal antagonism, but a deepening crisis arising from the absence of a clear-cut policy which would furnish direction and greater impetus to the growing number of suffragists clamoring for action.

For five years thereafter — until 1916 — each national convention witnessed major changes among the officers. Women of widely differing outlook — the wealthy Socialist Jessie Ashley, the sociologist Sophonisba Breckenridge, Jane Addams (who took a lead-

ing part in organizing the Progressive Party in 1912), and socialites
such as Katherine Dexter McCormick and Harriet Laidlaw — succeeded one another in efforts to achieve stable leadership, an effort
foredoomed to failure under Dr. Shaw's ambiguous and faltering
direction.

During part of this time Mrs. Catt was far removed from the
national scene, although in 1912 she resumed an active role in
connection with the campaign taking shape in New York for a
suffrage referendum. She was on a world tour on behalf of the
International Alliance during some of the bitterest divisions in
1910–1911, and wrote to a friend with what proved to be rare
acumen:

> I do not think there will be a split. If the difference is over per-
> sonal matters, it is better policy to stay in and change them. There
> seems to be no great difference of opinion on tactics. I am glad the
> National is quarreling; it betokens life and alertness. A few years ago
> nothing could rouse the convention from a dead calm . . . something
> is doing and I am glad of it.

> I daresay the National *is* rotten, but give a calf rope and it will
> hang itself. Just wait until it is dead. Its successor will then inherit
> its field, its good will, and its property, and no resentments and ill
> feeling. Patience . . . the National will either die or come to. Give it
> time.[14]

Despite all the dissension, some promising changes were taking
place. Beginning in 1910 the National Association had functioning
headquarters in New York, due initially to gifts from Mrs.
O. H. P. Belmont and later from other benefactresses. The battles
working women were engaged in had their impact: convention
meetings devoted to women in industry became standard events,
and Margaret Dreier Robins, Leonora O'Reilly, Rose Schneiderman, and others were now familiar figures, although they never
attained leadership in suffrage councils. When Miss Schneiderman spoke at a Cooper Union meeting in answer to the fears expressed by a New York state senator that women would lose their
feminine qualities if given the vote, she was educating not only
the legislators, but the women of all classes who listened to her:

We have women working in the foundries, stripped to the waist, if
you please, because of the heat. Yet the Senator says nothing about
these women losing their charm. They have got to retain their charm

and delicacy, and work in the foundries. Of course you know the reason they are employed in foundries is that they are cheaper and work longer hours than men. Women in the laundries, for instance, stand for thirteen or fourteen hours in the terrible steam and heat with their hands in hot starch. Surely these women won't lose any more of their beauty and charm by putting a ballot in a ballot box once a year than they are likely to lose standing in foundries or laundries all year round. There is no harder contest than the contest for bread, let me tell you that.[15]

The growing common cause between women of all classes was visible in the parades which had become a regular spring feature in New York. The reaction of onlookers had slowly changed from hostility or amusement to friendly interest and even respect; witness the report of an out-of-town correspondent sent to his newspaper in 1912:

Women who usually see Fifth Avenue through the polished windows of their limousines and touring cars strode steadily side by side with pale-faced, thin-bodied girls from the sweltering sweat shops of the East Side. Mrs. O. H. P. Belmont walked but a few steps ahead of Rebecca Goldstein, who runs a sewing machine in a shirtwaist shop.

All along Fifth Avenue from Washington Square, where the parade formed, to 57th Street, where it disbanded, were gathered thousands of men and women of New York. They blocked every cross street on the line of march. Many were inclined to laugh and jeer, but none did. The sight of the impressive column of women striding five abreast up the middle of the street stifled all thought of ridicule. They were typical, womanly American women . . . women doctors, women lawyers, splendid in their array of academic robes; women architects, women artists, actresses and sculptors; women waitresses, domestics; a huge division of industrial workers; women of the seven suffrage states in the Union; a big delegation from New Jersey; another from Connecticut . . . all marched with an intensity and purpose that astonished the crowds that lined the streets.[16]

Optimism was in the air, for that year six referendum campaigns were under way, in Arizona, Kansas, Oregon, Michigan, Ohio, and Wisconsin, the last three heavily populated, where the outcome would have an impact on eastern industrial states.

For weeks following Election Day, the suffragists thought they had won four states: Arizona, Kansas, Oregon — at last! — and Michigan. Only gradually did it become clear that the returns in Michigan were undergoing the kind of treatment which the California women had feared in 1911, but had been able to prevent:

The early returns showed favorable figures and the suffrage majority climbed steadily to 8,000. But many scattered precincts mysteriously withheld their returns, without explanation. One by one these were released, cutting the majority to 5,000, where it seemed established and Michigan was announced to the world as another suffrage state. Then the delayed precincts began sifting in their returns, each with a suspiciously large adverse majority, until the favorable majority became a slightly adverse one. Many weeks had been consumed in the process and nerve-racked suffragists, knowing precisely what was taking place, stood helpless before the deliberate theft of an election.[17]

Despite tremendous public uproar and attempts by the Governor to insure a fair count, including a public statement in which he accused the brewers of complicity in the fraud being perpetrated, the final official figures gave a bare majority of 760 to the opponents of the suffrage bill. It was almost immediately resubmitted, and once more defeated; Mrs. Catt pointed out the interesting anomaly that the increase in the total vote and in the "no" vote was exactly the same, down to the last digit: 16,747.[18] The affirmative vote fell off badly, and the measure lost by almost a hundred thousand. Understandably discouraged by such brazen skullduggery, the Michigan suffragists gave up on state referenda for a few years.

In Ohio and Wisconsin the margin of defeat was much greater than in the first Michigan vote — the liquor interests were too strong and the women too weak to require the kind of blatant fraud practiced in Michigan. In Ohio, where the vote took place at a special election held in September on amendments to the state constitution, the liquor forces were so strong that they boasted openly they had been responsible for the defeat of woman suffrage.

A suffrage victory in the far northern territory of Alaska, where the first act of the Legislature, after territorial status had been established in 1912, was the passage of a woman suffrage bill, did not materially alter the situation.[19] An objective nation-wide survey of the suffrage scene early in 1913 would have revealed the following:

1. The victories in Washington and California had aroused an opposition to woman suffrage which was not likely to be caught napping again.
2. Women had full suffrage in nine states, with a combined popu-

lation of about six and a half million. The three states won in 1912 had eighteen electoral votes, making a total of 45 in suffrage states, but none were states of decisive political importance.

3. It was legitimate to assume that the opposition's strength would mount in direct proportion to a state's political importance.

4. Under such circumstances, was the state-by-state "route" to woman suffrage the preferable and most promising one?

The growing number who doubted such a course were bolstered by the experience in Illinois in 1913. Here, despite broad support for suffrage, the Governor flatly refused to submit the issue to the voters; suffragists therefore turned instead to the possibility of obtaining a measure of suffrage, in this case the vote for president of the United States, through action of the state legislature. They based their reasoning on Article II, Section 2, of the Federal Constitution, which states that: "Each State shall appoint, in such Manner as the Legislature thereof may direct, a Number of Electors, equal to the whole number of Senators and Representatives to which the State may be entitled in the Congress." That year the Progressive Party, which had achieved large gains in a number of middle-western and western states in the wake of the older Populist movement, held the balance of power in the Illinois Legislature. Grace Wilbur Trout and Elizabeth K. Booth led a carefully organized campaign, down to the last detail of insuring that every legislator known to be favorable was in his seat when the count was taken.[20] The Hull House contingent worked tirelessly, the downstate counties were heard from in floods of telegrams to their representatives, and for once the vigorous opposition of the brewers and liquor interests came to naught. Twenty-nine electors were added to the suffrage column, for a national total of 74.

Yet however impressive this figure, and however encouraging the fact that woman suffrage had at last won a toe-hold, even in limited form, east of the Mississippi, the favorable circumstances which had brought it about were not immediately duplicated elsewhere. Confronted with another prospective stalemate, the eyes of more and more suffragists began turning to Washington, where in the nation's capital, a new suffrage venture was under way.

Chapter XX

NEW LIFE IN THE FEDERAL AMENDMENT, 1914–1916

If the years from 1896 to 1910 were a period of unrelieved "doldrums" as far as woman suffrage was concerned, those from 1910 to 1915 were a contradictory mixture of awakening, confusion, and continued paralysis. The growth of insurgent, reform-minded Progressive parties in middle-western and far western states had been a real factor in winning a number of referendum victories. Yet, despite the fact that the newly formed national Progressive Party made woman suffrage a plank in its 1912 presidential election platform behind the candidacy of Theodore Roosevelt (with Jane Addams seconding his nomination, and women in many states working for the party), it is hardly valid to claim, as suffrage historians have done, that woman suffrage had become an issue of national political significance in 1912. The politicians were aware that close to a million women would be eligible to vote in six states, but it is doubtful whether Roosevelt's advocacy of woman suffrage won him many votes, or if the failure of the major parties to do so lost them any.

In point of fact, interest in the Federal woman-suffrage amendment was at an alltime low. The annual hearings on the bill before Senate and House Committees had become routine, since nothing was expected to come of them. Woman suffrage had not been debated on the floor of the Senate since 1887, and had never reached the floor of the House; the suffrage bill had not received a favorable committee report in either house since 1893, and no report at all since 1896.[1] The chairman of the National Association's Congressional Committee for 1912, Mrs. William Kent, was given $10 for expenses connected with the hearings, and refunded change at the end of her term!

The credit for transforming this situation in a few months goes to a young woman who had undergone a vigorous apprenticeship in the militant wing of the British suffrage movement. Alice Paul was a Quaker and a social worker who had gone to England in 1907 to pursue her studies further. She was not only jailed for her suffrage activities, but went on a hunger strike and suffered the ordeal of forcible feeding. She came home in 1910 and began speaking to American suffrage groups on the lessons of the British movement. She also worked with Pennsylvania suffragists while completing her Ph.D. at the University of Pennsylvania, and took part in launching open-air meetings, already adopted in other states, in Philadelphia.

In Great Britain Miss Paul had made friends with Lucy Burns, another American who was working with the militants; they renewed their friendship in this country, and in 1912 the two women discussed with Jane Addams and Anna Howard Shaw the possibility of their undertaking work for the Susan B. Anthony amendment. The Board of the National Suffrage Association appointed them to its Congressional Committee, and Miss Paul succeeded Mrs. Kent as chairman, with the understanding that the Committee was to raise its own funds.

Miss Paul and Miss Burns came to Washington in January 1913. They gathered a few more women around them — Mrs. Lawrence Lewis, Crystal Eastman, and Mary Beard. In no time at all it became clear that there was a reservoir of great interest and energy in a suffrage amendment waiting to be tapped, and a spectacular campaign began to develop.

Within two months the tiny group had organized a parade of 5,000 women. With that dramatic sense which always characterized her suffrage work, Miss Paul chose the day before Woodrow Wilson's inauguration, since Washington would be filled with visitors from all over the country. When Mr. Wilson reached Washington and found the streets bare of any welcoming crowds, he is said to have asked where the people were; he was told they were over on Pennsylvania Avenue, watching the woman suffrage parade.

As it turned out, they were doing more than just watch. Miss Paul had a police permit for the parade, but received no help of a more practical nature when matters degenerated into a near-riot, and the crowds administered a very different kind of treatment from that which suffragists had become accustomed to in New York and other cities:

Five thousand women, marching in the woman suffrage pageant today, practically fought their way foot by foot up Pennsylvania Avenue, through a surging throng that completely defied Washington police, swamped the marchers, and broke their procession into little companies. The women, trudging stoutly along under great difficulties, were able to complete their march only when troops of cavalry from Fort Myers were rushed into Washington to take charge of Pennsylvania Avenue. No inauguration has ever produced such scenes, which in many instances amounted to nothing less than riots.[2]

"The women," said another newspaper story, "had to fight their way from the start and took more than one hour in making the first ten blocks. Many of the women were in tears under the jibes and insults of those who lined the route. At Fourth Street progress was impossible. Commissioner Johnson called upon some members of a Massachusetts National Guard regiment to help clear the way. Some laughed, and one assured the Commissioner they had no orders to act as an escort. At Fifth Street the crowd again pressed in and progress was impossible. The Thirteenth Regiment, Pennsylvania National Guard, was appealed to and agreed to do police duty. . . . Very effective assistance was rendered by the students of the Maryland Agricultural College, in guarding the women marchers. It was where Sixth Street crosses the avenue that police protection gave way entirely and the two solid masses of spectators on either side came so close together that three women could not march abreast. It was here that the Maryland boys formed in single file on each side of the 'Pilgrims' and became a protecting wall. In front a squad of the boys locked arms and formed a crowd-breaking vanguard. Several of the 'war correspondents' were forced to use their fists in fighting back the crowd. . . . The parade itself, in spite of the delays, was a great success. Passing through two walls of antagonistic humanity, the marchers, for the most part, kept their tempers. They suffered insult, and closed their ears to jibes and jeers. Few faltered, though some of the older women were forced to drop out from time to time."[3]

Public opinion was sufficiently outraged by the episode to bring about an investigation by the District Commissioners, and the Washington Chief of Police eventually lost his job. Tremendous publicity accrued to the suffragists, and the Congressional

Committee picked up fresh momentum. Pilgrimages were organized to Washington from all over the country with petitions collected at the grass-roots level, culminating in an automobile procession to the Capitol on July 31 which presented a group of senators with suffrage petitions carrying 200,000 signatures. Delegations began to visit President Wilson, whose early pronouncements on woman suffrage — beginning with his famous remark that the matter had never been brought to his attention — were not promising.

Suffrage Association leaders, while welcoming the tremendous upsurge of interest in the federal amendment which the Congressional Committee's work had evoked, were beginning to have an uneasy feeling that they had released a force they would have difficulty in controlling. Nevertheless, when Miss Paul and Miss Burns formed a national organization in April 1913 for the sole purpose of working for the federal suffrage amendment, it was still with Dr. Shaw's blessing. It took the name of the Congressional Union, and on November 15 began issuing its own weekly publication, *The Suffragist*. Miss Paul was the Union's chairman, and also retained her position as chairman of the National Association's Congressional Committee; no one could really tell where the activities of one began and the other left off, especially where finances were concerned.[4]

Such vagueness was not, in itself, surprising: suffragists had never been noted for meticulous organizational procedures. The real difficulty arose from the rift growing between the parent body and the new organization, which had been inevitable from the time when Miss Paul first assumed leadership of the Congressional Committee, a rift between dynamic and static methods of work and aims, which resulted in an open collision on the floor of the 1913 suffrage convention.

The Congressional Union group demanded an all-out campaign for immediate passage of the federal suffrage amendment on the ground that its passage and ratification by three fourths of the states was a practical goal, provided all efforts were concentrated on it. The National leadership felt that such a program was entirely premature. Mrs. Catt, on the scene once again, and preparing for the referendum New York suffragists hoped to win in 1915, led a movement for greater centralization of the National's scattered activities, which included making the Congressional Committee responsible for its policy to the Association's National Board.

The program pressed by Miss Paul and her co-workers did not receive the support of the convention, which, instead, voted to give the National Board the powers necessary to delimit the spheres of the Congressional Committee and the Congressional Union. There were prolonged negotiations in which the National's officers endeavored, in all sincerity, to retain the invaluable energies of Miss Paul and Miss Burns, while restricting their freedom to contravene established National Association policy. Yet the compromise offers put forward would not have proved workable even if they had been acceptable to Miss Paul, who never for one moment deviated from her original position. The differences in regard to policy were too deep, and they continued to grow:[5]

1. The original, and most basic area of disagreement was the Union's insistence that all suffrage work be limited to pressure on Congress and the President for a federal amendment.

2. Refusal by the Union to submit to limitations imposed by existing National policy. This included the above, and also the issue of whether the Union could send organizers into states where existing suffrage associations were already functioning. The Union felt that in many cases work for the amendment could only be done through by-passing such state associations as wished to engage only in state referendum campaigns. The National held to what it claimed had always been one of its cardinal principles, that "outsiders" could only go into a state to do suffrage work when invited by the state association to do so.

No solution to this impasse being possible, Miss Paul was removed as chairman of the Congressional Committee; Miss Burns and other members resigned. The influential Mrs. Medill McCormick was appointed the new chairman. The Congressional Union asked to change its status from an "affiliate" of the National American Woman Suffrage Association to that of an "auxiliary" on the grounds that the fee was smaller. In February 1914 the National Board voted against such an arrangement, 54 to 24, and thereafter the two organizations went their separate ways.

Although attempts were subsequently made to heal the split, always originating with the National, they became increasingly futile in the light of fresh differences. One was the Congressional

Union's insistence on holding "the party in power" responsible for failure to pass the woman suffrage bill or to act to further its passage through Congress. This principle had originated with the British militants and arose from the British parliamentary system where one party could actually be held responsible and ousted from power for defeat or inaction on specific legislation. Orthodox American suffragists contended that no party could be held similarly responsible under the American form of government and that an additional argument against it was that the issue of woman suffrage cut straight across party lines; both the Democratic majority and the Republican minority in Congress contained supporters and opponents.

The Congressional Union felt that in view of the Democratic majority, and the president's titular leadership of his party, the Democrats must bear responsibility; to implement this concept they tried to hold the women's vote in the enfranchised states over the Democrats' heads. Beginning in 1914 the Union, and later its successor, the Woman's Party, campaigned against Democratic candidates for Congress regardless of their attitude toward woman suffrage; in 1916 they opposed Wilson's re-election. The National Association held that such a policy alienated needed votes of both parties and would result in driving Wilson further away from the suffragists instead of winning his support.

Within two months after the final split still another issue widened it, and at the same time increased the paralysis which was afflicting the National Association. On March 2 another woman suffrage measure was placed before Congress, the Shafroth-Palmer amendment, principally the brainchild of Mrs. McCormick and some of the Senators advising her, which would require any state, 8 per cent of whose voters at the last election signed an initiative petition to hold a referendum on woman suffrage.

Its supporters claimed that this measure would not only make it easier to get state referenda held (pointing to the long list of states where endless campaigns had so far failed to secure a vote); they also argued that the Shafroth-Palmer amendment would gain the support of those senators who, while favoring woman suffrage in principle, opposed the Anthony amendment on the grounds that it was an invasion of states' rights.[6] Opponents of the Shafroth-Palmer amendment, many of them members of the National who remained loyal to the older organization despite their mounting exasperation with its ineffectiveness, branded the measure as cumbersome and confusing. Even admitting that it might be passed and ratified, and more state referenda thus made possible, each single one would still have to be fought and won; the Shafroth-Palmer bill committed the National anew to the state-by-state road to woman suffrage, one that seemed increasingly hopeless.

Events during 1914 certainly appeared to substantiate this view. Seven states voted on woman suffrage; only two, the sparsely populated and politically unimportant states of Montana and Nevada, were in favor. On the other hand grueling and costly campaigns were waged and lost in the two Dakotas, Nebraska, Missouri, and once again in Ohio. Mrs. Catt branded the lot as "tediously similar." Suffragists in growing numbers asked, what on earth was the use of one more unsuccessful campaign in South Dakota? Where was there evidence of any planning, of the weighing of one possible campaign's chances of success against another's — in short, of competent leadership?

Another wholesale turnover of national officers, six out of nine, took place at the close of 1914. Throughout 1915 the National appeared virtually bankrupt. When it attempted to compete with the Congressional Union in lobbying in Congress, the results were pitiful; at one time the disparity in numbers ran as high as forty-one to three. The only areas where signs of life were evident were the four eastern states where referenda were coming up in the fall: the National pinned all its hopes on a breakthrough in New York, Pennsylvania, Massachusetts, and New Jersey.

The Congressional Union, in sharp contrast, was moving into higher gear right across the country. During the 1914 election campaign it sent organizers into the nine western states which had won full woman suffrage, to swing the women's vote against Democratic candidates regardless of the fact that many were suffrage advocates:

If the party leaders see that some votes have been turned they will know that we have at least realized this power that we possess, and they will know that by 1916 we will have it organized. The mere announcement of the fact that the Suffragists of the East have gone out to the West with this appeal will be enough to make every man in Congress sit up and take notice.[7]

Whether or not this prophecy was substantiated, the Union claimed at least partial credit for the defeat of twenty-three out of forty-three western Democrats. It also continued to ply President Wilson with varied delegations of college women, working women, professional women, and western voting women.

Every step of this program was aimed at achieving one goal: to bring the woman suffrage amendment, with or without the President's support, and whatever its chances of passage, out on the floor of Congress. It succeeded; on March 19, 1914, the Senate voted, 34 in favor to 35 opposed, and on January 12, 1915, the measure came up in the House of Representatives, where it was defeated, 204 to 174.[8]

In the spring of 1915 the Congressional Union began organizing in every one of the forty-eight states in the country. As part of this plan it carried out an elaborate national demonstration in the form of an automobile pilgrimage which, starting from the Panama-Pacific Exposition in San Francisco, progressed through a series of meetings across the country to Washington. Meanwhile half a million signatures were being gathered, with amazing speed, to another suffrage petition. A rally in a Washington theater and a march to the Capitol on May 9th led up to still one more delegation to President Wilson to present the petition.[9]

To trace the suffrage bill's progress in these two years — to unravel the procedural tactics which were used to block it in the Rules Committee, the Judiciary Committee, and finally in Woman Suffrage Committees of both houses, tactics which varied from trying to bury the bill in committee to calling it up at the worst possible moment — makes dull reading now. At the time it made for killing, unrewarding work by those who were trying to push it forward and to focus national attention on the amendment's fate.

In weighing the role of the Congressional Union and of its successor, the Woman's Party, and evaluating their contribution to the winning of the vote, attention has too often been concentrated on the phase of their activity which began in 1917, when they went over to "militant" tactics adapted from the British suffragists, such as picketing the White House, hunger strikes in protest against being arrested, bonfires, etc. To do so is to overlook the long years of work they had put in beforehand, during three of which they were the only effective group working for a federal suffrage amendment. They took up that issue when it was dead, and brought it very much to life, a service for which even Mrs. Catt gave them credit.[10]

The four eastern suffrage referendum campaigns conducted during 1915 constituted a showdown unlike anything that had gone before. New York, Massachusetts, and Pennsylvania had been home to the great pioneers of the woman's rights movement; New Jersey women had been the first in the United States to vote, for a brief period in the early nineteenth century. All four were industrial states with large populations, of prime political importance. If these states, or some, or even one of them, could carry for woman suffrage, the national situation would be drastically affected.

This was fully realized on both sides. The suffragists made heroic efforts; the opposition stopped at nothing to defeat them. Nothing had previously approached these campaigns in concentrated effort, organizational detail, imaginativeness of the propaganda and educational work, and dogged, slugging "footwork" by thousands of dedicated supporters, men and women who went from door to door in the cities, held outdoor meetings in every small town, and spoke at every crossroads. They nerved themselves for an unparalleled effort — and they lost, in all four states.

They lost by respectable, not to say impressive, margins. Each defeat had some elements not present in the others. The best showing was made in New Jersey, which polled 42 per cent of the total vote in favor of suffrage. Here a potent cause for defeat lay in the fact that the election was held on Registration Day, October 19; many regular voters did not go to the polls, and it was possible for a large number of unregistered "floaters" who came from New York across the river to help vote the measure down.[11]

The New Jersey defeat did not help the other three referenda, all of which were held on November 2. In neighboring Pennsylvania the women were optimistic, due to brilliant leadership by Miss Hannah Patterson and Mrs. Frank M. Roessing, both of whom achieved national prestige from their work. For the first time large industrial areas, Alleghany County and seven others, carried for suffrage. But Philadelphia, stronghold of the saloon vote, went against, with a margin of more than 45,000, accounting for 80 per cent of the adverse margin. Even so, 46 per cent of the vote was cast in favor of the suffrage amendment, which might have given grounds for hope in the future. Unfortunately both Pennsylvania and New Jersey had state constitutions which provided that a defeated amendment could not be resubmitted to the voters for five years. This put the states with the best numerical chance of an early victory out of the running.

Massachusetts, where only 35.5 per cent of the total vote was in favor, suffered the worst defeat, due largely, the suffragists felt, to the fact that the state had been the origin and home of the anti-suffrage movement for thirty years. It also had a large body of Catholic voters, and while the Church took no official position, strongly worded statements by leading clerics were issued in opposition to the proposed bill for the Massachusetts Anti-Suffrage Committee and by the National Association Opposed to Woman Suffrage.[12] Suffragists saw evidence of "dirty work" in the fact that the total vote was the largest ever cast on an amendment in the state's history, that it was uniformly adverse in every county in the state, and in all but two towns and cities. The outcome left Massachusetts suffragists with little taste for another attempt by the state method.

In New York, where a masterly campaign had built up an indomitable spirit, the reaction was altogether different, although here the adverse majority was 194,984, numerically the largest of the four contests. Not that the workers who thronged headquarters in New York City on election night listening to the returns did not react in bitter disappointment to the figures which gave the outcome. Some cried outright; but those who commandeered automobiles and went out to address the after-theater crowds, promising that the new campaign was already underway, were more representative of the general feeling. An overflow meeting at Cooper Union just two nights later pledged $115,000 toward a new drive, and actually announced the opening of the campaign for another referendum, which would necessarily not be held until 1917, two years away.[13]

One reason for the resilience of the New York suffragists was the enormous confidence they had in their leader. They were, however, not alone in believing Mrs. Catt to be the best organizer in the suffrage movement. Out of the bankruptcy and mounting confusion in the National's affairs and its increasingly disastrous competition with the dynamic Congressional Union had come wide recognition of the fact that there must be a change in policy and in leadership, and that no one would fill the need of the hour except Mrs. Catt. After Anna Howard Shaw's announcement on November 20, one month before the annual suffrage convention, that she would not be a candidate for re-election to the presidency, the movement to draft Mrs. Catt began to pick up momentum.

There is evidence that Mrs. Catt herself had no such idea. She was obsessed by the movement's paucity of leadership and had always sought out promising material for training and opportunity. She looked constantly for one who would lead the National out of the wilderness, and in 1912 wrote to a friend: "Some day she'll come. Perhaps she is growing up now and maybe she is nearly ready for her task and will step forth directly." [14] Even after the New York referendum she still did not see herself in the role. She thought she was too old at fifty-five to be capable of such an effort, and she also felt honor-bound to lead the New York suffragists to final victory in 1917.

The 1915 convention of the National early in December decreed otherwise. It confronted Mrs. Catt with a summons on terms she was too stalwart a fighter to refuse. The New York State Suffrage Association was persuaded to release her; her international responsibilities, already diminished by the European war and now largely financial, were taken off her hands by a committee which pledged itself to raise the sum of money needed to maintain the International Woman Suffrage Alliance headquarters in London. Finally she was told that she could write her own ticket as far as her Executive Board was concerned.

Two other factors contributed to Mrs. Catt's decision, unwilling though it was, to take the National's presidency. One was the action, taken by the outgoing National Board, to drop the vexing Shafroth-Palmer amendment (although it took a good deal more hard work finally to lay its ghost). The other was the knowledge that in the foreseeable future the National would have money with which to put up the kind of campaign needed to insure victory. In September 1914 Mrs. Catt had personally received a legacy in the neighborhood of $2,000,000, bequeathed to her by Mrs. Frank

Leslie, the wealthy publisher of *Leslie's Weekly*. Mrs. Leslie had been considered eccentric — a beautiful woman, married four times, who had become a highly successful editor and business executive. For years she had given the suffrage cause sums, never exceeding $100 at a time; her bequest to Mrs. Catt contained the wish that her fortune be expended "to the furtherance of the cause of woman suffrage." Although nearly half the estate was subsequently consumed in litigation or out-of-court settlements, and the first payments were not made to Mrs. Catt until early in 1917, the money finally made available was of inestimable aid.[15]

Mrs. Catt's assumption of the presidency of the National American Woman Suffrage Association marks a significant turning point. At the moment, it must have appeared the last hope of the women who chose her for the post, and *how* she would bring order out of chaos and victory out of apparent stagnation could hardly have been clear to anyone, including Mrs. Catt herself. She wrote bitterly to a friend:

Taking on a concern "bankrupt" in various matters and letting go a concern brimful of ideas . . . I am off to Washington Monday. O, how I loathe it. . . . I've moved from a comfortable office to an uncomfortable one; from a job I understand to one I don't. . . . I do need something more than human help. If you have any influence with the divinities please implore their aid on my behalf.[16]

One would never have guessed her feelings from the profound, almost overnight change that took place in the affairs of the National. Immediately after the New Year, a series of communications to the presidents of the state suffrage associations began crackling out from the New York headquarters. The women back in the states who, having no sympathy for the tactics and thinking of the Congressional Union, had been sticking to their posts without any real perspective or hope, took a new lease on life when they began receiving precise, imaginative directives regarding policy and program. Renewed activity in Washington on behalf of the federal amendment, conferences between state and national leaders, schools for organizers, ideas on fund-raising — best of all, real planning, based on specific questionnaires sent to every state association — all gave promise of a new era in suffrage work.

One reason Mrs. Catt could promise and then accomplish so much was that the Board she picked at the time of her election was a *working* board. Its members were women with independent means who had the ability as well as the willingness to devote themselves single-mindedly to their new jobs. These requirements were to be mandatory for suffrage leadership for the next five years. As soon as a woman's health or family responsibilities precluded such full-time activity, neither sentiment nor gratitude for past achievement stood in the way of her replacement. This of course had been true of Miss Paul's methods of work and organization from her first days in Washington, and a good deal of the startling progress made by the Congressional Union was due to it. It did not make for a socially representative leadership in either group; but it provided two brilliant leaders with trained and experienced staffs who measured up to any demands that were made upon them, and it was one of the reasons why American women at last won the vote. The day for the amateur reformer had given way to the professional organizer, just as was becoming the case in the labor movement. Susan Anthony would have welcomed the change.

It was not easy for Dr. Shaw to step aside and learn to work with this new group. That she was able to do so is testimony to her largeness of spirit and devotion to the cause. Once she had finally been brought to see that she could make her best contribution in other ways than in the post her beloved "Aunt Susan" had willed her, she gave Mrs. Catt unstinting loyalty: "The new group is taking hold and doing things splendidly. . . . I realize that my day except for speaking and 'inspiring' has gone by, and this is all right; I will speak and 'inspire' my best. I might do worse, I suppose." [17]

It took months of hard work to get the old National back on its feet. At first the national officers fanned out into the states to do a combination of surveying and re-organizing, some of the fruits of which Mrs. Catt presented to her Board in a grimly realistic report three months after she had assumed the presidency:

A serious crisis exists in the suffrage movement. A considerable number of women in the various states have turned to the Federal Amendment as the most promising avenue. The victory of the Federal Amendment especially appeals to the women of those states with constitutions which make a successful referendum well-nigh impossible. A considerable number of women in the South are dead set against the Federal

Amendment. The first anti-suffrage organization of importance to be effected in the South has been formed in Alabama with the slogan: "Home Rule, States Rights, and White Supremacy." A considerable number of other women wish to work exclusively for suffrage within their own states. The Congressional Union is drawing off from the National Association those women who feel it is possible to work for suffrage by the Federal route only. Certain workers in the South are being antagonized because the National is continuing work for the Federal Amendment. The combination has produced a great muddle from which the National can be freed only by careful action.[18]

It was Mrs. Catt's unique contribution to the achievement of greater democratic opportunities for American women that she was able to weld so many of these seemingly disparate elements into a potent political force. Her greatest gift, outranking even her excellence as an organizer, was the statesmanlike vision which enabled her to conceive a plan of action, in which each group could play a role and thus help to achieve the desired goal. Having created such a plan, she could also assure its implementation, because she had developed a corps of lieutenants who could carry every last detail into execution. Such was the caliber of her leadership that it is no overstatement to say that Carrie Chapman Catt stands beside Miss Anthony and Mrs. Stanton in stature.

Only the Congressional Union and Woman's Party, led by Miss Paul, could not fit into her flexible and comprehensive program, and went its own way. It in no way detracts from the value of the work accomplished by Miss Paul and her associates from 1913 through 1916 to say that it was fortunate, for the United States and for its women, that they were not the sole group from 1916 on that was working for suffrage, and that Miss Paul's way was no longer the only effective way in which women could work to win the vote.

Chapter XXI

THE TURN IN THE TIDE, 1916–1918

In the summer of 1916 the United States faced a presidential contest with the entire House of Representatives and one third of the Senate at stake. The Democrats, headed by Wilson, went to the polls on a strong reform record, bolstered by the theme of "He Kept Us Out of War"; the Republicans nominated Charles Evans Hughes.

The Congressional Union met in Chicago June 5–7 (immediately preceding the Republican convention) and organized the National Woman's Party in the twelve states where women had the presidential vote. Said the keynote speaker, Miss Maud Younger:

With the foundation of the Woman's Party, a new force marches on to the political field, a new cry rings out in the national campaign. For the first time in a presidential election, voting women are a factor to be reckoned with. Four years ago, women voted in six states — today in twelve, including Illinois. These states with their four million women constitute nearly one-fourth of the electoral college and more than one-third of the votes necessary to elect a President. With enough women organized in each state to hold the balance of power, the women's votes may determine the presidency of the United States.[1]

Fear of such a possibility probably was a factor in influencing both parties to include, for the first time, some reference to the desirability of woman suffrage in their election programs; but on the all-important question of how it should be achieved, both were silent.[2]

The Woman's Party maintained an anti-Democratic position throughout the campaign, but it directed its principal attack against Wilson:

The effort of the Woman's Party will be directed toward the defeat of Mr. Wilson and the national Democratic ticket in the twelve equal suffrage states. . . . The Woman's Party has been accused of "being out to punish Mr. Wilson." They are very indifferent indeed about Mr. Wilson. In thirty-six states they are not attempting to harm a political hair of Mr. Wilson's head. They would view with composure the re-election of Mr. Wilson — but *not* in the equal suffrage states and *not* by the help of women's votes. One thing we have to teach Mr. Wilson and his party — and all on-looking parties — that the group which opposes national suffrage for women will lose women's support in twelve great commonwealths controlling nearly a hundred electoral votes; too large a fraction to risk, or to risk twice, even if once risked successfully. If that is made clear, it is a matter of total indifference to the Woman's Party — so far as suffrage is concerned — who is the next President of the United States.[3]

Having so explicitly defined its aims, the Woman's Party had to face the fact that the election results fell short of administering the desired lesson with sufficient clarity either to Wilson or his party. The President carried ten out of twelve "suffrage states," losing only Oregon and Illinois. The Woman's Party was even less successful in defeating Democratic candidates for Congress. It had to admit that the impact of the women's vote could only be accurately gauged in Illinois; there it was counted separately, since women cast only presidential ballots, and their majority for Hughes ran ahead of his overall majority in the state. Elsewhere the Woman's Party relied on the assertions of its organizers that the women had voted for Hughes or other candidates, and that Wilson owed his election only to the combined forces of Progressives, labor, and farmers (all presumably male!). [4]

Whatever the weakness of its logic, the Woman's Party continued to assert that its election policy had been successful. When its failure to influence the progress of the suffrage measure through Congress any further became undeniable, it was forced to turn to other tactics, and it chose the one on which its latter-day fame has come to rest: militancy.

The logic of the National Suffrage Association's policies, as evolved by Mrs. Catt during 1916, led in a diametrically opposite direction. She was disappointed in the Republicans' failure to include in their platform a suffrage plank that had any teeth in it,[5] particularly after the heroic demonstration which the National staged in Chicago during the convention, when 5,000 women marched in a suffrage parade in a cold, drenching rainstorm, buffeted by gale winds from the lake front. The Democratic plank, favoring "the extension of suffrage to women, state by state, on the same terms as men," pleased her no better. Feeling in both suffragist groups resulted in stormy outbursts from the gallery. The *New York Times* described the scene when the vote on the Democratic Resolutions Committee report was taken, in somber vein: "The galleries ruled the convention and the women ruled the galleries. It was like the French Convention of the Revolution . . . and the women with the rollcall blanks, noting down their enemies and the way they voted, suggested the knitting women of the Reign of Terror." [6]

Instead of unleashing any militant onslaught, Mrs. Catt evolved a program whose most obvious and first step was to win over Mr. Wilson to support of a federal amendment. Considered anti-suffrage while still governor of New Jersey, the President passed through successive phases in which he pleaded that he could do nothing unless his party acted, since he was solely its representative and spokesman (although he had *led* it on other controversial issues); that he could do nothing until Congress acted and could not invade the province of a Congressional Committee to hasten its action (although he had done so in other cases); finally, that the issue was one solely up to the several states.

The manifest difficulties of the state path in the face of such political realities as the stealing of the Michigan vote in 1912, the opposition of the corrupt machines in Ohio, Wisconsin, and New York, not to mention the impossibility of getting anywhere by such means in the "Solid South," were brought to Wilson's attention by repeated delegations from the Woman's Party and by Mrs. Catt and her gifted lieutenant, Mrs. Helen Gardener. Mrs. Catt herself presented him with verified reports of election frauds in Michigan, Nebraska, and Iowa and argued that states' rights could hardly be considered slighted by a federal amendment which required ratification by three fourths of the states. Above all, she kept the door of communication between the National and the White House open so well that the President himself, accompanied by Mrs. Wilson, appeared at the National's Atlantic City convention in September 1916 at the height of his own campaign for re-election. He did not finally commit himself on this occasion, although it seemed to his eager listeners that his address stopped only just short of it: "I have not come to fight anybody but with somebody. . . . We feel the tide; we rejoice in the strength of it, and we shall not quarrel in the long run as to the method of it." [7]

Mrs. Catt believed that the moment which marked his "conversion" to the federal amendment came when Dr. Shaw, replying to his address, uttered the words: "We have waited so long, Mr. President, for the vote — we had hoped it might come in your administration," and the entire audience of women rose silently and turned toward him. Although it was another year before Wilson took the position, as leader of the Democratic Party, that Congress should act on woman suffrage, he never thereafter refused to grant the National aid when asked, and he gave it in ways the public never learned.[8]

Along with winning presidential support went the necessity of making suffrage as pressing a political issue as dozens of others. In addition to innumerable domestic problems, war was an immediate issue, first with Germany, then with Mexico, and finally with Germany again. To threaten the Democratic Party, or both major parties, with the wrath of women voters in a dozen western states was in Mrs. Catt's eyes so idle a threat as to be worse than useless; nor did she see any sense in forcing the federal amendment toward a showdown in Congress without working to increase the number of favorable votes the measure could count on. To do so the National had to mobilize its scattered and often dissident forces and convince its members that, at long last, it knew where it was going. When Miss Paul revived the suffrage amendment as a political issue in 1913, the cause took a long step ahead. It took another with the presentation and acceptance of what came to be called Mrs. Catt's "Winning Plan" — a step no less decisive because for years it remained a secret. To the women on whom fell the burden of implementing it, the Plan and the appearance of the President were elements of major significance at the 1916 convention.

Mrs. Maud Wood Park, one of the ablest of Mrs. Catt's aides, has left a brief sketch of the occasion at a pre-Convention meeting: "The crowded stuffy room . . . the tired faces of the women; the map of the United States on the wall . . . Mrs. Catt's calm demeanor when the routine business was over and she outlined the work that must be done." [9] As she talked to the jaded women, each the president of a state suffrage association, each filled to brimming with the vexations of work back in her own bailiwick, she spared them nothing — one of the ways in which Carrie Chapman Catt challenged and won the loyalty of those whom she worked the hardest: she talked about the disintegration that had gone on, unchecked, for years in the National; she demanded a whole new approach to the work ahead, the election of national officers who would stick to their jobs until the end,[10] and, above all, the adoption of a program which would enable lobbyists in Washington and campaigners in the field to feel a united organization behind them:

When thirty-six state associations, or preferably more, enter into a solemn compact to get the [Federal] Amendment submitted by Congress and ratified by their respective legislatures; when they live up to their compact by running a red-hot, never-ceasing campaign in their own states designed to create sentiment behind the political leaders of the states and to aim both these forces at the men in Congress as well as the legislatures, we *can* get the Amendment through, and ratified. We cannot do it by any other process. No such compact has ever been made, and no virile intention exists in the minds of the majority of the Association to back up a Washington lobby. Whether this is due to a prevailing belief that a lobby, assisted now and then by a bombardment of letters and telegrams, can pull the Amendment through, or to a lack of confidence in suffrage by the Federal route, or to sheer, unthinking carelessness, I am not prepared to say. I am inclined to believe that all three of these causes exist. . . .

This Convention must not adjourn, should it sit until Christmas, until it creates a logical and sensible policy toward the Federal Amendment. . . . If it be decided that we *do* want enfranchisement by the Federal route, then at least thirty-six states must sign a compact to go after it with a will. . . .

National Boards must be selected hereafter for one chief qualification — the ability to lead the national fight. There should be a mobilization of at least thirty-six state armies, and these armies should move under the direction of the national officers. They should be disciplined and obedient to the national officers in all matters concerning the national campaign. This great army with its thirty-six, and let us hope, forty-eight divisions, should move on Congress with precision, and a will. . . . More, those who enter on this task, should go prepared to give their lives and fortunes for success, and any pusillanimous coward among us who dares to call retreat, should be courtmartialled.

Any other policy than this is weak, inefficient, illogical, silly, inane, and ridiculous! Any other policy would fail of success.[11]

Not content with generalities, however sobering or inspiring, Mrs. Catt was ready with detailed plans:

When a general is about to make an attack upon the enemy at a fortified point, he often begins to feint elsewhere in order to draw off attention and forces. If we decide to train up some states into preparedness for campaign, the best help which can be given them is to keep so much "suffrage noise" going all over the country that neither the enemy nor friends will discover where the real battle is. . . .

We should win, if it is possible to do so, a few more states before the Federal Amendment gets up to the legislatures. . . . A southern state should be selected and made ready for a campaign, and the solid front of the "anti" south broken as soon as possible.

Some break in the solid "anti" East should be made too. If New York wins in 1917 the backbone of the opposition will be largely bent if not broken. . . .

By 1920, when the next national party platforms will be adopted, we should have won Iowa, South Dakota, North Dakota, Nebraska, New York, Maine and a southern state. We should have secured the Illinois law in a number of other states.*

With these victories to our credit and the tremendous increase of momentum given the whole movement, we should be able to secure planks in all platforms favoring the Federal Amendment (if it has not passed before that time) and to secure its passage in the December term of the 1920 Congress.

It should then go to the legislatures of thirty-nine states which meet in 1921, and the remaining states would have the opportunity to ratify the amendment in 1922. If thirty-six states had ratified in these two years, the end of our struggle would come by April 1, 1922, six years hence. . . .

It will require, however, a constructive program of hard, aggressive work for six years, money to support it, and the cooperation of all suffragists. It will demand the elimination of the spirit of criticism, back-biting and narrow-minded clashing of personalities which is always common to a stagnant town, society or movement, and which is beginning to show itself in our midst. Success will depend less on the money we are able to command, than upon our combined ability to lift the campaign above this sordidness of mind, and to elevate it to the position of a crusade for human freedom.[12]

The compact Mrs. Catt asked for was signed by the officers of more than thirty-six state suffrage associations.[13] It remained secret, but its provisions were within the framework of larger

* The "Illinois law" was presidential suffrage by act of the legislature.

policy decisions made by the convention: concentration on the federal amendment, and submission of state to national leadership and direction. Every state was assigned a specific role to play. States which already had woman suffrage were to get their legislatures to memorialize Congress on behalf of a federal amendment; those where favorable opportunities existed for a referendum for amending the state constitution were to prepare for such campaigns (subject to decision by the National Board, in order to put an end to hopeless campaigns); a third group, primarily in the South, were to work for presidential, or at the least, primary suffrage.

Life speeded up Mrs. Catt's timetable. It took only four years, instead of the six or more she envisaged, to accomplish the job: factors came into play which, although perhaps dimly foreseen at the time, could not have bulked as large in her reckoning as they did in actuality — such as the entry of the United States into the World War.

But what is remarkable is how closely the unfolding drive by the National American Woman Suffrage Association followed the blueprint she had drawn, the degree to which it made possible speedy ratification in many states, once Congress had passed the amendment, and the way in which a lag on one front could be made good on others, once the machinery began to roll in high gear. Before very many months the first fruits of the new strategy began to appear, although at first they appeared haphazard and accidental.

On January 10, 1917, the first suffrage pickets stood outside the gates of the White House, notice that the Congressional Union and Woman's Party (which had been united under the name of the latter) were no longer satisfied with delegations to the President and lobbying recalcitrant congressmen (although they continued to pursue these avenues as well). They were silent pickets, and they stood motionlessly, holding banners which asked "Mr. President, What Will You Do For Woman Suffrage?" and "How Long Must Women Wait for Liberty?" [14] The technique of "Silent Sentinels" had been employed by the Women's Political Union in Albany in attempting to get a suffrage referendum bill before the New York legislature in 1912; the technique of picketing was familiar from countless labor disputes. However, picketing the White House was novel, and the authorities were not quite sure where it would lead or how to handle it. For the time being the police were passive, and the President, driving out with Mrs. Wilson in the afternoon, courteously raised his hat to the motionless women who stood on either side of the gates with unfailing regularity day after day, regardless of the weather. The crowds were curious, often sympathetic in their comments on the placards, whose slogans varied from time to time. Even a moving picket line, which circled the White House on Inauguration Day, March 4th, provoked no difficulties.

The 65th Congress opened its special session on April 2, 1917, and among the new members presented formally at the bar of the House was the first woman to take her seat in the nation's legislative body. She was Miss Jeannette Rankin of Montana, who had headed the women of her state in their successful fight for suffrage in 1914. Miss Rankin led an uneasy Congressional life between the two suffrage factions, who celebrated her formal admission to the House by a joint luncheon in her honor — probably the last instance of cooperation between them — at which Miss Rankin sat as guest of honor with Mrs. Catt on her right and Miss Paul on her left.[15] Whatever her tribulations — the merciless criticism she was subjected to by suffrage adherents for not doing enough for the cause and from its opponents for representing women more than the full electorate which had sent her to Congress — she was a visible embodiment on the House floor, among 421 men, of the growing pressure on that body for political legitimacy for her sex.

Meanwhile relations with Germany were deteriorating, and the possibility of the United States becoming involved in the global war which for two years had been decimating Europe became increasingly acute. Mrs. Catt watched the situation anxiously, aware of the repercussions that such a development would have on the suffrage cause, even within the ranks of the National, now more unified than in many years. As early as February 25, the organization's services were tendered to the Administration in the event of war, but it never, as the Woman's Party charged, abandoned suffrage work for war work, and Mrs. Catt continuously emphasized that suffrage was the National's first concern.

Behind this viewpoint lay her belief that, while war could never settle any issues, the women could not stick their heads in the sand and pretend it was not going on. Moreover, they needed political standing more than ever in order to make their contribution toward the right kind of peace; and, lastly, there was no incongruity between winning the vote for women, and the "war aims" which the Wilson administration gradually developed as the months passed, summed up in the phrase "make the world safe for democracy." Realist that she was, Mrs. Catt knew that the ability of suffragists to plead their cause successfully would depend in some measure on whether they too had joined in the national war effort.

Not so the Woman's Party. With a large proportion of Quakers among its most active members and leaders, it took no steps toward organizing war work (although individual members did engage in it). Its sole acknowledgment of the war was the use it made of passing events in its banner slogans, which grew steadily sharper; these in turn began to provoke reactions from crowds affected by the high-powered propaganda campaign aimed at arousing patriotism, which sometimes evoked something nearer hysteria. "Democracy Should Begin at Home," said the banners; others referred to "free Russia," where women had received the vote after the overthrow of the czarist regime, in invidious comparison with the United States and "Kaiser Wilson." Mob violence first broke out on the day when the banners told envoys from the Kerensky government, calling at the White House, that this country was a democracy in name only. Thereafter it flared repeatedly among onlookers, who included servicemen in uniform as well as outright hoodlums; on June 22, the arrests began.

The charges under which the pickets were brought into court reflected the dilemma confronting the Commissioners of the District of Columbia and the Wilson Administration to which they were directly responsible.[16] The only charge ever made was that of obstructing sidewalk traffic; the truth was that the women were violating no law, perpetrating no crime. Their actions could legally be classed only as committing a nuisance.

Too much emphasis has been put, subsequently, on the merits of the picketing — its aid or harm in winning votes for women — and too little on the fact that the pickets were actually among the earliest victims of the abrogation of civil liberties in wartime. Most discussions of this issue confine themselves to the Government's actions under the Espionage Act, its treatment of the I.W.W., Socialists (like Eugene Debs), and conscientious objectors. The fact remains that, once the suffrage arrests began, they were invariably confined to the pickets and never included the men who tore the banners from their hands and destroyed them, and often physically maltreated the women. While their slogans obviously were inflammatory, the women were never once arrested for disturbing the peace, inciting to riot, or jeopardizing the security of the country or its Chief Executive.

At first the pickets were dismissed without sentence. But as picketing and violence continued, the District courts began to sentence the women to jail, gradually increasing the term from a few days to six weeks and eventually to six months. A total of 218 women from 26 states were arrested during the first session of the Sixty-fifth Congress; 97 went to prison. Their jail terms were served in the infamous Occoquan workhouse in near-by Virginia or in the only slightly less obnoxious District of Columbia jail. When the women protested against the illegality of their arrests, the bad conditions, and the brutality of their treatment by going on hunger strikes, the authorities, having learned nothing from the bitter experience of the British government, resorted to forced feeding, and made martyrs wholesale. [17]

Nor could the women who underwent these trials be considered as remotely near the lunatic fringe. Many among them, in addition to Miss Paul and Miss Burns, were professionals — some, like sixty-year-old Lavinia Dock, long a co-worker of Lillian Wald's at the Henry Street Settlement and internationally known in the nursing field, well established in their professions. Others were wealthy, such as Mrs. Lawrence Lewis, or the wives of leading Washington newspapermen, such as Mrs. Gilson Gardner, or of prominent public servants, such as Mrs. Harvey W. Wiley. A considerable number came from respected Quaker families; many were eager young college graduates, others working women, including a near dozen workers from a Bridgeport munitions plant.

To add to the complexity of the dilemma, the men whose problem they became were not for the most part anti-suffrage. (In Wilson's entire cabinet there was only one opponent to woman suffrage, Secretary of State Lansing.) There is good reason to believe that many were appalled at what they sincerely thought was the harm being done to the suffrage cause by such tactics as picketing.

This was of course the chief concern of the National, which spared nothing, by public statements or personal visits by its leaders to newspaper editors and congressmen, to make clear that the pickets had nothing to do with that organization, which abhorred their actions. Mrs. Catt saw to it that the marchers in New York's last suffrage parade in 1917 carried signs disavowing the pickets, and Wilson's message to the voters of New York on the eve of the referendum election there urged them not to allow themselves to be adversely influenced by their feelings on the picketing question.

What such suffrage adherents completely overlooked, in their zeal for the cause, was the injustice being done to the women on the picket lines and in prison. Even after police joined the mobs in attacking the women, and after conditions at Occoquan and the District jail became widely publicized, as well as the illegality of their transfer to Virginia without access to counsel or friends, and indeed of all the proceedings against them, condemnation was still mainly directed against the women themselves.

Matters could not continue so indefinitely, and the pickets showed no inclination of giving up; there were always more, ready to replace the women hauled off in the police wagons, or those who appeared in court at long last, after a court order had been secured, too ill and emaciated to stand on their feet. President Wilson could not continue to claim ignorance of the conditions of their imprisonment; he heard the full details from Dudley Field Malone, Collector of the Port of New York and a friend and political supporter of long standing, as early as July. To the women's demand that they be given the status of "political prisoner," the Administration answered that to do so would set up all kinds of hazardous wartime precedents. But since it could not terminate the outcry which widespread publicity had aroused by now against their treatment, or put an end to the hunger strikes, all pickets were unconditionally released on November 27th and 28th.[18]

Months later, on March 4th, 1918, the District of Columbia Court of Appeals invalidated every single one of the prison sentences and the original arrests as well. No disagreement as to the merits of the picketing and hunger strikes should be allowed to obscure this outcome, or the fact that, with all too few exceptions, the leaders of the National suffrage association, including Mrs. Catt, tacitly acquiesced by their silence in the injustice done.[19]

However, without impugning the motives or detracting from the courage of the women who endured the ignominy and sufferings of forcible feeding and other forms of maltreatment, the question must be asked: Was the judgment behind this form of protest a valid one? What did all the heroism and suffering accomplish? Were they responsible, as the Woman's Party has always maintained, for the forward movement of the suffrage amendment which began during 1917?

Certain gains were undeniably taking place. The Senate Committee on Woman Suffrage issued a favorable report on the measure September 15th, the very day after Senator Jones of New Mexico, chairman of the committee, had visited Occoquan workhouse to see conditions there. A House Committee on Woman Suffrage was finally appointed on September 24th. The pickets were released a week before Congress reconvened, and one week after the session opened, the House set a date, January 10, to vote on the amendment. All these developments, the Woman's Party claimed, were the outcome of the picketing.

It is impossible not to conclude, from the impact reflected in the press from day to day that the issue of suffrage for women did gain enormous publicity from the picketing, the arrests, the jail sentences, and the hunger strikes. But while some support was gained by the women's gallantry, other support, in Congress and outside of it, was alienated. It is true that the pickets apparently posed the Administration with a problem whose eventual solution lay only in granting women the vote. But to say that the Woman's Party was the sole cause of the breakthrough which finally occurred is to ignore history. Other forces were at work; among the most obvious were the role of women in a country now totally at war, and the mounting crescendo of suffrage work under the leadership of the National Suffrage Association.

Like the Civil War, World War I brought women out of their homes into new spheres of action, and thousands more into work no longer new to them. The enormous influx of women into industrial work and public service sharply altered their standing in the community. It also furnished them with a new, heightened moral argument: if democracy began at home, surely the most immediate application must be to those who were shouldering, and competently discharging, every kind of social responsibility, and by so doing, proving once and for all their competence to assume political responsibility as well.

In the light of the more recent and much greater influx of women into industry during World War II, their numbers in the earlier struggle may seem unimpressive. Yet it took four pages of small type in a government publication to list those occupations in which, in varying degrees, women substituted for men in 1917 and 1918. They took jobs in blast furnaces, in the manufacture of steel plate, high explosives, armaments, machine tools, agricultural implements, electrical apparatus, railway, automobile, and airplane parts; they worked in brass and copper smelting and refining, in foundries, in oil refining, in the production of chemicals, fertilizers, and leather goods. Thousands of additional women operatives poured into the textile mills producing uniforms for the armed services, the transport services, and other occupations.[20]

The wholesale employment of women in occupations where hitherto few or none of them had labored raised the question of whether they could properly work unlimited hours, and whether the conditions under which they worked should be otherwise safeguarded. This led to the creation of special agencies for this purpose and the appointment of women to positions in them. The Women's Bureau of the Department of Labor goes back initially to the needs of women workers in munition and ordnance plants, which led to setting up the Women's Division of the Ordnance Department, and subsequently to the establishment in June 1918 of the Woman in Industry Service of the Department of Labor. It was headed by Mary Van Kleeck. Her assistant was Mary Anderson, who succeeded her in the post in 1919 and became the first director of the Women's Bureau in 1920. [21]

Women were also making their appearance for the first time on

Government bodies connected with the general war effort. Dr. Shaw, as chairman on a nearly full-time basis, and Mrs. Catt both served on the Women's Committee of the Council for National Defense, which tried to swing the nation's women into farming, kitchen gardening, food conservation, nursing, selling Liberty Bonds, and other kinds of war activity.

The National maintained an Overseas Hospital in France, which it financed, and somehow the busiest suffrage leaders were also those who found it possible to raise food, can it, knit, and work for the Red Cross. It was Mrs. Catt's incessant theme that while they must do *both,* suffrage must remain their number one *war* job. The dual aspect of their work was never more vividly displayed than in the last great suffrage parade in New York on October 27, 1917. Smaller by far than that of 1915, it was perhaps even more effective. Along with 2,500 women carrying placards enumerating the signatures of more than a million women to a suffrage petition came divisions of farmerettes, women workers in industry, doctors, and Red Cross nurses for overseas service. What the parade dramatized was taking place in life in every city and at every cross-roads in the country. How then, by any manner of logic, could women still be denied the rights of citizenship?

Yet the history of the last three years of the suffrage movement is emphatic evidence that logic was not enough; though the fruit might be ripe for plucking, it was not just going to fall from the tree. While it became clear from the first months of 1917 on that the "Winning Plan" and steadily mounting Woman's Party activity being organized in the states were beginning to produce results, and that these were having their slow effect on Congress, the going continued increasingly difficult. To the double load of suffrage and war work were added a near-breakdown of the country's transportation system, the influenza epidemic, and incessant charges of anti-patriotism. A few days after the signing of the Armistice, Mrs. Catt reported to her Board:

The work of the past two years has been the most trying and difficult of my experience. All antisuffragists in the country did their utmost to make the public believe that suffragists were traitors to their country since they did not lay down their work when the U.S.A. went to war. They had an extensive press bureau which advertised this theory from the Atlantic to the Pacific. It appeared in the most subtle way, in speeches, articles, letters, and all other means of spreading propaganda. It was a constant irritant. It so far affected our own people as to lead many of them to throw up their suffrage responsibilities entirely. . . . To have held the work in the middle of the road in the midst of these trying circumstances has been a more stupendous undertaking than most of you realize. It has cost more nerve stress than anyone not at Headquarters can possibly know.[22]

To assess the forces working for woman suffrage at such a time one must bear in mind not only the White House pickets, but the increasingly spectacular results which began to develop in the states. In January 1917 North Dakota granted its women presidential suffrage by legislative action (the "Illinois law"), followed in impressive succession by Ohio, Indiana, Rhode Island, Nebraska, and Michigan (the last three in the space of just one week), while the first historic breach in the Solid South was made on March 6, when the Arkansas legislature gave women the "primary vote."

A referendum on a suffrage amendment held in Maine in September 1917 proved a defeat, but Mrs. Catt's comment was "A battle has been lost. Forget it. Others lie ahead." [23] Her eyes were fixed on the crucially important referendum coming up again, after a two-year interval, in New York. Here, next to the enormous effort that went into collecting the signatures of more than a million women to a suffrage petition — irrefutable evidence that women wanted the vote — the most significant development was the eleventh-hour decision of the powerful Democratic "machine," Tammany Hall, to abstain from opposing the suffrage measure. Its leaders had apparently come to the conclusion that it was too dangerous to alienate the oncoming women voters; many of them had wives and daughters working in the Woman Suffrage Party, even leading it, who would be able to "deliver votes" once they were enfranchised. Tammany's action was conclusive: a margin of more than 100,000 carried suffrage in New York City while the vote in the rest of the state almost broke even.

The special war session of Congress, which ran from April until October 1917, had been barred by action of the Democratic caucus from considering any but war measures. But when Congress reconvened on December 3, it was bound by no such limitation, and its members had a good deal to ponder, where woman suffrage was concerned: not only the picketing, or the 100,000 margin for the women in New York, or the growing string of state victories. At its convention meeting in war-time Washington, December 12–15th, the National American Woman Suffrage Association served notice that it too, was losing patience:

If the Sixty-fifth Congress fails to submit the Federal Amendment before the next congressional election, this association shall select and enter into such a number of senatorial and congressional campaigns as will effect a change in both Houses of Congress sufficient to insure its passage. The selection of candidates to be opposed is to be left to the Executive Board and to the boards of the States in question. Our opposition to individual candidates shall not be based on party considerations, and loyalty to the Federal Amendment shall not take precedence over loyalty to the country.[24]

A vote on the Anthony amendment was scheduled in the House for January 10, 1918. The day before, the President made his long-awaited declaration in favor of the amendment to Congressman Raker, chairman of the House Committee on woman suffrage — indication that, whatever the outcome of the vote, the President had committed himself to leadership of his party in favor of the measure.

The vote in the House proved, if proof were needed, that not all the heroes in the long struggle were women. Endless lobbying and tallying by both suffrage groups had shown that the vote would be painfully close and that no one could foretell the outcome. It was with real anguish that the women keeping their tallies up in the galleries saw the hair-line finish shaping up, and their supporters rounding up every possible vote. Four of them — determining votes — came from sick-beds. Sims of Tennessee, with a broken arm and shoulder, which he refused to have set for fear he would be incapacitated from attending, and who, despite excruciating pain, stayed till the end trying to influence uncertain colleagues; Republican House Leader Mann of Illinois, who had been in a Baltimore hospital for six months and who appeared, pale as a ghost and hardly able to stand upright; Crosser of Ohio; and Barnhart of Indiana, the latter carried in on a stretcher on the very last roll call. Representative Hicks of New York kept faith with his wife, an ardent suffragist, who had just passed away; he left her death-bed to come to Washington for the roll call, and then went home to attend her funeral.

Thanks to such devotion, the amendment passed, 274 to 136, exactly the two-thirds majority required to pass a constitutional amendment, with Speaker Champ Clark's favorable vote in reserve in case of a deadlock. Such bedlam reigned around the clerk's desk down on the floor that three rollcalls and a recapitulation were needed before the outcome was certain. The women in the galleries were finally reassured by the cheering and waving of their supporters down below. A voice out in the corridor began to sing "Old Hundred"; others took it up, and the familiar hymn echoed through the marble Capitol. Some of those present must have thought of the women all over the country who, not yet knowing the outcome, worked doggedly to the last possible moment to make it sure. Months later, Mrs. Ben Hooper of Wisconsin wrote to her state association president:

I was frightfully tired from my work when I returned from [the December Washington convention] but I started right in to secure the vote of Mr. Davidson of this district and of Mr. Classon of the Ninth District after Christmas.* I traveled over a good deal of their districts not making public speeches but seeing men who were politically prominent and talking the question out with each one of them, putting my best efforts into making them see the situation from our viewpoint. Some days I got up at 5.30, took an electric train, and did not get home until midnight, talking the question out with from six to eight men and going from office to office all during the day. The day I was in Appleton it was ten below. The day I was in Marinette there was a very bad snow storm. I spent the night there and got to Oconto before any of the walks were clean, so had to wade through snow up to the tops of my shoes. There are no street cars in Oconto. As far as I could see there were no taxis. I worked up until the last moment, until I knew nothing more could reach Washington, and then I gave it up. There is nothing the matter with me except nervous and physical exhaustion. I am not complaining because I would do it all over again to get the result even if I were in bed for six months.[25]

An analysis of the House vote is revealing. Fifty-six of the men who voted against the amendment the only previous time it came up, on January 12, 1915, changed their votes to "aye." The New York delegation of more than forty representatives, with a stinging mandate from its constituents fresh in mind, voted in favor, with

---

* Both men voted for the amendment.

only four exceptions. The West and Northwest, by now almost solidly "suffrage," voted in favor with few exceptions. The border states, Kentucky, Tennessee, and Maryland, split almost evenly. Arkansas, and surprisingly, Florida broke away from the southern bloc to vote aye (the Florida delegation split).

The bulk of the "nay" votes came from an otherwise Solid South, and from the still unregenerate and largely industrial states of Massachusetts, Pennsylvania, New Jersey, and Ohio.

The vote cut sharply across party lines. But political observers saw signs that the "hungry" Republicans, with their eye on the coming 1920 elections, wished to win as many women as possible to their banner: while the Democrats divided almost evenly, 104 ayes to 102 nays, one hundred and sixty-five Republicans voted in favor in contrast to only 33 against.

Chapter XXII

WHO OPPOSED WOMAN SUFFRAGE?

Why did it take the women of this country so long to win the vote? Fifty-three years elapsed from the first state suffrage referendum held in Kansas in 1867 (from which we can date serious attempts to achieve woman suffrage) to the final ratification of the Nineteenth Amendment in 1920. The last ten of these, in particular, saw rapid social change, accelerated by the War, during which all kinds of taboos and restrictions against women crumbled away. How can one acount for the fact that instead of weakening, overt opposition to woman suffrage actually stiffened, becoming more active and more articulate?

By comparison, opposition to women in education or professional work was guerrilla-like in nature — sporadic, largely concealed, and evinced in obstacles and restrictions which tough-minded women could overcome. Some of the opposition to the enfranchisement of women was obviously based on the prejudices of individuals. But the more closely one looks, the clearer it becomes that suffragists faced far more than mere conservative opinion; no distaste for women in new social roles, no feeling about the sanctity of motherhood or the sacredness of the home could account for the animus that expressed itself in highly organized and articulate form against women as voters, becoming increasingly intemperate as woman suffrage spread slowly from one state to another.

Where did the multitude of anti-suffrage organizations, male and female, that cropped up across the country come from? Who supplied the organizers and the witnesses at legislative and Congressional hearings, so often masculine in gender? Who paid the bills for the stream of newspaper articles and advertisements, the hoardings and handbills? Who bought the referendum votes that were stolen from the suffragists in Michigan in 1912, in Iowa in 1916, and, very nearly, in California in 1911? Who paid for the immigrant and saloon vote in city after city, state after state, in suffrage elections from the Dakotas to New Jersey?

What were the interests which, with such intensity, fought women suffrage, and why? None of the suffrage leaders ever fully answered this question. Even Mrs. Catt, who gave it considerable space in her book, *Woman Suffrage and Politics,* was inclined to stress only one aspect of the opposition, largely to the exclusion of any other.[1]

Inevitably the main source of opposition varied from one part of the country to the other. In the South the source of sentiment lay in fear of the Negro vote — in fear of strengthening any attempts to overthrow the system of Jim Crow restrictions (including the poll tax) which, in defiance of the Fourteenth and Fifteenth amendments, disfranchised the colored population. In the Middle West much of the opposition stemmed from the brewing interests; in the East from industrial and business sources.

The original "anti" leaders were women of irreproachable social position, like the wives of General Sherman and Admiral Dahlgren, who as early as 1872 headed one thousand signers to a petition to the United States Senate against granting woman suffrage. In 1882, in opposition to the campaign for the municipal vote for women in Massachusetts, two women "remonstrants" appeared at a legislative hearing on the bill, but preserved their modesty by presenting a written statement instead of verbal testimony against the proposed bill.[2] A Boston Committee of Remonstrants was organized and began to extend its activities further afield with the Oregon suffrage referendum campaign of 1884, and successively to counteract the work of suffragists in the Dakotas, Rhode Island, Vermont, and Kansas. They sent telegrams, distributed literature, and in 1887 began hiring "male counsel" to represent them at legislative hearings. Beginning in 1889, the ladies received the acknowledged assistance of a group of "gentlemen," one of whom became the secretary of the Boston Committee of Remonstrants and editor of the earliest "anti" publication, *The Remonstrance,* the first issue of which appeared in 1890. (Until 1908 this continued to be the sole publication of its kind, and it did yeoman duty.)

In 1895 to combat the drive to put woman suffrage into the revised New York state constitution (an attempt which failed), anti-suffragists, men and women, organized in New York, and the Massachusetts group re-formed itself into the Massachusetts Association Opposed to the Further Extension of Suffrage to Women; it continued the most active and vocal, although similar organizations eventually appeared in some twenty states. In 1911 a National Association Opposed to Woman Suffrage was formed in New York, headed by Mrs. Arthur M. Dodge.

Almost without exception the women in these organizations were ladies of means and social position. The main burden of their argument was that woman suffrage placed an additional and unbearable burden on women, whose place was in the home; the fact that this argument came largely from women whose housework was done by an adequate force of servants and that they presumed to speak for women less fortunately placed, never seemed to disturb the "antis," who also argued that they did not need political suffrage since their menfolk represented them and cared for their interests.

No one in the suffrage camp credited the "antis" with great effectiveness. Their arguments seemed too puerile and roused more than one woman who eventually became a suffrage leader to thought and action.[3] While the antis' appearance at hearings and in print, through a flood of pamphlets and letters to the newspapers, did furnish legislators with the excuse that a body of respectable women did not want the vote, their real role in the opinion of the women working with Mrs. Catt was to serve as a front for more potent forces working against woman suffrage, principally the liquor interests. Mrs. Catt declared categorically that "a trail led from the women's organizations into the liquor camp and it was traveled by the men the women antis employed. . . . These men were observed in counsel with the liquor political managers too often to doubt that they laid their respective plans before each other so far as cooperation could be of advantage." [4]

The anonymity in which the brewers preferred to carry on their opposition to woman suffrage was punctured in 1918 by a Senate Judiciary Committee investigating charges of propaganda carried on by them during the war in both Bolshevik and German interests. The complaints which had for years flooded suffrage headquarters after every referendum received unexpected authoritative documentation when the subpoenaing of the files of Percy Andreae, who masterminded much of the brewers' publicity, turned up such letters as one marked "confidential" to a Milwaukee brewing concern in 1914:

In regard to the matter of woman suffrage, we are trying to keep from having any connection with it whatever. We are, however, in a position to establish channels of communication with the leaders of the anti-suffrage movement for our friends in any state where suffrage is an issue. I am under the impression that a new anti-suffrage association has been organized in Illinois and is a retail liquor dealers affair. I consider it most dangerous to have the retailers identified or active in any way in this fight, as it will be used against us everywhere.[5]

A brewers' strategy conference on October 13, 1913, whose minutes unaccountably survived (since it was the practice of the brewers' organizations to keep neither minutes nor financial records), revealed their role in more than one woman suffrage referendum defeat. An organizer for the brewers declared that in Nebraska, woman suffrage was defeated in 1911 at tremendous expense. His report for Wisconsin stated: "We have had the usual bills, like every other state — county option (liquor selling), women's suffrage in about six different forms and we have had everything else, which were all defeated; and I say that can be done only by organization and by active work of the brewers being on the job all the time and not leaving it to somebody else." [6]

From South Dakota: "So far . . . we have defeated women's suffrage at three different times, and I want to say that this association, the U. S. Brewers' Association, through the efforts of one gentleman, Mr. Edward Dietrich, has been able to cope with it, and he has always been fortunate in winning." [7] And in June 1915 at another strategy gathering, the general counsel of the Iowa Brewers Association asserted that "We are of the opinion that woman's suffrage can be defeated, although we believe that the liquor interests should not be known as the contending force against this campaign." [8]

The means employed by the liquor groups to achieve their goal went beyond buying editorial support for their "educational campaigns" or open editorial opposition, or allocating quotas to saloon keepers and bartenders of the number of customers for whose appearance and "no" vote at the polls they would be held accountable. Their influence reached openly into the halls of legislation. The Lieutenant-Governor of Wisconsin, as one instance alone, told Mrs. Ben Hooper, one of Mrs. Catt's most active coworkers, that he had seen the Milwaukee lawyer who "lobbied" for the brewers "sit in the gallery of the Senate and tell his men

"Well, boys, we saved the home."

(Rollin Kirby's famous cartoon in the New York World
on November 3, 1915.)

with his hands how to vote." [9] As late as 1918, with Prohibition staring them in the face, lobbyists for the brewers were still lobbying against the woman suffrage amendment in Washington.[10]

It is more difficult to pinpoint some of the other elements in the opposition to woman suffrage. Easiest to identify, after the liquor groups, were the political machines, whose weight was invariably thrown against votes for women until Tammany Hall gave up in 1917. Machine men were plainly uncertain of their ability to control an addition to the electorate which seemed to them relatively unsusceptible to bribery, more militant, and bent on disturbing reforms ranging from better sewage control to the abolition of child labor and, worst of all, "cleaning up" politics. The arguments many suffragists used in their own behalf, such as the inherent interest of women in such improvements as better schools or protective legislation for women workers, sounded in the ears of the machine bosses like the trumpet of doom.

While both sides enlisted the support of clergymen of all faiths, the anti-suffrage forces made marked use of Catholic opponents. Although the Papacy was reticent in committing itself explicitly on the issue of women and the vote, Cardinal Gibbons sent an address to the National Anti-Suffrage Convention held in Washington in 1916; reference has already been made to leaflets aimed directly at Catholic voters in Massachusetts, and the same tactic cropped up elsewhere.[11]

Most difficult of all to link with the opposition to woman suffrage were the business interests. The proceedings of the annual conventions of the National Association of Manufacturers and the U. S. Chamber of Commerce, or the pages of the *Wall Street Journal,* do not contain a word of protest against granting women the vote. There was no nation-wide mobilization of Big Business against woman suffrage. Yet some business groups fought suffrage tenaciously and bitterly, albeit with the greatest circumspection. One suffrage organizer after another reported the presence and activity of railroad, oil, and general manufacturing lobbies, whenever suffrage was up for legislative action or referendum.

In March 1916 Mrs. Catt was in Iowa, with a state referendum scheduled for June and what looked like a good chance of victory. Yet already a cloud no bigger than one man's hand was visible:

That man Maling is in Iowa doing dirty work. I had a talk with him myself, and I have now written to every Congressman, and to each newspaper, and to all the women I know, and I think I shall have succeeded in stirring up a hornet's nest. I have called on one and all to institute an investigation as to who or what is backing this man. He is saying that it is the business interests of Colorado. I half believe it. I am a bit fearful that the banks, mine owners and other big business are really sending along an official warning to the men of the other states to beware of this terrible menace of woman suffrage, but, if it is so, it is better to smoke our enemy out and know where he is.[12]

There were other instances. In the course of a Congressional investigation into the affairs of Swift & Company, the meat packers were shown to have made secret contributions to the "antis" — secret because the company recognized that eventually woman suffrage was likely to "sweep the country." [13] An appeal to Nebraska voters to vote against the woman suffrage referendum in that state in 1914 carried the signatures of nine railroad and municipal transit executives, seven bankers, and other assorted businessmen, leavened by those of two Episcopalian ministers.[14]

In Oklahoma, where the opposition went to almost unprecedented lengths in what proved to be one of the closest of suffrage referendum victories, a National organizer wrote to Mrs. Catt that she was reliably informed the antis were drawing on an unlimited fund through Mr. Pat Malloy who was temporary chairman of the Democratic state convention and who empowered them to draw on the oil company for which he worked at Tulsa. [15]

One of the most intriguing combinations to come to light was a Texas Businessmen's Association. It was extremely active in the issuance of "boilerplate," articles sent free to newspaper editors, which covered a wide range of issues, from the Adamson Act (instituting the eight-hour day on the railroads) to prohibition and woman suffrage. Public attention had already been drawn to some of the interests involved in this organization, during the eastern suffrage referenda campaigns which took place in 1915; they included not only a number of brewers, but the Gulf Refining Company (oil), Swift & Company (meat-packing), the Santa Fé Railroad, the American Express Company, and the Southeastern States Portland Cement Company.[16]

Subsequently the 1918 Senate Committee investigation into the brewers' propaganda activities uncovered the relation between this association and a "National Farmers Union," some of whose funds came from the above concern, other contributions from additional railroads (Union Pacific, Illinois Central, M-K-T, and Southern Pacific), and large amounts through a single individual, identified as Eric P. Swenson, who divided his interests between banking in New York and large ranch holdings in

Texas.[17] The Farmers Union likewise issued material which included articles opposed to woman suffrage.

Mention has already been made of the frequency with which women "antis" came from moneyed circles. Their ties were often with leading figures in the business world. Two directors of the national women's anti-suffrage organization were wives of directors of railroads. There was a strong railroad and corporation tinge to the board of the Man Suffrage Association, which included J. P. Morgan's son-in-law and directors of the Southern, Northern Pacific, and M-K-T roads, as well as municipal traction corporations. The moving spirit of the Man Suffrage Association, considered by suffragists to be the evil genius of the opposition, was Everett P. Wheeler, who made his livelihood as a corporation counsel.

In Massachusetts, where the "antis" were so entrenched that defeat of the state referendum in 1915 left suffrage workers hopeless of progress by the state method, the *Woman's Journal* looked into the election expense reports which the law required be filed with the Secretary of State. Reports from three anti-suffrage organizations showed the majority of their contributions coming from individuals, four fifths of them from men. An amount of $31,695 was reported from 135 men, an average of $235 apiece. The outraged *Journal* asked, "What sort of man can afford to sign a check for $235 with which to fight the enfranchisement of women?" and answered its own question: "the powerful directors of the moneyed section of Boston." [18]

It is not too difficult to see why such corporate interests as railroads, oil companies, and other manufacturers were opposed to giving women the vote. The Federal Income Tax, which had been authorized by the Sixteenth Amendment to the constitution in 1913, had been bitterly opposed as "communistic"; so had popular election of United States Senators, provided by the Seventeenth Amendment in the same year. Other elements of the "New Freedom," such as the institution of the Federal Reserve banking system, the Tariff Commission and the Federal Trade Commission, along with new anti-trust legislation and a widespread movement for the initiative and referendum, all appeared as cumulative threats to vested interests. In such circumstances, the addition of a large body of new voters, control of which appeared uncertain and many of whose leaders were vocal in the cause of further reform, presented a fresh menace. What might not such an infusion into the body politic do to the enormous advantages concealed in grants to railroads, franchises of various kinds, and rate schedules? [19] Mrs. Maud Wood Park, who came to know the members of the United States Senate all too well during the four years in which she headed the National's Congressional Committee, wrote of some of the Senators that they "were not really in favor of our form of government. They believed in an oligarchy of the well-to-do and they were fearful that tariff schedules might be reduced or railroad regulation extended if women had a chance to vote." [20]

There was also a strong feeling, particularly in some of the industries that would be most closely affected, that women would use the vote to improve the conditions of working women. The National Council of Women Voters, which had been organized in 1911 as an abortive attempt to gather together the voting strength of the enfranchised women in the West, had stated as its threefold purpose: extension of equal suffrage to other states; changing conditions in the suffrage states to improve conditions for women, children and the home; and "to claim justice for women in the political and economic world." [21] The legislative record of some states which had enjoyed woman suffrage for a number of years could be used to substantiate such a view; so could innumerable speeches and articles by women like Florence Kelley, Margaret Dreier Robins, Leonora O'Reilly, and others, as well as publications issued by the National itself.[22]

The men from northern states who led the fight against the suffrage amendment on the floor of the United States Senate were spokesmen for business interests, and the fact was spread out in their voting record on a score of measures. Senator Wadsworth of New York who did not alter by one jot his opposition to suffrage after his state gave its women the vote in 1917 also voted against the income tax, the direct primary, the taxation of war profits, and an investigation of Wall Street. Senator Weeks, leader of the Republican machine in Massachusetts, voted against the direct election of senators, the income tax, taxation of war profits, and the establishment of the Federal Trade Commission. The father-in-law of Saulsbury of Delaware, Victor Du Pont, "throughout his entire career was the legal guide and adviser of the family business, the E. I. Du Pont de Nemours Powder Co." [23] The reputation of Brandegee of Connecticut was such that even the impersonal Dictionary of American Biography noted that "his influence was largely negative, if not reactionary in effect"; he opposed the direct election of Senators, extension of parcel post, the Federal Reserve system, and the income tax.

These men alone would not have been able to delay the suffrage amendment as long as they did without the support of the large majority of southern Democrats. For decades the question of woman suffrage had carried, for politicians and the dominant interests in the South, some of the same explosive impact of desegregation today, as a threat to established social, economic, and political patterns. Fear, thought Mrs. Park, was the basis of such unyielding opposition:

Like some of the business groups in the North, which had managed to arrive at satisfactory terms with existing political machinery, they were terrified at the possibility of any considerable change in the voting body . . . the 14th amendment, which provides for the reduction of the basis of representation of a state denying the right of suffrage to male citizens for any cause except rebellion or crime, might be enforced if women had the vote. For this reason they [the southern senators] dreaded anything that called attention to the right of suffrage.[24]

This keynote sounded through most of the speeches in the Senate against the amendment in the closing battle, as in the words of Senator Smith of South Carolina, who was assailing the few southerners who supported woman suffrage by constitutional amendment:

I warn every man here today that when the test comes, as it will come, when the clamor for Negro rights shall have come, that you Senators from the South voting for it have started it here this day. . . . If it was a crime to enfranchise the male half of this race, why is it not a crime to enfranchise the other half? You have put yourselves in the category of standing for both amendments [the 15th and 19th], and when the time comes, as it will, when you meet the results of this act, you cannot charge that it was a crime to pass the 15th amendment. . . .

By thus adding the word "sex" to the 15th amendment you have just amended it to liberate them all, when it was perfectly competent for the legislatures of the several states to so frame their laws as to preserve our civilization without entangling legislation involving women of the black race.[25]

Nor were the Southerners alone in voicing this point of view. Senators Wadsworth of New York and Reed of Missouri took the states' rights position to the point where they declared they would vote against a federal amendment *forbidding* woman suffrage! And Borah of Idaho, who always based his opposition on the states' rights issue, declared that he had no wish to add to the already heavy burden borne by the South. Some of his words have a strangely contemporary ring:

I want to ask my friends upon the other side of the Chamber, if this Amendment is passed, do you propose to go home to your people and say, "We now have the Fifteenth Amendment, which inhibits discrimination on account of race or color, and the Eighteenth Amendment, which inhibits discrimination because of sex, and the power under each amendment in Congress to enforce the rule, and we propose to see these guaranties of the Constitution of the United States faithfully carried out?" Does anybody suppose that this amendment is anything but a white amendment? . . . Do you propose to put the South under Federal control as to elections? If you do you have a great task which you seem lightly to contemplate. . . . Nobody intends that the two and a half million Negro women of the South shall vote, unless . . . party expediency compels action for the sheer purpose of party advantage.[26]

Borah was not the most striking example of the strange coalition which, despite everyday partisan alignments, faced the suffrage amendment down to the final vote. With regard to the tacit filibuster which prevented a vote on the amendment a whole year before the end, the *Woman Citizen,* in the person of Alice Stone Blackwell, commented acidly:

It was clear that Senator Lodge (Rep.) of Massachusetts was the leader and general floor manager for the opposition, but the loving camaraderie between the "wilful few" Republicans and the "wilful few" Democrats who in normal relations do not waste time in each other's company, was an amazing sight to the galleries. Mr. Lodge of Massachusetts and Mr. Ellison Smith of South Carolina, Mr. Brandegee of Connecticut, Mr. Martin of Virginia, Mr. Wadsworth of New York, Mr. Underwood of Alabama, as divided as the Kaiser and the King of

England in most matters, were as united as twin brothers in defending the nation against the "awful disaster to the nation should women be enfranchised by the Federal Amendment." The Congressional Record prints for the most part what the Senators say, but it cannot record the pictures of Republicans and Democrats with arms around each other's necks, with Democrats slapping Republicans on the back in token of a common jubilation that they had scored a mighty victory in preventing the Senate from taking a vote! [27]

"The unholy alliance," Mrs. Catt christened this combination after she and Mrs. Park, watching from the gallery, had once seen Lodge of Massachusetts and Martin of Virginia standing arm-in-arm at the back of the chamber, comparing notes.[28] It did not in the end prevent women from getting the vote, but it caused far more delay and difficulty than one would ever imagine from reading the usual phrase in the history books, announcing that American women were enfranchised after World War I.

Chapter XXIII

A HARD-WON VICTORY, 1918–1920

The women who left the galleries of the House on January 10, 1918, singing "Old Hundred," thought that the end of their struggle was just around the corner. They were wrong. It took all of 1918 and half of 1919 and the election of a new Congress to get the suffrage amendment through the United States Senate. Its ratification took fourteen months more. The end did not come until August 1920. The story of the year-and-a-half delay in the Senate is a shabby one and reveals clearly what forces were most potently obstructive and how they worked through both parties.[1]

Immediately after the favorable House vote, matters looked hopeful: Mrs. Catt had a new dress made for the "ratification tour," which she planned in order to spur action by the states. But the astute Helen Gardener cautioned, "You can't hustle the Senate," and suffragists learned the hard way that she was right.

One reason was that although the "winning plan" was showing impressive results, it had not as yet made sufficient headway, something apparent to anyone who studied the "suffrage map" objectively. Early in 1918 it showed eleven "full suffrage" states, but the only one east of the Mississippi was still New York. The sole breach in the Solid South had been the winning of the primary vote in Arkansas. Four more states had joined Illinois in the presidential suffrage column, but except for Rhode Island these were in the Middle West: North Dakota, Nebraska, and Michigan. Significantly, action by the legislatures of three other states granting presidential suffrage had been canceled: in Indiana by court action declaring the measure unconstitutional; in Ohio by a referendum — the same day as the victory in New York! — and in Vermont by veto of the governor. If presidential suffrage was going to prove so vulnerable, there was additional incentive for pushing the federal amendment; but to be successful, fresh gains would first have to be made in the states.

Meanwhile the "unholy alliance" in the Senate was aided by the death of ten senators, of whom seven had been pro-suffrage; their replacements could not be counted on to share their views. Although President Wilson made repeated attempts to win additional senatorial support, these were unsuccessful, and the Woman's Party remained highly dissatisfied with his efforts.[2] They felt that once again he was doing too little too late, and they resumed militant demonstrations — burning his speeches (including the statements he made on behalf of woman suffrage, which they thought inadequate) and setting "watch fires" in front of the White House. New arrests took place, followed by jail sentences, and a fresh spate of publicity.

Leaders of the National, on the other hand, felt that Wilson was proceeding as vigorously as circumstances permitted. The war was now in its final crucial stage on the western front; after the last big German push in July of 1918 had been stopped and the Allied armies went over to the offensive, the problems of peace began to assume mounting importance; the domestic situation was critical, with a fuel shortage, a near breakdown in transportation, and the influenza epidemic, all major factors.

Wilson chose not to risk leadership of his party on woman suffrage, at least until September. Then the opposition suddenly changed tactics; apparently believing they could defeat the measure, they allowed it to come up, and five days of debate were scheduled before the vote. Great pressure was then brought to bear on Wilson to intervene personally. On the 27th of September he telegraphed six Senators, known to be doubtful, asking them to vote for the bill.[3] On the 29th, Secretary of the Treasury McAdoo urged the President to address the Senate, not because of any illusion that the needed votes could be won by such a step, but because of the public impression it would create, thus aiding the election of Senators favoring woman suffrage in November.[4]

At this point the President decided to intervene by taking the sensational step of addressing the Senate on a measure it was then in the act of debating. A number of considerations undoubtedly entered into his decision and were reflected in his speech. There was a chance that the bill, given the added weight of his support, might pass, and that Democratic leadership in securing its passage might enhance the party's chances in the Congressional elections only a few weeks away. He could thus strengthen backing for his cherished peace program, which he must have believed that many women voters would also support.

Nor could he be unmindful of the contradiction between the role claimed by the United States as a leader in a world-wide democratic effort, and the fact that it was lagging in democracy at home while other countries were taking steps to give their women representation. On the crest of war time liberalism and gratitude, women had won the vote in most of the provinces of the Dominion of Canada.[5] In Great Britain, where the suffrage movement had for so long paralleled that in the United States, the hide-bound opposition against which militancy had availed nothing crumbled before women's help in a war which had seemed for a time to be threatened by defeat. The British House of Commons had passed a woman suffrage bill as early as November 20, 1917, and on January 10, 1918 (the same day the suffrage amendment first passed the American House of Representatives), resistance had given way in that stronghold of conservatism, the British House of Lords.[6]

Wilson spent a Sunday afternoon writing his speech on his own typewriter. So closely were the leaders of the National in touch with the White House that they knew in advance of his decision.[7] On Monday morning September 30, with only half an hour's notice to that body, the President appeared before the Senate and appealed to it to pass the woman suffrage bill as a war measure:

I had assumed that the Senate would concur in the amendment because no disputable principle is involved, but only a question of the method by which the suffrage is to be extended to women. There is and can be no party issue involved in it. Both of our national parties are pledged, explicitly pledged, to equality of suffrage for the women of the country. Neither Party, therefore, it seems to me, can justify hesitating as to the method of obtaining it, can rightfully hesitate to substitute federal initiative for state initiative, if the early adoption of this measure is necessary to the successful prosecution of the war and if the method of state action proposed in the party platforms of 1916 is impracticable within any reasonable length of time, if practicable at all.

This is a peoples' war and the peoples' thinking constitutes its atmosphere and morale. . . . Through many, many channels I have been made aware of what the plain, struggling, workaday folk are thinking upon whom the chief terror and suffering of this war falls. . . . They think in their logical simplicity, that democracy means that women shall play their part in affairs alongside men and upon an equal footing with them. . . .

We have made partners of the women in this war; shall we admit them only to a partnership of suffering and sacrifice and toil and not to a partnership of privilege and right? This war could not have been fought, either by the other nations engaged or by America, if it had not been for the services of the women — services rendered in every sphere — not merely in the fields of effort in which we have been accustomed to see them work, but wherever men have worked, and upon the very skirts and edges of the battle itself. . . .

I tell you plainly that this measure which I urge upon you is vital to the winning of the war and to the energies alike of preparation and of battle.

And not to the winning of the war only. It is vital to the right solution of the great problems which we must settle, and settle immediately, when the war is over.[8]

His speech was an eloquent plea, but it made not the slightest impression on the opponents of woman suffrage. In fact McAdoo noted that the President's appearance was "bitterly resented by all those opposed to the amendment, and that even those who favored it were influenced by senatorial tradition and the feeling that the Chief Executive should not plead for any particular measure which the Senate had under consideration."[9]

The debate contributed little that was new to the ideology of the suffrage question. It did however reflect the changes that had taken place over half a century; the opposition spent little time worrying about preserving femininity and the home, and more on political issues such as that of states' rights. A McCumber from North Dakota could still declaim:

Whether the child's heart pulses beneath her own or throbs against her breast, motherhood demands above all tranquility, freedom from contest, from excitement, from the heart burnings of strife. The welfare, mental and physical, of the human race rests to a more or less degree, upon that tranquility.[10]

But the theme to which senator after senator harked back was the right of a state to decide for itself which of its citizens could vote, a theme pursued not only by the majority of the Southerners and those who, like Borah, chose to dwell largely on the problem of the South, but also by Pomerene of Ohio, Reed of Missouri, and Wadsworth of New York. "States' rights" had become the magic touchstone which united all the opponents of votes for women, despite the fact that, as suffrage supporters reminded the Senate time and time again, the Constitution had already undergone eighteen amendments which had been ratified by three fourths of the states, who could hardly therefore be said to have been deprived of a voice in these matters.

On the day after Wilson's speech, woman suffrage was defeated, 62 in favor to 34 opposed, just two votes short of the two-thirds majority required to pass a constitutional amendment. Thirty Democrats and thirty-two Republicans voted in favor, with twenty-two Democrats and twelve Republicans opposed. Said the *Woman Citizen:*

A decent respect for the opinions of mankind requires that the exact responsibility should be located. Locating it is not difficult. . . . New England and the Democratic South stood together, and the Atlantic seaboard from Maine to Louisiana cast twenty-eight of the thirty-four opposing votes. This section of our country is notoriously conservative. New England Republicans, plus Pennsylvania, with nine votes, followed the lead of Senator Lodge.

The South, although in all but two states the number of adult white women outnumbers the total adults, male and female, of the colored race, cast nineteen "noes," southern Senators taking the ground that they were afraid of the Negro woman vote. . . . As a matter of fact the cotton industry, north and south, with their employment of thousands of women, and in the South, children, furnished a more correct demonstration of motives.[11]

At least the vote served to clear the air; the women knew where they stood. For the National, it meant swinging quickly into action on the decision, first made at its 1917 convention and since then more carefully planned by Mrs. Catt, to take a hand in retiring certain Senators up for re-election just four weeks away. Those marked for defeat, if possible, were Weeks of Massachusetts and Moses of New Hampshire, Republicans, and Saulsbury of Delaware and Baird of New Jersey, Democrats. The Woman's Party also campaigned against Moses and Baird.

Weeks and Saulsbury were well entrenched machine leaders;

yet both were defeated. (Senator Weeks' vote against the confirmation of Louis Brandeis, the first Jew to be nominated to the Supreme Court of the United States, was well aired throughout the Jewish community of Massachusetts.) Senator Moses barely got back his seat, and Baird's majority was sharply reduced.

The same election saw four state suffrage referenda come up, of which three were victorious, South Dakota, Michigan and Oklahoma, while the fourth, Louisiana, lost by only a few thousand votes, a showing of some consequence in a southern state. The three victorious campaigns deserve more than passing mention because they demonstrate so clearly the adversities still confronting woman suffrage, less than two years away from final victory. All three campaigns were carried on despite nearly insuperable transportation problems, the influenza epidemic, and growing weariness among suffragists themselves, most of those who were not on the paid staff of the National being active war workers as well. Against these odds were pitted increasing experience, a highly trained group of full-time organizers, and great tactical skill.[12] The Leslie bequest also furnished the National with close to a million dollars, beginning in 1917, but an amazing amount, considering the demands made by the Liberty bond and other war fund drives, was raised by both the National and the Woman's Party.

Yet the outcome in any referendum was still never certain. In Michigan, Mrs. Catt later told her board,

There threatened to be no campaign at all. . . . We literally browbeat the state into taking up the campaign. . . . It was a very difficult task to persuade them that suffrage at this time was a necessary piece of war work. It may be said that in all the campaign states a very large number of women never saw the point and refused to give time or attention to the campaign.[13]

South Dakota's campaign — the fifth — drew from her merely the tart comment that "the state presumably had accumulated some education on the subject from campaign to campaign. The general feeling around this office is: 'The Lord be praised that South Dakota is out of the way.' "[14]

The difficulties encountered by the suffragists in the Oklahoma referendum probably represented the worst in unprincipled opposition in any suffrage campaign. There were innumerable special

local problems, not the least of which was a complete breakdown
of the state suffrage organization after the campaign was underway. This was particularly serious because the Oklahoma state
constitution required that the number of votes in favor of an
amendment must exceed the total, not only of the negative votes,
but also of those ballots not marked either for or against. The
Governor, Lieutenant-Governor, Attorney-General, and Secretary
of the State Elections Board left no stone unturned to defeat the
suffrage amendment. They even went to such lengths as printing
only half as many ballots on the amendment as regular ballots and
withholding them altogether from the soldiers voting in the army
camps in the state. The National kept two of its best organizers,
the Shuler mother-and-daughter team, in Oklahoma for months
and spent more money on the campaign — nearly $20,000 — than
in any other state.[15] Flagrant efforts were made after election day
to count out what was clearly a suffrage victory, and the last
National organizer did not leave Oklahoma until December 3,
one month later, when the Governor finally surrendered to the
facts of life and proclaimed the measure passed.[16]

The three 1918 victories raised the electoral "barometer" of
states where women would vote in the next presidential election
to twenty, with 237 electoral votes. The defeat of Senators Weeks
and Saulsbury meant that (barring further deaths among pro-
suffrage senators) the suffrage amendment would pass the Sixty-
sixth Congress.

There were several reasons why such a situation did not constitute the millennium. Passage of the amendment in 1919 meant
that relatively few legislatures would be in regular session and
that thirty governors would have to be convinced to call special
sessions if women were to vote in the 1920 presidential elections.
Moreover, the end of the war had finally come. The more far-
sighted feared that seemingly imminent victory might slip through
their fingers if it were delayed too long and caught in the inevitable post-war conservative reaction.[11]

There was therefore every reason to press for passage in the
so-called "lame duck" session of the Sixty-fifth Congress, and the
appointment of a pro-suffrage senator from, of all places, South
Carolina, to replace the deceased and hostile Senator Ben Till-
man, was an added source of hope. Apparently the opposition

thought the same and made every attempt to keep the measure from coming to a vote until they could be certain of the outcome.[18] When they finally desisted and permitted a vote on February 10, 1919, they did so only because they knew defeat was assured:

Rumor had it that if the miracle were about to happen, that is, if the extra vote had been won over to the suffrage side, the opponents would attempt a filibuster. Therefore, all eyes attended the movements of Senators Lodge and Martin, leaders of the opposition. Senator Jones of New Mexico, chairman of the Senate Suffrage Committee, moved unanimous consent to consideration of the suffrage amendment. Immediately Senator Lodge was on his feet. "There is no objection," he said suavely. With his words, suffrage hopes died.[19]

The woman suffrage amendment was defeated by one vote. During the month of January and the first days of February, twenty-four state legislatures memorialized Congress, asking for submission of the suffrage amendment to the states, clear evidence of their approval had the amendment been submitted to them in regular session; other senators received majority petitions from their legislatures to the same effect. Yet nine of the "no" votes came from states that had so expressed their wishes: Wadsworth of New York and Borah of Idaho (both from full suffrage states); Pomerene of Ohio; Hitchcock of Nebraska and Reed of Missouri; Fletcher and Trammel of Florida; Moses of New Hampshire; and Hale of Maine.

The vote on February 10 left no further alternative except to await the Sixty-sixth Congress, and in the meantime leave no stone unturned to secure early passage of the amendment and, beyond it, ratification. More than 500 resolutions poured in on Congress from civic, church, labor, educational, and farm bodies and became so irksome that an old ruling was revived prohibiting the printing of such material in the *Congressional Record*.[20] Six more state legislatures gave women the presidential vote: Iowa, Minnesota, Missouri, Ohio, Wisconsin, and Maine, the last-named causing Senator Hale, who had voted against suffrage on February 10, to switch to its support. President Wilson himself was generally credited, during his labors at the Peace Conference in Paris, with securing the last needed vote, that of Senator Harris of Georgia.

The Sixty-sixth Congress convened in special session at President Wilson's summons on May 20, 1919. In his cabled address from Paris to both Houses of Congress, he once again recommended passage of the federal woman suffrage amendment.[21] That same day the House re-passed the amendment, this time by the spanking majority of 304 to 89, a margin of 42 over the necessary two-thirds majority. The tremendous increase arose in good part from the election of 117 new members to the House; of those pledged to vote for woman suffrage, only one went back on his commitment.

The showdown in the Senate lacked the drama of earlier occasions. The debate dragged through portions of two days, June 3 and 4, although most suffrage supporters, anxious to hurry the vote, refrained from oratory. The bulk of the speeches came from the opposition and belabored the states' rights theme, primarily as it affected the South, and the enfranchisement of the Negro woman. Three amendments were offered with no other apparent purpose than to cause further delay, but all were defeated. There were long speeches by Brandegee of Connecticut, Underwood of Alabama, Smith of South Carolina, Wadsworth, Borah, and Reed of Missouri, who spoke for five hours and whose verbosity, the *Woman Citizen* calculated, cost the taxpayers around $6,000.

No saving votes were carried in on stretchers, and no last-minute switches disturbed those who kept tally, for the last time, up in the gallery. So many opponents were absent that senators who wished to be recorded as voting for the bill, but who were even more anxious to see it finally passed, yielded to the demand for pairs.[22] Voting went fast and smoothly:

Ashurst's "aye" was followed by 4 "noes" in succession from Bankhead, Beckham, Borah and Brandegee. Then came five C's in favor: Capper, Chamberlain, Culberson, Cummins and Curtis. I had no need to check the list that time, for I knew the expected votes by heart and my ear would have caught instantly any deviation from our poll. Through the F's and K's, which, with the exception of Knox, belonged to us, everything held firm; through the M's and N's, P's and S's, where our largest number of votes was to be found; and, up to the last favorable vote, which was Watson's, nothing slipped. Then the five pairs, including 10 supporters and 5 opponents were read. Every senator was on record. Not one of the sixty-six men whom we had counted on had failed us.[23]

Although the Senate of the United States had finally accepted political equality for women, those present in the galleries did not leave this time singing a hymn. The victory had been too long delayed to evoke such an outburst of rejoicing; and ahead stretched the ratification campaign, which, thanks to the "unholy alliance," had been made as difficult and as uncertain of outcome as it could possibly be.

Once again, any thoughts that the worst was over and ratification would prove a simple matter were soon dispelled. The initial response to the telegrams sent to the governors of the forty-eight states by both Mrs. Catt and Miss Paul was encouraging. The first to promise prompt action were Governor Alfred E. Smith of New York and Governor Henry Allen of Kansas, who had been a volunteer speaker in New York's unsuccessful campaign in 1915. During the first week after the amendment was submitted, three mid-western states ratified. Illinois and Wisconsin, whose legislatures were in session at the time, ran a close race to be first. Illinois edged out Wisconsin by a few hours, but it was then discovered that the Illinois ratification bill had been wrongly worded by a clerk, and so Wisconsin had the honor of first filing its formal ratification resolution with the Secretary of State in Washington. Michigan had the distinction of being the first to call a special session of its legislature, and came in third; all three acted on June 10.

It looked deceptively easy, yet such quick action represented long and careful preparation. For years Mrs. Catt had been hammering home the necessity of keeping suffrage organization intact in states which had already won the equal franchise, for the purpose of getting action as soon as the amendment was submitted, and once again she was proved right. The states in which ratification lagged were often those in which the women had disbanded too soon. In Wisconsin, on the other hand, suffragists had long been at work, organizing, tallying the legislators in both houses, lobbying, "registering" the women back in the districts for such work, and raising money. The results amply justified their pains. Before the end was in sight elsewhere, the woman who had served as president of the Wisconsin Woman Suffrage Association for six grueling years, could write to a friend that they were so used to bearing the burden of campaign that they found it difficult to realize that the burden had been removed.[24]

It might have been assumed that those states which had already won the vote would ratify most expeditiously and with the least effort from national suffrage leaders. With the exception of Michigan, and New York and Kansas, both of which ratified on June 16, such was not the case. Eventually it seemed to exasperated suffragists as if those states where women had had the vote longest were the slowest in ratifying. Montana was the first western state to act, on August 2. Thereafter no "suffrage state" acted until Utah ratified on September 30, the thirteenth state to do so. California and Colorado did not act until November 1 and December 12 respectively; Wyoming was an inexcusable twenty-seventh, ratifying on January 26, 1919, and the state whose enfranchisement of women had marked the "breakthrough" for woman suffrage back in 1910 — Washington — was the thirty-fifth state to act, on March 22, when frantic suffragists had been reduced to counting remaining states where ratification could be won, on the fingers of one hand.[25]

But it was not the suffrage states which, in the last analysis, constituted the real ratification problem; they were merely an added irritant. When it came down to listing actual possibilities, it seemed altogether likely that the opposition might prevent thirteen states from passing the amendment. Six months before the Senate victory, Mrs. Catt warned her board:

There are some terrible hazards ahead which render it impossible to make positive predictions. I count that Maryland, Virginia, North Carolina, South Carolina, Florida, Georgia, Alabama, Mississippi, Louisiana and Delaware will not ratify, at least the first year. If the opposition could hold Pennsylvania and New Jersey, and one other state in addition to these ten, we would be beaten on ratification. . . . [The situation] has possibilities in it . . . of prolonging the suffrage struggle for many years in this country.[26]

In the same report she foresaw as difficult but probable: Maine, New Hampshire, Vermont, Massachusetts, Wisconsin, West Virginia, Ohio, and Iowa.

Eight months later, after the amendment had been passed by

Congress, the picture was clearer, and she wrote to young Marjorie Shuler:

The plan of the antis is to find thirteen states which they can hold out against ratification. They have been good enough to give us the list of the states. They are the solid south states: Maryland, Virginia, North Carolina, South Carolina, Georgia, Alabama, Mississippi, Louisiana, Florida, Kentucky, Tennessee and Delaware. I do not think they would have very much trouble in holding all of these out. Now they will get their thirteenth state in New Jersey, Connecticut, Vermont or New Hampshire. They tell us so, and they have given up all the others.[27]

Miss Shuler was being dispatched to stir up New Hampshire, and Mrs. Catt added, with that challenge which bound devoted suffragists to her with deep loyalty: "You thought you had a real job in Vermont — that was only a pleasure trip. This is a job. Come through with your shield or upon it." [28]

Mrs. Catt was no soothsayer; Pennsylvania and New Jersey both ratified, the former in less than three weeks. What counted was not the exactitude of all her predictions, but the fact that her method of work made it possible to correct her estimates in time. No southern state was written off (Texas obviously could not be considered part of the Solid South since it had given its women presidential suffrage by referendum in May of 1919; it was the ninth state to ratify the amendment). The border states of Kentucky and Tennessee proved decisive. Kentucky, led by the beloved Madeline Breckinridge, ratified on the very first day of its regular legislative session, January 6; Tennessee was to be the most fateful battleground of all.

The tactics used to bring the laggards into the fold varied according to the reasons for the delay. States which held back because the governors were reluctant to call special sessions because of the expense involved were brought to terms when the legislators (needled by the women) offered to serve without the extra pay to which such a session entitled them, and the women undertook the clerical and page work involved in the session itself, also without pay.

The Governor of Oregon, despite the fact that women had won the vote in his state in 1912 insisted that a special session called to ratify the amendment undertake no other legislation whatever.

When the legislators understandably balked at such a limitation, he announced he would call them into special session only if Oregon were necessary as the thirty-sixth state to ratify. Visits from national leaders were required, including Mrs. Catt herself, to galvanize the action needed to compel him to call the legislature, so that Oregon became the twenty-fifth state to act.

One woman gave her life for ratification of the amendment. Oklahoma was one of the dilatory states, thirty-third to ratify. A number of Democratic county conventions, called to elect delegates to the state convention, passed resolutions urging the governor to call the legislature, which he had been adamant in refusing to do. The secretary of the Oklahoma women's ratification committee, Miss Aloysius Larch-Miller, was scheduled to address such a convention. Although ill with influenza, she disregarded her doctor's orders and made her address, which carried the meeting with her. Two days later she died.

There had been another death during these months, which, while it did not result from the ratification fight, was certainly the cumulative result of a lifetime of devotion to the cause of women's progress. On July 2, 1919, Dr. Anna Howard Shaw had died from pneumonia contracted during the over-exertions of a speaking trip, made jointly with former President Taft and President Lowell of Harvard, to urge the adoption of the much-discussed peace treaty and specifically of a League of Nations. The old warhorse, seventy-two-years old and bone-weary from work on the Women's Committee of the Council of National Defense during the war, answered the summons just as she had responded to every other call to duty for fifty years. Coming on top of the long years of incessant travel and speaking, always with the cause of women foremost in her mind, the effort killed her. She was already ill when the amendment passed the Senate, and lived just long enough to know that the ratification campaign had gotten off to a good start.

The thirty-fourth state was West Virginia, in March. Here the opposition worked, not through the Governor, but within the legislature, and the vote in the Senate resulted in a tie. The legislature was held in session, and tireless suffragists from both organizations rode herd on the legislators while the winning suffrage vote, in the person of Senator Jesse A. Bloch, made a spectacular five-day dash across the country from the Pacific Coast to cast his vote for ratification. A few days later Washington followed and ratified, the thirty-fifth to do so.

Such a recital can do no justice to the mounting virulence of the opposition, the lengths to which suffrage supporters had to go in many states to bring unwilling governors or legislators into line, or the paltriness of some of the arguments advanced against calling special sessions, of which expense was only one. There were only rare instances where real difficulty developed in states which ultimately ratified, once the legislature was in session. The significance of the West Virginia episode lay in the fact that the opposition saw the showdown approaching.

Of the Solid South, the only vestige of hope now appeared to be in North Carolina, where the Democratic party convention voted in April 1920 to recommend that its members support the suffrage amendment, and the Governor appeared before the legislature to speak in its favor. Yet in August both houses voted to defer action.

After March 25, the date when the Washington legislature took action, the most promising remaining possibilities were Connecticut, Vermont, Delaware, and Tennessee. The governors of the two New England states had compacted not to call their respective legislatures (both of which were eager to ratify), and nothing could budge them from their stand. Connecticut was toured from end to end by an "Emergency Corps" of distinguished women, one from every state in the Union, which derived its name from the Governor's statement, wrung from him in April, that he would call the legislature into session if he received proof that an "emergency" existed; but no amount of pressure could apparently provide the requisite "proof."

In Vermont the Governor took refuge in the specious argument that the matter should only be acted upon by an Assembly elected with such a decision as an issue. He was not even moved by a deputation unique in the annals of the state:

Twelve of the fourteen counties were represented by four hundred women who went to the State Capitol, overcoming the obstacles of long distance, almost impassable roads and poor train service. Many came from towns remote from railroads, one woman walking five miles to the station. Others ploughed through deep snow and over muddy and rocky roads before daylight. Reaching the Capitol they marched, a silent army of loyal soldiers, through cold drenching rain and took their places before the Governor's chair. One by one, in a sentence or two, they presented Vermont's case. His response was that "he did not care to make a decision at once." [29]

Nor did he, until the amendment had been ratified without the aid of Vermont.

To understand the full extent of suffragists' anxieties, it must be realized that the struggles for the last few states were going on concurrently. It was impossible from day to day to tell whether or not any one state would be the final, crucial one; this applied equally to the campaigns raging at the same time in Vermont, Connecticut, North Carolina, and Delaware.

Although both Mrs. Catt, the Woman's Party, and the "antis" had originally considered Delaware a fairly certain holdout, circumstances had combined to change the outlook there. The state Republican and Democratic committees and the Republican Governor were pro-suffrage. The National committees of both parties, with an apprehensive eye to the coming election, threw their full weight behind ratification in Delaware. The state capital of Dover was besieged by lobbyists from brewing, railroad, and other business groups on the one hand and by suffragists on the other. The upper house of the legislature actually did vote in favor of ratifying. But on June 2 the lower chamber voted to refuse to consider the bill, and that eliminated Delaware as a possible thirty-sixth state. With Vermont and Connecticut still deadlocked, and the situation in North Carolina degenerating, there was only one other possibility left, the "border" state of Tennessee.

The day before Delaware dashed suffrage hopes, another, more momentous event occurred, and a favorable one. Ratification was under severe court challenge, with the opposition contending that constitutional amendments were necessarily subject to review by referendum. The crucial test came in Ohio where the State Supreme Court had ruled in September 1919 that a referendum on the already ratified Prohibition amendment was valid. As a result, efforts to secure referenda on the ratification of the suffrage amendment were already underway in widely scattered states — Massachusetts, Maine, Missouri, Texas, Oklahoma, and Ohio. But on

June 1, 1920, the United States Supreme Court unanimously ruled referenda on constitutional amendments invalid, unnecessary, and in conflict with constitutional provisions empowering state legislatures to ratify such amendments. This decision stopped what might have become a serious counter-attack on the suffrage amendment. It did more. It removed what had been heretofore considered an all but impassable barrier to ratification by Tennessee, whose constitution contained the following provision: "No convention or general assembly of this State shall act upon any amendment of the Constitution of the United States proposed by Congress to the several States, unless such convention or General Assembly shall have been elected after such amendment is submitted." (Article III, Section 32)

Opinion slowly grew that the Supreme Court decision abrogated this clause of the Tennessee constitution. The problem of convincing the state's governor of this fact was not solved until the Wilson administration itself intervened. The Department of Justice handed down its opinion on June 24 that the Court ruling permitted Governor Roberts to call a special session for the purpose of ratification, and on the same day President Wilson wired him: "It would be a real service to the party and to the Nation if it is possible for you under the peculiar provision of your State Constitution, having in mind the recent decision of the Supreme Court in the Ohio case, to call a special session of the Legislature of Tennessee to consider the Suffrage Amendment. Allow me to urge this very earnestly." [30]

Cabinet members, national party committeemen, leading Constitutional lawyers, all added their weight to the argument, while members of both suffrage organizations within the state dug in for a bitter battle, and their national leadership sent in help. Governor Roberts yielded to the overwhelming demand and called a special session for August 9.

The story of that session reads today like fiction; while later events showed that women would have gotten the vote anyway through action by the Connecticut legislature, nothing looked less likely in August. The political situation within the state was chaotic, with the dominant Democratic party split in two. The situation in the legislature, which had appeared promising before the session was called, deteriorated rapidly, a development that was hardly surprising in view of the flood of suffrage opponents that poured into the state capital, Memphis. Said the *New York Times:* "Virtually every Southern State and many States in the East are represented in the forces opposed to ratification." [31]

Mrs. Catt came with an overnight bag in response to a frantic S.O.S. from Marjorie Shuler — and stayed two months. Sue White led the Woman's Party forces, and both groups covered the state in their attempts to build up support to bolster those legislators who, at first polled in favor of woman suffrage, began melting away under a barrage of threats and actions whose blatancy could hardly be paralleled. Legislators who had expressed favorable sentiments toward woman suffrage were threatened with the ruin of their business and political careers, some were all but kidnapped, and they were all systematically plied with liquor. Mrs. Catt was an eye-witness to the scenes on the night before the session was to open:

During the evening groups of legislators under the escort of strange men had left the foyer and gone to a room on the eighth floor. As the evening grew late, legislators, both suffrage and anti-suffrage men, were reeling through the halls in a state of advanced intoxication — a sight no suffragist had before witnessed in the sixty years of suffrage struggle. . . . Suffragists were plunged into helpless despair. Hour by hour suffrage men and women who went to the different hotels of the city to talk with the legislators, came back to the Hermitage headquarters to report. And every report told the same story — the Legislature was drunk! In agony of soul suffragists went to bed in the early morning, but not to sleep.[32]

Next morning the lawmakers had regained some measure of sobriety, and the Senate passed the Amendment with relative promptness, 25 to 4. The last stand would be made in the House, and during the entire 10 days of the session no human being could foretell the outcome:

We now have 35½ states. We are up to the last half of the last state. . . . The opposition of every sort is here fighting with no scruple, desperately. Women, including Kate Gordon and Laura Clay,* are here, appealing to Negrophobia and every other cave man's prejudice. Men, lots of them, are here. What do they represent? God only knows.†

* Former members of the National's board, from Louisiana and Kentucky respectively, who had broken with it on the issue of "states' rights."

† Later she identified them as liquor, railroad, and manufacturing lobbies. See Catt and Shuler, p. 446.

We believe they are buying votes. We have a poll of the House show-ing victory, but they are trying to break a quorum, and God only knows the outcome. We are terribly worried, and so is the other side. We hope our fate is decided this week but God only knows that. I've been here a month. It's hot, muggy, nasty, and this last battle is desperate. . . . We are low in our minds. . . . Even if we win, we who have been here will never remember it with anything but a shudder.[33]

When the bill finally reached the House floor on August 18 after endless postponements sought by the opposition, and despite unheard of efforts to round up favorable voters (down to patrol-ling railroad stations to prevent their leaving town!), the suffrage cause appeared to be still short two votes, although one supporter came from a hospital to cast his ballot.

But on the opposition motion to table the bill once more, there was a sudden, unexpected tie. Representative Banks Turner, on whose support the women had not relied, but who was a friend of the Governor's and apparently swayed by Democratic Party arguments that the country would hold it responsible for defeat in Tennessee, voted against tabling. A tie meant that the measure itself must come up for a vote.

The two questions in the minds of the agonized women in the galleries were, how would Turner vote on the bill itself, and where would their other vote come from? Before Turner's name was called, came that of twenty-four-year-old Harry Burn, youngest member of the House, from a rural district in east Tennessee. He had promised only that he would vote in favor if his vote was necessary for ratification; the political leaders of his districts were opposing ratification. But his mother was a staunch suffragist, who had written her son: "Hurrah! And vote for suffrage and don't keep them in doubt. I notice some of the speeches against. They were very bitter. I have been watching to see how you stood, but have noticed nothing yet. Don't forget to be a good boy and help Mrs. Catt put 'Rat' in Ratification." [34]

In the most intense stillness Harry Burn voted "yes." Minutes later, Banks Turner also voted "yes." The amendment carried, 49 to 47, and the woman suffrage amendment had been ratified.

There was an aftermath which would have been pure *opera-bouffe* if it had not shown, once again, the extent to which the anti-suffrage forces were willing to go. Unable, despite threats and bribery, to bring the bill up for reconsideration, thirty-eight members of the losing minority crossed the state line into Alabama to try and prevent a quorum until the majority had somehow been undermined. Their hosts in Decatur had even wired those planning the move: "Send them on. We will be proud to entertain Seth Walker and his opponents of suffrage as long as they wish to remain and it will not cost them a penny." [35]

The action was promptly ruled illegal. The opposition then attempted to enjoin Governor Roberts from signing the ratification certificate, and the Secretary of State from issuing the proclamation certifying ratification when the Tennessee certificate reached him. Both moves likewise failed, and the proclamation certifying final adoption of the Nineteenth Amendment was signed by Bainbridge Colby in the early morning of August 26.[36] Twenty-six million women of voting age had been enfranchised, and subsequent court action by die-hard "antis" had no effect on women voting at the polls in November 1920 or on subsequent history.

CONCLUSION

Almost forty years after adoption of the Nineteenth Amendment, a number of promised or threatened events have failed to materialize. The millenium has not arrived, but neither has the country's social fabric been destroyed. Nor have women organized a political party to elect only women candidates to public office.

The nearest they have come to such political organization has been through the establishment of the Women's Joint Congressional Committee, through which a dozen of the largest women's organizations united to press legislation on Congress, such as the Child Labor amendment. Yet even this loose aggregation was effective only in the years immediately following the enfranchisement of women, in the twenties and early thirties.

Instead, women have shown the same tendency to divide along orthodox party lines as male voters. They have, it is true, voted in steadily increasing numbers, to the point where the Gallup Poll found women voting in equal numbers with men in the 1956 presidential elections.[1] Nevertheless, such an increase still does not match their growth in the total population (they now outnumber the men), nor does it adequately reflect their potential political power. There has not been more than a handful of women representatives in any Congress, and Senator Margaret Chase Smith remains the only woman elected thus far to her post (in contrast to several appointed to fill vacancies caused by death, usually that of their husbands).

No woman has yet been elected governor of a state, and not many as mayors, particularly of larger cities. There have been only two women in the Cabinet, and a handful in higher administrative posts, or serving as ambassadors or special envoys abroad.

Yet the Nineteenth Amendment did release fresh interest and energy into political life at the local, ward, and regional level. Women have exercised some of the healthy influence dreaded by the machines in favor of "good government," even though in most cases they are limited to "women's jobs" and "women's subjects" (such as health and education) which politicians consider theirs especially by virtue of aptitude or interest based on sex. Their political influence, such as it is, has so far been most effectively exerted through their own organizations — the League of Women Voters (born of the National American Woman Suffrage Association in 1919, even before suffrage was won), Parent-Teachers Associations, clubs, etc.[2]

In 1920 Mrs. Catt warned suffragists that the franchise was only an entering wedge, that they would have to force their way through the "locked door" to the place where real political decisions are made, whether on issues or on candidates: "You will have a long hard fight before you get behind that door, for there is the engine that moves the wheels of your party machinery. . . . If you really want women's vote to count, make your way there." [3]

The task of cracking the political machines has proved an arduous and, on the whole, still an unsuccessful one, in which women have faced such varied obstacles as their own distaste, born of social usage and breeding, for the unladylike rough and tumble (not to say corruption) of machine politics; the prejudices of the male politicians, who, having been compelled to accept woman suffrage, set up a whole new system of defences against a female invasion of their prerogatives. In addition there are the problems encountered by every woman who attempts, in addition to making a home and rearing children, to carry on a business or professional career or any kind of job.[4]

It is doubtful whether Mrs. Stanton or Miss Anthony, returning to the scene of their labors, would take more comfort if they looked elsewhere than politics to see how their sex was faring. The truth is that while most of the legal barriers are down, others remain, some of them rooted in physiology, others arising more from prejudice than fact. The problem of the child-bearing mother who wishes to bring up her children, but must interrupt her career to do so, seems likely to remain a continuing one in the foreseeable future despite labor-saving devices, new educational concepts, and the growing willingness of fathers and husbands to take on a share of household and family responsibility after they come home from work.[5]

The unmarried woman, or one widowed or divorced, without

children, continues to pay a heavy forfeit for her sex. Because so many women do marry and bear children, business firms or educational institutions are reluctant to train or promote a talented young woman who is likely, they feel, to cancel their investment in her by marrying and either following wherever her husband's career leads him, or raising a family, or both. While there is wide disagreement on this problem, there seems to be a valid basis for the complaints made by women that they need to be better than the best to get ahead.

Whatever the cause — fact, and myth or prejudice — men still comprise between 95 and 97 per cent of our lawyers, architects, natural scientists, and engineers, and 95 per cent of the doctors in the United States.[6] In her autobiography, Virginia C. Gildersleeve, dean for a quarter of a century of Barnard College of Columbia University, stated that opportunities for women in the higher academic posts were shrinking rather than increasing.[7] Men are presidents of many women's colleges and of all coeducational institutions of higher learning; no woman has headed a men's college. The proportion of women on the boards of trustees of such institutions does not seem to be growing; the privately endowed colleges need corporate funds for endowment, and state institutions have to wrestle with politicians. Although much is made by feminists of those women who do head business enterprises or hold high posts in others, business is still very largely "a man's world"; no better evidence exists than the presence of only a handful of women on the boards of directors of large banks and corporations.[8]

At the same time, however, more women are going to work, and working for longer periods in their lives. There are now about 22 million women workers, more than one third of all United States women, and nearly one third of the labor force [9] Although the relationship between the employment of women and family income is complex and variable, the increase in the number of women workers in such groups as young married mothers with small children and of older women shows that at least a large proportion work because they must, either as their principal means of support or as a necessary supplement to the family income. Yet the differential between men's and women's earnings continues to widen, in the face of mounting taxes and still rising price levels. Median annual fulltime earnings for women in 1956 (as distinguished from income from other sources) totalled $2,827 while for men the figure stood at $4,466.[10]

There is the widest possible divergence of opinion among women themselves as to how these continuing disparities are to be overcome. The Nineteenth Amendment made it possible in the two decades succeeding it to pass a host of state laws equalizing or at least improving the position of women with regard to guardianship of her children, jury duty, inheritance, property, citizenship, and many other legal rights. But one group, led by the National Woman's Party under Alice Paul, would like to wipe out all such remaining discrimination, as well as inequities in pay and employment, by a constitutional amendment prohibiting any discrimination on account of sex.

Division on such a measure follows largely, although not entirely, the lines of income and social status. Wage-earning groups have argued that a real danger exists in such a measure being used to nullify existing protective legislation for women workers; at best such laws, limiting women's working hours or defining their working conditions, could be rendered inoperative by years of litigation, law by law and state by state. Proponents of the amendment admit they desire nothing more, since they feel that the very existence of such legislation constitutes discrimination in itself (if it forbids women to work at night, or more than a certain number of hours, or in specified industries), and is an indignity to all women. To which opponents reply that, while women are *equal* with men, they are by no means identical, and that as long as women bear children and show certain other physiological differences, it is folly to rob them of what protection has been painfully won for them, frequently in the absence of adequate union protection.

Here lies a crucial point in the controversy. However acute the discrimination against women, in both earnings and employment, the question is whether, under existing conditions, it can best be overcome by statute. So far, the results of state legislation have not been encouraging. Even in the seventeen states where equal pay laws are on the statute books, unequal pay continues to be the rule for women.[11] A parallel suggests itself with an earlier period, when the first factory laws designed to protect women from certain abuses were passed. The laws remained largely a dead letter because, as Florence Kelley tirelessly reiterated, those most deeply concerned were disfranchised and had no weapon to compel enforcement. Today, equal pay laws in states like New York remain largely ineffectual, not because women cannot vote, but because they are so inactive and so little represented in the leadership of precisely those organizations of voters which could compel the enforcement of equal pay legislation — the trade unions.

The backwardness of women in trade unions continues to be a very real problem. Vast numbers of women workers are still unorganized because, as in an earlier day, they work at low-paid trades in which men have little interest, and which present special problems of organization. One field is office work, another retail, and a third domestic work. In all three, pay lags far behind the levels in those industries where organized male unionists have won massive improvements and from which women, by and large, except in wartime crises, are excluded.

Most unions have disregarded the need to educate and activate their women membership, a fact they may regret if they come under sharper attack at some later date. Even in those trades where women predominate and where large numbers of them are organized, they are only sparsely represented in union leadership. Figures for 1956 show they are overwhelmingly in the majority in the International Ladies Garment Workers Union (338,000 out of a total membership of 451,000), and in the Amalgamated Clothing Workers (288,000 out of 385,000). Yet the I.L.G.W.U. executive board of eighteen includes only two women, and the A.C.W. board of seventeen has also only two women members. The Communications Workers of America, in the telephone industry, have 168,000 women members (60 per cent of their total membership); yet only one woman sits on the executive board, and two others with top organizing jobs meet with the board, without a vote.

The Hotel and Restaurant Employees Union, with about 200,000 women (nearly 45 per cent of total membership) has two women vice-presidents. The only other unions with large bodies of union members which have any women on their top governing bodies are the International Union of Electrical, Radio and Machine Workers, which reported a woman membership of approximately 40 per cent, and the Laundry, Dry Cleaning and Dye House Workers Union (recently suspended from the AFL-CIO on charges of corruption and racketeering) with approximately 45,000 women; both of these organizations reported one woman each on their executive boards. Some of the others reported the presence of women on their national organizing staffs (in very small numbers), and of course they are present in scattered numbers in district and local posts. But it is significant that no women are to be found in leadership in the textile unions, or in the Retail Clerks International Association, where almost half the members are women and vast numbers remain unorganized.[12]

Once again, special note should be taken of the Negro woman worker's position, since she encounters a double measure of discrimination, as Negro and as woman. Census figures of 1950 gave non-white women in the United States an annual median income of $474, as opposed to $1,060 for white women.[13] Figures for 1956 showed an increase to $970 for the non-white woman as against $2,179 for the white woman.[14] While progress is being made, Negro women are still heavily concentrated in the lowest paid categories of employment, as domestic workers, farm workers, and in the northern and central states, in such lines as garment manufacture and laundry work.[15]

There is wide disagreement among authorities no less than among the general public, in other areas than the Equal Rights amendment. There are established scholars who insist that the women in the United States run things and get the best of everything — that our country is, in fact, a matriarchy.[16] Other critics blame women themselves for not taking greater advantage of their hard-won opportunities. Still another segment of opinion, whose idiom frequently resembles that of the arguments used for decades against each step toward enfranchising women, contends that the more women do go into business, politics, the professions, or any kind of work outside the home, the greater the ultimate cost to our society, the higher the rate of juvenile delinquency, and the larger the number of men psychologically disturbed by changing social patterns.

Discussion of these and a host of other issues is not properly the realm of the historian, who can do no more than indicate their existence, and suggest, however tentatively, that the efforts and sacrifices of more than a hundred years have not been wasted or misguided because new difficulties have arisen. It seems necessary to repeat that women's position in our time, their relationship to their families, their ambitions and frustrations are not only the result of the new opportunities before them or the new responsibilities placed upon them but arise from other factors as well, such as the increasing tempo of industrialization, automation, urbanization, and — possibly — atomization! [17]

Today's woman, armed with her ballot, her diploma, her union card, faces a dizzily complex world; inevitably she is often confused and paralyzed by it. So, one might add, is her male opposite, who also stays away from the polls on election day in large numbers, rarely goes to union meetings (thereby permitting racketeers to fasten their grip on his organization), and, if he achieves a B.A. or Ph.D. does not always make the most of it.

Whatever its hazards, it is doubtful if the world which women face today can appear to them any more hostile or bewildering than that which confronted the early nineteenth century woman with aspirations. Freedom and uncertainty seem to go together. It might help if we remembered more often, not only the lonely vigils of Washington at Valley Forge and Lincoln in the White House, but the doubts and fears that racked an Angelina Grimké or the seemingly intrepid Elizabeth Cady Stanton when she stood up to make her first public speech in the tiny Wesleyan chapel at Seneca Falls. Perhaps in learning more of the long journey these, and hundreds more, made into our present time, we can face our own future with more courage and wisdom, and greater hope.

ACKNOWLEDGMENTS

A book such as this draws heavily, not only on the work of other writers and authorities whose contributions are itemized in the reference notes, but on the help of the highly trained, and usually anonymous librarian and archivist. Such aid, and the patience, resourcefulness, and interest with which it is given, are all too often taken for granted by the reading public and the scholar. Behind each reference note dealing with a manuscript collection or only a single item in a particular library lies the work of one or more painstaking and skilled librarians, whose contribution I gratefully acknowledge.

My deepest thanks go to Mrs. Margaret S. Grierson, director of the Sophia Smith Collection, not only for her endless practical help but for her unflagging encouragement and faith in this book. Valuable aid was also rendered by many others: Mrs. Elizabeth B. Borden, director, and Miss Mary E. Howard, archivist of the Radcliffe Women's Archives; Mrs. Dorothy Porter, librarian of the Negro Collection, Howard University; Mrs. Jean Blackwell Hutson, curator of the Schomburg Collection of the New York Public Library; Mr. Ransom Waterman and Miss Elizabeth S. Duvall, of the Sophia Smith Collection; and Mrs. Kathleen Doland, reference librarian of the Forbes Library of Northampton.

I would like to express a special measure of appreciation, as a resident of Northampton, Massachusetts, with no connection with Smith College, to Miss Margaret L. Johnson, librarian, for the privilege of using the Smith College Library, and to its staff for their unremitting helpfulness and patience.

Among those who took part in some aspect of the woman's rights movement and who gave me the benefit of their experience and opinions were Miss Mary Anderson, the late Mrs. Thomas S. Cullen, Miss Mary Dreier, Miss Florence Luscomb, Miss Alice Paul, Miss Rose Schneiderman, Miss Doris Stevens, Miss Olive Van Horn, Miss Mary Van Kleeck, and Miss Alda Wilson.

I am also variously indebted, for suggestions regarding specific points in the manuscript or for general criticism, to Professor Samuel Flagg Bemis, Professor Gwendolen M. Carter, Mrs. Mildred Adams Kenyon, Mrs. Everett C. Kimball, Mr. David Lawrence, Professor Arthur Mann, and Professor Dale L. Morgan; to Mrs. Arthur C. Holden, for access to her invaluable library of books dealing with the history of women; to Mrs. Edna L. Stantial, for access to the papers transmitted to her for arrangement and transfer to the Library of Congress by the executors of Mrs. Carrie Chapman Catt, by Miss Mary Gray Peck and other suffragists, and for her permission as Mrs. Maud Wood Park's executor, to read and quote from "Front Door Lobby," Mrs. Park's autobiography; to Miss Alma Lutz and the Beacon Press for making available the proofs of Miss Lutz' biography of Susan B. Anthony; to Miss Otelia Cromwell and the Harvard University Press for letting me see the proofs of Miss Cromwell's biography of Lucretia Mott; to Mrs. Berthold Strauss and Miss

Alda Wilson, executors of Carrie Chapman Catt, for permission to quote from Mrs. Catt's unpublished letters and reports; and to Mrs. Ralph K. Miner for permission to quote from the Myrtilla Miner Papers.

Too often editors, like librarians, are anonymous, despite the invaluable contribution they make; I am grateful to Mrs. R. M. Hainer of the Harvard University Press for the skill and understanding with which she has worked on this book.

My greatest debt is to my friend Helen Terry, not only for her practical aid with the manuscript and proofs, but for her understanding and encouragement.

BIBLIOGRAPHICAL SUMMARY

Material on the history of women, both primary and secondary, is to be found today in practically every large library in the country. Despite its volume, in the form of letters, journals, organizational records, newspapers and other publications, relatively little use has been made of it, either by the general historian or the specialist. Consequently a rich field awaits any student looking for new, unploughed ground.

There are unfortunately large gaps in the sources available, which constitute a real loss. A great deal of material has been dissipated and lost, reflecting not only the low worth put on it by historians and sociologists, but a general attitude of the relative unimportance of women and their activities. Other factors have been the inexperience of women in keeping records, and their financial inability to publish such material as convention reports, newspapers, and magazines.

Moreover, society long demanded of women a standard of gentility which decreed that it was "unladylike" to make known differences of opinion or to criticize others: hence the "editing" of journals and letters, or their preservation only in copied and highly emended form, or their wholesale destruction.

A few of the older women's organizations have been successful in preserving their records. Inexplicably, and despite the historical sense of Mrs. Catt, the official records of the National American Woman Suffrage Association were scattered at the time that organization closed its New York headquarters in 1923. Diligent search and communication with as many of the older suffrage leaders as this writer was able to locate have failed to reveal the bulk of its records, including office correspondence and organizers' reports. Some material was returned to the states where key campaigns were waged and has found its way to the historical societies; some was taken by Mrs. Catt to her home. Of this last collection, sections were distributed on a rather arbitrary basis to the New York Public Library, Smith, and Radcliffe; the remainder is now being prepared for the Library of Congress by Mrs. Edna L. Stantial of Melrose, Massachusetts, including transcripts of speeches and reports made by Mrs. Catt, and the records of the Leslie Commission on Woman Suffrage. The letters over a period of forty years from Mrs. Catt to Miss Mary Gray Peck are also in the possession of Mrs. Stantial for transmittal to the Library of Congress.

A unique task of gathering together letters, clippings, and accounts of suffrage campaigns and their leaders was performed by Mrs. Maud Wood Park. She added her own voluminous suffrage correspondence and presented it, as the Woman's Rights Collection, to Radcliffe College.

Among the growing number of women's archives, those at Radcliffe and Smith are today outstanding. The Women's Archives, which is separately housed from the college library and the Woman's Rights Collection at Radcliffe, contains a unique collection of suffrage correspondence, including many letters from Mrs. Catt from 1895 to 1920 and the papers of Anna Howard Shaw. It also possesses the collected papers of a number of distinguished women such as Leonora O'Reilly, Mary Anderson, Dr. Alice Hamilton, and others. In addition the Women's Archives is building up an index, in card file form, of the location of source materials relating to women throughout the country.

The Sophia Smith Collection at Smith College covers the history and position of women on an international scale. Its American section includes the vast Garrison family papers in which are to be found letters from most of the important woman leaders in the nineteenth century. Its collection of published works dealing with women is integrated with the general college library, but separately catalogued. The card index of secondary material covers, not only books, but articles from a wide selection of periodicals published here and abroad, arranged by subject heading as well as by country, and is an invaluable aid to the researcher.

Since it has been manifestly impossible to write an account on a scale such as this one entirely from primary sources, I have made use of published works, particularly where certain periods and individuals were concerned; some ground has been well-ploughed, especially the earlier phases of the woman's rights movement. The only accounts that make any claim to covering the subject matter comprehensively are *Ladies in Revolt,* by Abbie Graham (New York, 1934) and *Angels and Amazons,* by Inez Haynes Irwin (Garden City, N.Y., 1933). Neither author had access to anything like the source material now available to the scholar; the benefit of having been able to talk to many women who lived through some of the most dramatic phases of the movement is partially balanced by the participants' inevitable lack of objectivity. One must be grateful to Miss Graham and Mrs. Irwin, however, for tackling a subject so thoroughly neglected by all others.

A large number of published biographies exist, and these are for the most part listed in the reference notes. The outstanding work of this type has been done by Miss Alma Lutz, who has covered a hundred-year span in the woman's rights movement by her biographies of Emma Willard, Elizabeth Cady Stanton, the latter's daughter Harriot Stanton Blatch, and most recently Susan B. Anthony. (Unfortunately only the most recent biographies of women as leaders are footnoted, nor does it seem possible for most authors to deal with such subject matter without calling the women by their first names!)

A significant present-day trend in the literature about women should be noted. During the first quarter of the twentieth century when suffrage was being won, or was still new, as was organization among working women, there were a number of sociological and economic studies published; today's new literature, however, is largely psychological in nature. While this reflects a general trend, as a whole new science of human behavior develops, it is hardly sufficient by itself when so few factual studies are being added to the earlier work of Mary Van Kleeck, Edith Abbott, Sophonisba Breckinridge, and their contemporaries. The recent National Manpower Council publications, *Womanpower,* and *Work in the Lives of Married Women,* are welcome exceptions. The deficiency is all the more serious when taken in conjunction with the virtual abandonment of the original role of the Women's Bureau, which made invaluable studies, based on actual field-work by trained personnel, for more than twenty-five years under the leadership of Mary Anderson.

Special account must be taken of existing books dealing with the suffrage movement. The monumental six-volume *History of Woman Suffrage* stands in a class by itself. Its first three volumes were put together — the phrase is used advisedly — by Mrs. Stanton, Miss Anthony, and Mrs. Mathilda Gage. These women were not professional writers; but they were inveterate hoarders of newspaper clippings, speeches, and letters. What they lacked in literary craft, objectivity, and style, they made up by creating an immense grab-bag of source material, much of which would otherwise have been lost or remained difficult of access to the later writer. The women made some mistakes and omissions, but no scholar has done better up to now.

The later three volumes are of a different caliber. Volume IV was the joint product of Mrs. Ida Husted Harper, and Miss Anthony. A professional writer and publicist, Mrs. Harper's work bears the stamp of greater literary smoothness, but unfortunately volume IV, and to an even greater extent volumes V and VI the greater part of which she edited rather than wrote, contain far less original material reprinted in full, and are lacking in objectivity. They become a chronicle of campaign and convention dates, of speakers (all of whom apparently made excellent addresses), and committees. Nevertheless, as a record of events and legal gains in the separate states, they contain much helpful information.

The books written by participants in the closing years of suffrage campaigning all suffer from serious bias, a defect heightened by the split within the suffrage movement. The story of the Woman's Party has been told both by Doris Stevens in *Jailed for Freedom* and by Inez Haynes Irwin in *The Story of the Woman's Party;* one would hardly know from either account that anyone else was working for suffrage. Mrs. Catt on the other hand, aided by Mrs. Shuler, endeavored in *Woman Suffrage and Politics* to write a narrative of the suffrage movement beginning with the Seneca Falls Convention; her work is more scholarly, and of particular interest in highlighting the role of the brewing and liquor interests in opposing suffrage. But these women too saw chiefly what they themselves were engaged in day by day and are therefore less than just in their estimate of the Woman's Party. That Mrs. Catt herself became aware of this deficiency is indicated by a letter she wrote to Alice Stone Blackwell near the end of her life:

> During the last few years . . . I began to realize how very difficult it would be for a serious investigator to get at the real essence of all our history. I am inclined to think that the suffragists, who have written their own history, have not always known all the facts at the time of writing and perhaps they have not been free enough from prejudice to tell the whole truth. A person without such prejudices in the future, with access to all sources of information concerning the woman's movement, might tell a better story than has yet been told. (August 28, 1943, ST.)

The student wishing to pursue the history of Negro women faces a most difficult task, despite the efforts of the Schomburg Collection of the New York Public Library and the Negro Collection at Howard University to amass material in this field. The early records of the National Association of Colored Women have been largely scattered; some are to be found in the Terrell Papers in the Library of Congress. An interesting record is furnished by the archives of the National Association of Colored Graduate Nurses (1908–1952) which have been preserved intact and are now in the possession of Mrs. M. K. Staupers of Washington, D. C.

But generally speaking the Negro woman and the white working woman both lacked the means with which to leave a printed record; not until the advent of the Women's Trade Union League is there any unified body of material through which the student may begin to trace the rise of organization among working women. The labor press needs to be far more thoroughly explored than has yet been the case to yield the story of their early efforts; so do other sources, such as state and national census material, the records of church and benevolent organizations, and material still untapped in local historical societies.

NOTES

HWS   *The History of Woman Suffrage* was published in six volumes. Volumes I to III were edited by Elizabeth Cady Stanton, Susan Anthony, and Mathilda Joslyn Gage. The first two volumes were published in Rochester, New York, in 1881; the third in 1886. Volume IV, edited by Susan B. Anthony and Ida Husted Harper, was published in Rochester in 1902. Volumes V and VI were edited by Ida Husted Harper and published in New York in 1922.

LC   Library of Congress, Manuscripts Division

NYPL   New York Public Library, Manuscripts Division

SSC   Sophia Smith Collection, Smith College, Northampton, Massachusetts

RWA   Women's Archives, Radcliffe College, Cambridge, Massachusetts

WHS   State Historical Society of Wisconsin, Madison, Wisconsin

ST   Material in the possession of Mrs. Edna L. Stantial, Melrose, Massachusetts

CHAPTER I
The Position of American Women up to 1800

1. Charles and Mary Beard, *The Rise of American Civilization* (New York, 1930), I, 44.

2. See Edmund S. Morgan, *The Puritan Family: Essays on Religious and Domestic Relations in Seventeenth-Century New England* (Boston, 1944).

3. Alexis de Tocqueville, *Democracy in America* (New York, 1954), II, 364.

4. Anna Howard Shaw, *The Story of a Pioneer* (New York, 1915), pp. 24–26. Quoted by permission of the publisher, Harper & Brothers.

5. *The Lawes Resolutions of Womens Rights; or The Lawes Provision for Women* (London, 1632) pp. 124–125.

6. See George Elliott Howard, *A History of Matrimonial Institutions* (Chicago, 1904), II, ch. xv. In New England, "a dissolution of the bond of matrimony was freely granted for various causes, such as desertion, cruelty, or breach of the marriage vow; and usually, though not always, the husband and wife were dealt with as equals before the law." Yet even here, Howard quotes Governor Hutchinson with respect to the inequity that existed in practice: "Female adultery was never doubted to have been sufficient cause; but male adultery, after some debate and consultation with the elders, was judged not sufficient" (pp. 330–331). See also Julia C. Spruill, *Woman's Life and Work in the Southern Colonies* (University of North Carolina Press, 1938).

7. Mary S. Benson, *Women in Eighteenth-Century America,* Columbia

University Studies in History, Economics and Public Law, no. 405 (1935), pp. 244–249.

8. See Elisabeth A. Dexter, *Colonial Women of Affairs* (Boston and New York, 1924).

9. *Antinomianism in the Colony of Massachusetts Bay, 1636–1638,* Prince Society Publications, XXI (1894), 158. One of the charges made against Mistress Hutchinson was that she failed to teach other women "that which the Apostle commands, viz., to keep at home" (p. 167).

10. *Ibid.,* p. 168.

11. *Ibid.,* p. 284.

12. *Ibid.,* p. 324.

13. *Ibid.,* p. 293.

14. Alice M. Earle, *Colonial Dames and Goodwives* (Boston and New York, 1895), p. 256. See also Elizabeth Commetti, "Women in the American Revolution," *New England Quarterly,* 20: 329–346 (September 1947).

15. Benson J. Lossing, *Pictorial Fieldbook of the American Revolution* (New York, 1850) I, 488.

16. *Familiar Letters of John Adams and His Wife Abigail Adams During the Revolution* (New York, 1876), pp. 286–287, letter dated July 31, 1777.

17. William Reed, *Life and Correspondence of Joseph Reed* (Philadelphia, 1847), II, 260–271, and *Life of Esther De Berdt, later Esther Reed of Pennsylvania* (Philadephia, 1853); Elizabeth F. Ellet, *Women of the American Revolution* (New York, 1848–1850), I, 52.

18. *Pennsylvania Magazine,* August 1775, p. 363.

19. Adams, *Familiar Letters,* pp. 149–150, letter dated March 31, 1777. On Mercy Warren, see *First Lady of the Revolution,* a life of Mrs. Warren by Katharine Anthony (Garden City, N. Y., 1958).

20. See Vena B. Field, *Constantia,* University of Maine Studies, 2nd Ser., no. 17 (Orono, Maine, 1933).

21. Constantia, "The Equality of the Sexes," *Massachusetts Magazine* (March-April 1790), pp. 132–133. Constantia was Mrs. Murray's pen name.

22. *Ibid.,* p. 134.

23. Constantia, *The Gleaner* (Boston, 1798), III, 188–189.

24. Benjamin Rush, *Thoughts on Female Education* (Philadelphia, 1787), pp. 6–7.

25. Frank Tannenbaum, *Slave and Citizen: The Negro in The Americas* (New York, 1947), pp. 28–33; John Hope Franklin, *From Slavery to Freedom* (New York, 1947), pp. 56–57.

26. So-called because originally the crossing from Africa to America was the second leg of a triangular journey for the traders which began in Europe with goods to be sold on the African coast and ended with goods — molasses, cotton, and rum — for the European market.

27. E. Franklin Frazier, *The Negro Family in the United States* (Chicago, 1939), p. 44.

28. George F. Dow, *Slave Ships and Slaving* (Salem, Mass., 1927), pp. 244–246.

29. *Ibid.,* p. 242.

30. *Ibid.,* p. 151.

31. The most recent work on slavery is Kenneth Stampp, *The Peculiar Institution* (New York, 1956), a dispassionate and careful analysis whose con-

clusions are nonetheless uncompromising. At the other end of the scale are the earlier writings of Ulrich B. Phillips, which are far less critical of slavery, with a host of authorities in between.

32. American Anti-Slavery Society, *American Slavery As It Is: Testimony of a Thousand Witnesses* (New York, 1839), p. 175. This compilation was the work of Theodore Weld and his wife, Angelina Grimké Weld.

33. Stampp, p. 321.

34. *The Letters of Theodore Weld, Angelina Grimké Weld and Sarah Grimké, 1822–1844* (New York, 1934). Quoted by permission of the publisher, Appleton-Century-Crofts and the American Historical Association. Hereafter, this book will be referred to as the *Weld-Grimké Letters*. A. W. Calhoun quotes the sister of President Madison: "We southern ladies are complimented with the name of wives; but we are only the mistresses of seraglios." *Social History of the American Family From Colonial Times to the Present* (Cleveland, 1917–1919), III, 308. See also Allan Nevins, *Ordeal of the Union* (New York, 1947–1950), I, 453–454. A vivid account of one slave woman's fate occurs in Pauli Murray's *Proud Shoes* (New York, 1956), ch. iii.

35. Frazier, p. 125; Stampp, pp. 334, 360.

CHAPTER II

Early Steps Toward Equal Education

1. Jean-Jacques Rousseau, *L'Emile or A Treatise on Education,* ed. W. H. Payne (New York and London, 1906), p. 263.

2. Hannah Mather Crocker, *Observations on the Real Rights of Women* (Boston, 1818), p. 41. Mrs. Crocker was a granddaughter of Cotton Mather, the mother of ten children, who did not publish any of her writings until after her husband's death. She was one of the earliest women interested in Masonry, and was the matron of a lodge patterned on its principles. (See *Dictionary of American Biography*.)

3. *Ibid.,* p. 20.

4. *Ibid.,* pp. 5–6, 56.

5. Quoted in Alma Lutz, *Emma Willard* (Boston, 1929), p. 56. For additional discussion of Mrs. Willard's role and that of other pioneer educators, see Willystine Goodsell, *Pioneers of Women's Education in the United States* (New York, 1931).

6. Lutz, p. 181.

7. See A. J. G. Perkins and Theresa Wolfson, *Frances Wright: Free Enquirer* (New York, 1939).

8. Frances Wright, *Course of Popular Lectures* (New York, 1829), p. 44.

9. *Ibid.,* p. 72.

10. "It will help us to understand the intellectual equipment of Americans in 1848–1860 . . . if we bear in mind that according to the census of 1840, four-fifths of the children did not go beyond the primary grades, and only three-quarters of one per cent went to college." Allan Nevins, *Ordeal of the Union,* I, 53.

11. The standard work in this field is still Thomas Woody, *History of Women's Education in the United States* (New York and Lancaster, Pa., 1929), in two volumes, but it needs to be supplemented. Eleanor W. Thompson,

Education for Ladies, 1830–1860 (New York, 1947), goes beyond the area suggested by its sub-title: *Ideas on Education in Magazines for Women,* and has an excellent bibliography.

12. Quoted in Robert S. Fletcher, *History of Oberlin College to the Civil War* (Oberlin, Ohio, 1943), I, 373.

13. *Ibid.,* p. 291. Lucy Stone refused to write a Commencement essay because it would have to be read to the audience by a male student.

14. See Mae E. Harveson, *Catharine Beecher: A Pioneer Educator* (Philadelphia, 1932).

15. Catharine Beecher, *The Evils Suffered by American Women and Children* (New York, 1846), p. 12. Miss Beecher opposed women's participation in anti-slavery and other reform movements.

16. Mary Sharp College at Winchester, Tennessee; Georgia Female College at Macon, Georgia; Wheaton Seminary. See Woody, I, 137–142.

17. "Mary Lyon's name was nowhere more honored than among the Lowell mill girls. . . . Mount Holyoke Seminary broke upon the thought of many of them as a vision of hope." Lucy Larcom, *A New England Girlhood* (New York and Boston, 1889), p. 223. See also A. G. Violette, *Economic Feminism in American Literature Prior to 1848,* University of Maine Studies, 2nd Ser., no. 2 (Orono, Maine, 1925).

18. Mary Lyon to Hannah White, February 26, 1834. Quoted in *The Power of Christian Benevolence, Illustrated in the Life of Mary Lyon,* compiled by Edward Hitchcock and others (Northampton, Mass., and Philadelphia, 1852), pp. 186–187. This work is commonly known as the Hitchcock Memoir of Mary Lyon, and is the sole source of many of her letters, of which the originals were destroyed in a fire. *Mary Lyon Through Her Letters,* ed. Marion Lansing (Boston, 1937) is a recent compilation based on those in the Memoir and others in the Mount Holyoke College Archives. There is no adequate biography of Mary Lyon, since the earlier ones overstress the religious motives in the founding of Mount Holyoke, to the exclusion of others. Beth Gilchrist in *The Life of Mary Lyon* (Boston, 1910), draws on the personal recollections of early students who knew Miss Lyon. See also Arthur C. Cole, *A Hundred Years of Mount Holyoke College* (New Haven, 1940).

19. Mary Lyon to her mother, Mrs. Jemima Lyon, May 12, 1834 (Mount Holyoke College Archives).

20. Mary Lyon to Zilpah Grant, February 4, 1834, quoted in Hitchcock, p. 172.

21. Hitchcock, pp. 244–245.

22. Alice Blackwell, *Lucy Stone* (Boston, 1930), p. 20.

23. Gilchrist, pp. 258–261.

24. First Annual Catalogue of Mount Holyoke Female Seminary, 1837, pp. 8–9.

25. There were some 200,000 free Negroes in the "free states," of whom Allan Nevins has written that they were "kept in menial positions, debarred from the intellectual professions and skilled handicrafts, denied equal educational facilities in many communities, and subjected to legal and political discrimination. They were in fact little better than outcasts." *Ordeal of the Union,* I, 519.

26. Laura Haviland, *A Woman's Life Work* (Chicago, 1889), p. 35.

27. Dorothy Porter, "Organized Activities of Negro Literary Societies, 1828–1846," *Journal of Negro Education,* 5: 555–576 (October 1936).

28. See *Memoirs and Poems of Phillis Wheatley* (Boston, 1834). Shirley Graham's *Phillis Wheatley* (New York, 1949) is a fictionalized biography.

29. See "Prudence Crandall: Champion of Negro Education," by Edwin W. and Miriam R. Small, *New England Quarterly*, 17: 506–29 (December 1944).

30. Fifty years later the state of Connecticut attempted a measure of restitution. Largely at the instigation of Mark Twain, the Legislature voted the widowed Prudence Crandall Phileo, then living in Kansas, an annual pension of $500. Mrs. Phileo was still in the vanguard of thought; she was an ardent suffragist.

CHAPTER III

The Beginnings of Organization Among Women

1. Elizabeth Buffum Chace and Lucy B. Lovell, *Two Quaker Sisters* (New York, 1937), p. 31.

2. Blackwell, *Lucy Stone*, p. 40.

3. Porter, in *Journal of Negro Education*, 5: 572.

4. *Weld-Grimké Letters*, I, 388, letter of Sarah and Angelina Grimké to Theodore Weld, May 18, 1837.

5. Henrietta Buckmaster, *Let My People Go* (New York, 1941), p. 89.

6. Harriet Martineau, *The Martyr Age in the United States* (Boston and New York, 1839), pp. 29–30.

7. Martineau, *Autobiography* (London, 1877), II, 28.

8. See Elisabeth A. Dexter, *Career Women of America, 1776–1840* (Francestown, N. H., 1950), pp. 50–51: "Women in America have always contributed their full share to church work, but few at any times have preached or held office in the organized churches. . . . In general, the stronger the ecclesiastical tradition and more compact the organization, the less place for women. Loosely organized fellowships sometimes accepted them, and new sects and revivalistic movements often allowed women the same opportunities as men." Mrs. Dexter is here referring, among others, to Jemima Wilkinson, who organized a sect, and to Ann Lee, the founder of Shakerism in America.

9. I Tim., ii: 11–12; I Cor., xiv: 34–35.

10. Mrs. Stewart was born in Hartford, Conn., in 1803. At the age of five she was "bound out" for domestic service in the family of a clergyman, where she had access to books. She was married in 1826 but her husband died three years later. William Lloyd Garrison printed a pamphlet of her religious writings in 1832, entitled *Meditations,* and published her speeches in the *Liberator.* Both, with added biographical material, re-appeared under the title of *Meditations of Mrs. Maria W. Stewart* (Washington, 1879).

11. "Farewell Address," October 21, 1832, in *Meditations,* p. 58.

12. *Ibid.,* pp. 76–78.

13. Not all the women reformers favored the anti-slavery cause, or women's advocacy of it. In addition to Catharine Beecher, there were other dissidents: Mrs. Willard excused, or temporized on the issue of slavery until the Civil War; Mary Lyon severely reprimanded Lucy Stone, during the latter's brief time at Mount Holyoke, for leaving copies of the *Liberator* in the students' reading room. (In all probability she did not wish her school racked by the kind of dissension which had crippled Lane Seminary in 1834.)

14. *HWS,* I, 61.

15. Wendell Phillips, one of the great orators of that highly articulate age, bore witness to her powers: "She swept the chords of the human heart with a power that has never been surpassed and rarely equalled. I well remember, evening after evening, listening to eloquence such as had never then been heard from a woman." (Address, *Memorial Meeting for Angelina Grimké Weld,* 1880, p. 28.)

16. Sarah Grimké, *The Equality of the Sexes and the Condition of Women* (Boston, 1838), pp. 9–10.

17. *Ibid.,* p. 10.

18. *Ibid.,* p. 122.

19. *Ibid.,* p. 41. In these Letters, Sarah Grimké went far beyond women's role in the anti-slavery movement. She ranged over a wide area, from social relations between the sexes, to equal pay for equal work (one of the earliest arguments by a woman for this principle); from the effect on white women of the white man's treatment of slave women, to women's right to enter the ministry, and their legal disabilities. Six years before the far more widely known *Woman in the Nineteenth Century* by Margaret Fuller, this pamphlet deserves the honor usually bestowed on the later work, of being known as the first serious discussion of woman's rights by an American woman. When Elizabeth Cady Stanton and Lucretia Mott visited England in 1840, they found it well known there.

20. *Weld-Grimké Letters,* I, 429–430, letter of Angelina Grimké to Theodore Weld and John Greenleaf Whittier, August 20, 1837.

21. Quoted in *HWS,* I, 82–83.

22. Quoted in Catherine Birney, *The Grimké Sisters* (Boston and New York, 1885), p. 124.

23. *Weld-Grimké Letters,* II, 564, letter of Angelina Grimké to Theodore Weld, February 21, 1838.

24. L. Maria Child, *Letters* (Boston, 1883), p. 26.

25. See Gilbert H. Barnes, *The Anti-Slavery Impulse, 1830–1844* (New York and London, 1933), pp. 140–144; Samuel Flagg Bemis, *John Quincy Adams and the Union* (New York, 1956), Chs. 17 and 18.

26. John Quincy Adams, *Speech . . . Upon the Rights of the People, Men and Women, to Petition* (Washington, 1838), p. 65.

27. *Ibid.,* pp. 67–68, 76. Subsequently, in speaking to a group of women from his own Congressional district, he somewhat modified such liberalism, saying that "I made some remarks on the right of women to petition, and on the propriety of their taking a part in public affairs. This was a point to be left to their own discretion, and there was not the least danger of their obtruding their wishes upon any of the ordinary subjects of legislation — banks, currency, exchange, Sub-Treasuries, internal improvement, tariff, manufactures, public lands, revenues and expenditures, all of which so profoundly agitated the men of the country; the women, so far from intermeddling with them, could scarcely be prevailed upon to bestow a thought upon them; and, knowing that, it was scarcely consistent with civility so much as to name them in their presence. I now alluded to them only to discard them. But, for objects of kindness, of benevolence, of compassion, women, so far from being debarred by any rule of delicacy from exercising the natural right of petition or remonstrance, are, by the law of their nature,

fitted above all others for that exercise." *Memoirs of John Quincy Adams* (Philadelphia, 1874–1877), X, 37.

28. Child, *Letters,* p. 31.

29. Maria Weston Chapman, *Right and Wrong in Massachusetts* (Boston, 1839), p. 12.

30. House Archives, National Archives, Box 72.

31. Edith Abbott, *Women in Industry* (New York and London, 1910), pp. 66–70; also, Dexter, *Career Women of America, 1776–1840.*

32. Helen L. Sumner, *History of Women in Industry in the United States,* vol. IX of *Report on the Condition of Woman and Child Wage-Earners in the United States* in 19 volumes, U. S. Sen. Doc. 645, 61 Cong., 2 Sess., p. 14. An account of how this monumental inquiry came to be made will be found in Chapter 15.

33. *Ibid.,* p. 27.

34. Grimké, *The Equality of the Sexes,* pp. 50–51.

35. Sumner, p. 129.

36. *Ibid.,* p. 23.

37. *Ibid.,* p. 63.

38. *Ibid.,* p. 74. Another factor which pulled down women's earnings was the prevalence of child labor. It has been estimated that in 1831 in the six New England states and New York, New Jersey, Pennsylvania, Delaware, Maryland, and Virginia, 7 per cent of all employees were children. John R. Commons et al., *History of Labor in the United States* (New York, 1935), I, 173.

39. Quoted in Commons, I, 423.

40. Quoted in Harriet H. Robinson, *Loom and Spindle* (New York, 1898), p. 84.

41. Quoted in Vera Shlakman, *Economic History of a Factory Town, A Study of Chicopee, Mass.,* Smith College Studies in History, XX (1935), 121–122. Edmund Dwight was a leader in building up the textile industry in the Connecticut Valley; J. K. Mills was his partner.

42. See John B. Andrews and W. D. P. Bliss, *History of Women in Trade Unions,* vol. X of *Report on Condition of Woman and Child Wage-Earners,* U. S. Sen. Doc. 645, 61 Cong., 2 Sess., pp. 61–65.

43. The best account of this organization is in Hannah Josephson, *Golden Threads* (New York, 1949), ch. xii.

44. Miss Bagley's connection with the paper began with its third issue in June 1845 and lasted until her retirement in September 1846. Most of the time she was one of a three-member publishing committee, and for a brief period was the actual editor.

45. *Voice of Industry,* vol. 1, no. 48 (Lowell, Mass.), May 15, 1846.

46. *Ibid.*

47. *Ibid.*

48. *Voice of Industry,* vol. 2, no. 14, September 18, 1846.

49. Massachusetts House Documents, no. 50 (Boston).

50. *Ibid.*

51. *Ibid.*

52. *Voice of Industry,* vol. 2, no. 24, November 28, 1845.

CHAPTER IV
The Beginnings of Reform

1. See Willystine Goodsell, *A History of Marriage and the Family* (New York, 1935), pp. 463–465.

2. Jane Swisshelm, *Half a Century* (Chicago, 1880), p. 72. Mrs. Mary R. Beard has held that such devices as trusts, and other redress through equity court proceedings, largely nullified these forms of legal discrimination. (See Beard, *Woman as a Force in History* [New York, 1946], ch. v–vi.) But while some women were able to secure redress through equity, the procedure was too cumbersome and expensive to help them all, or those who often needed assistance most, as working women did.

3. Child, *Letters,* p. 74.

4. *HWS,* I, 175–176. In this instance Mrs. Nichols' quick wit saved the day. She prevailed upon the train conductor to order the train to proceed across the Massachusetts state line, only a few minutes away, where the sheriff no longer had jurisdiction.

5. *HWS,* I, 670. When this enumeration was read at a woman's rights convention, one woman remarked that a widow ought also to be granted a coffee-pot; another commented that Ohio was more generous than New York, in that it allowed a widow *twelve* spoons.

6. *HWS,* I, 295.

7. Quoted in *HWS,* I, 260–261. Helen W. Papashvily, *All the Happy Endings* (New York, 1956), discusses the inequalities of nineteenth century marriage as they are portrayed in the widely read "domestic novels" of the period, almost entirely written by women.

8. See Yuri Suhl, *Ernestine L. Rose* (New York, 1959).

9. *HWS,* I, 99.

10. Ruth Finley, *The Lady of Godey's* (Philadelphia, 1931). This is a biography of Mrs. Hale.

11. The more romantic aspects of some periods of Miss Fuller's life have encouraged several biographies. The only scholarly treatment is Mason Wade's *Margaret Fuller, Whetstone of Genius* (New York, 1940). Mr. Wade has also edited the valuable *Writings of Margaret Fuller* (New York, 1941), which includes *Woman in the Nineteenth Century* and some of her letters.

12. William Ellery Channing, to whose liberating influence Transcendentalism owed a great deal, defined it as "an assertion of the inalienable integrity of man, of the immanence of Divinity in instinct. . . . Amid materialists, zealots and sceptics, the Transcendentalists believed in perpetual inspiration, the miraculous power of will, and a birthright to universal good." *Memoirs of Margaret Fuller Ossoli* (New York, 1869), II, 12–13.

13. *Writings of Margaret Fuller,* ed. Mason Wade, p. 125.

14. *Ibid.,* pp. 214–215.

15. *Ibid.,* p. 124.

16. *Ibid.,* p. 123.

17. "To her, I, at least, had hoped to confide the leadership of this movement. It can never be known if she would have accepted it; the desire had been expressed to her by letter." Paulina Wright Davis at first national woman's rights convention in Worcester, Mass., 1850. *HWS,* I, 217.

18. So thought Elizabeth Cady Stanton and Susan B. Anthony: *HWS*, I, 801.

19. Blackwell, *Lucy Stone*, p. 9. This biography by Mrs. Stone's daughter is still the only one, and needs to be supplemented by a new study based on the Blackwell family papers, now in the possession of Mrs. Stantial.

20. *Ibid.*, p. 3.

21. *Ibid.*, p. 67.

22. *Ibid.*, p. 91.

23. *Ibid.*, p. 161.

CHAPTER V

The Seneca Falls Convention, 1848

1. William Lloyd Garrison, who reached the convention too late to take part in the debate, registered his protest by refusing to be seated as a delegate in the main hall, and by remaining in the gallery with the women instead. Less well known is the refusal of a Negro delegate, Charles Remond, to be seated: he wrote to a friend that he was "almost entirely indebted to the kind and generous members of the Bangor Female Anti-Slavery Society, the Portland Sewing Circle, and the Newport Young Ladies Juvenile Anti-Slavery Society, for aid in visiting [England]." Remond to Charles B. Ray, June 30, 1840, in *Documentary History of the Negro People in the United States*, ed. Herbert Aptheker (New York, 1951), p. 196.

2. Otelia Cromwell, *Lucretia Mott* (Cambridge, 1958). This is a carefully documented study.

3. On the occasion when Mrs. Mott testified, with Mrs. Stanton and Mrs. Rose, on a bill pending before the New York state legislature to permit divorce on grounds of drunkenness, Mrs. Mott asked her companions not to be too radical in their statements. Out of deference for her they were unusually temperate in their remarks. However, after hearing all the testimony, Mrs. Mott rose once more for a further statement, and her anger at all she had heard of women's plight under the existing legislation was such that she made the most extreme speech of anyone present. *HWS*, I, 425.

4. Alma Lutz, *Created Equal: A Biography of Elizabeth Cady Stanton* (New York, 1940). This is one of the best existing biographies of the women leaders. However, it is uncritical of Mrs. Stanton, who had her prejudices and human limitations.

5. Elizabeth Cady Stanton, *Eighty Years and More* (New York, 1898), pp. 147–148.

6. *Ibid.*, p. 148.

7. *HWS*, I, p. 67.

8. *Ibid.*, p. 70.

9. *Ibid.*, p. 71.

10. Lucretia Mott to Elizabeth Cady Stanton, July 15, 1848, Stanton Papers, LC.

11. Rheta Child Dorr, *Susan B. Anthony* (New York, 1928), p. 47.

12. *The First Convention Ever Called To Discuss the Civil and Political Rights of Women* (Seneca Falls, New York, 1848), p. 6.

13. *HWS*, I, 72.

14. Dorr, p. 51. In the uproar that ensued after the convention, with bitter attacks made on the signers by press and pulpit, many withdrew their names.

CHAPTER VI
From Seneca Falls to the Civil War

1. Katharine Coman, *Industrial History of the United States* (New York and London, 1905), p. 227; *Historical Statistics of the United States* (Government Printing Office, 1949), p. 179.

2. J. D. B. DeBow, *Statistical View of the United States, A Compendium of the Seventh Census* (Washington, 1854), table CXCV, p. 179. More than half of this number were in New England.

3. See James D. Hart, *The Popular Book: A History of America's Literary Taste* (New York, 1950).

4. Helen E. Marshall, *Dorothea Dix, Forgotten Samaritan* (Chapel Hill, 1937). This is a carefully documented study. Miss Dix took no part in the agitation for woman's rights.

5. *HWS*, I, 110.

6. See Harriot K. Hunt, *Glimpses and Glances* (Boston, 1856).

7. "She is not so ultra as some of us; we must accept her for what she is. We need every possible shade and variety of lecturers and workers in this great movement." Paulina Wright Davis to Elizabeth Cady Stanton, Sept. 1, 1851, Stanton Papers, LC.

8. Quoted in Ida Husted Harper, *The Life and Work of Susan B. Anthony* (Indianapolis and Kansas City, 1899), I, 78–79. Dr. Hunt never married, and both Lucy Stone and Rev. Brown were still single at the time of this onslaught.

9. See Bertha Stearns, "Reform Periodicals and Female Reformers," *American Historical Review*, no. 37, pp. 678–699 (July 1932); Eleanor Thompson, *Education for Ladies*, pp. 11–15; Arthur J. Larsen, ed. *Crusader and Feminist: Letters of Jane Grey Swisshelm* (St. Paul, 1934); Margaret Farrand Thorp, *Female Persuasion: Six Strong-Minded Women* (New Haven, 1949), pp. 70–88, 113–133. Among the abolition papers which gave the women the most help were Garrison's *Liberator*, the *Anti-Slavery Standard* (edited for a brief period by Lydia Maria Child), and Frederick Douglass' *North Star*.

10. Ernestine Rose compared organizations to "Chinese bandages"; Lucy Stone said she had "had enough of thumb-screws ever to wish to be placed under them again." *HWS*, I, 541.

11. Elizabeth Cady Stanton to Susan B. Anthony, February 19, 1854, Stanton Papers, LC.

12. The three-volume biography of Miss Anthony by Ida Husted Harper will always remain a classic source of information on the woman suffrage movement and on Miss Anthony's role in it. The first two volumes were written in Miss Anthony's lifetime and under her own roof, and have an immediacy which came from Mrs. Harper's knowledge of her subject and her own participation in suffrage campaigns. More recent is Katharine Anthony's *Susan B. Anthony: Her Personal History and Her Era* (New York, 1954), which has a Freudian slant, and Alma Lutz, *Susan B. Anthony: Rebel, Crusader, Humanitarian* (Boston, 1959).

13. Quoted in Harper, I, 104.

14. Dorr, *Susan B. Anthony*, p. 98.

15. Dorr, p. 109.

16. *HWS*, I, 629–630.

17. Not all these gains were lasting. In 1862, further legislation whittled some of them away, necessitating further work to have them restored.

18. Stanton, *Eighty Years and More*, pp. 165–166.

19. Quoted in Lutz, *Created Equal*, p. 104. Mrs. Stanton was sanguine but not quite sanguine enough. She lived to be eighty-eight, and Miss Anthony to be eighty-seven, and both can be said to have died with their boots on.

20. *HWS*, I, 115–117. For further biographical details, see Arthur Fauset, *Sojourner Truth: God's Faithful Pilgrim* (Chapel Hill, 1938).

21. *HWS*, I, 111–112.

22. *Ibid.*, p. 117.

23. *Ibid.*, p. 118. Mrs. Gage's final comment on "John" was: "He died young, worn out by his own enthusiasm and conflicts."

24. *Ibid.*, pp. 173–174.

25. *Ibid*, p. 184.

26. *HWS*, III, 365.

27. See Calhoun, *Social History of the American Family*, II, 344–355. While contemporary authorities, such as Helper and Olmsted, contain some references, there is little material available on the position of Southern white women other than those of the planter class. The term "Southern women" as used by historians and sociologists has come to refer almost exclusively to this group.

28. In the absence of any possible accurate tally of the number of slaves who escaped to free territory or the proportion that were women, estimates of the total annual number range from one to two thousand annually. See Russell B. Nye, *Fettered Freedom: Civil Liberties and the Slavery Controversy* (East Lansing, Mich., 1944), p. 213n. It is certain that fewer women than men tried to escape.

29. Harriet Beecher Stowe, *Uncle Tom's Cabin* (Boston and Cleveland, 1852), ch. xii.

30. Blackwell, *Lucy Stone*, pp. 183–184.

31. Adams, *Speech Upon the Rights of the People*, p. 79.

32. See Earl Conrad, *Harriet Tubman* (Washington, 1943).

33. Quoted in Benjamin Brawley, *Early Negro American Writers* (Chapel Hill, 1935), pp. 290–291.

34. Frances E. W. Harper, *Poems on Miscellaneous Subjects* (Boston, 1854).

35. Like many early Negro papers, few copies of this one survive. There is one in the Toronto, Ontario, Public Library, and a photostatic copy in the SSC.

36. Hallie Q. Brown, comp., *Homespun Heroines* (Xenia, O., 1926), p. 95.

37. The Myrtilla Miner Papers are in the Library of Congress. See also Sadie St. Clair, "Myrtilla Miner: Pioneer in the Teacher Education of Negroes," *Journal of Negro History*, 34: 30–45 (January 1949), and Ellen O'Connor, *Myrtilla Miner, a Memoir* (Boston and New York, 1885).

38. Special Report of the Commissioner on Education, District of Columbia (1871), p. 207. Although the slave trade was outlawed in the District of Columbia in 1850, slavery itself was not abolished there until 1862.

39. *Life and Letters of Frederick Douglass*, ed. Philip S. Foner (New York, 1950–1955), IV, 372, letter of Frederick Douglass to Ellen O'Connor, May 4, 1883.

40. Quoted in O'Connor, p. 56.

41. Letter from Myrtilla Miner to "Dear Friends," May 13, 1860, Miner Papers, LC.

42. Quoted in O'Connor, p. 41.

CHAPTER VII
The Civil War

1. Louisa May Alcott, *Her Life, Letters and Journals*, ed. Ednah D. Cheney (Boston, 1923), pp. 140–141.

2. Shaw, *Story of a Pioneer*, pp. 52–53.

3. Alcott, p. 146.

4. There is a large collection of Clara Barton's papers in the LC and another in the SSC. The most recent biography is Ishbel Ross, *Angel of the Battlefield: Clara Barton* (New York, 1956). The best account of Mother Bickerdyke is Nina Brown Baker, *Cyclone in Calico: The Story of Mary Ann Bickerdyke* (Boston, 1952).

5. A considerable literature has grown up around the Sanitary Commission. Among many contemporary accounts, see L. P. Brockett and M. C. Vaughan, *Women's Work in the Civil War* (Boston & Philadelphia, 1867), and Mary Livermore, *My Own Story of the War* (Hartford, 1889). Marjorie B. Greenbie's *Lincoln's Daughters of Mercy* (New York, 1944) is lively, but unfortunately interlarded with fictitious conversations. The Sanitary Commission Bulletins 1861–1865 are valuable source material.

6. Margaret Leech, *Reveille in Washington* (New York and London, 1941), p. 210.

7. See Giraud Chester, *Embattled Maiden: The Life of Anna Dickinson* (New York, 1951), based on the Dickinson papers, in the Library of Congress. Katharine Anthony, in her biography of Susan Anthony, lays considerable emphasis on Miss Anthony's attempts to secure Miss Dickinson as a leader of the organized woman's movement.

8. *HWS*, II, 42.

9. Quoted in Harper, *Susan B. Anthony*, I, 226.

10. *HWS*, II, 53n.

11. Said Mrs. Weld: "I rejoice exceedingly that the resolution should combine us with the negro. I feel that we have been with him; that the iron has entered into our souls. True, we have not had our hands manacled, but our hearts have been crushed. . . . I want to be identified with the negro; until he gets his rights, we shall never get ours." *HWS*, II, 60–61.

12. *HWS*, II, 81.

13. It is not clear why the League should have ceased its work before the amendment was finally ratified, which did not occur until December 18, 1865.

14. *Congressional Globe* (February 9, 1864), vol. 34, Part I, p. 536. There were 65,601 women's names on the first installment of petitions submitted by Sumner.

15. See Francis Simkins and J. W. Patton, *The Women of the Confederacy* (New York, 1936), pp. 88–90. This is a more comprehensive and authoritative treatment than the more recent *Heroines of Dixie*, by Katharine W. Jones (Indianapolis, 1955), and contains an excellent bibliography of source materials.

16. Simkins and Patton, pp. 116–118, 126–128.

CHAPTER VIII

The Intellectual Progress of Women, 1860–1875

1. Abraham Flexner, *Is Social Work a Profession?* (New York School of Philanthropy, 1915), p. 10.

2. Jane Swisshelm, *Letters to Country Girls* (New York, 1853), p. 78.

3. The Maria Mitchell Library in Nantucket contains many of her notebooks, diaries, and letters, the latter unfortunately pruned of any references deemed too personal by her sister. See Helen Wright, *Sweeper in the Sky* (New York, 1950).

4. Quoted in Wright, p. 200.

5. *Ibid.*, pp. 199–200.

6. T. L. Nichols, *Nichols' Health Manual: The Life and Work of Mrs. Mary S. Gove Nichols* (London, 1886), p. 22.

7. *HWS*, I, 37n.

8. Harriot Hunt, *Glances and Glimpses* (Boston and Cleveland, 1856), pp. 127–131, 139–140. In 1853 Dr. Hunt received an honorary degree from the three-year-old Philadelphia Female Medical College.

9. Elizabeth Blackwell, *Pioneer Work in Opening the Medical Profession to Women* (London, 1895), Everyman's Library, p. 23. See also Ishbel Ross, *Child of Destiny: The Life of Elizabeth Blackwell* (New York, 1949).

10. *Ibid.*, p. 160.

11. The Hospital is still in existence, as the New York Infirmary, on East 15th Street.

12. Dr. Zakrzewska later founded the New England Hospital for Women and Children in Boston. See Marie E. Zakrzewska, *A Woman's Quest* (New York, 1934).

13. Annual Report of the Infirmary for 1864, quoted in Blackwell, p. 169.

14. Cecil Woodham-Smith, *Florence Nightingale* (London, 1950; New York, 1951), pp. 231–236.

15. Address by Dr. Stephen Smith, *Memorial Meeting for Dr. Elizabeth and Dr. Emily Blackwell, January 25, 1911* (New York Academy of Medicine, 1911). Others who paid tribute to Dr. Elizabeth Blackwell on this occasion were Dr. William H. Welch and Dr. Abraham Jacobi.

16. Dr. Sophia Jex-Blake, the first woman to graduate from a British medical school, did so in 1877.

17. Shaw, *Story of a Pioneer*, pp. 83–84.

18. *HWS*, II, 611–612.

19. *Ibid.*, p. 613.

20. *Public Laws of the State of Illinois, 1871–1872*, p. 578.

21. M. Carey Thomas, "Present Tendencies in Women's Education," *Publications of the Association of Collegiate Alumni*, series III, no. 17, p. 47 (February 1908).

22. In 1952 there were some 12,000 women doctors in the United States, as compared with some 200,000 men physicians and surgeons. U. S. Department of Labor, Women's Bureau, Publication D-55: *Spotlight on Women in the United States, 1956–1957* (Government Printing Office, 1957), p. 22.

23. James Monroe Taylor, *Before Vassar Opened* (Boston and New York, 1914), p. 41. Chs. i and ii deal with southern seminaries before the Civil

War; see also Woody, *History of Women's Education in the United States,* II, ch. iv.

24. *HWS,* III 526-528; also letter to the author from Historical Collection of the University of Michigan.

25. Allan Nevins, *The Emergence of Modern America,* History of American Life Series, vol. VIII (New York, 1927), pp. 264-265.

26. Dr. Taylor's book contains a detailed account of the founding and early years of Vassar.

27. Taylor, p. 280.

28. The best account of Wellesley is that of Alice Payne Hackett, *Wellesley: Part of the American Story* (New York, 1949).

29. Wright, *Sweeper in the Sky,* pp. 181-182.

30. L. Clark Seelye, *Early History of Smith College* (Boston, 1923), p. 36.

31. *Last Will and Testament of Sophia Smith* (Northampton, 1871), pp. 10-11.

32. *Ibid.,* p. 9.

33. Frances E. W. Harper, "The Colored Woman of America," *Englishwoman's Review,* n.s. 57: 10 (January 15, 1878).

34. Anna J. Cooper, *A Voice from the South* (Xenia, O., 1892), pp. 75-79.

35. Atlanta University Studies, no. 5: *The College-Bred Negro (1900),* pp. 34-35, 53-57; no. 15: *The College-Bred American Negro (1910),* pp. 22-23, 49. In the later report, 107 "non-Negro colleges" reported a total of 114 Negro women graduates, the largest number (66) coming from Oberlin, and the next largest group from the University of Kansas. The Negro colleges, led by Howard and Fisk, had graduated 514 women by 1910.

36. Negro students to the present day continue to be a minority in the privately endowed colleges as contrasted with the larger number at state-supported institutions. Factors are inadequate preparation in segregated schools, lower costs, and a more democratic social climate.

37. Letter to the author from Howard University Law School.

38. Elizabeth H. Davis, *Lifting As They Climb* (National Association of Colored Women, 1933), pp. 294-295.

39. Sara W. Brown, "Colored Women Physicians," *Southern Workman,* 52: 584 (December, 1923).

40. Adah B. Thoms, *Pathfinders: A History of the Progress of Colored Graduate Nurses* (New York, 1929), ch. ii; see also Mary Ellen Chayer, "Mary E. Mahoney," *American Journal of Nursing,* 54: 429-431 (April, 1954).

CHAPTER IX

Women in the Trade Unions, 1860-1875

1. *Manufactures of the United States in 1860, Compiled from the Original Returns of the Eighth Census,* III, 742; *Twelfth Census of the United States (1900),* vol. VII: *Manufactures,* Part I, p. cxxvi, table XLIII A.

2. Quoted in John R. Commons et al., *Documentary History of American Industrial Society* (Cleveland, 1910-1911), IX, 72-73.

3. *Ibid.,* p. 138. See also Israel Kugler, "The Woman's Rights Movement and the National Labor Union, 1866-1872," Ph.D thesis, New York University, 1954. Perhaps no other aspect of the early woman's rights movement, with the exception of the Seneca Falls convention, has received more consideration than the presence of Mrs. Stanton, Miss Anthony, and several

other women as delegates at the National Labor Union convention in 1868. Actually this event had less significance than the organizing of women workers done by Augusta Lewis and Kate Mullaney.

4. Speech by Moses Beach at Twenty-Fifth Anniversary of the Working Women's Protective Union held in 1888, reprinted in *Report of the Working Women's Protective Union, 1863–1894* (New York, 1894), p. 8.

5. *The Revolution*, vol. II, no. 12, p. 181 (September 24, 1868).

6. *Ibid.*, p. 196.

7. G. A. Stevens, *New York Typographical Union No. 6: A Study of a Modern Trade Union and Its Predecessors* (Albany, 1913), p. 434n.

8. *The Revolution*, vol. II, no. 15, p. 231 (October 15, 1868).

9. *Ibid.*

10. Quoted in Stevens, p. 434.

11. Far more notice has been paid to the appointment of Kate Mullaney, leader of the Troy Collar and Laundry Workers union, as assistant secretary of the National Labor Union in 1868. However, there is no evidence that she ever carried out any duties in connection with this office.

12. President's Report, 19th Convention, International Typographers Union (1871), p. 12.

13. *Ibid.*

14. Quoted in Stevens, p. 437.

15. Andrews and Bliss, *History of Women in Trade Unions*, p. 91.

16. Abbott, *Women in Industry*, p. 236.

17. The story has been told in fictional form by Samuel Hopkins Adams in *Sunrise to Sunset* (New York, 1950).

18. From resolution quoted in *Troy Daily Whig*, June 19, 1869.

19. *Troy Daily Whig*, July 10, 1869 and August 5, 1869.

20. *Troy Times*, and *Daily Whig*, July 20, 1869.

21. *Troy Times*, August 2, 1869.

22. Andrews and Bliss, pp. 108–110.

23. *Ibid.*, p. 109.

24. Massachusetts Bureau of Statistics of Labor, *Third Annual Report*, pp. 434–436.

CHAPTER X

The Emergence of a Suffrage Movement

1. *The Revolution*, vol. III, no. 6, p. 88 (February 11, 1869).

2. Quoted in *Life and Writings of Frederick Douglass*, IV, 43.

3. *HWS*, II, 391–392.

4. *Ibid.*, p. 384.

5. Letters of William Lloyd Garrison II, to his father, May 13, 1867 and June 3, 1867, SSC.

6. *HWS*, II, 235.

7. *Ibid.*, p. 242.

8. Stanton, *Eighty Years and More*, pp. 248–249.

9. Carrie Chapman Catt and Nettie Rogers Shuler, *Woman Suffrage and Politics* (New York, 1923), p. 107. Subsequent quotations have been made by permission of the publisher, Charles Scribner's Sons.

10. Male white residents of the District of Columbia voted until 1874, when the territorial government of the District was abolished.

11. *Congressional Globe,* 39 Cong., 2nd Sess., Part I, p. 56.

12. *Ibid.,* p. 66.

13. *Ibid.,* p. 84. The House vote, on a similar measure on January 28, 1867, was 49 in favor to 74 opposed, with 68 abstaining. *Congressional Globe,* 39th Cong., 2nd Sess., Part II, p. 806.

14. *HWS,* II, 324–325, 333. Additional bills to enact woman suffrage in Territories (western lands not yet admitted to statehood, in this case Utah) and in the District, were proposed by Representative Julian, and Senator Henry Wilson of Massachusetts.

15. Just who was to certify suffrage groups as "legitimate" was never explicitly stated, but it was understood that the final decision rested with a Massachusetts group consisting of Mrs. Stone, Mr. Blackwell, Mrs. Howe, and Thomas Wentworth Higginson.

16. *Congressional Globe,* 41st Cong., 3d Sess., Part I, pp. 218, 272; also in *HWS,* II, 443–448.

CHAPTER XI

First Victories in the West

1. Georgia Willis Read, "Women and Children on the California-Oregon Trail in the Gold Rush," *Missouri Historical Review,* 39: 1–23 (October 1944).

2. *Diary of Mary Richardson Walker, June 10–December 21, 1838,* ed. Rufus A. Coleman, Sources of Northwest History, no. 13 (Missoula, Mont., 1931), pp. 8–9.

3. See George R. Stewart, *Ordeal by Hunger* (New York, 1936) for the most comprehensive account of the Donner party expedition.

4. Allan Nevins, *Emergence of the American Nation,* p. 377.

5. Nancy Ross, *Westward the Women* (New York, 1945). This is a vivid account of the pioneer women of the Pacific Northwest, with a bibliography of published journals and diaries.

6. Clifford Drury, *The Diary of Elkanah and Mary Walker, Pioneers Among the Spokanes* (Caldwell, Idaho, 1940), p. 187, ff. See also Ross, ch. iii.

7. Abigail Scott Duniway, *Pathbreaking: The Story of a Pioneer* (Portland, Ore., 1914), pp. 7–10. This autobiographical account is unfortunately poorly organized, but it remains a vivid firsthand account of Mrs. Duniway's active career. It is also highly biased on certain controversial points, and should be read in conjunction with the history of the suffrage movement in Oregon in *HWS,* VI, ch. xxxvi.

8. The most complete file of *The New Northwest* during the period Mrs. Duniway was its editor and publisher is in the Oregon Historical Society, Portland, Ore.; there is a microfilm in the SSC.

9. Anna Howard Shaw to Lucy Anthony, August 30, 1912, Shaw Papers, box 6, RWA. Dr. Shaw went to Oregon anyway!

10. Dr. Shaw, who knew Mrs. Morris, tells a story in her autobiography for which there appears to be no further verification: that Mrs. Morris helped a neighbor's wife during a difficult childbirth (as pioneer women often did) and that the grateful husband, a member of the Territorial Legislature, promised to introduce a woman suffrage bill, and did so. Shaw, *Story of a Pioneer,* p. 243.

11. The text of this historic bill read: "That every woman of the age of

twenty-one years, residing in the Territory, may, at every election to be holden [sic] under the laws thereof, cast her vote; and her rights to the elective franchise, and to hold office, shall be the same, under the elective laws of the Territory, as those of the electors." *HWS,* III, 727.

12. *HWS,* III, 739.

13. *Ibid.,* p. 731.

14. *Ibid.,* p. 734.

15. See E. W. Tullidge, *Women of Mormondom* (Salt Lake City, 1877); Susan Young Gates and Leah D. Widsoe, *Women of the Mormon Church* (Salt Lake City, 1926), and others.

16. Bernard de Voto, *Forays and Rebuttals* (Boston, 1936), p. 33; *Utah,* in the American Guide Series (New York, 1941), p. 66.

17. See Latter-Day Saints' *Millenial Star,* 32:102, 113–116, 130–134, 145–147, 163–165, and elsewhere (1870). *The Star* reprinted these articles from the *Deseret News.*

18. Leonard J. Arrington, "The Economic Role of Mormon Women," *Western Humanities Review* (Spring 1955); also the same author's *Great Basin Kingdom: An Economic History of the Latter-Day Saints, 1830–1900* (Cambridge, 1958).

19. Outside of Salt Lake City, the most extensive file of the *Woman's Exponent* is in the Widener Library at Harvard.

CHAPTER XII

Breaking Ground For Suffrage

1. E. R. Turner, *Woman Suffrage in New Jersey, 1790–1807,* Smith College Studies in History, I (1916), 165–187.

2. *The Revolution,* vol. II, no. 20, p. 307 (Nov. 19, 1868).

3. Negro women also went to the polls in 1870 in some South Carolina districts, encouraged by local Negro Reconstruction administration officials. See Benjamin Quarles, "Frederick Douglass and the Woman's Rights Movement," *Journal of Negro History,* 25: 35 (June 1940).

4. Catt and Shuler, *Woman Suffrage and Politics,* p. 92n.; *HWS,* II, 587–599. See also "Address Presented to Peter Hill by Nanette Gardner," *Woman's Journal,* vol. III, no. 51, p. 402 (December 21, 1872).

5. Another form of demonstration for woman suffrage should be noted — refusal to pay taxes. While this type of protest was never attempted by more than a few individuals, it aroused comment at the time. As early as 1858 Lucy Stone had her household goods sold because of her refusal to pay taxes (Blackwell, p. 195). Other tax-protestants were Abby Kelley Foster, Dr. Harriot K. Hunt, and best-known of all, the Smith sisters, Abby and Julia, of Glastonbury, Connecticut, whose repeatedly-sold cows became widely known. See Elizabeth G. Speare, "Abby, Julia and the Cows," *American Heritage,* vol. VIII, no. 4, pp. 54–57, 96 (July 1957).

6. Anthony, *Susan B. Anthony,* p. 281.

7. Mrs. Gage appears to have been the only one among Miss Anthony's friends and co-workers to have come actively to her aid at this time. The National did pass a resolution at its 1873 convention, condemning the proceedings as "a blow against the liberties of every citizen of this country" (*HWS,* II, 522n.), but they did little to implement it. The *Woman's Journal,* which spoke for the American, at first congratulated the ladies "on

their energy and success," but when they ran afoul of the law, dropped the issue except for a fair account of the trial from the pen of Mrs. Stone. She stressed that the women's work should be the creation of public sentiment in favor of woman suffrage. *Woman's Journal,* vol. IV, no. 26, p. 204 (June 28, 1873).

8. *Proceedings in the Trial of Susan B. Anthony* (Rochester, 1874), pp. 87–88.

9. Minor based his reasoning on Article I, Sections 2, 4 and 9; Article IV, Sections 2 and 4; Article VI; and the Fourteenth Amendment. The resolutions were first published in *The Revolution,* vol. IV, no. 17, p. 259 (October 28, 1869).

10. 21 Wallace 162.

11. In their brief the Minors pointed out that Chief Justice Taney, writing the famous decision in the Dred Scott case, distingushed between "the rights of citizenship which a State may confer within its own limits, and the rights of citizenship as a member of the Union." Taney was upholding the inability of any state to make a Negro, even a free Negro, a citizen; the Minors argued that by the same logic a state could not take away from a woman what she already had — her citizenship in the Federal Union. *HWS,* II, 726.

12. 16 Wallace 36

13. 110 U. S. 651 at 663–664, 665.

14. *HWS,* IV, 9.

15. *HWS,* III, 39.

16. *Ibid.,* pp. 31–33.

17. Blackwell, p. 253.

18. Catt and Shuler, p. 107.

19. Except for 1914–1915, when the so-called Shafroth-Palmer amendment was introduced as an alternative.

20. *HWS,* III, 93n.

21. *Congressional Record,* 49th Cong., 2nd Sess., vol. XVIII, Part 1, pp. 33–38.

22. *Ibid.,* pp. 980–1003. The question of suffrage for women had been debated twice previously in Congress: in 1866 in connection with the District of Columbia bill and in 1874, when the Pembina Territory (now part of North Dakota) was established.

23. *Ibid.,* p. 986.

24. *Ibid.,* p. 989.

25. Women voted in Washington Territory from 1883 to 1887, when the courts invalidated the law enfranchising them. The Territory was admitted to statehood in 1889 without woman suffrage.

26. National American Woman Suffrage Association, *Victory: How Women Won It — A Centennial Symposium, 1840–1940* (New York, 1940), p. 165.

27. Recognizing Kansas as the most liberal state in this respect, the National Association adopted the Kansas state flower, the sunflower, as its emblem, and it became a familiar sight during later suffrage campaigns.

28. *Congressional Record,* 51st Cong., 1st Sess., vol. XXI, Part 3, pp. 2663–2712.

29. My authority for this message is *HWS,* IV, 999–1000. There is no record of it in the Wyoming State Archives, which are incomplete for this period.

30. Here, too, the debate was anything but routine. Senator Morgan of Alabama rose to such heights as declaring that he would "leave a country where it is necessary for my wife and daughters to go to the polls to protect my liberties." *Congressional Record,* 51st Cong., 1st Sess., vol. XXI, Part 7, pp. 6574–6589.

CHAPTER XIII

The Growth of Women's Organizations

1. See Elizabeth M. Bacon, "The Growth of Household Conveniences in the United States from 1865 to 1900," Radcliffe Ph.D. thesis, 1942.

2. U. S. Dept. of Health, Education and Welfare, Office of Education, *Statistics of Higher Education, 1953–4* (Government Printing Office, 1956), ch. 4, sec. 1, p. 79.

3. U. S. Dept. of Labor, Women's Bureau, Bulletin no. 218, *Women's Occupations Through Seven Decades* (Government Printing Office, 1947) table IIA, p. 208.

4. See Jennie C. Croly, *History of the Woman's Club Movement in America* (New York, 1898) and Mary I. Wood, *History of the General Federation of Women's Clubs* (New York, 1912). In her introduction to the former, Mrs. Ellen M. Henrotin wrote: "The State Federations have in each case adopted, immediately on their formation, a special line of work, always educational in character, and embracing education from the kindergarten to the university, as represented in the state systems — public and traveling libraries, art interchanges, village and town improvement associations and constructive legislation." (p. x.)

5. See Ernest R. Groves, *The American Woman* (New York, 1944), pp. 258–264.

6. Mary Earhart in *Frances Willard: From Prayers to Politics* (Chicago, 1944) regards Miss Willard as the most important force in a rebirth of the suffrage movement after the ridicule and hostility into which the militancy of Mrs. Stanton and Miss Anthony had led it. She believes that it was Miss Willard who was mainly responsible for creating a national "woman's movement." Her biography is the only recent treatment by an author outside the W.C.T.U., of an important figure.

7. Frances E. Willard, *Home Protection Manual: Containing an Argument for the Temperance Ballot for Women* (Chicago, 1879). See this pamphlet for text of a Home Protection petition, p. 27. The slogans coined by Miss Willard might sound mawkish to already suffrage-conscious women, but they succeeded in endowing the issue of voting for women with an aura of respectability for the more backward, that not even the revered Lucretia Mott had achieved.

8. Catt and Shuler, pp. 300–302.

9. Fanny Barrier Williams, "The Colored Woman and Her Part in Race Regeneration," in *A New Negro for a New Century* (Chicago, 1900), p. 384.

10. Emma L. Field, "The Woman's Club Movement in the United States," Howard University M.A. thesis, 1948.

11. Mrs. E. C. Hobson, and Mrs. C. E. Hopkins, *Report Concerning the Colored Women of the South* (Slater Fund, Baltimore, 1896), pp. 6–7.

12. Fanny Barrier Williams, *The Present Status and Intellectual Progress of Colored Women* (Chicago, 1893), p. 8. Mrs. Williams gave it as her view

that the Negro woman in the South continued to need "protection," adding: "I do not wish to disturb the serenity of this conference by suggesting why this protection is needed and the kind of men against whom it is needed."

13. I am indebted for much new information, and corroboration of already known facts of the life of Mrs. Ida B. Wells-Barnett, to her daughter, Mrs. Alfreda Duster of Chicago, who allowed me to read the unpublished manuscript of Mrs. Barnett's autobiography.

14. A. S. Pride, *Register of Negro Newspapers in the United States, 1827–1950,* Northwestern University Ph.D. thesis, 1951, lists this publication with no copies known to be extant, a fate shared by innumerable other Negro papers.

15. *The Woman's Era,* vol. II, no. 319 (June 1895). A file of this publication is in the Rare Book Room of the Boston Public Library.

16. R. W. Logan, *The Negro in American Life and Thought: The Nadir, 1877–1901* (New York, 1954), p. 236.

17. Quoted in Davis, *Lifting As They Climb,* pp. 17–19.

18. *Woman's Era,* vol. III, no. 2: pp. 1–2. Clubs continued to join with the passage of time, and organized State Federations similar to those of the General Federation of Women's Clubs.

19. Mary Church Terrell, *A Colored Woman in a White World* (Washington, 1940). This is one of the few existing narratives of the lives of Negro women leaders. Negro women's archives have survived in only rare instances; it is fortunate that Mrs. Terrell's voluminous papers are preserved for further study in the Library of Congress.

20. Today the Association's program is somewhat more limited, and its leadership role is shared with other organizations, the majority of which are members of the National Council of Negro Women, founded by Mary McLeod Bethune in the era of the New Deal; the N.A.C.W. is not among its affiliates.

21. Logan, pp. 236–238.

22. See Ida Husted Harper's letter to Mary Church Terrell, March 18, 1919, in Terrell Papers, box 3, LC, and Mrs. Catt's report to the National Board of the National American Woman Suffrage Association, March 23, 1919 (ST), re admission to the National Association of the Northeastern Federation of Women's Clubs, a colored organization. Mrs. Harper wrote to Mrs. Terrell at Mrs. Catt's request, asking her to use her influence to persuade the Negro group to withdraw its application, in order not to jeopardize the final vote coming up in the Senate on the federal woman suffrage amendment when it looked as if the favorable margin was just one vote. Mrs. Catt told her board that in the event they wished to stand by the National's constitution, the colored group should be admitted, but that if they were, some of the southern state suffrage associations might withdraw from the National, and the suffrage amendment might lose the support of some southern Senators. (Minutes, Board of Directors meeting, March 23, 1919. ST.)

CHAPTER XIV

Women in the Knights of Labor and the Early A. F. of L.

1. U. S. Dept. of Labor, Women's Bureau Bulletin no. 225, *Handbook of Facts on Women Workers* (Government Printing Office, 1948), p. 1. The 1890 figures include almost 300,000 girls under 15 years of age.

2. Women's Bureau, Bulletin no. 218, *Women's Occupations Through Seven Decades*, pp. 208–223.

3. The best account of women in the Knights of Labor is in Andrews and Bliss, *History of Women in Trade Unions*, pp. 111–132. The organization did not limit its membership to wage earners, but took in housewives, professionals, small businessmen, and farmers.

4. Andrews and Bliss, p. 125.

5. Report of the General Investigator of Woman's Work and Wages, *Proceedings of the General Assembly of the Knights of Labor*, 1888, p. 15.

6. Andrews and Bliss, pp. 130–131.

7. *Proceedings of the Knights of Labor*, 1886, p. 163.

8. Frances Willard, *Glimpses of Fifty Years* (Chicago, 1892), p. 523.

9. *International Council of Women Report* (1886), pp. 155–156.

10. Andrews and Bliss, p. 116.

11. Report of the General Investigator of Woman's Work and Wages, *Proceedings of the Knights of Labor*, 1888, p. 14.

12. Leonora M. Barry to Terence V. Powderly, December 29, 1888, Powderly Papers, Catholic University.

13. Report of the General Investigator of Woman's Work and Wages, *Proceedings of the Knights of Labor*, 1888, p. 5.

14. *Ibid.*, p. 9.

15. *Ibid.*, pp. 9–10.

16. Report of General Instructor and Director of Woman's Work, *Proceedings of the Knights of Labor*, 1889, p. 2.

17. Mrs. Lake was a lecturer for the W.C.T.U. in the 1890's, and a speaker in the successful campaign for woman suffrage in Colorado in 1893.

18. Andrews and Bliss, pp. 155–196. For the organization of women in the A. F. of L. in this period, see also Alice Henry, *Women in the Labor Movement* (New York, 1923), pp. 51–56.

19. See Frances Howe, "Leonora O'Reilly, Socialist and Reformer," Radcliffe honors thesis, 1952. The O'Reilly Papers in the RWA are a largely untapped source of material on the history of women workers.

CHAPTER XV

The Reform Era and Woman's Rights

1. "Great American Millionaires," in the *Tribune Monthly*, vol. IV (June, 1892); reprinted in Sidney Ratner, *New Light on the Great American Fortunes: American Millionaires of 1892 and 1902* (New York, 1953), p. 91.

2. See Arthur Mann, *Yankee Reformers in the Urban Age* (Cambridge, 1954) for a study of the varied elements to be found in the social reform movement of 1880–1900, as it took shape in one area: Boston.

3. Certainly the new ferment did not touch all college girls, many of whom went through their four-year course with no consciousness of the stirrings in the world off campus. See Mary B. Gilson, *What's Past Is Prologue* (New York and London, 1940), pp. 10–19.

4. Grace H. Dodge, "The Association of Working Girls Societies," Report at the convention of Christian Workers in the United States and Canada, September 21–28, 1887, in Grace Dodge Scrapbooks, National Board of the Y.W.C.A., New York City. See also Abbie Graham, *Grace H. Dodge: Merchant of Dreams* (New York, 1926), chs. iv and v.

5. The most complete files, covering the years 1891 through 1894, are in the Labor Collection of the State Historical Society of Wisconsin, the Enoch Pratt Free Library in Baltimore, and the Brown University Library, with a microfilm at the SSC.

6. See articles by Grace H. Dodge in *Harper's Bazaar*, January 11 and 25, 1890; in the *Union Signal* (published by the W.C.T.U.), September 26, October 10 and 17, November 7 and 14, and December 5, 1890, in Grace Dodge Scrapbooks; also *Discussions of the Convention of the Association of Working Girls Held in New York City April 15, 16 and 17, 1890* (New York, 1890).

7. This fact is documented in the pages of *Far and Near*, in which occasional articles begin to crop up, with the passage of time, about settlement houses, labor unions, and the condition of women in industry, written by Vida Scudder, Katharine Coman, Mary Kenney, and Leonora O'Reilly.

8. Josephine Shaw Lowell to Mrs. Henry S. Russell, April 7, 1889, quoted in Rhinelander Stewart, *The Philanthropic Work of Josephine Shaw Lowell* (New York, 1911), p. 358.

9. Mrs. Lowell to her sister, May 19, 1889, *ibid.*, pp. 358–359.

10. *Ibid.*, p. 372. Collection of such statistics was most necessary, since only a few of the earliest state labor bureaus were beginning to attempt such work.

11. *Ibid.*, p. 344. One may disagree with this point of view, since the record shows that many such women were willing to act on their own behalf. Nevertheless these difficulties were present in organizing women then, and down to the present time, and are still especially true of the retail trades.

12. Maud Nathan, *The Story of an Epoch-Making Movement* (New York, 1926), pp. 1–14. The archives of the National Consumers League are in the Library of Congress, but they are scant for the earlier years of the organization.

13. *Ibid.*, pp. 26–28. Among the stores who made the list that first year (1891) were Altman's, Lord & Taylor's, and Arnold Constable. Best's made the list the following year.

14. The League's White Label on manufactured products was a guarantee that they had been produced in conformity with state factory and hour laws (however inadequate these were), not in sweatshops, and not by child labor. See Josephine Goldmark, *Impatient Crusader: Florence Kelley's Life Story* (Urbana, Ill., 1953), ch. v.

15. See the writings of Jane Addams, Lillian Wald, Vida D. Scudder, and others. Competent although by no means definitive biographies include James W. Linn, *Jane Addams* (New York and London, 1935); R. L. Duffus, *Lillian Wald, Neighbor and Crusader* (New York, 1938); and Howard E. Wilson, *Mary McDowell, Neighbor* (Chicago, 1928). Vida Scudder is discussed in some detail in Mann, *Yankee Reformers*, pp. 217–228; see also her *On Journey* (New York, 1937). The Lillian Wald papers cover the entire period of her activity, beginning with her earliest work on the East Side, and are in the New York Public Library. There is a large collection of Jane Addams papers in the Swarthmore College Peace Collection.

16. Lillian Wald, *The House on Henry Street* (New York, 1915), pp. 202–203.

17. The women whom Jane Addams drew around her at Hull House at different periods, comprised an astonishing galaxy. They included Florence Kelley (during the years she served as Chief Factory Inspector of Illinois — an

appointment of a woman by Governor Altgeld which was not duplicated until Governor Alfred E. Smith of New York appointed Frances Perkins to the same post thirty-five years later); Julia Lathrop, the first woman to serve on the Illinois State Board of Charities, who also became the first director of the Children's Bureau of the U. S. Dept. of Labor; Grace Abbott, who succeeded Miss Lathrop at the Children's Bureau; her sister Edith, the distinguished sociologist; Sophonisba Breckinridge, dean of the University of Chicago's pioneer School of Civics and Philanthropy; Dr. Alice Hamilton, pioneer in American industrial hygiene and medicine; Mary McDowell, first director of the University Settlement "behind the yards" in Chicago. It is not difficult to conclude that the existence and manifold activities of such a group was a real factor in speeding woman suffrage in Illinois. See, in addition to the titles listed above under no. 15, Jane Addams, *My Friend Julia Lathrop* (New York, 1935); Alice Hamilton, *Exploring the Dangerous Trades* (Boston, 1943); and E. A., "Grace Abbott at Hull House," *Social Service Review*, vol. 24, nos. 3 and 4, pp. 374–394, 495–518 (September and December 1950).

18. Mary Anderson, *Woman at Work* (Minneapolis and London, 1951), p. 32.

19. Mollie Daly to Mary McDowell, June 1, 1902, McDowell Papers, Chicago Historical Society.

20. The archives of the National Women's Trade Union League, going back to 1903, are in the Library of Congress.

21. Mrs. Kehew was associated with innumerable aspects of the woman's movement, and is an interesting figure. See Anne Livingston, "Mary Morton Kehew — An Appreciation," *Life and Labor*, vol. VII, no. 4, p. 83 (April 1918), and *Dictionary of American Biography*.

22. Women in Industry: Decision of the United States Supreme Court in *Curt Muller vs. State of Oregon*, and Brief for the State of Oregon by Louis D. Brandeis, published by the National Consumers League, New York City. See also Alfred Lief, ed., *The Social and Economic Views of Mr. Justice Brandeis* (New York, 1930), pp. 337–348.

CHAPTER XVI

The Unification of the Suffrage Movement

1. Shaw, *Story of a Pioneer*, p. 153.

2. Lucretia Mott died in 1880. During the last years of her life she had exerted her influence toward reconciling the two groups.

3. *HWS*, IV, 218–219.

4. Susan B. Anthony to Rachel Foster Avery, May 12, 1899, Anthony Papers, LC.

5. Catt and Shuler, *Woman Suffrage and Politics*, table on pp. 495–496.

6. Catt and Shuler, pp. 108–110.

7. Carrie Chapman Catt to Mary Gray Peck, December 15, 1910, ST.

8. Harper, *Life and Work of Susan B. Anthony*, II, 696.

9. *Ibid.*, ch. xliii. Nevertheless the vote in favor of suffrage was encouraging, having increased from one third of the total vote cast in 1867, to two fifths. The vote for the suffrage measure was 95,302, and against it 130,139.

10. *Ibid.*, II, 889.

11. *Ibid.*, II, 886–887.

CHAPTER XVII
Entering the Twentieth Century

1. Material on the legal position of women at this time, state by state, can be found in *HWS*, IV. See also Howard, *History of Matrimonial Institutions*, III.

2. *Women's Occupations Through Seven Decades*, table 3, p. 34. The figures show not only an absolute, but a proportional increase of women workers in the growth of the total labor force. These totals include "gainful workers 10 years of age and over;" the figure for women workers *over 14* for 1900 was 5,114,461, and for 1910 it was 7,788,826.

3. *Ibid.*, table IIA, pp. 208–223.

4. Bruce Bliven Jr., *The Wonderful Writing Machine* (New York, 1947), pp. 78–79.

5. *Women's Occupations Through Seven Decades*, table IIA, pp. 210–211.

6. Mary Putnam-Jacobi, *"Common-Sense" Applied to Woman Suffrage* (New York, 1894), pp. 17–18.

7. M. Carey Thomas, "A New-Fashioned Argument for Woman Suffrage," speech delivered to the National College League for Woman Suffrage, October 17, 1908.

8. Putnam-Jacobi, pp. 99, 180. Miss Thomas could also recall vividly "the awful doubt, felt by women themselves as well as by men, as to whether women as a sex were physically and mentally fit for (higher education) . . . I was terror-stricken lest I, and every other woman with me, were doomed to live as pathological invalids in a universe merciless to woman as a sex." "Present Tendencies in Women's College and University Education," *Publications of the Association of Collegiate Alumnae*, series III, no. 17, pp. 45–46 (February 1908).

9. Office of Education, *Statistics of Higher Education, 1953–1954*, table 1, p. 79.

10. Thomas, p. 47.

11. Mary E. Howard, "It Happened Seventy-Five Years Ago," *Radcliffe Quarterly*, November 1954. President Eliot gave his permission, and Mr. Gilman's efforts in organizing the new enterprise were shortly aided by a Committee of Ladies, among them Mrs. Elizabeth Agassiz, wife of the eminent naturalist, and Miss Alice Longfellow, daughter of the poet.

12. *Acts and Resolves of the General Court of Massachusetts, 1894*, ch. 166, pp. 141–142.

13. See Edith Finch's excellent biography, *Carey Thomas of Bryn Mawr* (New York and London, 1947); Cornelia Meigs, *What Makes a College?* (New York, 1956).

14. A vital and compelling personality who aroused antagonism by her impatience and self-assurance, Miss Thomas was known to some suffragists as "Her Holy Smokes." Letter from C. C. Catt to M. G. Peck, January 29, 1911, ST.

15. Thomas, "A New-Fashioned Argument for Woman Suffrage."

16. Mary Gray Peck, *Carrie Chapman Catt* (New York, 1944) is a warm and detailed account by a devoted admirer who was also Mrs. Catt's close friend for almost forty years. Because Miss Peck herself took part in some suffrage campaigns, her book catches the spirit of that great effort as few

others do. However it lacks the background and scope that a biography of Mrs. Catt now requires, and draws for documentation mostly on the letters the author received from Mrs. Catt, now in the possession of Mrs. Stantial. This correspondence is very nearly unique, for continuity and frankness, in suffrage annals.

17. At the time of their marriage the Catts made a pact (reminiscent of earlier couples): Mrs. Catt was to have at least two months each fall and again in the spring, for suffrage work. Needless to say this time limit soon disappeared.

18. See Catt letters for this period in the McCulloch and Harrison papers, and others, RWA.

19. C. C. Catt to Ella Harrison, April 10, 1896, RWA.

20. Shaw, *Story of a Pioneer*, pp. 141–142.

21. The excerpted letters in the RWA of Dr. Shaw to Lucy Anthony (Susan B.'s niece), who was her friend and secretary for a quarter of a century, give some idea of the magnitude of her endless journeys, and the burden of constant speech-making.

22. With the exception of Eliza Eddy's bequest of some fifty thousand dollars to Lucy Stone and Susan Anthony in the 1880's, which made possible, among other things, the publication of the earlier volumes of the *History of Woman Suffrage*, this was the first money gift of any size to the suffrage cause. The promise made by Miss Thomas and Miss Garrett was faithfully kept, and provided Miss Shaw with a modest livelihood until 1911. Thereafter, other gifts enabled her to continue giving her full time to woman suffrage.

CHAPTER XVIII

Into the Mainstream of Organized Labor

1. The Triangle Fire on March 25, 1911, in a loft building where New York University now stands, took the lives of 146 girl shirtwaist operatives; many died when they jumped out of windows from the eighth, ninth, and tenth floors, their clothing ablaze, because the stairway exits were barred. (One charge made against the company was that this had been done to prevent workers from stealing the merchandise; another, to keep the workers from leaving their machines in a sudden strike.) The employers were tried and acquitted; one partner was subsequently fined $20. See Martha Bruere, "The Triangle Fire," *Life and Labor*, I, no. 5: 137–141 (May, 1911); Tom Brooks, "The Terrible Triangle Fire," *American Heritage*, vol. VII, no. 5, pp. 54–57, 110–111 (August 1957); Hope A. Rockefeller, "The Triangle Fire, 1911: The Impact of a Disaster in an Era of Reform," Smith College honors thesis, 1959.

2. Described to the author by Clara Lemlich Leiserson. An account of conditions in trades employing women appears in Elizabeth Butler, *Women and the Trades*, vol. I of the Pittsburgh Survey by the Russell Sage Foundation (New York, 1909).

3. Louis Levine, *The Women's Garment Workers Union: A History of the International Ladies Garment Workers Union* (New York, 1924), ch. xxi. See also William Mailly, "The Working Girls' Strike," *Independent*, vol. LXVII, no. 3186, pp. 1416–1430 (December 23, 1909).

4. Levine, p. 154 (quoted from *New York World*, Nov. 23, 1909). The speaker was talking in Yiddish.

5. The New York State Department of Labor estimated there were 15,000

strikers in New York, of whom 11,000 were women. Mailly uses the figure 30,000; Levine and the union say 20,000.

6. Levine, p. 159.

7. Mabel Hurd Willett, *The Employment of Women in the Clothing Trade,* Columbia University Studies in History, Economics and Public Law, vol. XVI, no. 2 (1902) deals largely with conditions in the New York shops at an earlier date; union organization in the Chicago trade took place during and after the strike. Her account stresses legal protection for health and safety on the books of relatively advanced states such as New York, and passes over the problem of enforcement, and the actual conditions under which many women had to work.

8. Mary Dreier, *Margaret Dreier Robins* (New York, 1905), p. 75. Anderson, *Woman at Work,* p. 41. Miss Anderson was active in the strike, and subsequently served as representative of the Chicago Women's Trade Union League in helping to administer the Hart, Schaffner, and Marx agreement, which was the major outcome of the struggle.

9. First Constitution of the Women's Trade Union League, 1903. For accounts of the League's history, see: Gladys Boone, *The Women's Trade Union Leagues in Great Britain and the United States,* Columbia University Studies in History, Economics and Public Law, vol. 489 (1942); Dreier, *Margaret Dreier Robins;* and U. S. Dept. of Labor, Women's Bureau Bulletin no. 252, *Toward Better Working Conditions for Women — Methods and Policies of the National Women's Trade Union League* (Government Printing Office, 1953).

10. Leo Wolman, *The Growth of Trade Unions, 1880–1923* (New York, 1924), pp. 98–99.

11. Paul Brissenden, *Earnings of Factory Workers, 1899–1927* (U. S. Dept. of Commerce, Bureau of the Census, monograph X, Washington, 1929) estimates annual per capita earnings of women workers in 1899 at $267, compared to $498 for men. By 1904, this figure rose very little for women, to $289, whereas earnings for men had increased to $540. The gap had increased even further by 1909: $339 for women, $631 for men workers, and has continued down to the present. (See table 40, p. 103). Brissenden states that the differences in earnings "are often attributable less to the sex factor than to degree of skill"; he overlooks the fact that women, largely because of their sex, were, and are often still, denied the opportunity for on-the-job training, or for promotion, which would either enable them to acquire additional skills, or put such skills to use.

CHAPTER XIX

The Suffrage Movement Comes of Age, 1906–1913

1 See McCulloch papers, RWA.

2. *Proceedings,* National American Woman Suffrage Association Convention, 1908 (Warren, Ohio), p. 29.

3. Mrs. Blatch's initial service to woman suffrage had been when she insisted that a chapter on the history of the American Woman Suffrage Association be included in the *History of Woman Suffrage* being compiled by the leaders of the National Association. Although she was only four years out of Vassar College, Mrs. Stanton and Miss Anthony turned the job over to her; its inclusion in volume IV of the *History* (pp. 406–433) averted a slight that

would have made the eventual merger of the two organizations even more difficult than it was.

4. Harriot Stanton Blatch and Alma Lutz, *Challenging Years: The Memoirs of Harriot Stanton Blatch* (New York, 1940), p. 92. Quoted by permission of the publisher, G. P. Putnam's Sons. This depressing picture is born out by the reports delivered at N.A.W.S.A. conventions by state leaders from all over the country, or by a record such as that of the Oswego Political Society (in the collection of Mrs. Arthur Holden, New York City) which details, down to the unfailing tea and cookies, the routine reading of papers and other proceedings of such small groups, pursued month after month, year after year.

5. Blatch and Lutz, p. 93.

6. Ray Strachey, *The Cause* (London, 1928) is a balanced account of the suffrage movement in Great Britain, in the context of the broad movement for woman's rights, which weighs the contributions made by both the "militant" and the "constitutional" groups to eventual success.

7. Blatch and Lutz, pp. 93–94.

8. *Two Speeches by Self-Supporting Women* (published by the League of Self-Supporting Women, 1907), Blatch papers, LC.

9. Blatch and Lutz, pp. 131–132.

10. See Woman's Rights Collection at Radcliffe, especially files on Susan Fitzgerald and Florence Luscomb; Cullen Scrapbooks for 1908–1909, SSC; annual *Proceedings,* N.A.W.S.A. conventions.

11. Mrs. Blatch and Mrs. Catt clashed: Mrs. Blatch complained that Mrs. Catt was autocratic; Mrs. Catt occasionally tried to bring about cooperation between the Women's Political Union and the other New York suffrage groups, with no success. See Blatch and Lutz, pp. 207–208, and letter from C.C. Catt to Mary Gray Peck, Feb. 5, 1911, ST. Mrs. Blatch eventually joined the Congressional Union.

12. College Equal Suffrage League of Northern California, *Winning Equal Suffrage in California* (1913), p. 63.

13. Letter from Clara Schlinghyde to C. C. Catt, Nov. 11, 1911, ST.

14. Letters from C. C. Catt to M. G. Peck, December 13, 1911, and Nov. 23, 1912, ST.

15. Wage Earners' Suffrage League of New York, "Senators versus Working Women," speech by Rose Schneiderman, March 20, 1912, p. 5.

16. *Baltimore American,* April 5, 1912. The reporter was in error; there were still only six suffrage states.

17. Catt and Shuler, pp. 180-181.

18. *Ibid.,* p. 185.

19. The bill giving Alaska formal territorial status, which was passed by Congress August 24, 1912, contained a clause empowering the newly established Legislature to enfranchise women, *Statutes at Large,* vol. XXXVII, part I (Washington, 1913), 62 Cong., 2 Sess., ch. 387, sec. 9, p. 515. No demand for woman suffrage existed in the area, but the National Suffrage Association sent literature to the legislators, and the woman suffrage bill was the first act of the Alaska Legislature. It passed unanimously, with only one absent, and was signed by the Governor on March 21, 1913. Since a territory sent only a nonvoting delegate to Congress, and had no presidential electors, the step did not materially affect the progress of woman suffrage elsewhere.

20. Grace Wilbur Trout, "Sidelights on Illinois Woman Suffrage History,"

Illinois State Historical Society Journal, vol. XIII, no. 2, pp. 145–179 (July, 1920).

CHAPTER XX
New Life in the Federal Amendment, 1914–1916

1. Catt and Shuler, pp. 495–496.
2. *Baltimore American*, March 4, 1913.
3. *Baltimore Sun*, March 4, 1913.
4. *Proceedings*, N.A.W.S.A. 1913 Convention (New York): financial reports of Congressional Committee and Congressional Union, pp. 66–70. Over $25,000 was raised — and spent — in less than twelve months.
5. Inez Haynes Irwin, *The Story of the Woman's Party* (New York, 1921) and Doris Stevens, *Jailed for Freedom* (New York, 1920). These books give no details of the breach, nor is it documented in the otherwise comprehensive papers of the Woman's Party from 1913 to 1920 on deposit at the Library of Congress. There is documentation for the National's position in an undated headquarters letter from Anna Howard Shaw, then president of the N.A.W.S.A., to state auxiliaries, apparently sent in January 1914 (a copy is in the Radcliffe Women's Archives), and in an extensive typewritten memorandum, undated and unsigned, but apparently meant for the members of the National Board, which covers the progress of discussions between Board representatives with Miss Paul and Miss Burns, in the N.A.W.S.A. papers in the Stantial collection.
6. This was the position of Senator William E. Borah of Idaho, who, although representing a state which gave women the vote back in 1896, consistently opposed the federal suffrage amendment, down to and including the last Senate vote in 1919.
7. Speech by Alice Paul at Newport, Rhode Island, on August 29, 1914, reprinted in *The Suffragist*, September 12, 1914.
8. In both cases the leaders of the National bewailed bringing the measure to a vote as ill-advised, since they felt defeat was inevitable; all things considered, however, it made a surprisingly good showing. It must always be borne in mind that a two-thirds majority in both houses is required to pass a constitutional amendment.
9. The National cooperated in these demonstrations, one example of the efforts made by both groups at first to work together on a limited scale.
10. "There is no doubt but that the Congressional Union has pushed the Federal Amendment to the front, no matter what anybody says about it." C. C. Catt to presidents of state suffrage associations in suffrage states, January 12, 1916. Copy in the Woman's Party papers, LC.
11. Leaders of the opposition were reported by suffragists to have claimed that the defeat of the bill was a sure thing, once the vote was fixed for Registration Day. *HWS*, VI, 425.
12. "Eminent Catholic Prelates Oppose Woman Suffrage," and "Some Catholic Views on Woman Suffrage" — leaflets in SSC. See also Lois B. Merk, "Boston's Historic Public School Crisis," *New England Quarterly*, 31: 172–199 (June 1958) for some of the basis of Catholic opposition to woman suffrage in Massachusetts.
13. A vivid first-hand account of the New York 1915 campaign occurs in Peck, *Carrie Chapman Catt*, pp. 221–234; Miss Peck worked in the speakers'

bureau at suffrage headquarters. Also *HWS*, VI, 459–475. For a description of the early stages of the Pennsylvania campaign, a year before the referendum took place, see Jennie B. Roessing, "The Equal Suffrage Campaign in Pennsylvania," *Annals of the Academy of Political Science*, vol. LVI, no. 145, pp. 153–160 (November 1914).

14. C. C. Catt to M. G. Peck, June 8, 1912, ST.

15. See Rose Young, *The Record of the Leslie Woman Suffrage Commission (1917–1929)* (New York, 1929).

16. C. C. Catt to M. G. Peck, December 30, 1915 and January 10, 1916, ST.

17. Anna Howard Shaw to Lucy Anthony, June 1916, RWA.

18. C. C. Catt, Report of Survey Committee to Board of Officers, March 1916, ST.

CHAPTER XXI

The Turn in the Tide

1. *The Suffragist*, June 24, 1917.

2. Mr. Hughes came out personally for the federal suffrage amendment in July. Politicians were astute enough to realize the truth of Mrs. Frank M. Roessing's statement to the Republican Platform Committee that, in the four eastern states which had defeated woman suffrage the previous November, nevertheless more votes had been cast for woman suffrage than had been cast for William Howard Taft, Republican presidential candidate in 1912. (*Chicago Examiner*, June 8, 1912.)

3. *The Suffragist*, September 30, 1916.

4. *The Suffragist*, November 11, 1916.

5. A states rights' rider was the work of Senator Borah of Idaho.

6. *New York Times*, June 17, 1916.

7. Ray Stannard Baker and William E. Dodd, eds. *The Public Papers of Woodrow Wilson: The New Democracy* (New York and London, 1925–1927), II, 300.

8. Wilson re-wrote statements following suggestions from Mrs. Catt, helped to secure an Administration spokesman for the National's convention in 1917 (Secretary of the Interior Lane), and never refused to see a National representative or delegation; needless to say, both Mrs. Catt and Mrs. Gardener were discreet in their demands on him. See Helen H. Gardener Papers, Woman's Rights Collection at Radcliffe.

9. Maud Wood Park, "Front Door Lobby," manuscript written in 1936–1937, telling the story of the National's Congressional Committee's lobbying from 1916 to 1919. Copy in Stantial papers.

10. The two officers on whom Mrs. Catt leaned most heavily during her first year as President, Mrs. Roessing and Miss Patterson, both resigned their posts for personal reasons at this convention.

11. C. C. Catt, Report of Survey Committee to National Board; this report was actually delivered at a joint meeting of the Board and the heads of all the state suffrage associations. The pages of Mrs. Catt's copy, in the Stantial papers, are deeply marked with crayoned underlinings, to drive home her points.

12. *Ibid.*

13. Like so many of the National's archives, there is no trace of this document.

14. On December 4, 1916, on the occasion of the President's address to the opening of the final session of the 64th Congress, five members of the Congressional Union let down a banner from the gallery carrying the first of these slogans. Pages tore it down, while the President went on speaking, and the women were not molested.

15. *Woman's Journal*, vol. 48, no. 14, p. 79 (April 4, 1917).

16. *The Suffragist*, March 3, 1918. It is impossible to level a blanket charge of opposition to woman suffrage against the District Commissioners. The Chief Commissioner, Louis Brownlow, was in favor of it; his son-in-law, Representative Sims of Tennessee, was to make suffrage history on the floor of the House.

17. It is difficult to locate the break in the chain of command which permitted such conditions in the prisons to continue so long after they were known by the President. See Wilson's memo to his secretary, Joseph P. Tumulty, in Ray Stannard Baker, *Woodrow Wilson; Life and Letters* (Garden City, N. Y., 1927–1939), VII, 321, 362.

18. The Woman's Party held that an interview secured by the journalist David Lawrence with Miss Paul while the latter was still in prison paved the way for the releases, since Mr. Lawrence was thought to be close to Administration circles. One account has Mr. Lawrence telling Miss Paul that the Administration was prepared to support the suffrage amendment in Congress, and asking whether the Woman's Party would be satisfied — and call off the pickets — if there were action in one House during the present session of Congress and in the other House during the next session. (Irwin, *The Story of the Woman's Party*, pp. 254–255.) In a letter to the author (May 15, 1956), Mr. Lawrence has denied this version of the interview. His published story of the interview appeared in the *New York Post* over his by-line, November 29, 1917.

19. One of the National's leaders, Mrs. Norman deR. Whitehouse of New York, did protest directly to Wilson. Baker, VII, 362.

20. U. S. Dept. of Labor, Women's Bureau Bulletin no. 12, *The New Position of Women in American Industry* (Government Printing Office, 1920), pp. 137–148.

21. Welfare leaders and women trade unionists had long urged establishment of such an agency. The A. F. of L., however, took little interest in the new Bureau; it did not support its founding, nor oppose early attempts to discontinue it. See Anderson, *Woman at Work*, pp. 92–93, and the National Women's Trade Union League Papers, box 27, LC.

22. C. C. Catt to Board of Directors, November 14, 1918. ST.

23. *Woman Citizen*, September 22, 1917, p. 306.

24. *HWS*, V, 542.

25. Jessie J. Hooper to Theodora M. Youmans, June 31, 1918, WHS.

CHAPTER XXII
Who Opposed Woman Suffrage?

1. Catt and Shuler, *Woman Suffrage and Politics*, chapters x, xiv, xv, and xviii: pp. 270–278. Also *HWS*, V, 678–682.

2. I am indebted for material on the anti-suffrage movement in Massachusetts to those sections of Mrs. Lois Bannister Merk's Ph.D. Thesis, "Massa-

chusetts and the Woman Suffrage Movement," Radcliffe, 1956, which have been made available through the Women's Archives at Radcliffe.

3. Mrs. Maud Park, among others, attributed her first interest in woman suffrage to her presence by invitation at an "anti" parlor meeting.

4. Catt and Shuler, p. 276.

5. *Brewing and Liquor Interests, and German and Bolshevik Propaganda*, Report and Hearings of the Subcommittee on the Judiciary, United States Senate, 65th Cong., 1st Sess. vol. I, p. 1032.

6. *Ibid.*, p. 1170.

7. *Ibid.*, p. 1179.

8. *Ibid.*, p. 1015–1016. The Iowa referendum was lost.

9. "Autobiography of Jessie Jack Hooper," p. 11: WHS.

10. C. C. Catt to state suffrage association presidents, May 14, 1918, WHS.

11. *A Message from His Eminence James Cardinal Gibbons*, issued by the National Association Opposed to Woman Suffrage, SSC. While the opposition of leading Catholic churchmen arose from concepts which were basic to the church's tenets, they were also probably reinforced by the increasing attention attracted by the question of birth control, due to the efforts of Mrs. Margaret Sanger. Mrs. Sanger returned from abroad in October 1915 and at once launched into a campaign to legalize the dissemination of information about birth control through medical channels. See Lawrence Lader, *The Margaret Sanger Story and the Fight for Birth Control* (New York, 1955), and Margaret Sanger, *My Fight for Birth Control* (New York, 1931) and *An Autobiography* (New York, 1938).

12. C. C. Catt to Anna Howard Shaw, March 16, 1916, ST.

13. *Government Control of the Meat-Packing Industry*, Hearings on S.5305 Before the Committee on Agriculture and Forestry, U. S. Senate, 65 Cong., 3d Sess., Part 2, pp. 1750–1752 (testimony of Mr. Henry Veeder, counsel for Swift & Co., February 8, 1919).

14. *HWS*, VI, 875.

15. Marjorie Shuler to C. C. Catt, October 19, 1918, SSC.

16. *New Republic*, vol. IV, no. 42, pp. 62–64 (August 21, 1915).

17. *Brewing and Liquor Interests*, pp. 2541–2544, 2550–2552, 2574–2578, 2604. Mr. Swenson was at this time not only a partner of Swenson & Co., but a director of the National City Bank of New York; from 1921 to 1929 he served as chairman of the Board of the National City Bank. At the time of his death in 1945, the *New York Times* obituary described him as "a retiring man who was seldom mentioned in the newspapers," and listed among his directorships in addition to the National City Bank, the Southern Pacific Railroad, Pacific Oil Company, and Pacific Mail Steamship Company.

18. *Woman's Journal*, vol. 47, no. 3, p. 17 (January 15, 1916).

19. The Boston and Maine Railroad divided its energies between, among other matters, opposition to woman suffrage and to adoption of the initiative and referendum. See New Hampshire Public Service Commission Reports, vol. 5: "Investigation . . . on April 21, 1915, of payments made by the railroads with a view to influencing legislation in New Hampshire," pp. 377–379.

20. Maud Wood Park, "The Front Door Lobby," ch. xii, ST.

21. *The Vanguard*, I, no. 1 (1916) published by the National Council of Women Voters, Tacoma, Washington. In League of Women Voters Papers and Correspondence, box 3, LC.

22. See as an example, *Woman Suffrage: History, Arguments and Results*, published by the N.A.W.S.A. (New York, 1913). Strenuous efforts were also made to link woman suffrage with socialism, by publicizing the participation of Socialist groups in suffrage parades and Socialist speakers' appearances on suffrage platforms.

23. *National Cyclopedia of American Biography*, XXI, 408.

24. Park, ch. xii.

25. *Congressional Record*, 66th Cong., 1st Sess., vol. 58, Part I, p. 619.

26. *Ibid.*, p. 563. The senator was in error when he referred to the "Eighteenth" as the woman suffrage amendment. The Eighteenth was the Prohibition Amendment, which was passed by Congress in December 1917 and ratified in January 1919. (It was repealed by the Twenty-first Amendment in 1933.)

27. *Woman Citizen*, July 6, 1918, p. 106.

28. Park, ch. xiv.

CHAPTER XXIII

A Hard-Won Victory, 1918–1920

1. The Woman's Party continued to insist that the major opposition came from the Democratic Party. Nevertheless those senators who wished to force the issue to a vote were blocked by a Democratic filibuster, for which the responsibility was shared by Republican leaders such as Senators Lodge, Borah, and Weeks, to name only a few.

2. See Baker, *Woodrow Wilson; Life and Letters*, vol. VIII, for examples of Wilson's efforts, by letter and interview, to gain needed votes in the Senate.

3. *Ibid.*, p. 427n.

4. William G. McAdoo, *Crowded Years* (Boston, 1931), p. 498.

5. See Catherine L. Cleverdon, *The Woman Suffrage Movement in Canada* (Toronto, 1950).

6. The suffrage secured by British women at this time was limited to householders, wives of householders, and women of thirty and over. This meant enfranchising less than six million out of a possible eleven million adult females. Full equalization of the franchise in Great Britain did not take place until 1928. See Strachey, *The Cause*, chapter xix, and pp. 383–384.

7. Anna Howard Shaw to Lucy Anthony, September 28, 1918, Shaw Papers, RWA.

8. *Public Papers of Woodrow Wilson: War and Peace*, I, 263–267.

9. McAdoo, p. 498.

10. *Congressional Record*, 65th Cong., 2nd Sess., vol. 56, Part 2, p. 10774.

11. *Woman Citizen*, October 26, 1918, p. 429.

12. At peak, there were some two hundred organizers on the National payroll, mostly younger women whose resourcefulness and judgment had been trained, first in the organizers' schools established by Mrs. Catt, and then in a succession of campaigns. They were paid on a carefully worked out scale, and received a month's vacation, usually during the winter holiday season: "This work is the most wearing that can possibly be put on young women, and consequently we give them more vacation than is usual in other occupations." (C. C. Catt to Theodora Youmans, October 4, 1918, WHS.) The Woman's Party organizers were fewer in number, and they were not put through any formal training. The hallmark of both groups was unflagging energy and devotion to their work. The work of these organizers is described in widely

scattered suffrage archives in state historical society records, in the correspondence of women like Marjorie Shuler and Eleanor Garrison in the SSC, and in the Woman's Party papers, LC.

13. C. C. Catt to Board of Directors, November 14, 1918, ST.

14. *Ibid.*

15. In Mrs. Frank J. Shuler of Rochester, N. Y., Mrs. Catt found a successor to Mrs. Roessing as an organizer and second-in-command in the field. Later she was co-author, with Mrs. Catt, of the best short history of the suffrage movement to date. Her daughter Marjorie was one of Mrs. Catt's most trusted younger aides.

16. See *HWS*, VI, 529–535, and Catt and Shuler, pp. 305–313.

17. The fate of the amendment to abolish child labor is an example. It passed both houses of Congress, with a speed which made the progress of the suffrage measure seem glacier-like, by ample margins in 1924, only to have its ratification blocked within a year. Said the *New Republic:* "For the present, the tide is running irresistibly against any proposed progressive legislation which the business interests now in control of American politics have any sufficient interest in defeating." *New Republic,* vol. XLII, no. 546, pp. 330–331 (May 20, 1925).

18. It required unanimous consent to bring up the suffrage bill again, and for weeks Senators Wadsworth and Weeks (both Republicans) spelled one another, so that one of them was always on the Senate floor to block action.

19. *New York Tribune,* February 11, 1919.

20. *Woman Citizen,* April 5, 1919, p. 942.

21. *Public Papers of Woodrow Wilson: War and Peace,* I, 494.

22. The practice of pairing — matching votes of absentees who wished to have their position recorded — required, when a constitutional amendment was being voted on, that two "pairs" in favor be secured to offset every "pair" in opposition, so as to secure the necessary two-thirds majority required for passage.

23. Park, "Front Door Lobby," ch. xviii.

24. Theodora Youmans to Sara Van Dusen, June 13, 1919, *WHS.*

25. Mrs. Catt's correspondence with suffrage leaders in the lagging states makes pithy reading, and is fortunately among the National's headquarters material which has been preserved. See C. C. Catt Papers, NYPL.

26. C. C. Catt to Board of Directors, November 14, 1918, ST.

27. C. C. Catt to Marjorie Shuler, July 1, 1919, SSC.

28. *Ibid.*

29. Catt and Shuler, pp. 404–405. Governor Clement of Vermont was a businessman, whose interests were centered in the building and management of railroads, as well as newspapers and hotels.

30. *Public Papers of Woodrow Wilson: War and Peace,* II, 497. Wilson had been inactive for several months, following the stroke which he suffered on October 2, 1919, while on his western speaking trip on behalf of the Versailles Treaty and the League of Nations. Later, as he began to convalesce, he urged action for ratification on the governors of southern states, as well as those of West Virginia, Delaware, and Tennessee.

31. *New York Times,* August 9, 1920. See A. Elizabeth Taylor, *The Woman Suffrage Movement in Tennessee* (New York, 1957).

32. Catt and Shuler, p. 442.

33. C. C. Catt to M. G. Peck, August 15, 1920. See also Taylor, pp. 110–114.

34. *Baltimore Sun,* September 5, 1920, which also contained a story on the Burn family. Mrs. Burn deserves to be better known. According to the *Sun* reporter, she did her own housework and dairy work, and read several daily papers and other publications. When the wife of the former governor of Louisiana came to urge her to get her son to reconsider his vote, Mrs. Burn put her to rout!

35. *Baltimore Sun,* August 22, 1920. Many of these legislators left their hotels in the middle of the night.

36. There were belated ratifications by the legislatures of Connecticut and Vermont, but to the women of ten states, Mrs. Catt and Mrs. Shuler wrote, even this pride was denied: "One of the ten was Delaware, the only one north of the Mason-Dixon line. The other nine were Virginia, Maryland, North Carolina, South Carolina, Georgia, Alabama, Louisiana, Mississippi, and Florida." Catt and Shuler, p. 463.

CHAPTER XXIV

Conclusion

1. George Gallup, Director, American Institute of Public Opinion, press release, "Analysis of '56 Vote by Groups," no. 3, January 20, 1957.

2. See Valborg Fletty, *Public Services of Women's Organizations* (Chi Omega Service Fund Publication, 1951).

3. C. C. Catt, "Political Parties and Women Voters," Address at first Congress, League of Women Voters, Chicago, February 14, 1920.

4. See Eleanor Roosevelt and Lorena B. Hickok, *Ladies of Courage* (New York, 1954) and Marion K. Sanders, *The Lady and the Vote* (Boston, 1956). Both books argue that there is no short cut for women in politics that can by-pass the neighborhood party organization. Both emphasize the difficulties of the game, but insist that it is well worth the candle!

5. See National Manpower Council, *Work in The Lives of Married Women* (New York, 1958).

6. National Manpower Council, *Womanpower* (New York, 1957), p. 124.

7. Virginia C. Gildersleeve, *Many A Good Crusade* (New York, 1954), p. 108.

8. See Max Lerner, *America As A Civilization* (New York, 1957), p. 603; Bernice Fitz-Gibbon, "Tips For Would-Be Women Bosses," *New York Times Magazine,* September 23, 1956.

9. *Womanpower,* p. 110.

10. U. S. Dept. of Commerce, Bureau of the Census, *Current Population Reports: Consumer Income,* series P-60, no. 27 (Washington, April, 1958), table 27, p. 46.

11. To date, equal-pay legislation is on the statute books in Alaska, Arkansas, California, Colorado, Connecticut, Illinois, Maine, Massachusetts, Michigan, Montana, New Hampshire, New Jersey, New York, Oregon, Pennsylvania, Rhode Island, and Washington, but the coverage afforded varies widely from state to state. See Digest of State Equal Pay Laws (Revised as of December 1, 1957), Women's Bureau, U. S. Dept. of Labor.

12. Information and figures from letters to the author from union sources, and from Directory of National and International Labor Unions in the

U. S., 1957, U. S. Dept. of Labor, Bureau of Labor Statistics (Government Printing Office, 1957), pp. 11, 56–57.

13. Bureau of the Census, *Current Population Reports,* series P-60, no. 9, table 17, p. 33.

14. Bureau of the Census, *Current Population Reports,* series P-60, no. 27, table 28, p. 47.

15. U. S. Dept. of Commerce, Bureau of the Census, 1950 Census of Population, vol. II: *Characteristics of the Population,* Part I: United States Summary, table 159, pp. 399, 402.

16. See Henry Steele Commager, *The American Mind* (New Haven, 1950), pp. 23, 424.

17. The literature covering this area is vast and highly controversial. Among the more balanced discussions are Kate Hevner Mueller, *Educating Women for a Modern World* (Minneapolis, 1954), and Sidonie M. Gruenberg and Hilda S. Krech, *The Many Lives of Modern Woman* (Garden City, 1952). See also Lerner, pp. 599–611, and Miriam U. Chrisman, "The Changing Role of Women in an Industrial Society, with Emphasis on the Development of Their Higher Education," M.A. thesis, Smith College, 1955, pp. 226–230 and throughout; the latter has a comprehensive and up-to-date bibliography.

INDEX

Eleanor Flexner

Eleanor Flexner was born in New York City in 1908. She was graduated from Swarthmore College and studied at Somerville College, Oxford. Her first book, *American Playwrights, 1918–38: The Theatre Retreats from Reality* (1939) resulted from experience with the theatre during the depression. Trade-union membership and an interest in the problems of working women led to *Century of Struggle* (1959). Miss Flexner has contributed to the Radcliffe College-sponsored *Notable American Women, 1609–1950,* to appear in 1968. In 1966–67 Miss Flexner received a Guggenheim Fellowship for a biography of Mary Wollstonecraft, the first English feminist.

Atheneum Paperbacks

HISTORY—AMERICAN

Atheneum Paperbacks

STUDIES IN AMERICAN NEGRO LIFE

Atheneum Paperbacks

HISTORY

HISTORY—ASIA

Atheneum Paperbacks

LAW AND GOVERNMENT

DIPLOMACY AND INTERNATIONAL RELATIONS

Atheneum Paperbacks